The
Winter Game

Professor Robert Pascoe is the foundation Dean of
Arts at Victoria University of Technology. Author
and historian, his work in Australian social history
includes the story of immigration, ethnic relations,
local history, sport and popular culture

On any clear winter's Saturday his voice may be
heard raised in barracking tones across the wide,
open expanse of the MCG.

The
Winter Game

Over 100 years of Australian football

Robert Pascoe

MANDARIN

Published 1996 by Mandarin
a part of Reed Books Australia
22 Salmon Street, Port Melbourne, Victoria 3207
a division of Reed International Books Australia Pty Limited

First published in Australia in 1995
by The Text Publishing Company

Typeset in Berkeley Book by Bookset Pty Ltd
Printed and bound in Australia by Griffin Paperbacks

National Library of Australia
   cataloguing-in-publication data:

Pascoe, Rob. 1953– .
The winter game: over 100 years of Australian football.

   New ed.
   Bibliography.
   Includes index.
   ISBN 1 86330 597 1

   1. Australian football — History. I. Pascoe, Rob, 1953–. II. Title.

796.336

Memorabilia kindly provided by Just Collectables!
212 Chapel St, Prahran, Victoria
Ph (03) 9510 4556
Fax (03) 9510 4557

Contents

Acknowledgements   vii

Introduction *Divided by the*
Barassi Line: Why Sydney plays
Rugby and Melbourne plays Rules   xii

Part One *Preliminaries*
  1 The laws of the game   3
  2 Teams, positions and players   21
  3 Origins   45

Part Two *The 1870s to the 1920s*
  4 Breaking from the pack   55
  5 Victoria's decade of crisis   63
  6 Class identity   71
  7 The Anzac heritage   91

Part Three *The 1930s to the 1960s*
  8 Depression football   109
  9 Social mobility   121
 10 The Golden Rules   139
 11 New skills   159

Part Four *The 1970s to the 1990s*
 12 'Going the long bomb'   183
 13 Balanced attack and defence   201
 14 Possession at all costs   219

Future Prospects
 15 Zones and set plays   239

Writing Your Own Club History 249

Statistics *Premiers and*
Runners-Up, Medallists and
Leading Goalkickers   251

Notes   281

Bibliography   293

Index   303

Acknowledgements

This book is dedicated to the memory of the late Lance Betros, who passionately followed Essendon and the Tennant Creek Eagles. I would like to thank all those who agreed to be interviewed, my colleagues at Victoria University, my friends in the Melbourne Cricket Club library coterie, many others who put up with incessant football chatter, and my family, whom I continue to embarrass each Saturday afternoon in the Outer.

I wish to thank: Ron Adams, Neil Balme, Alf Batchelder, Stephen Betros, Central District Football Club, Wilf Christensen, Rose Clerehan, Graham Dunkley, Ron Fear, Martin Flanagan, Geoff Gallop, research assistant Michael George, Geoffrey George, Heather Gridley, Robin Grow, Peter Haby, John Hennessy, Rob Hess, Michael Heyward, Jennie Hooke, David Huggins, Col Hutchinson, Just Collectables!, Launceston Football Club, Eric Lund, Clem Macintyre, Chris McConville, Annie McGlade, John McLaren, Stuart Macintyre, Kevin Madden, Mike Martin, Bill Meaklim, the late Fred Morton, Dave Nadel, the National Film and Sound Archive, Janice Newton, Val Noone, Norwood Football Club, Paul O'Brien, the late Dinny O'Hearn, Denis Pagan, Ross Peacock, Pioneer Books, Jim Poulter, Harvey Reese, Norm Sowden, Tom Stannage, Bob Stewart, Sturt Football Club, Tom Wanliss, and Sharon Welgus. Jennifer Lord, my editor, and the people at Reed were enthusiastic and supportive.

Introduction

Divided by the Barassi Line

Why Sydney plays Rugby and Melbourne plays Rules

The winter game in Australia is football. Football in Australia can mean one of two things: the codes of Rugby played in Sydney, in Brisbane, and throughout their hinterlands, or the strange indigenous game known as Australian Rules, which dominates Melbourne, Hobart, Launceston, Adelaide, Kalgoorlie, Perth and the towns in between.[1] Drawing on the surname of the Australian game's most famous player, the late historian Ian Turner once declared: 'Australia is divided by a deep cultural rift known as the Barassi Line. It runs between Canberra, Broken Hill, Birdsville and Maningrida [Arnhem Land] and it divides Australia between Rugby and Rules.'[2] To the east of this imaginary Barassi Line, Rugby Union and Rugby League are by far the most important versions of football played, producing players equal to the best from New Zealand, Great Britain, South Africa and France. But to the west of this dividing line, a home-grown form of football was invented in Melbourne and spread widely after its official origins in 1858. Closer to Gaelic football or speedball than other variants of football, Australian Rules is a quick, high-scoring game which demands strength at ground level and athletic aerial abilities above the turf. It is not only a historical puzzle how such a unique game could have developed in Australia – a small nation of 18 million people and derivative in most things – but why a continent with so few cultural or linguistic differences should have become divided so completely between Rugby and Rules.

The first clue to distinguishing between Sydney and Melbourne is to recognise the significance of their dates of founding, one in 1788 and the other in 1834. Between these two dates in British history, enormous changes in economy and polity took place. This half-century was characterised by the industrial revolution, the end of slavery in British possessions, dramatic developments in the history of science, and the emergence of working-class movements. The first British settlers of Melbourne were far removed in background and experience from their grandparents who had established Sydney. The 'fragment thesis' holds that colonial cultures are powerfully conditioned by the fragment of metropolitan culture which caused them to exist in the first place. The styles of economic development and political culture which typify Australia's two major cities are as divergent as those separating New York from Boston, Glasgow from Edinburgh, and St Petersburg from Moscow. The Sydney–Melbourne rivalry is equally intense as a result.[3] Briefly put, Sydney's politics have always been uncompromising, with a winner-take-all attitude to the spoils. Melbourne, the headquarters of both national trade unionism and the nation's conservative political party, has had a richer and more participatory political history. Sydney has had Tammany Hall and secret civilian militias; modern Melbourne is better known for its mass demonstrations and soap-box orators. This difference in political style can be explained by differences in social conflict between the two cities.

Sydney's elite made its money from the city's entrepot role in Southeast Asia. As a commercial elite, it has always valued entrepreneurial skills ahead of liberal education, and Sydney's private school system is not well developed. Sydney's elite was also overwhelmingly Anglican, and its working class has historically been strongly Roman Catholic. Its two codes of Rugby correspondingly divide along class lines – the amateur Rugby Union developed in the 1870s while Rugby League, proletarian in its social base, emerged in conjunction with the development of working-class organisations towards the end of the nineteenth century. Sydney's Rugby competition started in earnest only in the early 1870s, and developed across the suburbs much more slowly than Melbourne's football competition, not reaching fully-fledged form until 1900. There was undoubtedly more scope for an aquatic culture to flourish in Sydney, with its abundance of harbours and bays. Sydney lacked a network of private schools – King's School (1831), Sydney Grammar (1857) and Newington College (1863) were the only major schools in colonial

Sydney. It also lacked the wide open spaces of Melbourne's plains and Melbourne's flat terrain, necessary conditions for playing areas and transporting fans by cable-tram. Generous parklands and cheap transport fares were crucial to Australian football's early appeal. It has also been claimed that Sydney's elite was less skilled at the administration of sport.[4] This insight can be expressed in different terms: that for Sydney's gentry, sport was an exclusive rather than inclusive activity (dramatically so in the case of polo or yachting) and did not call for the same complexity of administration as mass sport.

The Melbourne story is quite different. Its elite was as much Presbyterian as Anglican in background, and more sympathetic to the possibility of self-improvement for the lower orders. Melbourne's initial growth was triggered by a massive influx of immigrants during the 1850s goldrush – this was a highly skilled and literate population with advanced political ideas. In Melbourne in 1856 organised labour won the right to an eight-hour working day, and other industrial or political reforms followed. Melbourne developed as a mercantile, financial and manufacturing centre – enterprises based on white-collar professions – and so prized more highly than Sydney the graduate skills developed through education. Melbourne life was dominated by schools such as Scotch College (1851), Geelong Grammar (1855), Melbourne Grammar (1858), Geelong College (1861), Wesley College (1866), and Xavier College (1878). Sydney remained a more international city, open to external influences, while Melbourne became a culturally closed city once the goldrush population settled down. Melbourne housed the Federal Parliament from 1901 to 1927, when Canberra was built. Melbourne was fundamentally liberal: politically progressive, but socially conservative. At its heart Melbourne was a more inclusive city, and its own football code developed and grew as a Saturday afternoon recreation for players and spectators from all social classes. Rugby and Rules suited Sydney and Melbourne respectively because of these very different histories.

The connection between the culture of a city and its preference for one sport above another is to be found in the value of organised recreation for the onlookers and the participants alike. Team sports like football are a powerful metaphor for social conflict. Each time a group of spectators watch a football match, they are looking at themselves mirrored in the play and learning something about their own lives. The sense of catharsis, of profound emotional release, which comes at the

end of a football game, is the signal that some deeply significant reaffir-
mation of one's place in the larger social order has taken place. Organised sporting contests call up emotions as profound as that powerful
sense of Good versus Evil in the ceremonies of organised religion. This
larger link between a city and its game has within it a smaller link
between the players and the coach: the players are us, the citizenry, and
the coach embodies the wisdom of the game. Watching or playing a
football match is not merely a technical exercise, it also engages us
because the game contains meaning. The content of that meaning is to
do with social conflict and struggle.

What exactly is the social struggle to which football refers? The two
codes are quite different in appearance. One passionate observer gave
this poetic description of Australian football: 'Aussie Rules is an exhila-
rating balletic spectacle, high-leaping artistry. The bladdery objet d'art is
wrenched from the sky five metres up in a catatonic twist of the body
. . . A magnificent pas de deux of man and ball terminating in a graceful
somersault to the earth . . .' This spectator had a different impression of
Rugby: 'Overdeveloped beef-cakes galumphing a few steps, in gangs of
threes and fours, towards the obliteration of a witless plodder clutching
with ten thumbs the oval pigskin to an ample belly . . .'[5] Stripped of its
embellishments, this description conjures up the contrasting images of
the two codes. The attraction of Rules is the athleticism and agility of
individual players, while Rugby's appeal is rather more the strength and
power of players working in groups. The laws governing each code pre-
serve and regulate these fundamental differences between Rules and
Rugby. The laws are refined and recodified according to arbitrary (that
is, anthropological) principles. The laws can be (and are) changed and
modified from one season to the next, but these refinements are undertaken by regulatory bodies which are mindful of community expectations
and assumptions. A good example of this occurred at the conclusion of
the 1993 season, when the Australian Football League (AFL) conducted
a mail questionnaire of its members in order to test the popularity of
proposed rule changes.

There are five basic laws governing Australian Rules which distinguish
it from Rugby and reflect Melbourne's different social history.[6] A basic
feature of the Australian game which puzzles aficionados of Rugby (and
of English football) is the absence of an off-side rule. In cultural terms,
no particular privilege attaches to those who are defending property. The

off-side rule only makes sense if one presupposes that those who are defending their goal (for which read one's own property) should have some particular advantage. In cultural terms it is analogous to feudal assumptions about the inviolability of aristocratic land ownership. Before the emergence of capitalism, for land to change hands was the exception rather than the rule. Australian football, to the contrary, traces its cultural origins to mid-nineteenth-century *laissez-faire* capitalism, and presumes that defending teams in any kind of contest deserve no particular advantage.

Australian Rules differs from Rugby in a second respect. Its laws concentrate much more on ball-handling and rather less on man-to-man tackling. Kicking, marking and handballing are all features of the Australian game; the conventions controlling these aspects of the play have been carefully codified and consistently regulated to a far greater extent than the laws relating to shepherding, tackling and interfering with the movement of other players. It is in this man-to-man area that the greatest degree of ambiguity exists in Australian Rules. Exactly when an attempt to mark from behind another player concedes a free kick, to offer a notorious example, is inconsistently umpired. In short, the individual's actions with the ball provide the focus of the game – in terms of the political culture of Melbourne, this focus derives from the notion of the individual as a free agent which began to dominate Western discourse in the mid-nineteenth century. The triumph of individualism was at the expense of the estates, the earlier notion of society made up of collectivities, and it is this older view of social life that Rugby extols. Rugby's rules about man-on-man conflict are not nearly so ambiguous, and require the players to form scrums, line-outs and other group actions which give expression to the notion of collectivity.

Like the English and American codes of football, Rugby may be distinguished in another decisive way from Australian Rules, namely in its clear delineation of property. Property in the pre-capitalist mind-set is fixed and given, marked out in zones and in a rectangular field of precise dimensions. English football similarly presumes a regular pitch of invariant dimensions. Not so in Australian football: the playing field is oval and rather carelessly measured. Australian Rules fields of play vary quite considerably in terms of their length and width, depending in fact on how much open space had originally been allotted. This *laissez-faire* attitude to property reflects the assumptions of a post-feudal society, a key one of which is that land can be readily bought and sold. Similarly, the internal markings within the oval are a great deal less restrictive than the English and American equivalents. The Rugby field is uniformly 75 yards wide by 110 yards long, marked out with 10 and 25 yard lines; the internal dimensions vary slightly between Rugby League and Rugby Union, but they both operate on basically the same principles. Land is presumed to be finite, and the territory of contest unchanging. Significantly, American baseball, which emerged in the 1840s in similar political conditions to those prevailing in Melbourne in the 1850s, shares with Australian Rules a careless indifference to the outer measurements of the field.

Then, perhaps most striking of all the contrasts, there is the fundamentally different attitude to authority in the Australian game. While the 'referee' in Rugby and in the English football game came to enjoy a send-off power, no such entitlement attaches to the 'umpire' in the Australian Rules context (at senior levels), and attempts to introduce it have always been resisted. The former case mimics the absolutist state, the latter the negotiability inherent in modern democratic societies. Once again, this curious difference can be traced back to colonial conditions in Melbourne – Australian Rules, after all, was codified only four years after the Eureka rebellion in Victoria. Umpires were added later and were given very limited powers. In the English case, adopted by Sydney, the state has an omnipresent authority; in the other, indigenously Australian variant, the whole point of the game sometimes appears to be the crowd's quarrel with the 'man-in-white'. Laws about many aspects of the Australian game, especially about free kicks, are almost perversely ambiguous. To make matters even more ambiguously democratic, the number of Australian umpires has been increased during successive periods, leading to shared rather than despotic decision-making.

Where this cultural analysis leads is to a provocative suggestion – that Melbourne's football game very deeply reflects the liberal social democratic milieu in which it was formed. The class struggle the game unobtrusively mirrors is one in which the contending forces are engaged in hegemonic struggle rather than knock-down battle. There is no fixed centre, there is a curious interweaving of the two teams, and the players move as interdependent individuals. In the other codes, notably in the case of Sydney's Rugby, battle is joined on either side of a centre line, and the underlying motif is brute force. Each team operates as a bloc rather than as a group of individuals. The social struggle reflects conditions in pre-industrial Britain and the early years of the penal colony in New South Wales. Early Rugby was closely associated with the military regiments based in Sydney.[7] It is a game enjoyed mostly by people who believe that life's essential struggle is one of force, and who live in a city whose political life is built around the same assumptions. In the terms of Italian Marxist Antonio Gramsci, the Sydney Rugby style is a triumph of *dominio* (coercion), Melbourne's football a contest around *egemonia* (consent).

Sydney's international outlook has opened it to the world. Appropriately, the only successful indigenous game produced in Australia developed in the rather more inward-looking manufacturing city which grew up further south fifty years later.

This broad-brush comparison between Rugby and Rules can be used to explain many other features of the codes. Women are far more numerous in a Rules crowd because the game belongs to an era of greater participation by women in the struggle between the haves and the have-nots. Also, the rule changes permitted in each code over the intervening decades tended to reinforce rather than challenge the basic cultural assumptions in each game. The role of the umpire in Australian Rules, for example, has consistently been made ambiguous and contestable due to the number of changes to the rules governing 'free kicks'. For it to be otherwise would be to concede to the state an absolutism which the citizens of goldrush Victoria found repugnant. The laws of the games are inherently conservative and help to fossilise the cultural meanings embedded in each game. We now turn to examine those laws of Rules more carefully.

part one
Preliminaries

The Laws
of the Game

The Scene

The Boundary Line

Encircling every Australian football oval is a glistening white line marked out against the emerald field. It is a thin strip of lime-chalk, separating one reality from another. As the players jog across it onto the field, they are infected with 'white-line fever', and undergo a change of character. They are separated utterly from us now, and have entered a space where the laws of civil society are not meant to hold. Over the next one hundred minutes they may become involved in an 'incident' or two – a moment where an angry fist flies into another's face or when two bodies crunch together. The word 'incident' is actually police shorthand for an episode, such as a public commotion, which calls for the intervention of the authorities.[1] Yet it is extremely rare for the police to prosecute any player who commits acts of violence on the football field.

That boundary line changes the rules altogether; it gives permission for men who might indeed be good friends off the playing field to engage in quite vigorous conflict on it. On the field they are called upon to perform for us, the spectators, and in doing so they act out the roles and rituals we expect of them. The laws of the game are actually a collective script written by the spectators as to what we expect to see each time a serious game of football is played. The boundary line separates us, the throbbing Id of passions and undisciplined energy, from the Ego of our own team's players regulated by the dour Super-Ego of the men-in-white.[2] Players like Melbourne full-forward Allen Jakovich threaten conventionality by breaking through this membrane which separates player from spectator (by, for example, exchanging a high-five with a supporter at the fence after a goal). But most times the separation is complete.

It is this boundary line which provides the key distinction between those who are ruled by the laws of the game and those who observe those laws being played out. In the nineteenth century, spectators kept surging onto the field during exciting moments of play. A clear separation between players and the crowd took several decades to effect. In the 1902 season peanut vendors would take short-cuts across the field when play was sufficiently distant.[3] During the 1920s separating off the crowd from the playing field required diligent effort from the VFL (Victorian Football League, forerunner of the AFL).[4] Trainers were not allowed to run onto the field to counsel players until 1956. It was not until 1964 that coaches were permitted to go on to the field to give the quarter-time and third-quarter addresses. Before that season, players merely changed ends in silence at the end of those two quarters. Coaches had begun to recognise the psychological advantage of crossing the boundary line onto the field and addressing their players. In 1989, when Victorian Football Association (VFA) coach Harold Martin was barred from entering the field for ten weeks, he crossed the boundary line by means of a cherry-picker to address his Box Hill players.

No other aspect of the laws has been subject to so much change as the boundary line. Boundary umpires were first used at Ballarat in 1891; they were introduced in the VFL competition in 1903 to perform the throw-in of the ball on behalf of the central umpire. Then, in the 1920s and 1930s, forcing the ball out of play (in any way) conceded a free kick; in 1939 this rule was dropped and boundary throw-ins were reintroduced. The rule that kicking the ball out of bounds on the full conceded a free kick reappeared in 1969. The surname of the 1950s Melbourne captain Johnny Beckwith is used to describe the skill of knowing where the boundary line is: 'doing a Beckwith' entered the football argot to indicate a perfectly placed kick which skims around the back pocket, just inside the boundary line, before going over the line and out of play.

The Oval

The boundary line encircles a playing field whose dimensions are not regular, except for the fact of being oval. Australian Rules is unlike any other football code in that grounds may measure between 135 and 185 metres in length, and anywhere between 110 and 155 metres in width. All other codes require a smaller playing area, and allow less local variation. In Australian Rules, the only official stipulation is that these fields must be elliptical in shape. Originally, the game was played on the huge expanses of Melbourne's parklands, such as Yarra Park, half a mile long; in 1866 it was agreed that the distance between goals should be no more than 200 yards, and the width of the (then oblong) playing space should be no more than 150 yards. The size of the ovals now varies greatly, with respect both to the playing area (and thus how much turf each player covers in the course of a game) and to the space between the playing field and the encircling spectators. Victoria Park and Windy Hill had a cosy intimacy for the home sides; the adoring Collingwood and Essendon fans (from 1922 to 1991) were almost close enough to touch their players, while for visiting teams the effect was more like a cauldron of hostility. Measured within boundary lines (not the fence) the Melbourne Cricket Ground (the MCG) is 159 metres long by 136 wide; Waverley Park 180 by 142; Princes Park 151 by 137; Victoria Park 164 by 133; the Western Oval 176 by 123; and Kardinia Park is 171 by 117. Older VFL grounds differed even more dramatically: Glenferrie Oval was 160 metres long but only 105 metres wide, Windy Hill was 154 by 129, a tight playing space, while Brunswick Street was hardly elliptical, measuring 147 by 130.[5] Grounds in Western Australia are generally even bigger than Waverley: the official dimensions of the WACA, for example, are 188 metres by 174 metres.

The irregularity of the Australian Rules field means that every oval, even at senior level, has its own peculiarities. Take the matter of wind. The conventional wisdom is that when the wind blows across the oval, the windward side is used for attack, the leeward side for defence. Before the building of the Great Southern Stand in 1992, the MCG tenants learnt to favour the outer side in attack, because it was better protected from Melbourne's spluttering sou'-westerlies (and because it was a shorter distance goal to goal – this error in the ground's dimensions was not corrected until 1993, and from then the goal squares at the MCG have been regularly moved to keep the ground in better condition). Geelong's original home, Corio Oval, was situated in a pretty vantage overlooking Corio Bay – the on-shore breeze was a constant 2-goal advantage in the years before Geelong moved inland to Kardinia Park in 1941. Footscray's Western Oval has always been blasted by a fierce northerly which gives the Geelong Road end about a 4-goal advantage. Footscray has a good record against many clubs at home; against Fitzroy, for example, it had won thirty-four out of fifty-two games played at the Western Oval until 1993. The wind patterns buffetting the inner Melbourne suburbs have proved surprisingly regular over the decades.[6]

Another factor left unspoken in the laws of the game consists in whether the grounds are north–south or east–west, and which is the usual orientation in any particular league. Most of the WAFL's grounds, for example, are north–south; because Bassendean Oval runs east–west, it takes local knowledge to have a chance against Swan Districts at home, as the play of the late-afternoon sun in the eyes of the footballers can catch them unawares. Swan Districts have liked to kick to the Guildford end of their ground in that last quarter (unless wind conditions dictate otherwise) because the oval's east–west alignment means that the late-afternoon sun suddenly appears over the R. A. McDonald Stand.[7] The Melbourne captain of the 1990s, Garry Lyon, likes to win the toss and kick to the Punt Road end at the MCG, because by the last quarter the forwards standing at this end have trouble with the sun over the Members stand. The light-towers around grounds like the MCG are placed away from the central corridor so that a ball at the zenith of its flight is unlikely to be hidden in the glare of any one bank of lights.

Goal and Behind Posts

The goal posts must be at least 6 metres high; the behind posts 3 metres. The space between each post is 6.4 metres. Behind posts originated as the corners of the oblong English football pitch. Indeed, the straightness of the line connecting the four posts is the only remaining clue that the game was once played on a regular oblong field. Twenty yards to each side of the original goal posts were kick-off posts. When the ball travelled across this line, 'behind' the goal (as it were), the defending team had the right to kick out. The first time behinds were noted was in 1878, but they did not become part of the official score until 1897. Interestingly, the cross-bar has never been a feature of the Australian game. As soon as the season ends, literally the morning after the Grand Final, these sets of posts are unceremoniously pulled out of the ground by curators across Australia, and the cricket season commences. Throughout the long summer recess, it is only at those ovals not used for cricket (such as Waverley Park in Melbourne) that these posts stand guard as lone sentinels of the game.

The Goal Square

Lines are drawn out 9 metres in front of each goal post and connected by the kick-off line to make a rectangular space nonetheless called the goal square. For a few seasons in the 1890s, when behinds were first added to the score, a wider goal square was drawn to include the behind posts. It then took on its present pattern, which has remained unchanged. The goal square is the site for the traditional rivalry between the attacking team's full-forward (originally known by the less imposing name of the goal sneak) and the defending full-back. It contains as much intensity of conflict as a boxing ring. These two players are the ones least likely during a match to venture far from their original starting positions. It is also the place where some football fans want their ashes sprinkled.[8]

Centre Square

The centre of the oval, exactly halfway between the two goals, is surrounded by a circle 3 metres in diameter; around this is a larger square, its sides 45 metres in length (roughly one-third of the oval's width). This rather complicated arrangement was devised in 1975 after a compromise idea of a smaller diamond was trialled in the VFL over the previous two years. The purpose was to reduce the congestion of players at the bounce of the ball. The first experiment in the first decade of the twentieth century was a circle 5 yards in radius into which players could not enter until the ball was bounced. Now at the umpire's bounce only four players from each side are permitted in the centre square until the ball hits the ground; most of the others stand on the line and run in at this moment. Much of the strategy of the game is based on the idea of winning the ball out of the centre and holding possession.

The Ball

A football measures about 725 by 550 millimetres. The oval ball replaced the traditional round ball in 1880, early in the development of football, so the symmetry of the oval ball and the oval field was established early in the game's history. The first oval balls were 26 inches in circumference, somewhat larger and heavier than those used in the modern game. A dry ball now weighs about 475 grams. A wet ball is much harder to handle and to kick, so some players are chosen specially as 'wet-weather' experts, and relish the tougher conditions.

Before each game, the host team offers the visitors a choice of brands – Sherrin or Ross Faulkner in Victoria, Burley in Western Australia. Burley was a Victorian who moved to the West in 1903; in 1985 Burley joined forces with Sekem, the Perth company which dominates the guernsey business. The Sherrin family has been manufacturing footballs since 1879 and has been closely associated with the Collingwood Football Club. The Sherrin has proved so popular that it has become the standard nickname for an Australian football, but the company was sold to the foreign firm Spalding in 1972. Ross Faulkner, who started in Thornbury in 1921, has remained locally owned, but the Sherrin is the more popular choice because it is slightly smaller and more easily controlled.[9] Yellow balls are used in night games to improve visibility.

The Weather

There is no reference to weather in the Australian football laws, as it is assumed the game will always proceed – rain, hail or shine. None of the grounds are covered by a roof. Heavy rain caused rounds to be delayed in the early years of the VFL but Melbourne's temperate winters have kept postponements to a minimum. Matches played interstate ran the risk of tropical downpours; a notable example was the Saturday night game at Brisbane on 14 June 1952 between Essendon and Geelong – torrential rain forced the game to be postponed to the Monday night. It nonetheless drew a crowd of 28,000.

A VFA contest between Williamstown and Footscray in 1921 was abandoned due to hail. A 1922 match between Perth and East Fremantle was suspended for fifteen minutes during a vicious hailstorm. VFL Rounds in 1960 and 1963 were postponed owing to flooded grounds. Carlton missed the finals in 1971 because a freak fog drifted across the Junction Oval during the third quarter of a Round 21 match it should have won against lowly Fitzroy. (The Blues had won their sixteen previous encounters with Fitzroy.)

Night Matches

The idea of playing football at night can be traced to an exhibition game in Melbourne in 1879 which attracted 12,000 fans. The first VFL night game for premiership points was the postponed game between Essendon and Geelong at Brisbane's Exhibition Ground in Round 8, 1952. (Essendon won by 69 points.) The second home-and-away game under lights took place at the MCG on Friday 29 March 1985 between North Melbourne and Collingwood. Sunday night twilight games started in Adelaide when the Crows joined the AFL in 1991. The first AFL twilight game in Melbourne was a pre-season match at Princes Park between Collingwood and Melbourne on Wednesday 17 February 1993 – the ball was bounced at 5.15 p.m.

The Play

Length of Game

Originally the teams changed attacking ends when a goal was kicked, and the game was finished when one team was 2 goals ahead of the other. This meant that games could go on for successive Saturday afternoons until the score was reached. (The obvious analogy is with cricket.) Halves (1870) and quarters (1885) followed later, although quarters were for over a century measured as twenty-five minutes in duration. In 1994, owing to the increased speed of the game and the consequent pressure on players, AFL quarters were reduced to twenty minutes in length, not including 'Time On'. Teams generally prefer to kick with the wind in the first quarter, as it is unusual for the wind direction to change during an afternoon.

The tradition of the two teams both taking responsibility for time has been maintained. The two clubs' timekeepers sit side by side and press the buttons on their clocks together. Norm Hector has been the time-keeper at Footscray since 1937 – fifty-eight seasons to 1994. The timekeepers are responsible for determining the amount of 'Time On', the seconds and minutes added onto the quarter whenever the ball is out of play. The umpire indicates this period by raising one arm and blowing his whistle at the start and end of each period of 'Time On'. The most time-consuming episodes occur when the ball is out of play, is being returned to the centre after a goal, or when an injury to a footballer stops play. For fans at the ground 'Time On' adds to the excitement of football, because the exact moment when the match is to end cannot be known in advance. Televised football has included a 'countdown clock' since about 1985, and has taken away this element of anticipation for viewers. Unlike Rugby League and soccer, Australian football has an unusual concern with measuring time. This interest in the exact measurement of time may reflect the game's evolution in the industrial age.

The final siren has an air of finality. 'Ring the bell! Ring the bell!' exclaim the barrackers when their team is just in front during the dying moments of a match. The first use of a siren was in 1933, but the bell was still used in the VFL until the 1950 season. Sometimes accident plays a part. The champion Essendon failed to score in the last quarter of its Round 6 game against underdogs North Melbourne in 1947 because some Arden Street urchins managed to sound the bell early when the officials were not watching.[10] Sometimes the umpire does not hear the siren and raises both arms to indicate the match is over before another goal is scored. Officially, the match ends at this moment, not when the siren is sounded.

Starting the Match

Starting the match is a great ritual moment in the game. The umpire holds the ball up as he walks onto the field as a signal to the timekeepers that the start is only minutes away. They answer his signal by sounding the siren. The teams run out onto the field, crash through the banner made by the cheer squad on the Thursday evening, run around the oval, go through their warm-up routines, and wait while a short coin-tossing ceremony determines which end each team will kick toward in the first quarter. (Some captains are notorious for claiming to win the toss every time – since the coin is often lost in the mud, it is hard to read!) The umpire checks with both captains that their teams are ready, raises the ball above the centre to indicate to the timekeepers to sound the siren and start their clocks, and bounces the ball down to commence the match. The bounce-down was invented in 1887.

Kicks

A kick is defined as the striking of the ball by any part of the leg beneath the knee. The first rules allowed a goal to be scored by any means, but from 1872 a clean kick was required; otherwise the score is one behind. Securing the ball by hand and then kicking it is the essence of the game. For much of Australian football's history, the kick dominated play. The laws of the game allow kicking and handballing; technically speaking, there is a third ball action: the punch. No other actions, such as throwing the ball, are permitted, although from 1938 to 1949 the VFA did allow a two-handed Rugby-style throw-pass in an attempt to win back interest in its league.

The first kicks were punt, place, and drop. The history of the game's kicks is interesting in itself. The stab kick was developed by Collingwood during a 1902 tour of Tasmania. The place kick was the preferred method of several early forwards, including Melbourne's Harry Brereton (1909–12), but it had virtually disappeared by the 1930s, although it was used by Tony Ongarello at Fitzroy in the 1950s. The drop kick, a powerful kick when executed by a full-back like Fred Goldsmith (South Melbourne, 1951–59), faded from the game during the 1960s, and became an Australian idiom for someone with unfashionable ideas. The drop punt, popularised by Jack Dyer at Richmond, became the dominant kick, though the torpedo punt and the banana kick have their place in the game. The banana kick was popularised by Blair Campbell (Richmond and Melbourne, 1966–69). Perhaps the most famous exponent of the torpedo punt was Malcolm Blight (North Melbourne, 1974–82) who won a game against Carlton in Round 10, 1976, at Princes Park with a booming 70-metre torpedo after the siren. The first players to use the torpedo regularly were Carlton's Horrie Clover and 'Soapy' Vallence.[11] Distances of 85 metres can be managed by the game's long kickers, players such as Essendon champion Albert Thurgood, St Kilda's famed Dave McNamara, Paul 'The Swede' Vinar (Geelong, 1959–66) and 1980s full-forward Darren Bennett (West Coast, Melbourne).

Marks

A 'mark' is catching the ball from a kick of at least 10 metres, provided the ball has not been touched by another player in the meantime. The 'mark' is one of the highlights of the Australian game, and its derivation is not a Koori term, but the 'mark' of English rugby, so called because the position from which the ensuing kick took place was marked out by the player using the heel of his boot. Although the aerial mark was a feature of Aboriginal football (*marn-grook*), it was not part of the Australian Rules game until the 1889 season, when popularised by the Essendon player Charles 'Commotion' Pearson. As Pearson soared up, women barrackers swooned at the thought of the danger he was in of crashing to the ground. Before the handball developed, there was also a 'little mark', catching a short kick: this was taken in front of the player, and was abolished only in 1897. The high mark (the 'speccy') became more common, and has survived into the modern period – though some pundits predict its demise in the era of possession football of the 1990s. Possession football emphasises the safe receipt of the ball in the chest mark.

'Standing the mark' is the responsibility of the opposing player closest to where the mark was taken. In the closing minutes of a 1924 game, three Fitzroy players had the ingenious idea of forming a human pyramid as a Geelong player went in for the (winning) goal. This was the origin of the rule that only one man could stand the mark. A kick from a mark in front of goal is taken along the angle described from the centre of the goals through the spot where the mark was taken, not the direction from which the ball had travelled.

Handballs

Handballs, punches and tap-ons are closely related. A handball requires the player to hold the ball in one palm while punching it with a closed fist. The 'flick-pass', a curious backhand of the ball made popular in the 1950s by Ted Whitten and the Footscray club, is no longer allowed. If the handball is executed wrongly, the umpire calls 'Throw' and a free kick is awarded to the other team. Handballs were once a way of getting out of trouble if one could not get a kick in, but then gradually became an attacking manoeuvre. In the 1960s 'Polly' Farmer perfected the 40-metre handball, which was as good as a stab kick in effectiveness.

Out of Play

The ball must be wholly across the boundary line before it is defined as 'Out of play', as judged by the boundary umpire. It is possible for a player to be outside the line but holding the ball in play.

Running with the Ball

This is the least-known law of all. The rule that the ball must be bounced every 10 yards (9 metres) was introduced in 1859, and reinforced in 1866, so that the less athletic players had a chance to catch those who sprinted. The modern law stipulates 15 metres, whether the player is running in a straight line or weaving, but the interpretation varies. As the game sped up, the time permitted for any player to dispose of the ball shrank in the public mind, to the point where the cry 'Ball!' or 'How far?' goes up as soon as any player props, quite legally, with the ball, for more than a few seconds. The spirit of the law, however, is that a player in possession of the ball should have a clear opportunity to dispose of it. In the early years it was not uncommon for players to run almost the entire length of the ground. Instances include Billy McSperrin (Fitzroy, 1897), Bill Schmidt (St Kilda, 1912) and Bob Davis (Geelong, 1952 Grand Final), but as defences got tighter the opportunities were rare. Recent runs include Ray Gabelich (Collingwood, 1964 Grand Final), Phil Manassa (Collingwood, 1977 Grand Final Replay), Peter Matera (West Coast Eagles, 1992), Michael Long (Essendon, 1993 Grand Final) and Mick McGuane (Collingwood, 1994). McGuane's seven-bounce run was immediately hailed as a record, but this historical error suggests that insufficient statistics are kept on this aspect of the game. In the interpretation of running with the ball, 'Travel' will generally not be called by the umpire if the player ducks and weaves no more than seven steps, or if he is running into an open goal.[12]

Scoring and Signals

Goals count as 6 points and behinds as one. Australian football is a high-scoring game and the average score has increased over the years. Once the behinds counted toward the final score, from 1897 on, the scoring rate increased dramatically. If the ball hits one of the goal posts or is touched before it goes across the line by any defending player (or an attacking player above the knee) the score is 'Rushed', one point. If a ball hits a behind post, there is no score and the ball is out of bounds. There is no concept of 'own-goal' in Australian football – indeed, a backman under pressure is often happy to concede a behind because it means his team gets the consequent kick-out. Goal umpires, dressed in white from the 1920s, wave one flag to register a behind, two for a goal. This idea was invented by the Tasmanians in 1884. The two umpires perform their flag-waving ritual in perfect synchrony. From 1986, senior grounds were equipped with a 50-metre arc, a curved line describing the distance from goal in order to improve players' chances of kicking a score. No particular importance attaches to the zone thus created, although it does figure in most team plans. Following the basketball example, some pundits have argued that a goal kicked from outside this line should count for 9 points rather than 6.

Draws and Clutch Games

The notion of a draw, so common in cricket, became less acceptable in football. Once behinds were counted as part of the score, draws became far less likely, and as the capacity of teams to kick bigger scores developed, the chances of a draw shrank considerably. Draws are also arguably far more likely at the beginning of the season, when football sides are still developing their team plans. Since 1991, draws have been legislated out of the pre-season knock-out competition and in the finals matches leading up to the Grand Final. If scores are tied at the final siren, a pair of five-minute quarters is played to produce a winner.

A clutch game is one which is decided by only a few points. Some teams are renowned for winning 'the close ones', while others are notorious for letting these games slip. Unlike basketball, where close scores are the norm, in Australian football one team or the other usually achieves a 'run', that is, the players share a psychological sense that this or that particular game is one they are going to win.

Kick-offs

Once the goal umpire has finished waving a single flag to indicate a behind scored, any player of the defending team kicks the ball out from the goal square to commence an attack on the opposite goals. The full-back usually performs this role, but the 'kick-out' (as it is colloquially called) has become an important offensive gambit, and sometimes the coach will have appointed some specialist backman to undertake this kick. Curiously, this kick (not being earned) is traditionally not counted as a disposal in the official statistics of the game, even though its effec-tiveness normally affects both teams' immediate prospects of scoring. Any ball kicked out by the full-back which crosses the boundary line without being touched by any player concedes a free kick, an unusual event which occurs only a few times in a season.

Checking and Tackling

A bump using the hip, shoulder, chest, arms or open hand is permitted, but the ball must be no more than 5 metres away. This proviso was added because of the actions of players like Dermott Brereton in ironing out opponents when the ball was not close by. Tackles are legitimate provided the player with the ball is not thrown forward. A player must, however, have the opportunity to dispose of the ball.

Infringements

Free Kicks

A minefield of ambiguity, the laws governing free kicks are unwittingly designed to render the Australian Rules referee a mere 'umpire' – that is, an overseer of rules rather than the presiding officer. Umpires were a late addition to the game, and were not invested with much authority. The spirit of the law is that the ball should be kept in motion, so an advantage must be paid to the team which has possession. It also follows that players should have the chance to get the ball – hence the rule that shepherding others is not permitted when the ball is more than 5 metres away. A third element is that the player who has the ball should have a reasonable chance of getting rid of it.

These three principles underlie all interpretations of free kicks, but also mean that the notion of penalty is far more ambiguous in Australian football than in any other code. Episodes likely to cause controversy in American football only once a game occur with bewildering regularity during the course of every few minutes of an Australian match. A player being tackled can lead to the call of 'Holding the ball' (the umpire signals this by a downward spread of his hands) or 'Holding the man' (tugging his shirt-waist) or perhaps even 'Play on' (hands thrust upwards). A push in the back is indicated by two hands pushing forward, while a 'Ball-up' is signalled by the umpire gesturing to himself. Free kicks are given against a player for kicking the ball out of bounds on the full (without bouncing), a push in the back of another player, tackling 'round the neck' (too high), holding the ball (not getting rid of it correctly when tackled), throwing the ball (an imperfect handball), running too far (not bouncing the ball every 15 metres), charging (interfering with another player unfairly), striking (using a clenched fist), kicking in danger (the foot must actually strike), tripping, wilfully wasting time (taking more than about 15 seconds to kick the ball), running into the centre square before the ball is bounced, and in many other ways interfering with play (such as shaking a goal post). One of the more obscure rules forbids touching the ball after the boundary umpire has signalled 'Out of bounds' (law 12.9.3), a rule which is rarely enforced. The hand signals for the various kinds of free kick, and for 'Play On', were invented by South Australian umpire Johnny Quinn in the 1920s, and have been used ever since in all leagues (including the AFL) to improve communication between the umpire and the players, not to mention the spectators.[13]

50-metre Penalties

The 50-metre penalty rule replaced a 15-metre penalty which applied before the late 1980s, because the earlier penalty was not discouraging the 'professional free kick', a tactic to slow down play. The 50-metre penalty applies to encroaching over the spot where a free kick is to be taken, not passing the ball back directly to the opposing player, and knocking the ball out of the hands of someone with a free kick or mark. Each of these infringements is a secondary infringement. The most famous episode under this rule was when Melbourne's Jim Stynes ran across the mark of Hawthorn's Gary Buckenara in the 1987 Preliminary Final.

Reportable Incidents and Send-off Rules

Many of the episodes which incur a free kick, such as time-wasting, can also lead to a player being reported by the umpires to the tribunal. In practice the incidents reported are assault, 'unduly rough play', or abusive language toward an umpire. The umpires must immediately inform the player or his captain of the report and must not engage in discussion of the episode with club officials. The report is then examined by a tribunal and the players cross-examined. The tribunal traditionally meets on Monday evening at league headquarters. Only in extreme circumstances is a player ordered off the field. At senior level, trial by video has been added to this process.

Before trial by video, various methods were used to identify acts of violence behind play. In 1912, following the tradition of the racing industry, stewards were introduced for this purpose, but this only lasted until 1916. An independent tribunal was created in 1913. A Melbourne player was fined 5 pounds by the courts for assault in 1913, an episode which almost prompted a strike by his team-mates when the club would not pay the fine on his behalf. Even in the modern period the police contemplate laying charges, as in the 1965 Semi-Final case when Essendon's John Somerville was allegedly hit by Collingwood's Duncan Wright.[14] Legal action was taken against St Kilda's Jim O'Dea when he hospitalised Collingwood wingman, John Greening, 55 metres behind play in Round 14 of 1972. Greening's wife filed a Supreme Court writ which was only dropped when St Kilda endorsed a Greening Fund and played the Magpies in a 1973 pre-season benefit match.[15]

Season Fixtures and League Ladders

The laws do not make clear that games are played for four premiership points (or two in the case of draws) and that league ladder positions are determined by these in descending order and, in the case of even points scored, the percentage of scores kicked over scores kicked against each team. In leagues with an uneven number of teams, and the necessity of byes, the ratio of matches won to matches played determines ladder position. Each league uses different terminology to indicate the 'home-and-away' matches (Victoria) from the 'roster' games (Tasmania) and the 'minor' games (South Australia). What Victorians call the 'finals series' is the 'final series' in the West or the 'major' games in Adelaide. From 1994 the AFL made a conscious effort to use the fixtures as a means of equalising the competition: the higher-ranked clubs had to play each other twice in the subsequent season, while the lower-placed teams were given lighter schedules. This weighted fixturing probably had more of an equalising effect on the competition than the salary cap or the national draft.

By tradition, the final league ladder is determined at the end of the home-and-away season, and there is no Brownlow voting during the finals campaign. The Brownlow and the Magarey medals go to the 'best-and-fairest' player, but the Sandover is awarded to the 'fairest-and-best', an interesting reflection of each state's definition of footballing excellence. However, in most states the goalkicking tally continues right to the end of the season, which is an advantage for full-forwards in higher placed teams.

Payment of Players

The VFL was originally established so that players could play football professionally – other leagues followed suit. Players were paid under the counter until 1911, when the practice became open. The VFL's Coulter Law of 1930 attempted to provide a basic wage of 30 shillings to each player. It was the industry standard until the celebrated Tuddenham and Thompson case of 1970. For many players, however, the reward of professional football has been the entree to employment it has provided rather than the actual salary involved. John Tilbrook (Melbourne, 1971–75) earned the nickname 'Diamond Jim' because of what it cost Melbourne to import him from Sturt; his career became a symbol of the escalating expenses of the 1970s. In the 1980s, rules about the draft and the salary cap introduced by the VFL were an innovation prompted by

American example. These changes were a belated attempt to prevent a wages explosion, and there is some doubt about how well the salary cap is monitored. A player's position in the national draft has been a notoriously poor indicator of his eventual promise.

Transfer of Players and Father/Son Rule

Closely associated, and one of the most contentious aspects of the game, is the set of conventions and rules about the transfer of players. The draft system was introduced in 1981 in an attempt to regularise the annual anarchy of players and clubs negotiating willy-nilly, and in 1985 the salary cap was imposed. A legal challenge in 1983 by Silvio Foschini to permit his move from the Sydney Swans to St Kilda was successful. Zoning and other regulatory mechanisms have been tried over the years.

Only one law among the flotsam and jetsam of discarded rules survives – the father/son rule. The father/son rule guarantees that a new player whose father played fifty or more games with a club can himself play for the same club. It can be described as a way of formalising the network of the one hundred 'royal' families across Victoria whose sons and grandsons have dominated the game. These family links are often not well recognised. 'Crackers' Keenan is related to the legendary Dave McNamara through his mother. Melbourne's exciting half-forward David Schwarz is related to Paul Couch through his mother. Tom Kavanagh is the illegitimate son of Brent Crosswell. The list goes on and on. In addition to connections by marriage, there are also several examples of grandfather and grandson connections, such as in the Beveridge family (Collingwood in the 1920s, Melbourne and Footscray in the 1990s). Famous father/son examples include: Kennedy (John, John); Cordner (Ted, David); Glendinning (Gus, Ross); Oates (Max, Michael); Barassi (Ron, Ron); Smith (Norm, Peter); Roberts (Neil, Michael); Tuddenham (Des, Paul); Whitten (Ted, Ted); Silvagni (Sergio, Stephen); Hudson (Peter, Paul); Fletcher (Ken, Dustin); Pert (Brian, Gary); Rose (Bob, Robert) and Dimattina (Frank, Paul). The Hirds (Alan, Alan Jnr, James) and the Bourkes (Frank, Francis, David) take it one generation further.[16]

It is not known exactly when the father/son rule was introduced. It is only known that it came into being sometime in the 1950s. The rule was first mentioned in VFL minutes in 1964. When the draft was intro-duced in 1981, the father/son rule was not mentioned. Given the com-mercial pressures on the traditions of Australian football, the survival of the father/son rule is significant.

The economics which underpin these laws and conventions of the game are occasionally revealed. One key idea is that Australian Rules is a public enterprise (privately owned clubs have not been successful). So continues the quaint convention of enumerating the size of the crowd and the gate receipts: the total money received at the ground is always published, along with the official attendance, the final score and other match details. As the size of the television audience increases dramati-cally season after season, the crowd size becomes economically irrele-vant. Nonetheless, disclosure of the official gate is most germane to understanding the culture of the game.

Teams, Positions and Players

Each senior professional team in Australian football has a particular character ascribed to it because of the club's social origins, playing style and history. Melbourne (1858) is seen as a silvertail club, because it is supported by the city's Establishment, although its recent return to form has increased the popular following of the Demons. Wearing a red yoke over navy blue, its players are well admired by a wide cross-section of fans, except in Perth (thanks to an intense rivalry with the West Coast Eagles). Attired in the AFL's most attractive guernsey, with blue and white hoops, Geelong ('The Cats', 1858) hails from a large country town, with an innocent enthusiastic style to match. Wearing a white CFC monogram against an Oxford blue guernsey, Carlton (1864) was a comfortably affluent club with a significant immigrant and university following until the mid-1960s, when the club ('The Blues') also became a bastion of the newly rich. Carlton is the league's most consistent performer – it plays a safe and reliable style of game. St Kilda (1873) is the league's least successful club; although the Saints (in red, white and black stripes) enjoyed recent success when based at Moorabbin (1965–92). Essendon (1873), the only colonial club not formed by cricketers, began as a patrician Protestant club which played out of Flemington and then East Melbourne, but picked up a massive popular following when it moved to Windy Hill in 1922 and has held on to this popularity since moving to the MCG in 1992. Wearing a red sash against a black background, the Bombers play fast and clever football.

Having been admitted to the league in 1925, and representing a staid middle-class area with little demographic shift, Hawthorn (1873) has struggled to build up a strong supporter base. This is ironic because the Hawks, in their brown and gold stripes, are the best team in the recent history of the league, a powerful combination of dour defence and disciplined aggression. During the 1980s they appeared in seven successive Grand Finals, equalling the record set by Melbourne in the 1950s. North Melbourne (1874) also joined the league in 1925, and was a notoriously rough team; leavened by fresh, skilled players in the mid-1970s, the Kangaroos won two flags and began their modern success story. Attired in blue and white stripes, they were a Catholic side with support across the western suburbs. The rugged Port Adelaide (1874) attempted to join the league in 1991; four years later its application was accepted, but its admission to the AFL depends on a vacancy among the sixteen clubs. Port's traditional black-and-white picket-fence guernsey will then require modification. The Sydney Swans began as South Melbourne (1877) but were relocated to Sydney in 1982 owing to financial difficulties. In their heyday the white and red Swans won three flags, but the last, in 1933, has become a distant memory.

The Footscray (1883) nickname, the Bulldogs, refers to its hooped red, white and blue colours, reflecting the inner-western locality's British and Protestant background. Once affluent, Footscray is a decayed industrial centre struggling to survive. Its football is appropriately hardy and unrelenting. Fitzroy (1884) also belongs to the aristocratic era, having been established by wealthy inner-suburban interests during the 1880s boom. Because Fitzroy was not the place for immigrants or mobile working-class families, the Lions have never enjoyed a large following, but funds provided by the Nauru government in 1994 will ensure its survival. Recently redesigned, the club guernsey is a gold lion monogram against a maroon and blue background. Fitzroy plays a quirky and unpredictable style of football. By the time it joined the league in 1908, Richmond (1885) had become a Catholic working-class team, sporting a yellow sash against a black background, and nicknamed the Tigers. As Richmond's people moved out to the eastern suburbs, they took their tribal loyalty to the club's larrikin ethos with them. Collingwood (1892) was from its very start the distinctive Catholic working-class club, probably the most famous sporting club in Australia, and is always guaranteed of large crowds wherever they play. The black-and-white Magpies play a tough brand of football.

The West Coast Eagles (1987) was a composite team of the best Western Australian players and, reflecting the state's strong footballing history, soon proved an ascendant force in the AFL. The blue-and-gold Eagles have perfected a tough possession style of football. The Brisbane Bears (1987) began as a scratch team in a city where Australian football did not have strong support, and are perceived as raw performers. Their colours are maroon and gold.[1] Adelaide (1991) is a composite South Australian side; the Crows play a high-possession game and wear dark-navy, red and yellow. At home games on Football Park they benefit from a parochial crowd of supporters. Fremantle (1995) is the AFL's sixteenth club and represents a port city which has dominated football in the West for more than a century. The Dockers are the first AFL side to include green and purple in their colours. Like the West Coast Eagles, Fremantle will quickly prove a dominant force in national football.

Apparel

The laws prohibit any gear which might cause injury, such as jewellery, surgical appliances, or sharp studs on boots. The traditional football boot was a deadly weapon, a heavy object capable of inflicting real damage on the legs of others, but it has been replaced by a lighter plastic equivalent. As Brent Crosswell playfully reminisced: 'The pre-1970 football boot was a real mongrel weapon, a hybrid, half football, half hob-nail boot, with a touch of ankle strap – not like that pair of "slippers" that Dermott Brereton wears, the ones with the moulded plastic marshmallow studs and the peaches and cream European soft-style toe. No sir, the pre-1970 boot was the real McCoy, the ultimate multi-purpose football weapon . . .'[2] The lighter boot has enabled the modern player to run faster. In a 1907 Semi-Final against Port Adelaide, West Torrens unsuccessfully experimented with sandshoes to achieve this effect, but these were not as sturdy as the modern plastic boot. The players in Australian football do not wear any protective gear, certainly none of the elaborate padding favoured by American and Canadian footballers. This is taken to extremes: Australian players are reluctant to wear helmets even when these might reduce the risk of head injury. The players have resisted any suggestion of head guards or other gear, although mouthguards to protect teeth became commonplace in the 1980s. The cultural explanation is straightforward: American footballers are dressed in a modern equivalent of medieval armour of a kind which would be wholly inappropriate in Australian football. (It is not clear why American football incorporated this particular cultural reference to the feudal period.) Teams in minor and country leagues often wear the uniform of an AFL club, partly for practical reasons, partly as a gesture toward the AFL's seniority. The guernsey fabric has become lighter and team colours have been altered for colour television.

The kinds of injuries sustained in Australian Rules are distinctive – the twists and turns of players moving fast and crashing into others produce knee and leg damage, with some likelihood of damage to the upper torso. The horrific neck and head injuries characteristic of Rugby League are less common in Australian Rules. There have been no deaths in the history of senior professional football.

The shorts worn by players became even skimpier in the 1980s; this was best exemplified by Sydney full-forward Warwick Capper. Sydneysiders, used to the baggy shorts favoured by Rugby players, were genuinely puzzled as to whether brief shorts were a technical necessity or a mere marketing ploy! Australian footballers began in knickerbockers with lace-up guernseys, and moved to shorts early in the twentieth century. Shorts were baggy until the 1950s. Marketing of players developed so much that by the 1980s the traditional dressing-gown used by interchange players to keep warm was replaced by specially tailored jackets in team colours. The dressing-gowns had been introduced by Collingwood in Round 5 of the 1930 season (the same year the Nineteenth Man was added). In 1994 Melbourne re-introduced dressing-gowns, but in a designer style. Experiments with caps in hot weather and gloves on muddy days have become more common.

The players are identified by numbers on the back of their guernseys, a convention which started in the VFL in 1912. Unlike in American sports, however, the surname of the player does not appear as well. As players are promoted within their club, they often change to a lower number, and each club has favourite numbers which reflect old heroes (5 at Hawthorn worn by the late Peter Crimmins; 29 at Richmond worn by Kevin Bartlett; or 2 at Melbourne worn by Robbie Flower). These numbers carry an emotional significance for the team and its supporters.

The Positions

Tradition dictates that the players are named on Thursday night in their playing positions for the Saturday, starting with the back pocket, and moving along each line. (In South Australia the players are named back-to-front, beginning with the forwards.) In what follows, each position is described historically and the best players associated with it are listed.[3] Our description follows the AFL convention, beginning with the back pocket (obviously each team has two of these), the full-back, the half-back flanker (again, two), the centre half-back, and so on, down the team-sheet. Fifteen separate playing positions are described, although of course with pairs of certain positions and the interchange players, the full team complement is twenty-one.

The rules say twenty-one 'named' players make up a team, of whom only eighteen are on the field at the one time. To have 'named' players does not always mean pseudonyms are not used. In 1903 the Collingwood champion Bill Proudfoot was obliged to use Bill Wilson as his playing alias when his employer, the Police Commissioner, withdrew permission for Proudfoot to don the black-and-white guernsey. The number playing has varied. When the VFL started in 1897, teams comprised twenty players, including five ruck-rovers. The team size was reduced to eighteen in 1899. One measure of a player's acceptability into the team is the use of a nickname. Nicknames are called out during play and follow Australian argot. So a redhead like Frank Adams (Melbourne, 1953–64) was only ever called 'Bluey'. 'Polly' Farmer got his nickname for the perverse reason that he did not talk much.

Back Pocket

Until the development of the attacking back pocket, exemplified by Alan Johnson (Melbourne, 1982–90) and Andrew Collins (Hawthorn, 1987–), this position was utterly defensive. Johnson was originally a winger and brought to the position drive and intelligent use of the ball out of the backline. If the team plan calls for rebound attacks along the left side, the more attacking style of back pocket takes that side, the more defensive the other. The back pocket was traditionally a stopper, assigned either to the opposition's small fast forwards or larger marking forwards.

This was a more important role than it sounds, because the forward pocket was traditionally the place where the opposition's best players – the ruckman and the rover – were rested. Nonetheless, the back pocket was not seen as a glamorous position, and demanded consistency and toughness over individualism and flair. It was often a captain's post, and has also produced an impressive array of senior coaches; these include Charlie Sutton (Footscray, 1942–56), John Beckwith (Melbourne, 1951–60), Tom Hafey (Richmond, 1953–58), David Parkin (Hawthorn, 1961–74), Tony Jewell (Richmond, 1964–70), Denis Pagan (North Melbourne, South Melbourne, 1967–76), Kevin Sheedy (Richmond, 1967–79), Michael Malthouse (St Kilda, Richmond, 1972–83) Terry Wheeler (Footscray, 1974–83) and Stan Magro (Collingwood, 1977–82). The explanation usually given for this phenomenon is that the back pocket sees the whole game and learns to appreciate the team plan. Early stars included Bob Rush (Collingwood, 1899–1908), Kevin O'Neill (Richmond, 1930–41), Max Oppy (Richmond, 1942–54), Wally Donald (Footscray, 1946–58), Bill Stephen (Fitzroy, 1947–57), the 1951 Brownlow medallist, Bernie Smith (Geelong, 1948–58), Bruce 'Bugsy' Comben (Carlton, 1950–61), Brian Walsh (St Kilda, 1956–64), Roger Dean (Richmond, 1957–73) and Ian Nankervis (Geelong, 1967–83). Only three back pockets have won Brownlows, including two of the best modern players, the 1985 medallist Brad Hardie (Footscray, Brisbane, Collingwood, 1985–92) and the 1993 winner, Gavin Wanganeen (Essendon, 1991–).

Full-back

The importance of full-backs is rarely noticed, as their attacking role is often not appreciated. They rarely do well in the Brownlow count, or in their club's best and fairest competition. It is the crucial defensive position, because the opposition will direct most of its attacking moves towards its full-forward. Full-back is an unforgiving position where any mistake can lead immediately to a goal. Most players who have succeeded in this position have known when to take a risk and attack the oncoming ball and when to stay with the full-forward. In many ways the full-back is the keystone of the defence, thwarting opposition attacks, bringing the ball to ground to be cleared by the pocket and flank team-mates.

Early champions in this position, such as Edward Officer (Essendon, 1897), Ted Rowell (Collingwood, 1901–15), Vic Thorp (Richmond, 1910–25), William Cubbins (St Kilda, Richmond, Footscray, 1915–34) and Jack Vosti (Essendon, Footscray, 1925–34) were famous for their long penetrating drop kicks. George 'Jocka' Todd (Geelong, 1922–34) was an expert spoiler, admired by Gordon Coventry. Casterton recruit Frank Gill (Carlton, 1929–42) perfected the tactic of getting in front of the full-forward and then reversing into him and knocking him off balance. The greatly admired Jack Regan (Collingwood, 1930–1943) was the 'Prince of Full-backs' who, instead of spoiling, confounded conventional wisdom by outmarking the full-forward.

The 1940s and 1950s were an excellent period for full-backs, notably 'Gentleman' Jim Cleary (South Melbourne, 1934–48), J.P. 'Shane' McGrath (Melbourne, 1940–50), Bill Brittingham (Essendon, 1943–52), Jack Hamilton (Collingwood, 1948–57) and Herb Henderson (Footscray, 1950–58). Just as Brittingham was switched from full-forward when John Coleman arrived at Windy Hill, a full-back like the 1955 Brownlow medallist Fred Goldsmith (South Melbourne, 1951–59) was switched from end to end depending on the wind direction. Fred Swift (Richmond, 1958–67) and Gary Malarkey (Geelong, 1977–86) were two of the shorter successful full-backs, relying on strength and judgement to avoid being outpositioned and outreached by taller forwards. Verdun Howell (St Kilda, 1958–68) in 1959 became only the second full-back to win a Brownlow.

Other modern champions in this position have included Wes Lofts (Carlton, 1960–70), Phil Hay, the Glen Iris lad with the thumping kick (Hawthorn, 1960–66) who shared the Hawk defence with brother Sted, Robert Murray (St Kilda, 1963–72), Barry Richardson (Richmond, 1965–74), David Dench (North Melbourne, 1969–84), Geoff Southby (Carlton, 1971–85), Peter McCormack (Collingwood, Richmond, Fitzroy, 1976–86), Gary Pert (Fitzroy, Collingwood, 1982–), Stephen Silvagni (Carlton, 1985–) and Dustin Fletcher (Essendon, 1993–). The modern era has seen possibly the least change in the role of the full-back compared to other positions. Rick Kennedy (Footscray, 1981–91) and Mick Martyn (North Melbourne, 1988–) are examples of full-backs who apply physical intensity to their opponents. Chris Langford (Hawthorn, 1983–), while an innovative attacking player, excels in beating his opponent in the one-on-one duels.

Half-back Flanker

The half-back flank position has been primarily defensive, demanding reliability and toughness. However, in line with the general trend in football, it has become a more attacking position. Many of the players who have been successful in this position could be described as defensive ruck-rovers, who clean up loose balls and break down opposition attacks – and who use pace and quality disposal to relaunch their team's attack. Creative flair was evident in some early champions, such as Jack Monohan (Collingwood, 1897–1907), while others, such as Charles Tyson (Collingwood, North Melbourne, 1920–29), Bob Chitty (Carlton, 1937–46) and Noel McMahen (Melbourne, 1946–56) were renowned for their toughness.

Others who relied on pace were Norm McDonald (Essendon, 1947–53), who was also a professional sprinter, Geoff Williams (Geelong, 1952–59) and Alex Epis (Essendon, 1958–68). Recent champion half-back flankers have included Barry Davis (Essendon, North Melbourne, 1961–75), who is often cited as the best of all time, the wiry John Rantall (South Melbourne, North Melbourne, Fitzroy, 1963–80), fearless Ian Bremner (Collingwood, Hawthorn, 1966–76), 'The Flying Doormat', Bruce Doull (Carlton, 1969–86), Stephen Wallis (Footscray, 1983–), Ken Hinkley (Fitzroy, Geelong, 1987–), who is the master of slow-motion grace, and Guy McKenna (West Coast, 1988–).

Centre Half-back

This is one position unmodified by the passage of time. The centre half-back dominates play to a surprising extent. They must be durable types, quite tall and well-built. Having a quality centre half-back is a great advantage to any side as it allows the team to break down opposition attacks before it gets the ball into a scoring position. Champion of the Colony in 1902, Hugh Gavin (Essendon, 1897–1902) was a mobile type whose effortless marking was a feature of his game. Other great centre half-backs in the early years included William 'Sonna' Thomas (South Melbourne, Richmond, 1905–19), Paddy O'Brien (Carlton, Footscray, 1913–26) and Bert Chadwick (Melbourne, Hawthorn, 1920–29).

George Clayden (Collingwood, 1924–33) was the 'enforcer' of the

Magpies backline and a part-time ruckman who played in the four premiership sides. Then came the cool and efficient Harold Matthews (St Kilda, 1925–32), the 1929 Brownlow medallist Albert 'Leeter' Collier (Collingwood, 1925–30, 1933–39), the Corio Bay institution Reg Hickey (Geelong, 1926–40), the 1947 Brownlow medallist Bert Deacon (Carlton, 1942–51), the brave Dennis Cordner (Melbourne, 1943, 1948–56) and the famous 'Mopsy' Fraser (Richmond, 1945–52), who inspired Dyer's defensive tactic, 'Ratbags to the backline!' when his kicking went astray. Brownlows continued to go to centre half-backs in the postwar era, including to Ron Clegg (South Melbourne, 1945–60) in 1949, Gordon Collis (Carlton, 1961–67) in 1961, and Ross Glendinning (North Melbourne, West Coast, 1978–88) in 1983.

Other notable players in this position have included Roy McConnell (Essendon, 1949–56), Ian 'Bluey' Shelton (Essendon, 1959–65), the attacking Peter Knights (Hawthorn, 1969–85), Bill Picken (Collingwood, Sydney, 1974–86), Jim Jess (Richmond, 1976–88), nicknamed 'The Ghost', the versatile Paul Roos (Fitzroy, Sydney, 1982–) and the reliable Glen Jakovich (West Coast, 1991–).

Defenders

Some players are moved around the backline during their career or, particularly in the modern game, during a match. Although there are some specialist backline positions, there are also utility roles for players whose responsibility in a particular match will depend on the height, pace and skill of opposing players. Early defenders were typified by champions such as the burly 16-stone Bill Proudfoot (Collingwood, 1897–1906), drop kick specialist James Sharp (Fitzroy, Collingwood, 1900–12, 1917), Stawell Gift winner Norm 'Hackenschmidt' Clark (Carlton, 1905–12), Martin Gotz (Carlton, 1906–11, 1913), Joe Slater (Geelong, 1906–14), killed in the war, and the high-leaping Wellesley Eicke (St Kilda, North Melbourne, 1909–26).

Then came players like Joe Murdoch (Richmond, 1927–36), the adaptable Frank Anderson (Carlton, 1934–44), Colin Austen (Hawthorn, Richmond, 1940–43, 1946–52), the 1949 Brownlow winner who left Hawthorn in a dispute, the courageous ukelele player Roy Simmonds (Hawthorn, 1950–61), John James (Carlton, 1953–1963), who took the Brownlow in 1961, Don Williams (Melbourne, 1953–59, 1964–68),

Albert Mantello (North Melbourne, 1954–62) and the 333-gamer, Kevin Murray (Fitzroy, 1955–64, 1967–74), whose distinction was recognised by the Brownlow in 1969.

Polished defenders of the modern era have included the flamboyant John Goold (Carlton, 1963–70), better known as 'Ragsy', the rangy red-haired Edward Potter (Collingwood, 1963–73), 300-gamer Francis Bourke (Richmond, 1967–81), the high-flying Alex Jesaulenko (Carlton, St Kilda, 1967–81), the dogged Laurie Fowler (Richmond, Melbourne, 1971–81), Rod 'Curly' Austin (Carlton, 1972–85), who once kept Hudson goalless, Gary Ayres (Hawthorn, 1978–91), who won two Norm Smith medals for best-on-ground in a Grand Final, Chris Mew (Hawthorn, 1980–91), another member of the 1980s Hawk backline who stands out in history, Ken Hunter (Carlton, 1981–89), Mark 'Bomber' Thompson (Essendon, 1983–), the rugged John 'Whoosher' Worsfold (West Coast, 1987–) and Ashley McIntosh (West Coast, 1991–).

Winger

The two wingers are the classic link players whose job is to cut loose. Each winger patrols the open spaces in the middle of the ground and has the responsibility of connecting the backline and forward-line game plans. There are usually no zonal restrictions for the wingers – they can run far more widely than any other player, apart from the on-ballers. Most top wingers have been fast and skilful players, ranging in build from rover-sized to the taller wingers typical of the 1960s and 1970s. Interestingly, wings were abolished by the VFA for many years, which had the effect of speeding up play and increasing the average team score. This experiment was not copied in other leagues.

Among early wingers, Lou Richards' grandfather, Charles Pannam (Collingwood, Richmond, 1897–1908) was a cunning and pacy winger who helped establish the 'short game' at Victoria Park. Edward Drohan (Fitzroy, Collingwood, 1898–1908) was skilful and accurate in all conditions; Mike 'Mad Mick' Longerigan (Essendon, 1907–09) relished a long run with the ball, one of the timeless motifs of wing play; Newton Chandler (Carlton, 1919–24) has served the Blues all his long life. The Tigers' flags in 1932 and 1934 owed a great deal to having two outstanding wingers, the stocky but elusive Alan Geddes (Richmond, 1925–35) and the 1930 Brownlow medallist, Stan Judkins (Richmond, 1928–36).

Other prominent wingers of the interwar era included the tall Ivan McAlpine (Footscray, Hawthorn, 1927–37), Magpie legend Bruce Andrew (Collingwood, 1928–34), the 1933 Brownlow winner Wilfred 'Chicken' Smallhorn (Fitzroy, 1930–40) and the 1940 Brownlow medallist Herb Matthews (South Melbourne, 1932–45).

In the postwar period, Des Healey (Collingwood, 1948–55) was a small man with a powerful stab pass, Thorold Merrett (Collingwood, 1950–60) also starred as a rover, Brian Dixon (Melbourne, 1954–68) was a durable and talented performer in five premiership sides (later a Victorian parliamentarian), Laurie Dwyer (North Melbourne, 1956–64) possessed great skill, Stan Alves (Melbourne, North Melbourne, 1965–79) was persistent and intelligent, while Richard 'Dick' Clay (Richmond, 1966–76) was the taller kind of winger, an excellent mark and long kick. In recent years, the fluid Keith Greig (North Melbourne, 1971–85) won Brownlows in 1973 and 1974, the rugged Bryan Wood (Richmond, Essendon, 1972–86) excelled in the one-on-one duels, the graceful Robbie Flower (Melbourne, 1973–87) could always make time for himself, Russell Greene (St Kilda, Hawthorn, 1974–88) was a vital cog in the Hawthorn machine of the 1980s, 245-game Michael Turner (Geelong, 1974–88) had blistering pace, the big Robert 'Dipper' DiPierdomenico (Hawthorn, 1975–91) shared the Brownlow Medal in 1986, Dennis Carroll (Swans, 1981–91) made his name on the wing before becoming a good backman, while the lean Nicky Winmar (St Kilda, 1987–) has an extravagance of talent. Finally, the dominance of the West Coast Eagles during the 1990s has had much to do with them having two of the game's greatest wingmen, the nuggety Chris Mainwaring (West Coast, 1987–) and the 1992 Norm Smith medallist, Peter Matera (West Coast, 1990–).

Centre

Size and pace are less important attributes to find in a champion centre-man than sharp anticipation, bursts of speed and pinpoint disposal. Although the centre player can move all around the ground, depending upon his team's game plan, the capacity to win at centre bounces is a vital element. Frederick Leach (Collingwood, 1897–1903) was exceptionally fast and possessed freakish anticipation; the legendary Magpie coach Jock McHale (Collingwood, 1903–20) liked to call the play from the centre; 227-gamer Rod McGregor (Carlton, 1905–20) was the key playmaker in the Blues triple premiership sides; William Schmidt (Richmond, St Kilda, 1908–21) was talented and pacy, and renowned for his baulking; the compact Colin Watson (St Kilda, 1920–25) worked hard in the packs; while Charlie 'Chooka' May (Essendon, 1922–26) was a rugged competitor. The first Brownlow Medal, in 1924, went to a centreman, Edward 'Carji' Greeves (Geelong, 1923–33), as did the 1930 Brownlow, won by the brilliant Alan Hopkins (Footscray, 1925–34). Other champion centre players of the period included quick Len Thomas (South Melbourne, Hawthorn, North Melbourne, 1927–40), the classy 1939 Brownlow medallist Marcus Whelan (Collingwood, 1933–42, 1946–47), the elusive and devastating Allan La Fontaine (Melbourne, 1934–42), who had the boxer's trick of keeping his eyes on the feet of opponents, and the quick and tough Les Foote (North Melbourne, St Kilda, 1941–57).

After the war came Ern Henfry (Carlton, 1944, 1947–52), the 1956 Brownlow medallist Peter Box (Footscray, 1951–57), the immensely talented Jack Clarke (Essendon, 1951–67), who represented the state twenty-seven times, Barassi's team-mate Laurie Mithen (Melbourne, 1954–62), William 'Bill' Serong (Collingwood, North Melbourne, 1956–62), fitness fanatic and devotee of circuit training Brendan Edwards (Hawthorn, 1956–63), the big quick Alistair Lord (Geelong, 1959–66), who took the Brownlow in 1962, and the triple medallist (1965, 1966, 1971) Ian Stewart (St Kilda, Richmond, 1963–75), who was a master at distributing the ball out of the centre. Then came 'Bill' Barrot (Richmond, St Kilda, Carlton, 1961–71), the Claremont recruit Denis Marshall (Geelong, 1964–68), the dazzling Barry Price (Collingwood, 1966–75, 1979), the clever Paul Sproule (Essendon, Richmond, 1968–75), the well-travelled Geoff Raines (Richmond, Collingwood, Essendon, Brisbane, 1976–89), the tireless Tony Shaw (Collingwood, 1977–94), the workhorse Terry Wallace (Hawthorn, Richmond, Footscray, 1978–91), and the hard-as-nails Brian Wilson (Footscray, North Melbourne, Melbourne, St Kilda, 1978–91), who won the Brownlow in 1982.

Current champion centremen are dual Brownlow medallist (1986, 1994) Greg 'Diesel' Williams (Geelong, Sydney, Carlton, 1984–), who dominates small ovals such as Princes Park, the quick-thinking 1989 Brownlow medallist, Paul Couch (Geelong, 1985–), the spectacular Derek

Kickett (North Melbourne, Essendon, Sydney, 1989–) and the extra-ordinary Michael Long (Essendon, 1989–), who plays the position with lightning anticipation.

Half-forward Flanker

The half-forward flank is one of the more difficult positions to play, as most team plans do not employ the flank as an attacking option. The flankers more typically get their goals by crumbing across the half-forward line or providing an alternative when the centre half-forward is blanketed. Champions include Firth McCallum (Geelong, 1897–1905), the fiery lightweight George Topping (Carlton, 1902–16), James Finley Stewart (St Kilda, Carlton, 1905–12), the crafty Percy Parratt (Fitzroy, 1908–17, 1920–23), who used a decoy centre half-forward, and the talented Gordon Rattray (Fitzroy, 1917, 1919–24, 1928). Because the new out-of-bounds rule dictated an emphasis on the central corridor in the 1920s and 1930s, champion flankers are hard to find in that era. The next true champion in the position was Robert 'Woofa' Davis (Geelong, 1948–58), who had pace and skill. Then came the tricky Graham Arthur (Hawthorn, 1955–68), who led the Hawks to their first flag, the solid Kenneth Turner (Collingwood, 1956–65), the MCG specialist Geoff Tunbridge (Melbourne, 1957–62), the dangerous Des Tuddenham (Collingwood, Essendon, 1962–75), John Sharrock (Geelong, 1963–68), John Northey (Richmond, 1963–70), whose nickname 'Swooper' best suggests what a great half-forward flanker does, Burnie lad John Greening (Collingwood, 1968–72, 1974–76), the very popular Syd Jackson (Carlton, 1969–76), and the graceful Subiaco recruit George Young (St Kilda, 1973–78). The dual-flag North Melbourne team of the 1970s, a decade in which all-out attack was the winning strategy, had both flanks patrolled by champions – the adaptable Wayne Schimmelbusch (North Melbourne, 1973–87), and the gifted Brownlow medallist of 1978, Malcolm Blight (North Melbourne 1974–82). Finally, working hard in an unproductive forward line is the brilliant Chris Lewis (West Coast, 1987–).

Centre Half-forward

The most difficult position on the field is the centre half-forward, because the player leads up the ground but is always turning back to his own goal. The centre half-forward is a tall, mobile target who must present himself as clearly as possible for team-mates kicking from several angles. Although not counted upon to kick the goals himself, he is usually the main avenue to the full-forward. Some teams play with two centre half-forwards spaced across the half-forward line.

Ballarat recruit Gerald Brosnan (Fitzroy, 1900–09) came to be recognised as the best centre half-forward of the early period. Dave Smith (Essendon, Richmond, 1903–14) was tall, fast and a good mark. One of the best players of all time, Dave McNamara (St Kilda, 1905–09, 1914–23) was renowned for his 90-yard place kicks from centre half-forward. Horrie Clover (Carlton, 1920–31) topped the Blues' goalkicking on four occasions. Small and durable, Jack Titus (Richmond, 1926–43) used speed and intelligence up forward; Laurie Nash (South Melbourne, 1933–37, 1945) was also small and had a raking long kick with either foot. Ken Hands (Carlton, 1945–57) was a tough competitor with a booming drop kick. Fred Flanagan (Geelong, 1946–55) was noted for his precision. 'Mr Football', Ted Whitten (Footscray, 1951–70), was skilful and ferocious; he represented Victoria on twenty-nine occasions. Murray Weideman (Collingwood, 1953–63) was big and high-marking. Fred Wooller (Geelong, 1954–64) was clever and intelligent, while Ken Fraser (Essendon, 1958–68) was extremely quick and had safe hands. Darrel Baldock (St Kilda, 1962–68) and Barry Breen (St Kilda, 1965–82) both played this key role in the Saints' best years. 'Breen's point', the winning score in the 1966 flag, was the butt of much good humour from 'Cowboy' Neale, who kicked the rather more significant tally of five goals that afternoon!

The high-scoring of the 1970s was made possible by some very talented centre half-forwards, including the inspiring Royce Hart (Richmond, 1967–77), the lightly-built Ross 'Twiggy' Dunne (Collingwood, 1967–78), the 367-goal Robert Walls (Carlton, Fitzroy, 1967–80), the four-flag Brent Crosswell (Carlton, North Melbourne, Melbourne, 1968–82), a forward also remembered for his rucking, David Cloke (Richmond, Collingwood, Richmond, 1974–91) and the high-flying Paul Van Der Haar (Essendon, 1977–90). Current players who excel at this position include Roger Merrett (Essendon, Brisbane, 1978–), the flamboyant Dermott Brereton (Hawthorn, Sydney, Collingwood, 1982–), the classic tall-marking Stephen Kernahan (Carlton, 1986–) and Stewart Loewe (St Kilda, 1986–), the mobile Barry Stoneham (Geelong, 1986–) and the strong Wayne Carey (North Melbourne, 1989–).

Forward

Some players are given a general role in the forward line, their exact position depending on the height and skills of the opposition backmen. They must trap the ball, set up goals, or kick goals themselves. Often these players put in eye-catching performances, such as Michael Grace (Fitzroy, St Kilda, Carlton, 1897–1900, 1903–08), who was judged Champion of the Colony in 1898, the long-kicking Fred Fontaine (Fitzroy, 1898–1907), and the celebrated Albert Thurgood (Essendon, 1899–1902, 1906), who was Champion of the Colony three times (1893, 1894 and 1901) as well as starring in the West. Vin Gardiner (Melbourne, Carlton, 1905, 1907–17) was diminutive and clever; Percy Martini (Geelong, Richmond, 1909–15, 1917–20) was big and strong; Roy Park (University, Melbourne, 1912–15), better known as 'The Little Doc', was the traditional goal sneak. Interwar forwards of note included Charlie Fisher (Carlton, 1914–21), Robert Makeham (Collingwood, 1923–32), Stan 'Bunny' Wittman (Melbourne, 1924–31), who was the last survivor of 'the spirit of '26' at Melbourne, Albert Morrison (Footscray, 1928–38, 1941–42, 1946), and the very talented Des Fothergill (Collingwood, 1937–40, 1945–47), who won the Brownlow in 1940.

Postwar champions on the forward line have included Fred Fanning (Melbourne, 1940–47), Len Fitzgerald (Collingwood, 1945–50), who won three Magarey medals, Ian Cooper (St Kilda, 1964–69), Kevin 'Cowboy' Neale (St Kilda, 1965–77), Allan Davis (St Kilda, Melbourne, Essendon, Collingwood, 1966–80), Gerard Healy (Melbourne, Sydney, 1979–90), who won the Brownlow in 1988, the quicksilver Peter Daicos (Collingwood, 1979–93), James Morrisey (Hawthorn, 1984–93) and the silken Garry 'Dollars' Lyon (Melbourne, 1986–).

Full-forward

It is difficult to win a flag without a champion at the business end of the ground. The full-forward position is normally the main goalkicking position – originally the position was called 'goal sneak'. The most profitable ploy used by full-forwards has been to lead into a defined area of the oval which team-mates recognise as part of the game plan. The most common area is 35 metres out, straight in front of the goals: this is nicknamed 'the Spot'. Other forwards run from this area in order to lead their opposing backmen out of the way. But even when team-mates up the field deliver the ball, 'laces up', correctly into this agreed area, the full-forward must receive the ball in a manner which defies the full-back's attempt to spoil. Another difficulty for the full-forward is the common tactic of an opposition ruckman dropping back into 'the Spot' and chopping off this supply. Hawthorn in the 1980s played a clever trident formation, with the two forward pockets advancing up the field on either side of Jason Dunstall and peeling off to create three options for receiving the ball.

Among the many outstanding players at full-forward, the best have included the vigorous James Grace (Fitzroy, 1897–1900), Walter 'Dick' Lee (Collingwood, 1906–22), who led the VFL goalkicking eight times, pacy and intelligent James Freake (Fitzroy, 1912–24), dual Brownlow medallist Ivor Warne-Smith (Melbourne, 1919, 1925–32), a utility who could play anywhere on the field, the game's record-holder, Gordon Coventry (Collingwood, 1920–37), Jack Moriarty (Essendon, Fitzroy, 1922–33), who was light and led well, the agile Harry 'Soapy' Vallence (Carlton, 1926–38), versatile angle kicker Wilbur 'Bill' Mohr (St Kilda, 1929–41), the big high-marking Bob Pratt (South Melbourne, 1930–39, 1946), the quick Claremont import George Moloney (Geelong, 1931–35), the solid and devastating Jack Mueller (Melbourne, 1934–50), whom some Demon fans regard as their best player of all time, Ron Todd (Collingwood, 1935–39), who wore Dick Lee's No. 13 guernsey until he went to Williamstown, Norm Smith (Melbourne, 1935–50), whose later achievements as a coach have overshadowed his talents at full-forward, and Lindsay White (Geelong, South Melbourne, Geelong, 1941–50).

In the postwar period the following deserve notice: George Goninon (Essendon, Geelong, 1948–54), Jock Spencer (North Melbourne, 1948–57), John Coleman (Essendon, 1949–54), whose first ton came up in twenty-one games, a feat not matched until the advent of Allen Jakovich, the loyal Jack Collins (Footscray, 1950–58), burly John Peck (Hawthorn, 1954–66), Doug Wade (Geelong, North Melbourne, 1961–75), who was the second man to kick a thousand career goals, the popular Peter McKenna (Collingwood, Carlton, 1965–75), ex-Port Melbourne Fred Cook (1967–69), Peter Hudson (Hawthorn, 1967–74, 1977), who equalled Pratt's 150 in a season, the 1981 Brownlow medallist Bernie Quinlan (Footscray, Fitzroy, 1969–86), who was appropriately nicknamed 'Superboot', mobile Michael Roach (Richmond,

1977–89), and the enthusiastic Mark Jackson (Melbourne, St Kilda, Geelong, 1981–86).

The 1990s are blessed with more champion full-forwards than any other decade in football history, especially if one considers the joint 1987 Brownlow medallist, Tony Lockett (St Kilda, Sydney, 1983–), Gary Ablett (Hawthorn, Geelong, 1984–), Jason Dunstall (Hawthorn, 1985–), only the third man to reach the 1000-goal barrier, and Tony Modra (Adelaide, 1992–).

Ruck

As with full-forwards, no side does well without an outstanding ruckman, but more ruckmen have come under the umpire's notice and won a Brownlow. A ruckman must be very tall and physically strong. In ball-ups and throw-ins he must outposition the opponent, palm, tap or punch the ball to the benefit of smaller team-mates around him, and at other stages of the game provide a reliable marking target for colleagues upfield. Because of these demands, most teams traditionally have two ruckmen and may also use other big men for throw-ins up the ground. In these team plans the centre ruckman patrols the middle of the ground, trying to keep half a kick behind the play (say, 30 metres) to offset any sudden attack.

The tireless Charles 'Tracker' Forbes (Essendon, 1897–1902) was Champion of the Colony in 1891, Peter Burns (Geelong, 1897–1902) was recruited from Ballarat Imperials, Jim Flynn (Geelong, Carlton, 1897–1910) was mobile and adaptable, Henry 'Tracker' Young (Geelong, 1897–1910) was an early palm ruckman, Jack McKenzie (Essendon, Melbourne, 1901–06) displayed flawless ruckwork, Jim Marchbank (Carlton, 1903–13) was big and forceful, Albert Franks (South Melbourne, 1906–13) was an aggressive recruit from the West who suffered several suspensions, Charlie Hammond (Carlton, 1906–09, 1914–18) was a burly five-flag player, Vic Belcher (South Melbourne, 1907–20) was a key member of the 1918 premiership side, Danny Minogue (Collingwood, Richmond, Hawthorn, 1911–16, 1920–26) was a good knock ruckman, Con McCarthy (Collingwood, Footscray, 1915–21, 1925–26) was a fitness fanatic who led the Tricolours in their first VFL seasons, Tom Fitzmaurice (Essendon, Geelong, North Melbourne, 1918–28, 1932–35) was a large man and the son of an Irish hurling champion,

Percy Rowe (Collingwood, 1920–24, 1927–28) had enormous strength and resilience, the 1927 Brownlow medallist Syd Coventry (Collingwood, 1922–34) led the Magpies during their four flags of the late 1920s, Perc Bentley (Richmond, 1925–40) gave excellent service both as a captain and as a captain-coach, Jack Dyer (Richmond, 1931–49) earned the nickname 'Captain Blood' but also had fine football skills and a good tactical sense, the 1941 Brownlow winner, Norman Ware (Footscray, 1932–46) was unusually mobile, Hugh Torney (Essendon, 1933–43) was an early innovator with handball, 'Phonse' Kyne (Collingwood, 1934–50) started his distinguished playing career as a centre half-forward, 1948 Brownlow holder William Morris (Richmond, 1942–51) was tall, thin and scrupulously fair, while 'Chooka' Howell (Carlton, 1942–54) had agility, good marking and a long kick.

Ruckmen of the postwar era include: Bob McClure (Essendon, 1946–51), who combined effectively with Hutchinson, Roy Wright (Richmond, 1946–59), who won the Brownlow in 1952 and 1954, was a talented tap ruckman, Jim Taylor (South Melbourne, 1949–61) was athletic and a spectacular mark, John Kennedy Snr (Hawthorn, 1950–59) was fiercely competitive and a good spoiler, Ray Gabelich (Collingwood, 1953–66) was a big man imported from West Perth, Robert Johnson (Melbourne, 1954–62) was also a great forward and later led East Fremantle with distinction, the 1965 Brownlow medallist, Noel Teasdale (North Melbourne, 1956–67) had determination and courage, Allan Morrow (St Kilda, 1957–66) was solid if not tall, John Nicholls (Carlton, 1957–74) inspired fear in his opponents and represented the state thirty-one times, Graham 'Polly' Farmer (Geelong, 1962–67) was the great innovator of the offensive long handball, Carl Ditterich (St Kilda, Melbourne, 1963–80) was talented and aggressive, 302-gamer John 'Sam' Newman (Geelong, 1964–80) was a Geelong Grammarian with a high leap and polished skills, the 1972 Brownlow winner Len Thompson (Collingwood, South Melbourne, Fitzroy, 1965–80) was giant and mobile, Peter Jones (Carlton, 1966–79) was courageous and skilful, Don Scott (Hawthorn, 1967–81) was tough and aggressive, 1975 Brownlow holder Gary Dempsey (Footscray, North Melbourne, 1967–84) was big and had safe hands, the stormy Neil Balme (Richmond, 1969–79) became a thinking man's coach, the winner of the 1981 Brownlow, Barry Round (Footscray, Sydney, 1969–85) continued his career with Williamstown, Peter 'Crackers' Keenan (Melbourne, North Melbourne, Essendon,

1970–80) had plenty of savvy and determination, Graham Moss (Essendon, 1973–76) was a Claremont hero who also won the Brownlow in his last VFL season, 1977 Brownlow medallist Graham Teasdale (Richmond, South Melbourne, Collingwood, 1973–83) was a strong-marking ruckman, dual Brownlow winner (1979, 1984) Peter Moore (Collingwood, Melbourne, 1974–87) was big and fast, Simon Madden (Essendon, 1974–92) was an outstanding mark, while Mike Fitzpatrick (Carlton, 1975–83) proved his worth whenever the Blues were trailing.

In the modern game, Justin Madden (Essendon, Carlton, 1980–) seems ungainly but is extremely skilled, Greg Dear (Hawthorn, Richmond, 1985–) has a wonderfully controlled aggression, the popular 1991 Brownlow medallist Jim Stynes (Melbourne, 1987–) is chasing the all-time record for consistency and also has the athleticism of a smaller man, 1992 Brownlow winner Scott Wynd (Footscray, 1988–) has youthful energy, while Damian Monkhorst (Collingwood, 1988–) provides the Magpies with match-winning vigour and strength.

Rover

Traditionally as small a player as the ruckman is tall, the old rover is not as central to the modern game as he once was. His job is to work with the ruckman and other followers in finessing the ball from the centre bounces, the throw-ins and other instances of congested play. The classic rovers were small men with great speed and dexterity. As with the other on-ballers, the rover has always been in the umpire's eye and is more likely to get enough votes for a Brownlow. Since the 1950s, the true rover has given way in many teams to the ruck-rover.

Among the champion rovers, mention must be made of the fast and immensely talented Richard Condon (Collingwood, Richmond, 1897–1909), the crafty Alec 'Joker' Hall (Essendon, St Kilda, 1898–1902, 1906), who was renowned for turning out of trouble, the explosively fast Percy Trotter (Fitzroy, 1901–06), the quick-thinking Ern Cameron (Essendon, 1905–12), who was named Champion of the Colony in 1911, the small and stocky Percy Ogden (Collingwood, Essendon, 1905, 1910–15, 1918–21), Percy Wilson (Collingwood, Melbourne, 1909–24), the muscular, wet-weather Tasmanian Viv Valentine (Carlton, 1911–18), Cazaly's partner Mark Tandy (South Melbourne, 1911–26), the stab pass specialist Frank 'Checker' Hughes (Richmond, 1914–15, 1919–23), who later became an outstanding coach, Minogue's receiver Donald Don (Richmond, 1917–28), the sure ball-handler Frank Maher (Essendon, 1921–28), the tenacious William Libbis (Collingwood, Melbourne, 1925–35), the freakish 1930 Brownlow medallist, Harry Collier (Collingwood, 1926–40), triple Brownlow winner (1931, 1932, 1935) Haydn Bunton Snr (Fitzroy, 1931–37), who also won three Sandovers, the quick Percy Beames (Melbourne, 1931–44), the tough-tagging Jack Hale (Carlton, 1933–41), the cheeky and vocal Albert Pannam (Collingwood, 1933–47), the masterly Dick Reynolds (Essendon, 1933–51), the reliable Alec Albison (Hawthorn, 1936–49), Alan 'Baron' Ruthven (Fitzroy, 1940–54), and the definitively cheeky rover Lou Richards (Collingwood, 1941–55) who earned his nickname 'The Lip' well before his media career.

Rovers were fewer in number from the 1950s onward, but some who stood out were the dual Brownlow winner in 1952 and 1953, Bill Hutchinson (Essendon, 1942–57), who had dazzling pace and wonderful anticipation, the hard-working Bob Rose (Collingwood, 1946–55), Neil Tresize (Geelong, 1949–59), later a state Labor parliamentarian, the devastating Stuart Spencer (Melbourne, 1950–56), later club president, the triple Brownlow medallist in 1959, 1963, and 1968, Bob Skilton (South Melbourne, 1956–71), who was best-and-fairest at South nine times, Bill Goggin (Geelong, 1958–61), whose teaming with Farmer was a highlight of the 1960s, the 1967 Brownlow winner Ross Smith (St Kilda, 1961–72, 1975), Kevin 'Hungry' Bartlett (Richmond, 1965–83) who was deadly accurate for goal even 50 metres out, Peter Crimmins (Hawthorn, 1966–75), who combined well with ruckman Don Scott, the bullocking 'Lethal' Leigh Matthews (Hawthorn, 1969–85), the Western Australian Aboriginal genius of handball, Barry Cable (North Melbourne, 1970, 1974–77), the elusive Garry Wilson (Fitzroy, 1971–84), Wayne Harmes (Carlton, 1977–88), the volatile Dale Weightman (Richmond, 1978–91), and the two brothers who found each other so easily they were nicknamed 'Sonar' and 'Radar', the master of pirouette Jim Krakouer (North Melbourne, St Kilda, 1982–91), and the languid Phil Krakouer (North Melbourne, Footscray, 1982–91). Currently playing are two champion rovers, the diminutive tackler and 1990 Brownlow medallist, Tony Liberatore (Footscray, 1986–), and John Platten (Hawthorn, 1986–), winner of the 1984 Magarey and the 1986 Brownlow.

Follower

A follower was traditionally a blocker or shepherder who assisted the ruckman and the rover at centre bounces. With a few exceptions, most teams do not have a player with a particular blocking role in the modern game. Instead they will 'tag' the playmakers of the opposition week by week. The old follower role disappeared in the 1950s, as the game sped up, and with the advent of the ruck-rover.

Champion followers of the old school included Harry 'Vic' Cumberland (Melbourne, St Kilda, 1898–1920), distinguished for his longevity as a player – he lasted until he was forty-three! – the courageous stalwart Fred 'Pompey' Elliott (Melbourne, Carlton, 1899–1911), William Dick (Fitzroy, Collingwood, 1908–18), Roy Cazaly (St Kilda, South Melbourne, 1910–27), whose surname became a by-word for high marking, big Dave Moffat (Richmond, 1912–20), Cazaly's team-mate Fred Fleiter (South Melbourne, 1919–25), the commanding Syd Barker (Richmond, Essendon, North Melbourne, 1908, 1921–24, 1927), the strong and long-serving Arthur Olliver (Footscray, 1935–50), the 1946 Brownlow holder, the dashing Don Cordner (Melbourne, 1941–50), and the inspirational, tough Alan 'Butch' Gale (Fitzroy, 1948–61).

Ruck-rover

Ron Barassi (Melbourne, Carlton, 1953–69) is celebrated as the game's first true ruck-rover, a role he carved out in the champion Demons team of the 1950s, and which has been copied elsewhere since. The role suits players who are too short to be genuine ruckmen but too tall for roving, and who are extremely physical. The ruck-rover breaks up congested play with his pack-bursting, gains possession, and directs the next attack by his short kick or handball. Skill is less important than physical build, durability and cool football brain. As the modern game progressed, the role became more mobile, and the ruck-rover was meant to stay with the play all afternoon. Champion ruck-rovers have included the hardy Sergio Silvagni (Carlton, 1958–71), 'Hassa' Mann (Melbourne, 1959–68), the talented Bruce Nankervis (Geelong, 1970–83), the durable and wiry Michael Tuck (Hawthorn, 1972–91), the star of soggy conditions, William Nettlefold (Richmond, North Melbourne, Melbourne, 1974–82), the effervescent and infectious Tim Watson (Essendon, 1977–94), the hard-contesting Wayne Johnston (Carlton, 1979–90) nicknamed 'The Dominator', the fleet-footed Craig Bradley (Carlton, 1986–), the unrelenting Gary 'Buddha' Hocking (Geelong, 1987–), the agile Michael McGuane (Collingwood, 1987–), the clever Dean Kemp (West Coast Eagles, 1990–), and the prolific Chris McDermott (Adelaide, 1991–).

Interchange Players

The Nineteenth Man was introduced in 1930 and the Twentieth in 1946 but these were not interchange players; players could be replaced only once – although to be selected as an emergency counted in the official statistics as a senior game played. The modern use of players as genuine substitutes was introduced as recently as 1978, and meant that players could be rested on the bench, as in other codes. In distant times the thought of being rested was an implied slight on one's capacity as a footballer.

Captains and Umpires

The rival captains originally managed each match. A field umpire was introduced in 1866, merely to arbitrate whenever the captains disagreed. Only in 1880 did the central umpire take charge of the match. Umpires originally had to share the same dressing-room as players. Now umpires are given their own changing room by law. The clear purpose in this rule is to remove the possibility of corruptive practices. In modern times, senior umpires are rarely intimidated off the playing field, although in about 1990 an umpire leaving a tribunal hearing was followed in his car by a disgruntled player and menaced.

Before the players run onto the field, the umpire visits each team's dressing-room and inspects the players' boots to check for dangerous spikes. (Richmond forfeited the 1904 VFA Grand Final because the umpire would not check the North Melbourne boots.) This ritual begins in junior football and continues all the way up to the most senior games. It also provides the umpires with an opportunity to establish personal contact with each player before the match starts. Umpires and players have at times had frosty relations. From about 1968 senior umpires began addressing players on first-name terms, so that 'Player Grinter' became 'Rod' (though never 'Balls'). In his newspaper column, Jack Dyer warned players not to be fooled by this feigned camaraderie: umpires were still umpires, no matter what! In the modern game it is extremely unlikely for retired players to become umpires, a practice of the early days.

During play, umpires are assumed to be invisible, as in other codes, and if they are struck by a ball, it is presumed to have passed through them. Not all umpires understand this notion, and sometimes call a ball-up after such an incident. Umpires are subject to disciplinary procedures at least equal in force to those endured by players in the tribunal. Mistakes, such as those made by goal umpires calling the wrong decision, can lead to suspension or reprimand. From time to time the AFL advises clubs and players that particular interpretations will prevail; during 1994, to cite a notorious example, 'tripping by hand' was singled out for attention. As these interpretations have become more contestable, and as play has sped up, the number of umpires has increased. In 1976 the VFL added a second central umpire, while in 1994 the AFL introduced a third field umpire. Together with the emergency umpire, who watches from the sidelines and can report a player, this now means there are eight umpires at every senior match.

Coaches and Trainers

Medical attendants have been allowed onto the field to tend injured players since the 1920s, but non-playing coaches could not use runners to relay messages until 1956. Coaches sat alongside the boundary line for many decades; only in the mid-1960s did coaches move up into the stand to get a better view of the entire game. (They have always sat on the wing, even though the view from one end might be more instructive of team play.) Coaches came into football around 1900, and have often been playing captains as well, particularly in junior ranks and the VFA. The longest number of years as a coach is thirty-seven, shared by Jock McHale (Collingwood 1913–50) and South Australia's Jack Oatey (Norwood 1945–56, West Adelaide 1957–60, Sturt 1962–82). The last captain-coach of a professional team was Graham Moss at Claremont in 1983. It is entirely symptomatic of the game's strong democratic ethos that a coach must enjoy the support of most players to remain at the helm. Once he ceases to have this support, the coach is unlikely to retain his job. This democratic element would not be tolerated in most professional sports, but hardly a season goes by without at least one AFL coach losing his position for lack of confidence by the club and the players.

The distinctive features of Australian football have been in a process of continuous evolution since the game was formally codified in 1858.

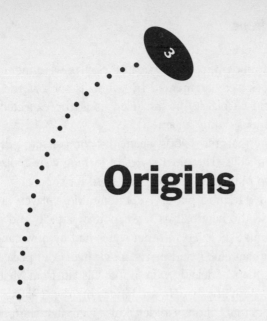

Origins

The laws of Australian football are an artefact of Melbourne's history, a codification of particular cultural traits associated with the city and its people. How these laws stand in the 1990s is a product also of historical contingency; that is, the rules and conventions governing football are a composite of developments within the history of the community and its game. In the 1990s Australian football was played professionally across five states, with teams in Victoria, Western Australia, South Australia, New South Wales and Queensland. It was still a game of individual skill, but set plays were more common than in the past, and the dominant clubs were those whose teams were good at possession. The possession game was based on the deceptively simple idea of reducing error and turnover.

The possession game relied on teams with outstanding ruck-roving skills. The West Coast Eagles won the 1994 AFL premiership without recognised players in many key positions: full-forward, ruck, centre half-forward, perhaps even full-back. Their players took to the next level of perfection a lesson of the 1980s: for the winning teams of that decade, notably Hawthorn and Essendon, were well balanced in attack and defence. Their backmen were good attackers, not merely dour defenders, and their forwards were skilled at trapping the ball in the forward line. This balance of attack and defence superseded the 1970s preference for putting constant pressure on the opposing team's backline: 'long bombs' were a particular feature of Richmond's play in that decade. This decade marked the start of modern football, because players were more readily traded, club revenues were augmented by windfalls such as the sale of television rights, and all players in the team could be expected to be moved to new positions during a game.

The decade before that, the 1960s, seems by comparison individual-istic and focused on skills. The older styles of kicking were replaced by the all-purpose drop punt, with the torpedo used for shots at goal, and the banana kick added to most players' repertoire. Most players at senior level could now use the handball as a weapon of attack, and run-on football was the norm. Skill levels in other states had by now caught up to those of the Victorian clubs, and interstate clearances of players were more common. Perth and Adelaide were not as distant from Melbourne as they had been. With the benefit of hindsight, the 1950s seem a simpler time. Len Smith's famous Golden Rules were just starting to be applied in the 1950s, and the game sped up to a discernible extent. Melbourne dominated the VFL with a combination of the fierce tackling which was once the signature of VFA clubs such as Port Melbourne, and the skills of Essendon, which had been the strong team of the previous decade. The 1940s, punctuated by war, was a decade in which only those clubs which could lay claim to some kind of continuity would prosper; South Fremantle and Essendon had precisely this long-term continuity in common. Other clubs which had been strong in the 1930s, such as Collingwood and Melbourne, fell away after 1941. The other factor was again the changing style of the game. The 1930s had belonged to teams whose players played a determined, physical game, with cour-age rather than skill the dominant ethos of Depression football.

Depression football in turn marked a whole new era in the game. The 1920s had been quick rather than physical – the decade was typified by Essendon's 'Mosquito Fleet', with the game speeding up and the scoring rate increasing dramatically. Players were much fitter and better co-ordinated on the field. Underlying this was the new motivational thinking of Collingwood, the club which was the first to adopt a con-sistent them-against-us ethos. This collective spirit, couched in Anzac language, made the Magpies the unbeatable side of the 1920s. Before World War I, football was rather more a kick-and-mark affair, a battle of individual heroes. Many of these heroes carried the hopes of localities which had lately found their working-class identity, like Footscray, Port Adelaide and Fremantle. These proletarian clubs sought to follow the professional path taken by wealthier clubs like Fitzroy and Essendon in the 1890s. The 1890s had seen the drama of professional versus amateur sport played out in the breakaway VFL. Professionalism developed in Australian football in the 1890s partly as a natural consequence of the game's popularity in the 1870s and 1880s. And this unprecedented popularity was shown in the size of crowds, with upwards of 10,000 Melburnians, rich and poor, clustered in the inner-urban parklands on Saturday afternoons from May to October every winter after 1858.

The official starting date of the game, known then as Victorian Rules, is 1858. But this is merely the year the middle-class schools of Melbourne decided to adopt the game. No-one can be entirely sure exactly where this strange new game came from. All that is clear, especially when we look back through the long span of about 140 winters in this southern Australian city, is that this curious version of football has continued to change, grow and develop each decade. The rapidity of these changes strongly suggests that the codified game is itself a product of the confluence of folk codes available to colonials in the 1850s, a most creative time in Victorian history. Those origins are worthy of detailed consideration.

The earliest surviving rules of Australian football are those set down in 1859 by the Melbourne Football Club. There is a handwritten copy in the possession of the Melbourne Cricket Club, and a printed version of the text was published in the *Australian Cricketer's Guide* for 1858–59.[1] The rules were devised by four men – J. B. Thompson, W. J. Hammersley, T. H. Smith, and the so-called 'father of football' T. W. Wills. (Wills' cousin, H. C. A. Harrison, was not involved at first.)

These rules were a mixture of the styles of the various codes with which Tommy Wills and the other three men on the committee were familiar. The striking fact is that these rules are the very first known codification of football in existence. The origins debate among football historians is mostly about what questions to ask in the first place. The keen interest in locating the precise origins of Australian football has obscured the importance of relating this 1859 formulation of the rules to the various types of football – codified or not – which were being played at the same time by people with whom Wills and others were in contact. These styles were the various kinds of folk football played in Ireland, the British public schools, Scotland, and Aboriginal Australia. It is a feature of a colonial society that it needs to define itself in relation to other societies, particularly its metropolitan core, and the ways in which the emerging Australian game would be explained to British society was important in itself. It was not merely a colonial adoption of a British game (as with cricket) or indeed an expression of immigrant European culture (as soccer would become in Latin America). This freed the game of external points of reference from the very start. So the fixity of rules in Rugby – or the disputes over professionalism in soccer – were resolved quite differently in Australian Rules football.

The four men on the Melbourne Football Club rules committee were elected to their positions because they were talented cricketers and therefore embodied the British idea of manliness. But they were also Cambridge-educated and were prepared to find a compromise among the different versions of football played at British schools which could be adopted in Victoria. The Rugby idea of carrying the ball, rather than merely kicking it, was adopted, but kicking other players in the shins ('hacking') was banned, and the 1866 version of the rules also insisted the ball had to be bounced every few yards. Hammersley and Thompson were English-born journalists who promoted the new game vigorously in the colonial press and helped insist that the Melbourne FC rules were followed. The Irish-born Smith was then Classics masters at Scotch and helped promote the game in schools. In short, the biographies of these lesser-known men reveal the game's true origins.[2] These men also embodied the liberalism of their day: by identifying rules for the game, rather than relying on traditions, they redefined sport as an open contest, not merely a ritual pastime for the leisured class. Codified rules were not sought (or needed) in croquet, royal tennis or other aristocratic pastimes in the colonies.

(There is no evidence for arguing that Australian football was invented by the Aborigines, but the idea is not preposterous. After all, lacrosse is recognised as the game of American Indians, surfing was devised by the indigenes of Hawaii, and the Australian Crawl style of swimming is regarded as an Aboriginal development. American Indians also played a version of football.[3] There are several reliable eye-witnesses who saw Australian Aborigines playing a ball game, *marn-grook*, as early as the 1840s. This game was a large-scale keepings-off, played with a round ball contested by two teams of as many as a hundred men and boys. The teams were intertribal, representing each moiety (half) and the players were paired off according to size and kin relation. The ball was kicked high, to be caught by men jumping up high, even onto the shoulders of others.[4] *Marn-grook* was important in the social solidarity of Koori society, for it was one of several games popular when groups of Victorian Aborigines met in their regular gatherings.[5] The level of violence among these groups was such that these occasions were essential to restoring peaceful relations between neighbouring peoples.[6] *Marn-grook* did not have goals.)

Melbourne's appearance in the late 1850s is important in understanding the game's origins. In a view taken looking south-east from the city in 1858, beyond the Treasury Building, Yarra Park was open land fringed by red-gums. (Several of these trees, protected by metal fences, were still standing in the 1990s.) The same photograph shows that the area which would become the Treasury Gardens was thickly wooded.[7]

Melbourne in the 1850s was surrounded by urban parklands. You could walk around the city from one park to the next, and hardly set foot on made ground. This emerald necklace adorned the city thanks to the availability of cheap land and the foresight of the planners. It was to Melbourne what Frederick Olmsted designed for Boston in the same period. Albert Park, Fawkner Park, Yarra Park, Princes Park – these overlaid stretches of cleared parkland had ancient associations with the indigenous Dreamtime. Onto these sacred grounds now thundered the boots of young footballers.

Before Pearson's high marking of the 1880s, the moment of aerial athleticism came at the start of the kick. (This movement can still be seen in some of the kicks in the 1909 Grand Final, preserved on film.) Players bounded into the air and simultaneously brought their foot up to the ball. It was such an elegant kick that a reporter in 1859 was moved to verse in describing W. J. Hammersley:

> *Swift as an eagle on the wing*
> *Holds fast the ball, then with a sudden spring*
> *He leaps high in air and kicks the volume round.*
> *The ball emits a hollow moaning sound.*
> *Obedient to this hero's skilful care,*
> *The foot-ball rushes whistling through the air.*[8]

In 1864 the Carlton Football Club was formed by local cricketers, who included Benjamin James and Tom Power. Carlton's first players were bedizened in orange and blue; its original home ground was nestled in the bushland setting of Royal Park, near the Gatehouse Street corner. (This was the spot where, three years earlier, Burke and Wills had gathered their entourage before setting off to the interior. Happily, in the 1980s the park was restored to its pristine condition, which rather reconstructs the mood of watching a colonial match through the screen of gum trees.)

Carlton was undoubtedly the dominant force in football in the 1870s. Its players switched to the famous Oxford blue colour in 1871, and that season culminated in its first flag. The club was growing with the suburb, which was filling up the bushland north of the city; the last locality of the suburb, Princes Hill, was established in 1876. Elegantly planned, Carlton was a 'Bloomsbury in the Bush' whose housing became affordable for immigrants only because of the 1890s crash.[9]

The mining communities which sprang up in south-eastern Australia in this period laboured all day six days of the week. These men found their amusement during the evening around prize-fighting contests under canvas or watching Lola Montez in Ballarat's pubs and theatres. Football existed only in a crude form as a folk game:

> The game was a kind of rugby, notable for the dominance of weight
> and strength, and for lack of rules. Games could last for three hours,
> with the players wearing wheat bags with holes cut for arms and head,
> to save wear and tear on ordinary clothes. Resin was used on the
> hands to make the ball stick, and twenty men played to a side. All in
> all it was a violent and rugged game, requiring great stamina.[10]

A similar style of game was played at Moonta, the Cornish mining community north of Adelaide.[11] The first recorded football club at Ballarat was not formed until 20 May 1860. From the 1860s, with the development of company mining, workers at Ballarat and elsewhere could devote their newly-won Saturday afternoons to the support of Australian football.

The beginnings of the game can be explained as the bringing together in this new colony of several important threads of the folk footballing which preceded it. There is no firm evidence which links *marn-grook* with Rules, but the new code played the same kind of role in promoting social harmony as indigenous football did. As with the indigenous code, the vitality of the new football was also understood to be related to the health of the society as a whole. This was pretty much a metaphysical connection: if the young men of the colony played to a high standard of fitness and sportsmanship, then the entire society would benefit. So this new game of Celtic fluidity, informed by deeply-entrenched notions of what was good for the young colony, was encoded within urban parkland spaces and a larger social structure which was essentially British. The moment of written codification in 1859 distinguished Rules from the styles of rugby then in evolution, and the game began to be diffused throughout the colony.

Population drift after the goldrushes carried this game into all parts of Victoria during the 1860s and 1870s. As the goldrush society settled down, this sport became an important event in the blank Saturday half-holidays. Idle young men in the suburbs of Melbourne and the back-blocks of country towns took up football on that one afternoon each week during winter. The localities where football took hold were often new communities in the first flush of family-building, and the game became inserted into the annual rhythm of these townships and suburbs. The building of Victoria's country network of train-lines coincided with this spreading enthusiasm for football. Country football leagues and their regular fixturing grew around these railway lines and the train timetables themselves.

We can turn now to examining this colonial development in more detail. From this point on, Australian football was not only codified in the technical meaning of that word – written down, subject to debate and refinement – but also, and perhaps more importantly, Rules was codified in a cultural sense. It became part of the colony's culture, a carriage for a variety of significant myths through which this new colonial society tried to define itself. Onto football could be foisted a range of hopes, aspirations, and anxieties around a variety of issues. The rural myth was one: kicking the proverbial football over a wheat silo was later to become a recognisable image of country-town life. Another was that cluster of ideas about health and sickness which bedevilled colonial masculinity: were these transplanted English men as virile and as capable as their cousins in Great Britain? Similarly, ideas about class conflict and the expression of working-class identity found ready expression in certain new clubs emerging or being transformed into proletarian institutions at the turn of the nineteenth century; in communities as various as Fremantle, Port Adelaide and Collingwood, to support the local team was to wear the proud badge of labour. Ideas about the Anzacs in the 1920s and social mobility in the 1950s likewise sustained and drew on aspects of football culture. (Every immigrant child wearing a VFL guernsey in the inner streets of Melbourne during the 1950s was a cause for celebration by the assimilationists.) Just as *marn-grook* had a paradigmatic role in Koori society, Australian Rules football, once established in the Long Boom (1860–90), became a powerful cultural force itself, shaping people's ideas of themselves as much as reflecting their sense of who they were in this new land.

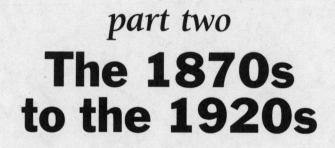

part two

The 1870s
to the 1920s

Breaking from
the Pack

Although Australian football began in the Colony of Victoria during Melbourne's early years, the crucial period in football's history is actually the half century from 1870 to 1920, an era which saw the creation of the major provincial and metropolitan leagues, and the organic interaction between particular communities (such as South Fremantle, Collingwood, Port Adelaide, Hawthorn) and the Australian game.

The development of the game accelerated in the 1870s and 1880s. It was a period of better regulation, with intelligent improvements to the rules and operation of the game. Harrison and Wills retired from playing and turned their attention to administration. New administrators such as T. S. Marshall came forward to steer the game. Crowds grew in size, and the development of new clubs and leagues meant that the total number of spectators increased dramatically. The strongest clubs were Carlton (which dominated Victorian football from 1871 to 1877), South Australia's Norwood (1878–89) and Geelong (1878–88).

The first efforts at taking the game across colony lines were made. In fact, the game was arguably more international by the end of this period than it would be a century later – the game's founders believed football would resemble cricket in reaching across national boundaries. They continued to put international competition on their agenda, but little came of these ambitions.

The population of the colony went from 500,000 in 1870 to approximately 1,100,000 in 1890. It was a boom period. As Melbourne grew as a metropolis, clubs sprang up in the new localities. In 1877 the strongest of these clubs formed the Victorian Football Association. The VFA proved a major force in Australian football from the 1870s to the 1930s. The foundation clubs of the VFA were Albert Park (renamed South Melbourne in 1879), Carlton, Hotham (which became North Melbourne in 1888), Melbourne and St Kilda. Geelong re-entered the senior competition in 1878, and was followed by Essendon in 1882, Fitzroy and Footscray in 1883, Williamstown in 1884, Richmond the next season, Port Melbourne in 1886, and Collingwood in 1892. Melbourne ran out of money in 1889 and affiliated themselves with the MCC – at the cost of financial independence, a price they were still paying a century later.[1]

During the 1870s and 1880s Melbourne's growth meant that new suburban clubs built on membership fees were formed across the metropolitan area. Britannia was founded in 1877 at the Crown and Anchor Hotel in Collingwood. The club played out of Willow Flat during 1878 and 1879, the Richmond Paddock (Yarra Park) in the next two seasons, and at Victoria Park (Dight's Paddock) from 1882. Success in the 1881 season led to increased membership receipts and the patronage of local worthies. Britannia applied to join the Victorian Football Association in 1887 and 1889,[2] but could not persuade the VFA it had the necessary backing.

Football started in Footscray in the late 1870s and by 1883 the Footscray Football Club had been formed. Footscray's colours and nickname, the Tricolours, imply genuflection to things British and monarchist. Their earlier title, the Prince Imperial Football Club, was similarly royalist, intended to honour the French prince martyred in the Zulu War while serving with the British. Footscray's first captain has left us a stirring account of how the game was played at that time.[3]

The play was slowly becoming more open, and a revision of the rules in 1872 helped speed this process up. Until the 1870s there were no set key positions, but now by deploying themselves more widely across the playing field players were able to outpace their opponents. The risk of losing possession by having fewer numbers at the ball was far outweighed by the benefits to be won by breaking from the pack. The scrummaging style favoured by traditional Rugby was on the way out. In 1876 *The Footballer* published a chart suggesting where the twenty players should be deployed, including a goal-to-goal line of seven players! In 1880 the handball was made legal by a rule which allowed the ball to be punched (not thrown); this remained a minor part of the game for several decades. From 1891 players were instructed to start in their playing positions at each centre ball-up rather than start from the centre-line.[4] Goal tallies which were unthinkable in the first decade of the game's existence were now being kicked. The traditionalists shook their heads in disgust as scores of five, six, and seven goals were kicked. Geelong Football Club became the dominant force in the 1870s and 1880s because its players had learnt to play in this more open style. Geelong's captain and long-time administrator was Charles Brownlow, who served the club for half a century before his death in 1924.

In the 1860s the English reached the same conclusion as their colonial cousins had during the preceding decade – that some codification of football's rules, however controversial, was necessary. But in the 1870s and 1880s, when the codified form of Rugby was making headway among Sydney's sporting fraternity, Melbourne resisted the English game. The English game simply did not fit the cultural anthropology of Melbourne life: 'Critics called the game "a task of strength and stupidity", scrummaging "like so many hungry dogs struggling for possession of a bone" and stated that "go-ahead Australians" would not find it "congenial to their natures". Soccer they recognised as having some of the openness they appreciated, but it was too tame and lacked handling.'[5]

In 1878 an intercolonial competition of sorts was played at the MCG between Carlton and the Waratahs (in a composite New South Wales team named after that colony's emblem and dressed in red and blue stripes). The teams played a Rugby game one week and Australian Rules the next. There was no doubt which code was the more popular with the Melburnians. A journalist at the time compared the 'cramped monotonous character' of one with the 'fine, free, dashing style' of the other. Rugby was not played again at the MCG until 1914, and then again in 1994.[6]

A local writer summed up the 1874 season:

> The football season is nearly over, for there are many unmistakable
> symptoms visible that summer is near at hand. This game has become
> very popular in this colony, and it is pursued with an ardour which
> would delight every lover of English sports. There are clubs
> innumerable, both in the metropolis and scattered about the country,
> and on Saturday afternoons the contests rage in all directions with

unexampled fury. It is very satisfactory to find that a pastime of this kind has become so perfectly acclimatised in our midst, for as long as our youths are addicted to football there is very little fear of their losing any of the physique or pluck their fathers brought with them from the 'sea-girt isle'. With the exception of a few *contretemps* the season has been an active and a pleasant one, and we have no doubt the reports of the various secretaries will tell of many doughty deeds and dwell with pride on the records of so many hard-fought fields. Exit football, enter cricket and boating, for both of which pastimes the prospects are good.[7]

There was an apologetic tone here. Although as many as 10,000 people were attending the premier matches between clubs such as Carlton, Melbourne and Albert Park, it was still necessary to define the game in relation to the colony's English origins. The English themselves had so little interest in Australian football that it was not mentioned at all in the pages of *The Times* during this entire period. Other sporting events in the young colony were reported in detail; football appeared, developed and flourished, all without any comment in London.

Football followed the upwardly mobile as they moved out into the suburbs during the 1880s, Melbourne's land-boom decade. The 'boys in blue' at Carlton won the praise of the journalists in the 1880s for their military-like demeanour and discipline.[8] Although Rechabite tents and lawn-bowls clubs followed the growth of respectable Camberwell in Melbourne's leafy east, football clubs were also formed – Canterbury in 1883 and Camberwell three seasons later.[9]

In regional centres the grip of football became evident from the 1870s. Ballarat Football Club (1862) played out of the Saxon Paddock (Western Oval) in red guernseys and white caps; Ballarat Cricket Ground was home to Ballarat South and the Imperials (sporting the same red, white and blue as Footscray). A local newspaper described the 'all conquering popular game' as reminiscent 'of the swoop of Goth and Hun upon the fair fields of civilised culture with all their delicate and tender delights'.[10] Ballarat's teams came to reflect the sectarian differences in the city, and its ovals (such as Golden Point) became picturesque highlights of the region.

Despite its wide reputation (and perhaps partly because its popularity is taken for granted) the success of Australian football has rarely been the subject of serious academic scrutiny. As long as its past and its meanings are not securely understood, the future of the game must always be hazardous. The local studies which do exist, and which may be thought of as pilot studies, indicate that a wealth of local material has been collected by club historians.

Each new development of Australian football was associated with the emigration of Victorians to other parts of the continent. In the depressed 1890s, for example, the thousands of Victorians who moved to the Kalgoorlie goldfields took the game with them, and then on to Fremantle and Perth. A map of Australia's internal population migrations in the 1870–1920 period is a map of this development. Each local history should be read in this context – for example, Western Victorian towns such as Port Fairy started playing football very early.

Where did each of these clubs get their capital? How was football funded? In many clubs there appears to have been both an informal and a formal funding system: for example, local businessmen who were supporters of a club would guarantee employment for players. Membership contributions were a significant element in this funding. It is clear that club hierarchies are a natural expression of the status and power distinctions within any community, and unless this were true a particular club would not survive. In Violet Town, for instance, the club was formed by the town's publicans, assisted by local parliamentarians and the owners of the butter factory and the coach works. An annual subscription of 2/6 was set, and the local shire secretary went around the town to drum up subscriptions.

The game also benefited from having been codified very early. Australian football enjoyed from the start the benefit of all organised recreation in that it has written rules. These laws have given it a quasi-judicial legitimacy. The Melbourne rules committee travelled around Victoria and insisted that the laws be followed.

Although the players may not reflect a given community exactly, the Australian game is significant socially in the way it makes room for men (and lately women) from different backgrounds and with different physiques. The average team reflects the variety of sizes and shapes of men: the short stocky ones are useful in the back pocket, tall thin men make excellent 'mark-and-kick' full-forwards, and so on.[11] The large variety of body shapes which make an Australian football team permits male spectators a variety of self-identifications.

Football also reflects a community's social class composition. Working-class people are given an opportunity. In many country towns Aborigines achieved some social mobility through football. Doug Nicholls got his games with Fitzroy in the 1930s, thirty years before his counterparts broke into Rugby. Each new immigrant group is represented in the game. Sergio Silvagni went from CBC Parade to Carlton in 1958. Dick Abikhair, of Lebanese extraction, played for Hawthorn and then North Melbourne during the 1930s and 1940s. A West Indian, William Albress, played eight senior games for Richmond in 1917 and 1918. Because football was such a local pursuit, real social mobility (defined as moving outside the immediate community) was by definition very rare; nonetheless, these men were important role models to young people from marginal circumstances.

The supporter is a vital element in the game, and in its success. Local or tribal identification with a football club began early. Football clubs and their supporters were closely linked to geography, sometimes within a specific factory or workplace. Working-class communities such as Fremantle found in Australian football a very powerful means of establishing local identity, especially during periods of economic hardship. As Melburnians moved out into the suburbs, they took their inner-suburban allegiances with them, and as new immigrants (such as the Jews and later the Italians in Carlton) came into the city, they attached themselves to the established clubs. So it mattered little that the inner suburbs which gave their names to the professional clubs began to decline in total population (and to change in ethnic character), because the fans took their tribal allegiances out into the new suburbs. A map of the home addresses of postwar members in each club is also a map of this secondary migration.

Closely connected to this cross-generational loyalty is the definite family element to football, in that women can also participate as supporters. In other codes football is more obviously a male-dominated activity: Rugby, especially in New Zealand, is accepted as predominantly a male interest. The popularity of football as a spectator sport is also partly attributable to the nature of the game. The spectators see their own individuality reflected in the players. This is why Australian spectators argue endlessly over the virtues and weaknesses of particular players. Football's style – a team game which allows individuals to display their talents – is less obviously disciplined than either code of Rugby, or soccer, or American football, which all tend to place more emphasis on team structures, and to have fewer opportunities for individual talent to be expressed. As well, it is a simple game, especially as it is viewed by the crowd, which is primarily concerned with outcomes ('Score-board!' is a favourite chant) rather than process ('Fine shot, sir!').

Finally, the game spread across southern Australia because it had a language of its own. New terms (such as 'barrack') were coined very early on in the history of football, and particular forms ('the rover snapped truly'; 'it was a physical encounter') make no sense outside the game. Like all great games, Australian football is buttressed by its own discourse, both spoken in the Outer and printed in the sports pages of the dailies. The term 'barracker' is perhaps the most distinctive of the new language constructed around the game. The word's origin appears to be in the vociferous supporters who accompanied the army team from the Victoria Barracks, though many other theories have been put forward.[12] This new urban sports fanatic was noted in other cities at the same time: in Boston the loud-mouthed fan was called a 'Krank'.

Once its language is mastered, Australian football provides an athleticism which is immediately obvious to the crowd: its high marking, hand-balling, kicking and running all create a flowing, skill-oriented game, rather than one which is predominantly defensive.

As early as the 1880s it was clear that Australian football ('Victorian Rules') was here to stay. The game had been successfully diffused throughout southern Australia. During the 1890s, however, it was to develop further, owing to the crisis of that decade.

Victoria's Decade of Crisis

The 1890s was a decade of crisis in Victoria, and the formation in 1897 of a professional league, the VFL, occurred to some extent as part of the unfolding logic of that crisis. The game had been born of a boom period which now suddenly ended. Crowds declined in size; players were as likely as other Victorians to quit the colony and head to Kalgoorlie or Fremantle; the attractions of amateur status were now weaker than ever. And yet football already possessed a cultural character of its own, exemplified by its irreverent humour.

Two clubs stood out in this decade – Essendon (1891–94) and Fitzroy (1889–1906). They had in common patrician origins, success on the playing field, and, most importantly, an enthusiasm to break away from the VFA and create a professional league. It was Essendon's Alex McCracken who served as the first VFL president (1897–1915).

Fitzroy had been admitted to the VFA in 1883 (in the company of Footscray), following the Association's rejection of the predecessor club, Normanby, two seasons earlier. Men like George Toms, Fitzroy's founder and a prominent local citizen, saw in football an avenue to build 'character'.[1] The young club, based in one of Melbourne's more affluent suburbs, set itself the challenge of attracting the best players from other areas. Nuggety rover Jack Worrall, for example, was persuaded by the club secretary to come down from Ballarat. Named Champion of the Colony in 1887 and 1890, Worrall led the charge for a professional league. Success came easily in the early years of the VFL: Fitzroy appeared in the finals nineteen times in their first twenty-seven years in the VFL, winning seven premierships in that period.

The Toms family history illustrates this new professional ethos. The original Toms had come out from Cornwall in the 1840s, first to Sydney and later to Melbourne. By 1883 George Toms was a prominent citizen of Fitzroy and called a meeting at the Brunswick Hotel to establish the Fitzroy Football Club. Fitzroy was one of the prosperous clubs which combined to form the first professional league, the VFL, at the end of 1896. In the meantime, young Edward Toms was playing for Melbourne (he appears in an 1890 team photograph) but switched to South Melbourne for the 1897 season, presumably because it paid. Although in the professional league, Melbourne Football Club remained amateur. Edward Vincent Toms changed sides in another sense: he left the Anglican faith of his Cornish ancestors and became a Roman Catholic. (One grandson was to become a priest.)

In 1890 the Britannia Football Club persuaded the municipality of Collingwood that it could charge spectators a modest admission at its Victoria Park ground. In 1882 the Collingwood Council had completed its controversial purchase of an old Aboriginal corroboree ground from the Dight family. The council reflected the interests of the slumlords who had developed the noxious and congested working-class suburb; this purchase was flawed from the start, and remained a source of controversy for more than a century. Was the paddock bought at a good price for the whole population to use for a range of recreational uses (including cricket) or was it virtually donated to the council to do with as they pleased? Although the legal issue was not resolved at the time, it was agreed in the 1880s that a well-organised sporting club would lend the locality some valuable civic pride. During 1890–92, after Britannia's application to join the VFA had been rejected a second time, the club's management was strengthened by new civic and property leaders organised around the idea of a Collingwood Football Club, which existed then only on paper. Some of the Britannia group deserted the Collingwood cause and went to Fitzroy. (Thus was born a great rivalry which persisted for the next century; long after Fitzroy ceased to be a great club it enjoyed the nuisance value of upsetting Collingwood.) They took their game bell with them, a relic of colonial football which was taken back by Collingwood in 1965. The Collingwood faction continued to battle to join the VFA, and was admitted to the VFA competition for the 1892 season, thanks partly to help from the Melbourne Football Club and local parliamentarian W. D. Beazley.[2]

Collingwood Football Club was born at the start of the 1890s depression. This depression was a rude shock for Victoria, after the young colony had coasted through three decades of prosperity. Other VFA clubs saw their memberships halve during this period, but Collingwood started with four hundred members, each paying their 5 shillings annual subscription. These barrackers were not at all dismayed when Collingwood finished its first VFA season sharing bottom spot with Williamstown: they loved their club through thick and thin. Part of the difficulty was that too few Britannia players had stayed with the club, although some returned to the fold in successive seasons. The club began winning consistently, however, under the captaincy of ex-Carlton player Bill Strickland. Leadership was also provided by local municipal officials, such as the rates collector Charles Wilson or clerks like Ern Copeland, from the Metropolitan Gas Company in Smith Street. One Collingwood official, E. L. Wilson, became the first VFL secretary in 1897, a post he held until 1929. Clubmen such as these gave professional football an important stability not often recognised by the fans. As for the Collingwood fans, paying numbers dropped in number to three hundred as the depression continued but all told, a thousand supporters attended the 1894 general meeting, filling Collingwood Town Hall. Copeland organised fund-raising functions to see the club through the depression.[3]

Britannia's colours had reflected its name – blue and white with a scarlet sash – but Collingwood had to abandon these when it joined the VFA owing to the clash with Footscray's guernsey, and did not return to them when the VFL started without the Bulldogs. So was born the black-and-white alternative, which was to become famous up and down the land. (Port Adelaide was then in magenta and blue, and did not adopt its very similar black-and-white stripe until several seasons later; Brunswick did not adopt black-and-white until 1900.) Collingwood's first nickname was the Purloiners, a pointed allusion to the suburb's class character as a den of thieves. The magpie, the common suburban bird with a proverbial talent for thieving, was a far better nickname, and was the brainchild of a Collingwood fan, W. S. Crawley, who got the idea from the magpie featured on the South Australian colonial crest.[4]

The move to professional football was closely tied to the development of betting, because one of the arguments in favour of paying players was that this made them less vulnerable to bribery. Playing dead to allow an unlikely team to win was first mentioned in 1894, and the Collingwood player Dick Langford was the first player to be dismissed for this reason. Cases were to continue until the 1920s – the practice was often called 'squaring' and was often (quite unreasonably) suspected when a favoured team lost in a boilover. Since sports medicine and sports psychology were then in their infancy as disciplines, contemporary explanations of a team's performance must not be taken too literally. However, those clubs which could stamp out the practice of 'squaring' among their players were more likely to inculcate a sense of team discipline. Essendon and the other VFA clubs which were to form the VFL at the end of the 1896 season resolved the issue by making unofficial payments to their players – much better to pay them yourself than have rival clubs pay them! It was a period of genuine hardship, when able-bodied young Victorian men were tempted to chase work in Kalgoorlie or Perth. Collingwood's answer was equally valid – to expel players like ex-Britannia rover Jack McInerney, found guilty of taking bribes in 1895. The following year brought the eventual reward for these five seasons of black-and-white discipline, Collingwood's first premiership. The ingredients of club success were all there: dedicated officials, such as head trainer Wal Lee (who served Collingwood until 1942), veteran players (Will Proudfoot, Charlie 'Buffer' Sime, Arch 'Snapper' Smith, Harry Dowdell, Eddie Murphy, to mention a few) and a large supporter base, as indicated by the 17,000 who thronged the East Melbourne Cricket Ground to see Collingwood defeat South Melbourne in the 1896 VFA Grand Final. The night before this game, Collingwood agreed to join with the seven other clubs who would make up the new VFL. Collingwood's Copeland was the brother-in-law of T. S. Marshall, the Association secretary whose stubborn refusal to allow professionalism led to the breakaway league: Copeland's reluctance to have Collingwood join the VFL was a lone voice. It was inevitable that a club as successful as the Magpies would form part of the VFL.[5]

Four rule changes introduced by the VFL in its maiden year sped up the game. Behinds had already been tallied; now they were added to the official score, reducing the chances of scrummaging play to force a draw. A kick-out which was not touched by any player before going out of bounds earned the other side a free kick. The boundary throw-in replaced a ball-up when the ball went out of play in regular play. (Boundary umpires were introduced in 1904.) The 'little mark', resulting from short kicks of two or more yards, was replaced by the 10-yard rule. The 'little mark' was a colonial version of the handball, which, though legal, was many years away from widespread adoption.[6]

Eight teams battled out the first VFL season in 1897. Their final order at the end of the season was: Essendon (Premiers), Geelong, Collingwood, Melbourne (these four were described as the 'finalists'), South Melbourne, Fitzroy, Carlton and (winless) St Kilda. Melbourne surprised the football pundits by winning its first six games, a record apparently not bettered in senior football until 1934, when Swan Districts joined the WAFL and promptly won their first seven matches. In Round 11 of 1897 South Melbourne kept Collingwood goalless (on a muddy Victoria Park ground), 2.5 (17) to 0.8 (8). Melbourne was kept goalless by Essendon in the round-robin finals competition. Low scores were not uncommon – in Round 3, St Kilda only kicked two behinds in a game against South Melbourne, 8.11 (59) to 0.2 (2). In Round 10, it managed only three behinds to a South Melbourne score of 8.16 (64).

In Round 5 of 1898 St Kilda finally kicked its first goal against South Melbourne. The rivalry between these two clubs was called the Lakeside Derby, because both home grounds faced onto Albert Park Lake. This year saw the introduction of the new sectional finals system, three rounds of matches among all clubs after the fourteen home-and-away games. One section was made up of the even-positioned teams on the final ladder (second, fourth, etc.) and the other of the odds. The minor Premiers had the right of challenge. In 1898 it was Essendon which unsuccessfully challenged Fitzroy in a Grand Final at Junction Oval.

Melbourne started the 1899 season well with eight wins out of its first nine matches, but then slumped badly and lost every match from then on. In one finals match St Kilda only managed to kick one behind – Geelong kicked 23.24 (162), a score which would stand as a record-winning margin for twenty years. In the 1899 Grand Final Fitzroy won another flag with a one-point win over South Melbourne.[7]

The Perth suburban clubs were growing in the 1890s, as typified by Subiaco. Subiaco 'was built on a Sunday'. It was settled and developed by ambitious tradesmen and clerks who had left Melbourne in the depressed 1890s and worked hard to establish themselves amid the sandy expanse. Many of the pretty cottages in Subiaco were built by their first owners, and the suburb has remained a comfortable haven since.

The reasons for the existence of its football club are not difficult to fathom: 'football was guaranteed immediate popularity in Subiaco because of the district's extremely high proportion of Victorian residents'.[8] It is also significant that Subiaco was on the new train line of the 1880s linking Fremantle with Perth and then Guildford. All eight of the permanent WAFL clubs share this characteristic. The Subiaco school headmaster, Sid Grace, was himself from Victoria and was tireless in promoting the game amongst his pupils; in 1897 Grace became the foundation secretary of the Subiaco Football and Cricket Club. Over at Cottlesloe State School, for two decades 'Mick' Riley played a similar role in furnishing recruits for the East Fremantle Football Club. It was this kind of network which sustained the growth of football in Perth and Adelaide.

The game was already exerting an influence on Australian culture. To begin with, no other sport in the world has produced the comic tradition associated with Australian football.

The French historian Theodore Zeldin has shown us that the joke is an important clue to how societies function. Humour plays a subversive role – it provides valuable distance from life's daily grind and enables us to see the machinations of everyday reality for what they are. Humour also helps us to join a group, for it gives us entree into the clique. Perhaps because Australian football has always been quintessentially tribal, it has lent itself well to humorous treatment. In Graeme Richmond's words, each football match is 'a meeting of the clans', and each clan is an assemblage of barrackers in the Outer who recognise each other partly by means of their humour.

The humour of football was not invented by the game's administrators; it came instead from the Outer, from the quips and barbs thrown by the barrackers. Football has always been a source of humour, right from its colonial origins. The journalist 'Vagabond' and other nineteenth-century writers give us snippets of these cries and whispers from the crowd. The umpire and police at the ground were freely parodied, and there was always a great deal of repartee between groups of supporters. (Standing in the terraced and crowded Outer provided barrackers with more anonymity than the fixed seating of the Members area or the lawned slopes of some suburban and interstate grounds.)

This humour inverted the existing social order – football humour gave the battler a moment of celebrity status and served to dethrone those in authority at the match. Jokes sparked naturally from each match and made their way into the footy pubs and then into print. Suburban newspapers developed an ironic style of reportage which meant that Australian football was reconstructed through quite a different language from that which explained cricket, horseracing, Rugby or other sports. (Daily newspapers carried factual quarter-by-quarter accounts – but the weeklies carried on the comic tradition.)

Australia has long enjoyed a lively tradition of black-and-white cartoons. Cartoonists picked up the easy-going banter associated with football and this humour was graphically represented in the pages of newspapers. Football cards have always presented the players in a dead-pan manner, but the newspaper caricaturists have had great sport with the same images.[9] Hugh McCrae ('Splash'), Dick Ovenden and Noel Counihan were early exponents; later caricaturists have incuded 'WEG' of the Melbourne *Herald* and Perth's Bill Mitchell.

The emergence of football humour coincided historically with the game's move to professionalism because Victoria's social crisis in the 1890s was the underlying factor in both trends. The game was moving from its respectable origins to become an outlet for the masses. It seemed fair that players should be paid at the senior level to play; at the same time, the humour of the Outer became a critique of players or officials who incurred popular displeasure.

Class Identity

Football emerged from the social crisis of the 1890s as the authentic working-class sport across southern Australia. It now became a badge of class identity, a source of local pride and an occupation for talented young men. The game had gone professional in Victoria, but in other states the pressures to maintain its amateur standing were stronger.

Football's popularity in the southern cities of Australia meant that it was seen to carry the responsibility for most of society's perceived ills. The elite in each city foisted onto the game their fears, anxieties and aspirations. In Perth, football was blamed for encouraging mob violence. Players who resorted to fighting on the field were blamed for inciting violence among the crowd. The 'Six Hungry Families', including the Lee-Steeres and their ilk, who dominated Western Australian life at the turn of the century, still clung to the idea that individual self-control was necessary to ensure social solidarity. The role of football in providing the Fremantle working class with a means of self-expression in a closed society was not acknowledged by the Perth conservatives. Kalgoorlie, Perth and Fremantle had been swamped during the 1890s by the inrush of Victorians and others escaping the depressed conditions of the eastern colonies. Football was both a consequence of this migration and a scape-goat for some of the potent effects of this demographic shift.

In Adelaide, the arguments were somewhat more concentrated on the vexed issue of player payments. The amateur tradition of the colonial period was maintained in South Australia by the artful expedient of creating a 'district system'. Players were tied by residence to one club rather than another; this early example of what would later be called 'zoning' was an effective means of keeping at bay any thoughts by players of demanding more money for their services, as clubs did not have to bid to enlist them.

It was therefore only in Melbourne that true professionalism took complete hold, and this did not occur overnight. Unlike the other states, Victoria had two metropolitan leagues, which meant that the question of amateur status did not disappear. Until at least the 1930s, attendances and interest in the VFA were strong enough to create a genuine rivalry with the VFL. The VFA, for example, created an identical club to Essendon, called Essendon Town until the locality became a city, and attired in the same red-and-black guernsey and later named Essendon A. Essendon Amateurs played out of the Essendon Recreation Ground (Windy Hill) while Essendon was based at East Melbourne. Also, there were two clubs in the VFL, Melbourne and University, which persisted with amateur status long after 1897.

Before moving to Windy Hill, which served the club for home games from 1922 to 1991, Essendon was based at the East Melbourne Cricket Ground. (This ground was taken over for the electrification and extension of the Jolimont Rail Yards in the 1920s.) Essendon's first nickname was the 'Same Olds', and they had played at Flemington from their founding in 1873 to 1881. In Round 15 in 1909 the 'Same Olds' and Collingwood attracted 36,000 spectators to a home game at East Melbourne, a record not beaten by Essendon until 1966. In all, East Melbourne hosted 225 matches for Essendon and the defunct University club.

University, which joined the VFL in 1908 in the company of Richmond, was made up entirely of players who were students or graduates of the University of Melbourne (hence their nickname, 'the Students'). Melbourne University was then the state's only university, and its students represented a tiny elite of future doctors, lawyers and other professional men. There was certainly no counterpart move to include a club based on the Workingman's College (RMIT). Wearing black and blue, University languished in the VFL competition precisely because its social base was so limited – a fully-fledged football club demands an enormous catchment from which to select its players. None of the nineteenth-century teams based on occupational groupings, such as the Warehousemen, survived into the professional era, and John Wren's attempt to professionalise the district Public Service team in the 1920s was similarly doomed. University Football Club closed down in 1915, owing to the war, and it did not re-enter VFL ranks after the war. In a sense, University merged with Melbourne.

Melbourne was the other VFL club clinging to amateur status during the first decades of the twentieth century. Its social base was a mixture of patrician and inner eastern suburban. Prahran residents, for example, were as likely to support Melbourne as St Kilda (then playing at nearby Junction Oval) or their own VFA side based at Toorak Oval. Melbourne Football Club could always survive on its potential to draw supporters from all corners of the metropolitan area, but its performance on the field was limited for as long as it remained amateur in a vigorously professional competition. Its first VFL flag in 1900 was a fluke, and its followers had to wait another twenty-six years before Melbourne's second premiership.

Professional payments to players were not, however, immediately made legal in 1897. Until the 1911 season, the payments to players were disguised in the clubs' accounts as 'expenses'.[1] Critics of professionalism were as much concerned with the effects of football betting as they were with the mere issue of player payments. There were several episodes of players 'playing dead' to prevent their team from winning.

Clubs formed around Australia were stronger in the opening years of the century than before Federation. In Western Australia, East Fremantle had taken over from Fremantle as the state's major footballing force. Another harbour locality, the South Australian city of Port Adelaide, dominated that state's football from 1910 to 1915. In the VFA, Footscray (1898–1900) and North Melbourne (1913–19) were doing well in this period, while Carlton (1906–10) had replaced Essendon and Fitzroy as the VFL's dominant club.

What these emerging clubs had in common was quite straightforward – they reflected the new strength of the organised working class. Football clubs provided suburbs with a new and potent source of identity. The process may be followed in detail at Port Adelaide. Port Adelaide had been a gentlemanly club in its first few decades. Its officials and players were shipping clerks and customs agents working at the Port. These gentlemen players were replaced by proletarian types who typified the new class-conscious mood of the locality.

The similarities in social development across Australia were not lost on contemporary observers, who recognised the strong pressures toward national unity reflected in the Federation movement. As an example, the magpie was adopted by Collingwood when one of its officials visited South Australia. Similarly, innovations in the game's strategy, tactics and organisation crossed state lines readily.

Collingwood was to become Australia's most famous sporting club, a notoriety which can be traced back to this period. Collingwood began with local men, but its real advantage was its club loyalty, which was more important to the Magpie hierarchy than the reputations of individual players. Indeed, five of the club's stars in this period were victims of this philosophy. Condon, rover-captain in 1900, possessed of great strength and agility, often disagreed with umpires; when he was threatened with life suspension by the VFL, the club did not initially contest his case. When he won readmission to the game in 1902, it was Condon who helped invent the team's 'short-game'. Ted Rowell (ex-Castlemaine and Kalgoorlie) was a specialist half-forward place-kicker whose first poor game in 1902 led to accusations of 'squaring': in fact he had been badly concussed. Charlie Pannam was cleared to Richmond (where Condon joined him after finally quitting Collingwood). Will Proudfoot and Jack Monohan left the Magpies to get better money elsewhere.[2] These five players were important to the team plan of the 1900s, but in another sense no individual player was more important than any other. They had been leading goalkickers and Champions of the Colony, but this did not matter. This was the great contribution Collingwood made to the game – professionalism was not merely a matter of money, but a commitment to the club and to a team plan. Collingwood's 'short game' was the first consistently applied team plan. One aspect of this team plan was the use of secret signals so that players knew where the ball was headed. This team plan was buttressed by an attitude to club loyalty which bordered on the theological.

A club is voracious in its appetite for young male talent, and so with Collingwood. In the 1890s, 60 per cent of its players were local boys, but in the years preceding the World War I, only 40 per cent were Collingwood born and bred. But of course the club's core values had already been formed and these newcomers were inducted into the Collingwood ethos. Local players also had the advantage that when their playing days were finished they were the ones who stayed in the district and regaled the local pub crowds with stories of their derring-do. The imports were dispersed across the Victorian countryside and were less likely to take a seat on the Collingwood committee or contribute to the club in other ways.[3] As the first VFL clubs grew out of their inner-suburban strongholds, this pattern was to be repeated many times. Thus did each of the old VFL clubs establish its own distinctive character.

There had been great rivalries in the colonial period, but Collingwood's clannishness led naturally to heroic hatreds, starting with a very fierce set-to with the Maroons, the nickname lent by Fitzroy's colours. Settling accounts with neighbouring Fitzroy became a major ambition for Collingwood each season after about 1895. The Magpie fans were so incensed by the strong-arm tactics of Fitzroy's 62-gamer, half-back Pat Hickey, that a female Collingwood supporter hit him on the head with an umbrella after an 1899 match. The 1903 Grand Final win over the Maroons was particularly savoured by Collingwood. This rivalry was the reason the VFL chose to field these two teams in the first Sydney exhibition match of that season. Even when Fitzroy was out of finals contention between 1907 and 1912, the Friday night taunts across Smith Street always presaged a vigorous match the next afternoon – and Fitzroy won five of the thirteen matches during those years.

The justly more celebrated Collingwood–Carlton rivalry started with their famous 1910 Grand Final, a brawl which led to several players being suspended for a year or more. Indeed, Carlton is the only club in VFL history to have defeated Collingwood more often than it has been beaten by the Magpies. Both clubs were already paying their players in the cloak-and-dagger professionalism which pervaded the VFL at the time. In 1910, Collingwood's annual wages bill for its players was about 500 pounds, while Carlton spent about twice that much. The VFL agreed to make player payments an open affair after a general meeting of seventy League players voted in February 1911 to endorse 'open professionalism'. The going rate was 1 pound 10 shillings per week, although at the time Collingwood paid only a pound.

Collingwood also had a policy of paying its players equally, both before and after wages became open and legitimate in 1911. This was one ingredient of the club-above-all recipe which Collingwood brought into the game, and was not common among VFL clubs. Essendon, for instance, paid greater amounts to its stars – the Magpies hierarchy interpreted claims for more money by its leading players as disloyalty to the black-and-white guernsey. Another symptom of this desire to create a fierce club tradition was the installation of honour boards at Victoria Park as early as 1904, just over a decade after Collingwood's formation.

Metropolitan zoning was introduced in 1915, against the opposition of clubs such as Collingwood which were beginning to recruit more widely.[4] Almost every year from 1896 to 1914, the Collingwood Football Club took a team trip to country Victoria or interstate. These trips were hugely successful: they increased the club's following, bonded the players, gave players an opportunity to try out new game-plans, made the players feel materially rewarded, and helped attract new talent.[5]

Relations between the club and the Collingwood Council remained contentious. The council owned the ground and vested its development in a trust controlled by the elected councillors. But the management of the ground on match days was of course a club responsibility, and the stated threat of taking the gate revenue to another suburban ground was necessary from time to time to keep the council and the club talking to each other. When the council tried to sack an incompetent groundsman and former full-forward, Ted Lockwood, in 1906, Magpie barrackers crowded into the council chamber and demanded that their hero be reinstated.

By 1902, Collingwood had built up a supporter base of 2000 members, among whom working-class locals predominated. Significantly, about one-sixth of these season ticket-holders were women. The colonial tradition of a mixed supporter base continued. Except for a few years when there was a separate ladies' pavilion (1902–09) all supporters barracked together from the same grandstands. Contemporary film indicates, however, that women and children sat in the front few rows, with the men behind. Grandstands had sliding ventilation panels at the back and sides to allow the men's cigarette smoke to escape. The new Victoria Park grandstand of 1909 was a replica of one at Maryborough admired by the Collingwood mayor of the day. The stand seated 1500 and featured a race from the rooms directly to the ground. Club membership by now had grown to 5000.[6]

In the years before World War I and until 1924, half-time at Victoria Park featured Aborigines giving boomerang displays to entertain the crowd. The last of the performers, Mulga Fred, was also adept with a whip. Male barrackers left the ground at half-time to have a few beers in one of several local pubs.[7]

The connections between football and the military would soon appear. An early indication came with Collingwood's famous club song, adopted in 1906, which is sung to the tune of a Boer War marching anthem, 'Goodbye Dolly Gray':

> *Good old Collingwood forever,*
> *They know how to play the Game.*
> *Side by side they stick together*
> *To uphold the Magpies' fame.*
> *Hear the barrackers a'shouting*
> *As all barrackers should.*
> *Oh, the premiership's a cakewalk*
> *For the good old Collingwood!*

Most of the innovations in football from this time were the result of changes in the VFL, and there is no doubt about the inexorable impact of professionalism in this regard. For example, the introduction of a finals competition was a VFL idea, copied in 1903 by the VFA. The creation of a national federation was another.

Following a meeting at Melbourne in the Cup week of 1905, in 1906 the game became federated with the creation of the National Australian Football Council. This provided a loose regulatory framework for the clubs and leagues which had formed in the colonial period. It was actually the third such attempt to create a national structure. In fact, the VFA was not to get a voice on the ANFC until 1949. The idea of federating the game typified the broad lateral thinking of the game's professional administrators.

Not that these Victorian administrators were always the first to come up with the ideas. Zoning existed in South Australia. The standard umpiring signals were invented in Adelaide in the 1920s, and so on. Attempts to get the game accepted in Sydney by playing exhibition matches there in 1903 were not successful. And at the playing level, simple mistakes were made more often than befitted professional sport. Umpires made mistakes; the 1900 finals campaign ended in farce when lowly Melbourne won the flag; and the rules on betting did not prevent players from taking bribes to 'play dead'. There were always suspicions about outside influences such as John Wren.

The VFA struggled to make its version of the game distinguishable from the VFL's (and thus better). The Association reduced the team size to eighteen in 1898 (which the VFL copied), to seventeen in 1908 and to sixteen in 1912 (neither reform being emulated by the League). The idea was to speed up play by dropping the wingmen from the game – they did not reappear until seven decades later – but the effect was to produce impossibly large scores for dominant VFA teams and lopsided results. The VFA also tried to give umpires a send-off power, but this also failed.[8]

Professional football was cleaner than the style which persisted in the VFA. The Association matches were marred by an excess of violence both on the field and around it, especially where North Melbourne and Port Melbourne were concerned. Richmond's dissatisfaction with this violent play was one of the reasons it sought to move across to the VFL in 1908. VFA teams were not developing new systems and strategies with anything like the ingenuity displayed by the fledgling VFL teams. Even after only a few seasons, clubs like Collingwood and Fitzroy were operating on a different level from VFA sides like Richmond or Prahran. The VFL clubs were developing their own styles, experimenting with new game plans. Fitzroy copied Collingwood's 'short game'; Melbourne devised a bullocking defensive style; Essendon built an aggressive attacking game around Thurgood.[9] Continual evolution was necessary if the game was not to descend to the brute force of rugby. The term 'professional' was subtly changing in meaning from 'playing for money' to 'business-like'. VFA teams were already on a lower plane. North Melbourne was particularly notorious for its reliance on violence and intimidation, and was nicknamed the Shinboners, partly because of the damage threatened to the legs of rivals! The Shinboners triumphed over Richmond in the 1903 Grand Final, played at the East Melbourne ground, in a match-winning effort rather ungraciously described by Richmond as 'brutality and ruffianism of the worst kind . . .'.[10] North Melbourne's version of this victory, its first flag, reads differently: 'All told, the Richmond combination just was not showing the judgment of its blue and white opponents.'[11]

The role of the mass media in the construction of football was still minor. The game relied far more on suburban folklore than on news-papers for its patronage. Indeed, in these early years of football, Mel-bourne's newspaper journalists were not treated particularly well by the game's administrators. In 1908 a writer in the *Age* complained that at the MCG, although 'most of the spectators were able to view the game in comfort', this was 'an advantage which, however, was not enjoyed by representatives of the press'. The writer went on:

> The inconveniently situated press box on the M.C.C. ground is a
> disgrace to the club, whose other appointments are irreproachable. In
> the compartment set apart for them the pressmen have their view
> intercepted by numerous iron pillars; one portion of the playing
> enclosure they cannot see, and on such an occasion as that they are
> annoyed by a constant stream of people passing in front of them or
> invading their compartment. This state of things is quite inexcusable,
> as the misplacing of the press box was pointed out when its present
> ridiculous position was first decided upon, and attention has since
> been frequently called to it without any alteration being made.[12]

The old press box symbolised the marginal role of the media in the formative period of organised football. A vestige of this period can be seen at the old Lakeside Oval in the form of the old wooden scorers-timekeepers-press box on the ground's southern side. In 1994 this double-storeyed structure was classified by the National Trust.[13]

The press made numerous suggestions about the game which were taken up by the administrators. Coverage was spotty – in 1908, for example, the Melbourne *Argus* published a diagram showing player posi-tions, but this practice did not become standard. Detailed statistics of matches were not published at all, merely the quarter by quarter scores, goal scorers, lists of the best players, and the crowd attendances. This fostered the view that Australian football patrons were only interested in outcomes and lacked knowledge of the game's tactics and strategies. In 1912 the VFL introduced the *Football Record* partly as a means of making up for the perceived shortfall in newspaper reporting. Listing the new guernsey numbers on each player's back, this slim publication was sold for a penny a copy outside each ground.

The 1900 season opened and closed in controversy. In Round 1 St Kilda won its first League match (after forty-eight losses in a row) by appealing successfully against a Melbourne behind kicked well after the third-quarter bell. Fitzroy dominated the season, and became the minor Premiers at the end of the home-and-away games, but the sectional finals system at the end of the year gave Melbourne the opportunity to knock off Fitzroy in a surprise Grand Final, 4.10 (34) to 3.12 (30).

The 1901 VFL season belonged to Essendon, off the boot of its champion Albert Thurgood. (Mistakes by officials were still common – a goal umpire's error gave Melbourne a 1-point victory over Collingwood, while Fitzroy missed the finals when a game was cut short by a timekeeper.) The Same Olds became the first team to kick 1000 points in a season, much to the disgust of old-timers; Essendon half-forward Fred Hiskins, the eldest brother in a famous footballing family, topped the 1901 goal-kicking list with 34 goals. The sectional finals system was abandoned.

In 1902 Collingwood discovered the stab kick during a famous mid-season trip to Tasmania – the Magpies became celebrated for their 'short game'. The Collingwood players discovered the value of the stab kick in moving the ball up the ground in herring-bone fashion, and they successfully introduced this strategy into their standard play. Now the 'Argus system' was used for the finals; the minor Premiers were given the right of challenge if knocked out of contention in either the Second Semi-Final or the Final. Collingwood won eleven games in a row, finished the season with only two losses, and, despite faltering against Fitzroy in the Second Semi-Final, went on to defeat Essendon in the Grand Final, 9.6 (60) to 3.9 (27).

In the following season the VFL decided to invade Sydney, with a match for premiership points between Fitzroy and Collingwood (Round 4) played at the SCG before a good crowd of about 18,000. Another match was played in Sydney later in 1903, and a third in 1904, but crowds fell away, and interstate home-and-away matches were not attempted again until 1952. The 1903 premiership was won (for the second year in a row) by Collingwood, when Fitzroy captain Gerard Brosnan failed to convert from a set shot 20 metres out at the final bell.

The season boundary umpires were introduced, 1904, was a year of upsets. In Round 7 at the Junction Oval, St Kilda defeated Collingwood for the first time in VFL history, having been thrashed on each of its eighteen previous encounters by an average of 53 points. St Kilda also defeated Fitzroy in Round 9. At the end of the home-and-away season,

South Melbourne missed fourth spot by merely 4.6 per cent, the narrowest margin since the VFL commenced – and smaller than in 1900, when the same team missed out only on percentage (that time 25.7) or 1902, when Geelong missed by 10.7 percentage points. (Thus the excitement in the last home-and-away round about qualifying for the finals has a long history.) Fitzroy won the 1904 flag with a Grand Final win over Carlton. After losing the 1903 premiership so narrowly, the Maroons were not about to let 1904 slip.

Fitzroy went on with it in 1905, winning ten of its fourteen home-and-away games, finishing second to Collingwood. This was champion place-kicker Dave McNamara's first season with St Kilda – in his debut against South Melbourne in Round 13, the Saints had defeated the Southerners for only the third time in VFL history, with McNamara kicking 4 of the team's 5 goals. This match was immortalised in an Edward Dyson short story:

> 'Wade into 'em Saints!' he yelled. 'Swing him on his ear, Cumby.
> Snatch th' 'air off him! Bring 'em down, you boshters! Jump 'em in
> the mud. Good man, Barwick! That shifted 'im. Give 'im another fer
> his mother!'
>
> Benno's 'appiest moments was when a S'melbin' player got busted,
> or took the boot in er tender place, 'n' curled up on the field,
> wrigglin' like a lamed worm. These affectin' incidents stirred th' clerk
> deeply.
>
> 'Oh, a bonzer, a bonzer, a boshter, a bontoshter!' screamed our
> Christian brother. 'Fair in the baloon, 'n' good enough for him! That's
> the way to tease 'em, the blighters! They're lookin' fer it, so let 'em
> have it wet 'n' heavy! Lay 'em out! Stiffen 'em. You can get better
> players fer old bottles anywhere!'[14]

Football 1905-style was still a kick-and-mark affair. In Round 14, Essendon's centre half-back, Michael Madden (sixty-five games) kicked the ball forward only to have it marked by his counterpart Magpie, Jack Monohan (170 games), who marked and kicked it back; this occurred eight times before Monohan in frustration kicked wide to the flank. Minor Premiers Collingwood challenged Fitzroy but were defeated 4.6 (30) to 2.5 (17). Melbourne won its first wooden spoon, and finished last again in 1906.

Carlton had enjoyed little finals experience, but in 1906 won its first of three flags in a row, a feat not equalled in the VFL until Collingwood's four-in-a-row from 1927 to 1930. Carlton was behind Fitzroy on percentage points going into the Grand Final (and thus had no right of challenge) but defeated the Maroons anyway. For the first time since the formation of the VFL, the first and second leading goalkickers were from the same team – Michael Grace, who had crossed from Fitzroy to Carlton, ended 1906 with 50 goals, while team-mate Frank 'Silver' Caine kicked 37. This achievement has never been equalled.

South Melbourne finally made it into the business end of the season in 1907, going down in the Grand Final against Carlton by only 5 points. South had finished fifth on the final ladder in 1906, 1905, 1904, 1902, 1900, 1898 and 1897. St Kilda also did well in 1907, breaking into the finals for the first time. It was such an even year that Essendon finished last with five wins: this was the best wooden-spoon performance until Geelong's effort in 1957.

The following season, 1908, saw two new clubs admitted to the VFL: Richmond, formed in 1885, played out of the Punt Road Oval, and University (1866) shared the East Melbourne Cricket Ground in Jolimont with Essendon. In 1908 Carlton became the first team to go though the home-and-away season with only one loss (defeated only by Essendon in Round 12). The evenness of the VFL competition from its earliest years continued to be one of the great strengths of professional football; it had taken twelve years to obtain this result, and no team has ever got through a VFL season without losing at least one match. This evenness distinguished Australian football from most other codes. Fitzroy had by now slipped from finals contention for a few seasons; in retrospect, the years from 1898 to 1906 had been glory days. Essendon would similarly take some years to assemble a team as fine as that of the 1890s. But as far as the VFL competition was concerned, Carlton's day had arrived. Premiers in 1906, 1907 and 1908, they were runners-up in both 1909 and 1910. From 1903 to 1922 Carlton missed the finals only once.

Carlton's secret was very obvious in retrospect – it was the first club to engage the services of a professional coach, the famous Jack Worrall. A star rover for Fitzroy in the 1880s and a right-handed opening bat for Australia, Worrall joined Carlton in 1902 as a secretary/manager and developed the position of coach. Carlton's glory days had been long ago, back in the 1870s; now, after Worrall, the Blues were destined to become the most consistent club in the VFL. Their finals record was one index of this success; the number of games won on end was another. In 1907 and 1908, Carlton won fifteen games in a row, still a club record. Worrall's coaching style was simple: he recruited men who were tall and could kick long; he joined them on the training track; he kept them to strict schedules and training regimes; and he repeated the same message over and again: 'Boys, booze and football don't mix!'.[15] Jack Worrall brought to his coaching the perspective of a veteran who could reflect on the not inconsiderable changes which had taken place over the preceding several decades. Later again, Worrall said that his Carlton players of 1906 were better than their counterparts in 1936 at the place kick and the drop kick; they and their colonial predecessors were not as quick, he conceded, but as far as Worrall was concerned they made fewer mistakes and they tackled each other cleanly, without using the elbow.[16]

Worrall did not last long into the next season, however, because the players went into open revolt against his disciplinarian methods. (Thus began an interesting tradition in Australian football, where the leadership of the team is determined by democratic means, a method which is puzzling to followers of other team sports.) Worrall was replaced by the Carlton captain, Fred 'Pompey' Elliott. ('Pompey' was a military nickname.) Carlton won the finals series, but South Melbourne exercised its right of challenge as minor Premiers and defeated the Blues by 2 points. So 1909 was South Melbourne's first premiership year. A film excerpt of this Grand Final survives. The players proceed onto the ground in an unhurried way. The crowd is well dressed by the standards of urban Melbourne in 1909. Many have come directly from the office, factory or shop for this Saturday afternoon treat. Children and women are near the front, while the men make up the remainder of the crowd. Play is very much kick and mark, with contests between pairs of players the standard feature of the game. The handball is still evolving and is represented here as a kind of knock-on motion, not yet formally recognised. Carlton, appearing in its fifth Grand Final in a row, goes down to South Melbourne. Its game plan is becoming tired and ineffective against fresher sides.[17]

The year 1910 saw St Kilda slip even further down the ladder, back to its winless ways of the late 1890s. Finally, in the last round of the home-and-away season, the Saints defeated minor Premiers Carlton for their only win of the year. Blues players were accused of being on the take, losing the Second Semi-Final as well. (This was also a period when concussed players were viewed with suspicion, so it is difficult to know how seriously these charges of bribery should be taken.) But the Carlton boys bounced back the next Saturday and fought a Grand Final not equalled for brutality in the VFL until the infamous Bloodbath Grand Final of 1945. This was meanwhile University's best year, with ten wins for the ill-fated team led by Harry and Ted Cordner (the latter was the father of the four boys who served Melbourne so well in the 1940s).

By 1911 Jack Worrall had gone to Essendon, and under his coaching the Same Olds won all but two games that season, with another match drawn. They went down to South Melbourne by merely 3 points, and to Carlton by 12 in a minor mid-season slump. Their final percentage was a mammoth 177.5, the best since Collingwood's in 1902. The Essendon achievement in 1911 would never again be bettered in the VFL competition – no side is ever again likely to compile as overwhelming a lead over its opponents. This is the answer to the old-timers who regret the passing of the days of low scores, that although the absolute results in Australian football doubled during the course of the twentieth century, in relative terms the competition became much tougher. The 1911 finalists were the same as in the two preceding years: Essendon, South Melbourne, Carlton and Collingwood. University slipped from sixth to last (tenth), while St Kilda was wracked by industrial trouble. This was the year when financial rewards for players were deemed legitimate, and the St Kilda committee's attempts to introduce economies by cutting the supply of dressing-room tickets brought about an open revolt by the players. In this regard the players reflected the society at large – the 1910s were a period of intense class conflict throughout Australia, and player dissatisfaction was one manifestation of this. Class identity unifying an entire club was another. St Kilda's industrial problems spilled onto the field: in Round 15, only six regular Saints stripped to play Carlton, so the club was forced to fill the team with ring-ins. Naturally they were thrashed, 18.21 (129) to 2.3 (15)!

The next year, 1912, saw Collingwood replaced in the finals by the Pivotonians (the nickname reflecting Geelong's pivotal role in Western Victoria). It was in fact the first time in VFL history that the Magpies did not make the final four (and it would only happen four more times in all the seasons leading up to World War II). Their failure was largely due to the absence through injury of star full-forward Dick Lee, who topped their goalkicking most years in his playing career between 1906 and 1922. His famous knee injury may well have been the origin of the expression, 'Dickie knee'; in any event, his cartilage operation of 1912 was the first one recorded in Australian football.[18] Lee overcame shin and knee problems to play 230 games, kicking 707 goals for Collingwood. When numbers were first allocated to all players in 1912 (on the basis of alphabet) Lee joked he would receive '13' owing to his bad luck with injuries – this proved to be true, and he went on to make the guernsey famous. Two of Lee's trademarks were running sideways off the opposition full-back and pulling in spectacularly high marks. Essendon held off a determined Fitzroy in Round 18 and then won all three finals games to win a second flag under coach Worrall.

The following season Essendon plummeted to eighth, a drop not seen again until Hawthorn's slide after its 1961 flag. Essendon's fortunes would not recover until it left East Melbourne for Windy Hill in 1922. Fitzroy, South Melbourne and Collingwood had raced away to lead the ladder by the end of the home-and-away season. Fourth spot came down to a battle between St Kilda and Carlton in Round 15, won by the Saints on the last kick of the day. Ironically, although his team was winless for the entire season, University's Roy Park headed the goalkicking tally at the end of Round 18. In the finals campaign, newcomer St Kilda kept winning but faltered in the Grand Final against the Maroons.

The 1913 finals campaign was the only one to have been missed by Carlton in the entire 1903–22 period; the team was not to let it happen again in 1914. That season opened with two draws in Round 1, another draw in Round 4 and a fourth in Round 12. By Round 14 only two wins separated the leading seven teams. In Round 18 Geelong played in an all-blue guernsey at Victoria Park to avoid confusion with Collingwood and won 8.10 (58) to 4.10 (34). (It was only the Pivotonians' fifth victory at Victoria Park since 1897.) The 1914 premiership as expected went to minor Premiers Carlton.

The four seasons dogged by war, 1915 to 1918, saw first the abolition of University, five clubs in recess during 1916, the return of Geelong and South Melbourne in 1917, then Essendon and St Kilda back from recess in 1918. (Melbourne did not return until 1919.) University's remaining players went to Melbourne, helping it to make the finals in

1915 – the Redlegs went down in the First Semi-Final to eventual Premiers Carlton. The shortened 1916 season, with only four teams competing, was won by Fitzroy, with only its fifth win for the year! The following year saw a fairer result, with Collingwood winning in a six-team competition. The 1918 flag was won by South Melbourne after it lost only one match all season, out of fourteen played.[19]

The call to arms in 1914 did not have the same urgency in working-class and Catholic clubs (Collingwood, Carlton, Fitzroy, Richmond) that it did in the better-heeled areas exemplified by Melbourne, South Melbourne, Essendon and the rest. L. A. 'Dicky' Adamson, the Wesley College principal who had not given up his fight against professionalism in football, remarked bitterly that the 1915 premiership team members (Carlton) should each receive an Iron Cross instead of the traditional medals. Recruiters who spoke at football matches during 1917 received a hostile reaction. At Brunswick Street they were physically assaulted.[20] There was a distinct cultural and social chasm between those clubs which stayed in and those which stayed out. It is a sign of the politically integrative power of football, however, that this cleavage did not lead to a permanent rift.

Out in the west, the 1900 season opened in Western Australia with four new district teams replacing the colonial competition dominated by Fremantle. East Fremantle and South Fremantle played out of the Fremantle Oval, while Perth and West Perth used the WA Cricket Association Ground as their base. Griff John started the South Fremantle club in 1900 after the financial collapse of the old Fremantle club the previous year. Subiaco and North Fremantle joined the Association in 1901, bringing with them new ovals at Shenton Park and North Fremantle. A Midlands Junction team entered in 1905, bringing the total number of teams to seven. In 1906 a new East Perth team entered the competition (nicknamed the 'Young Easts' in deference to East Fremantle), based on a confectionary workers' team called Unions. So from 1906 to 1910 there were eight teams in the WAFL. In 1908 Subiaco Oval was used for the first time (it later became the WAFL headquarters) and East Perth in 1910 moved to Loton's Park (Perth Oval). Fremantle Oval, with its new grandstand, was the game's showcase ground. Midlands Junction did not compete in the WAFL from 1911 to 1913, but returned in 1914. North Fremantle withdrew at the end of the 1915 season, after winning only one game out of twenty-one; Midlands withdrew at the end of a winless 1917 season. Neither side reappeared after the war, and the Western Australian competition started the 1918 season with six settled teams.

Fremantle's first football matches had been played on the Green, from 1906 the site of the railway station. Contests between Perth Boys School and Fremantle Christian Brothers traditionally 'ended up in a stand-up fight or two'. Fremantle Oval, further inland, was originally the parade ground for the Convict Establishment of the 1860s. Its grandstand, built in 1897 to the design of F.W. Burwell, is classified by the National Trust and is Australia's oldest football grandstand still in use. East Fremantle and South Fremantle both used the ground for many years, which did nothing to diminish the intense rivalry between the two teams. There was an ingenious suggestion that the centre of the trotting ground adjacent to what became East Fremantle Oval should be used for games, but the trotting fraternity were not keen on the idea. A derelict grandstand was demolished free of charge by the American military when they occupied East Fremantle Oval during World War II; in 1963 the Nipper Truscott Pavilion was built at the ground. The healthy rivalry between working-class South Fremantle and middle-class East Fremantle was to animate both clubs and spur them on in the Western Australian competition. The Foundation Day holiday (the first Monday in June) became permanently fixtured as a local Derby between Old Easts and the Bulldogs.

East Fremantle won most of the flags in the 1900–18 period, and even those it lost were usually lost only by accident. After winning the flag in 1900, Old Easts lost the last match of the 1901 season to West Perth. East Fremantle then convincingly won in 1902, 1903 and 1904. The 1905 and 1907 final matches were only lost following scoring disputes. (West Perth took the premiership in 1905; Perth in 1907 after appealing against a Charles Doig goal.) The years 1906, 1908, 1909, 1910 and 1911 were all East Fremantle years. Subiaco, under the presidency of Labor Premier John Scaddan, won the competition in 1912 and 1913. East Fremantle were Premiers again in 1914 and 1918. During the war years the reduced competition was won by Subiaco (1915) and by South Fremantle (1916, 1917).[21]

Football had also taken hold in the Kalgoorlie goldfields. The classic Kalgoorlie photograph taken by J.J. Dwyer 'Leaving a Football match, 22 September 1907' illustrates the power of this game to attract a generous-sized crowd. The crowd has been animated by the spectacle; it comprises women as well as men, young and old, all well dressed for the event.[22] The crowd forgets its normal inhibitions in front of Dwyer's camera. This match was played between local teams Hainault and Boulder – the tribalism in the VFL competition had its counterpart in regional centres typified by Kalgoorlie. Football started on the goldfields in the West because so many diggers were Victorians. It then took off, and even a junior competition developed on the goldfields. Mr A. Griffiths and the Kalgoorlie Junior Football Club posed for J. J. Dwyer in a set portrait of September 1914.[23] Football became an important element of Kalgoorlie life, a key to young men's socialisation. Goldfields people found in football a game which fitted naturally into the frontier conditions of Kalgoorlie.

Football was also developing well in South Australia. Despite some political difficulties, the electorate system of district football survived into the 1900 season, and with Sturt joining that year, it was now a contest among seven clubs – South Adelaide, Port Adelaide, Norwood, North Adelaide, Sturt, West Adelaide and West Torrens. North and Norwood each won the premiership three times in the 1900–15 period, Port five times, West Adelaide four times, and Sturt once. Every season from 1910 to 1915 Port Adelaide were Premiers or runners-up. Port's longest winning-run was thirty games; out of eighty-eight matches played over those six years, the Magpies lost only thirteen, drawing once and winning seventy-four.[24] The strength of Port Adelaide has been outstanding, even though the district idea underwrote the overall quality of the South Australian football competition. This ensured the success of the game in that state.

In 1915, Sturt won its first premiership, with a side that included centreman Bill Mayman. Mayman was to represent Western Australia, South Australia and Tasmania in Carnival football. Eventual Test captain Vic Richardson played at centre half-back.

The strength of football in three of Australia's six states meant that interstate Carnivals were regularly organised by the national football council. The success of Carnivals made up for the game's failure to win acceptance in New South Wales. Some football had also been played in New Zealand, but political dissension among its administrators saw its demise in 1911. It would not recover until the 1980s. The period from 1900 to 1918 saw Rugby League expanding across the suburbs of

Sydney, but Australian Rules by now had laid claim to Victoria, South Australia and Western Australia. The war had checked its progress, but it was about to emerge more strongly than ever in those communities where it had found devotees. Australian football was a potent source of community pride, particularly in working-class localities where proletarian organisations were taking shape.

The Anzac Heritage

Australians stumbled from the carnage of the Great War and sought to reconstitute the familiar rituals of Edwardian life in the new suburbs of the 1920s. The decade from 1919 to 1930 capped football's half-century of national expansion. Three clubs crossed from the VFA to the League in 1925, while University merged with Melbourne. Of the twelve clubs now making up the mature VFL, far and away the most powerful was Collingwood, which brought a new military-style discipline to the team and to its game plan. Before coming into the League, Footscray had dominated the VFA from 1919 to 1924 with similarly disciplined play, while over in Western Australia, another working-class team, East Perth, was the dominant force in the early 1920s (from 1918 to 1923). The Anzac Legend, as it came to be called, provided a new framework within which clubs, their players and the barrackers could understand the underlying discipline of the game. John Worrall welcomed the 1920 season of 'King Football' with explicit reference to World War I:

> The qualities that Australians were noted for at the war are all existent in our game. Dash – glorious dash – resource, determination, a never-say-die spirit, lasting power, gameness and 'help your neighbour' are essentials in our game that permeated the breasts of all our Australian boys at the war.[1]

Baldwin Spencer, professor of biology at the University of Melbourne, took over as president of the VFL and helped rectify what was regarded as an ill-administered game.[2] He was followed by another gentleman-scholar, the Melbourne Football Club's Dr William McClelland, who presided over the VFL for three decades.

It was not until the 1920s that newspaper accounts of Australian Rules began to take over the pages of Melbourne's dailies. A page somewhere in the middle of the *Herald* or the *Argus* would be given over to a summary of the previous Saturday's VFL and VFA matches. The *Sun News-Pictorial* burst onto the scene in 1925 with glorious photographs of the 'action'. Suburban weeklies such as the Richmond *Guardian* (to which historian Cec Mullen contributed) also devoted considerable space to football goings-on. Radio broadcasts of football also commenced in 1925, just two years after the 'wireless' began to appear in Melbourne households. The first broadcaster was Wally 'Jumbo' Sharland on 3AR, followed by Norman Banks in 1931 and 3UZ's Jack Gurry in 1932. These pioneers usually had to call the game from precipitous makeshift structures. (The MCC did not give permission for finals broadcasts to be made from the MCG until 1946.)[3]

This new interest in football coincided with the popularisation of the Anzac myth. Sports journalists began to construct more elaborate metaphors of football, especially around the theme of battle. The widespread Anzac values percolated through this coverage: individual players became heroes of battle, just as the common foot-soldier was seen to have won the day through particular acts of courage and tenacity.

Football had never sought Royal patronage: neither did it now seek legitimation through a connection with Australia's military elite. On those occasions when ex-servicemen played football, or when footballers went on to become servicemen, their military connection was usually left unrecognised – especially when they became high-ranking officers. Stretton, hero of the Darwin rebuilding, is not given his official title of Major-General when his days as St Kilda's full-back are remembered. (It was his unfortunate duty to play on Fred Fanning on the afternoon in 1947 when the latter kicked his 18 goals at the Junction Oval.)

A historian of Richmond Football Club during the 1930s Depression noted the strength of this Anzac theme during the interwar period, such as in descriptions of the team as a 'fighting machine' waging war against other clubs in battle.

Although many of the Richmond football team had no direct experience of the war, the tradition of Anzac was mediated and perpetuated. Many of the club officials and former players who were involved with the club during the Depression years, had, unlike those they coached, experienced active service in the war.[4]

Anzac images and actual strategies were a natural part of this generation's experience. But it was not widely known that these officials had military backgrounds, that Checker Hughes, for example, had been a Warrant Officer Class II during the war. In other words, football perpetuated the distinctively Australian notion that the nation's military heritage belonged to the foot soldier, not to the officers.

Another effect of the war was that St Kilda gave up wearing its original colours of black, red and white for the duration, since these were the colours of Imperial Germany. (The crest would be added in 1933.) Collingwood made no such change, even though black and white were the colours of Prussia.[5]

The war and the conscription debate had exposed the importance of religion in suburban Melbourne. Catholicism has always played a part in three working-class clubs: at Richmond it has pervaded the club, less vehemently than at North Melbourne, but with rather more passion than at Collingwood.

Richmond was a self-contained universe, bounded to the south and east by the Yarra River, protected to the west by the emerald expanse of Yarra Park, separated from Collingwood by Victoria Street. Richmond was the classic Irish–Australian locality, part of the working-class Catholic suburbs which then fringed central Melbourne in the inner east. North Melbourne and Collingwood were also proletarian and Catholic, but Richmond and its football club had some qualities which marked it apart. Some of these differences deserve emphasis and were reflected in its football. Richmond's blue-collar population shared a culture based around its hotels, the attendant street life (such as starting-price bookmakers, the racing industry, bingo nights in the front parlour) and semiskilled employment such as the Melbourne waterfront. It was a mix of the rough and the respectable, but above all tolerant – its full-back was an Aboriginal hairdresser, Vic Thorp; Dave Moffatt was as rugged as any other tough proletarian; while Barney Herbet was a gentle giant.

Richmond Football Club struggled in 1918 and 1919; indeed, some of its players were thrown out of the club for accepting bribes. (Bribery was common to the period: 1919 was the year the Chicago White Sox threw the baseball World Series.) The 1920 premiership side represented the new vigour of this community and the ethos of the selfless Anzac. Returned soldiers such as Hughes, Bill Thomas, Hugh James and Danny Minogue featured in this side.

Other dominant football clubs of the 1920s taking the Anzac fighting image to heart included those representing two suburbs which were industrialised in this period – East Perth and Footscray. Footscray's intense parochialism as a club can be explained by the suburb's relative isolation from the rest of the VFL competition. Footscray was already a strong club in its VFA days, before 1925, but shared the inner western area with VFA clubs Yarraville and Williamstown. In some ways it resembled East Perth in the Western Australian competition – both were localities in which noxious industries were located, conveniently adjacent to the central city but sufficiently removed from it.

Footscray was well-known for buying good players, such as Collingwood's McCarthy, and it was not long before this liberality with money was used to bribe other VFA teams to play dead. Footscray's ex-player Vernon Banbury was disqualified for life for his part in inducing several Port Melbourne players to lose the 1922 Grand Final.[6]

However, while Footscray's dominant values were Protestant, the quintessential working-class club was Collingwood, where Roman Catholic values played a bigger part. Collingwood's fierce local loyalty was moulded in the prewar days – but the real results of this club spirit were about to be seen. Indeed, Collingwood's reign from 1925 to 1930 has yet to be bettered by any AFL side. There were tangible reasons for Collingwood's success in the 1920s.

A major one was 'Jock' McHale. McHale's Scottish nickname was an ironic reference to his Roman Catholicism. An iron-man as a player, in the annals of the game he comes second only to Jack Titus in playing continuous VFL matches (191 in a row from 1906 to 1917) and he also served as Collingwood coach from 1913 to 1950, easily a VFL record. He left individual coaching to his assistants and concentrated on the main game. His philosophy was that each player should mind his man and not go too far from his own place on the field. His half-time speeches were always about the spirit of the club, designed to ignite the fire in the belly of the players.[7] McHale's game plan never changed from the 1920s to the 1940s, and it was devastating in the first decade, even if it was to become obsolete in later years.

Life-time supporter Tom Wanliss started following Collingwood in 1932, but not because of any particular champion heroes – 'There were blokes who wouldn't have got a game in another club, but they were a champion team!' His father was a Hawthorn supporter who took the tram from their Caulfield home to Glenferrie Oval on Saturday afternoons – but the Mayblooms were nowhere near as glamorous as Collingwood and did not succeed in building up a substantial supporter base in the VFL. (Their nickname was a pun on the hawthorn bush.) Collingwood did not have the same reputation for die-hard Catholicism as Richmond and North Melbourne; although Catholic at core, the club was welcoming of Protestants such as the Coventrys, the Colliers, and lanky centre half-forward Harry Curtis. The fact that North Melbourne survived, wedged geographically between Protestant clubs Essendon and Footscray, was partly due to its Catholic character.

Without runners, the playing captain enjoyed relatively more power than the non-playing coach in that period. Coaches began to exert more authority during the conduct of a match with the introduction of the quarter-time addresses in 1964 and the provision of runners. McHale was distant emotionally, even from the reserves coach Hughie Thomas. McHale did not shout at the players; he merely spoke quietly and firmly. He knew a great deal about preparation and fitness but had little interest in tactics: when 'Tubby' Edmonds kicked 5 goals in the 1929 Grand Final and Gordon Coventry played decoy, it was allegedly Edmonds and not McHale who had thought of the tactic. When Jack Regan early in his career apologised to McHale for missing an easy goal, the coach simply barked, 'Go jump in the bloody river!'[8]

Collingwood continued to receive plenty of political support from John Wren, the back-lane SP bookie who had made it. (His portrait hangs anonymously in the Social Club at Victoria Park.) Materially he gave 5 guineas each year in the period 1895 to 1900, but then gave nothing during the prewar years. The major donor during those years was Sir John Madden, the Chief Justice of Victoria. Wren's financial support for the club resumed after the First World War.[9]

The District Football League was introduced in 1919, and this encouraged a return to local talent in the side.[10] Many of the Collingwood seconds players were members of the Dons larrikin push; some of the seniors belonged to the Riley Street push. These young men were not strangers to violence; events in one spirited match against Carlton at Princes Park in 1922 led to the second civil charge arising out of a VFL game – Magpie full-back Harry Saunders was fined 5 pounds for assaulting Blue Alec Duncan.

The Collingwood–Fitzroy rivalry abated on the football field after the early 1920s, although the Maroons could still be relied upon to stage an upset against Collingwood when it was least expected or desired. A more public rivalry, however, now developed with Richmond, a club at last coming into its own in VFL ranks in the early 1920s. This new rivalry owed a great deal to Richmond's pretensions to becoming a champion club, but was triggered in particular by the Minogue incident of 1919. Dan Minogue, an erstwhile Collingwood captain, came back from the war with the desire to captain-coach the Tigers. To make matters worse, his new team defeated Collingwood in the 1920 Grand Final. Minogue's portrait was turned to the wall at Victoria Park. Collingwood did not mind its champions going to captain-coach a team in the VFA or in the bush, where in fact ex-Magpies could earn more money. Indeed, Collingwood helped Con McCarthy negotiate his job at Footscray. Others in this period went to Stawell (Bill Twomey Sr), Port Melbourne (Len 'Gus' Dobrigh), Northcote (Maurice Sheehy) and Benalla (Tom 'Chick' Drummond). Minogue's action was inexcusable, because Collingwood valued loyalty to the club above all else. No other captain deserted a VFL club until Barassi quit Melbourne in 1964.

Collingwood brimmed with confidence. Losing the 1926 Grand Final to Melbourne was such a shock because the Fuchsias were not taken seriously at Collingwood. (Melbourne's nickname reflected their guernsey colours and their pretty football.) Captain Charlie Tyson was even accused of playing dead.[11] The mid-season trip to Perth in 1927 was an important catalyst for the flag. The reintroduction of the out-of-bounds rule, from 1925 to 1939, helped strong teams like Collingwood by keeping the ball in the centre of the ground, shunning the wings. The new handball rule of 1927 stipulated the ball had to be held in the hand before it was punched. Collingwood also began to experiment with the punt kick, which began to win favour over the drop kick and the place kick.[12] Camaraderie among the Collingwood players was so strong that nothing came of a mooted strike in July 1928, when the 3 pound match payments were temporarily cut by 10 shillings.[13] These were all factors in Collingwood's extraordinary dominance during the period.

The 1919 season in the VFL was memorable for the return of Melbourne to what was now a nine-team competition, and for the creation of a Reserves competition. St Kilda had an up-and-down year, defeating Collingwood for the first time at Victoria Park – a success it would not repeat until 1962! – but going down to 1918 Premiers South Melbourne by 171 points. This would stand until 1979 as the VFL's biggest drubbing, and included a record 17.4 (106) final quarter by the Southerners. The Saints were down to fifteen through injury, and four other players left the field in disgust. As so often happens in professional football, however, St Kilda rebounded to win its next two matches, against Essendon and then against Geelong. Melbourne had very few of its 1915 players left and lost every match of the 1919 season. The shape of the final four was not determined until the end of Round 18, the last home-and-away matches. Fitzroy failed to beat Collingwood on a wet day at Brunswick Street and finished the season fifth. The Maroons would have made the finals if fourth-placed Richmond had defeated third-ranking Carlton at Punt Road in front of 35,000 people, but the Blues snatched the game in the last eight minutes of play. During the finals, upstart Richmond made it as far as the Grand Final, only to lose to minor Premiers Collingwood. The Magpies also won the inaugural Reserves flag, and with 56 goals Collingwood's Walter ('Dick') Lee topped the senior goalkicking list for the fifth time in six seasons, a VFL record. It was a portent of how thoroughly Collingwood would dominate the decade. From 1919 to 1930 Collingwood won five senior premierships (1919, 1927, 1928, 1929, 1930), including their record four-in-a-row, and four Reserves premierships (1919, 1920, 1922, 1925), which laid the foundations for the club's overall success.

Round 5 of 1920 featured a fine match at Punt Road between the previous year's Grand Finalists, in front of 30,000 people. The Magpies pegged back the Richmond lead until a mark was taken on the forward line in the last minutes by the cool Hugh James, who calmly steered through a goal despite the considerable distraction of a stand collapsing under the pressure of the excited crowd. (No-one was badly hurt.) Richmond went on to have a good season: in Round 9 it was trailing Essendon by 25 points with scant minutes remaining, yet kicked 7.3 (45) in fading light to win easily. In Round 13 at Victoria Park Richmond again defeated Collingwood, but only after the Magpies hit the post and then conceded a free kick in the Richmond forward line. On 28 August, Carlton thrashed Collingwood in front of 51,000 people at Princes Park. Fitzroy faltered in the finals despite having won the previous ten games. Melbourne improved on 1919 with five wins to its name at the end of the season. Richmond defeated Collingwood in the Grand Final, 7.10 (52) to 5.5 (35) to win its first VFL flag.

After losing only three matches in 1920, Fitzroy lost its first three matches in 1921 and managed only a draw in Round 4. Five draws and four 1-point results were recorded in 1921. Melbourne in particular was in several cliff-hangers for the season, finishing with six wins and two draws. Geelong, again at its own request, took the bye in Round 1 (as it did every year from 1919 to 1924). The final four were settled with several rounds to complete the season. Essendon won the 1921 wooden spoon, half a game behind St Kilda. With eight wins in a row, Richmond took the 1921 flag, and so its first two VFL flags were back-to-back. It was the fourth club to earn this distinction.

Essendon had its first season at Windy Hill in 1922 and christened its new ground in Round 1 with a triumphant win over Carlton, the 1921 runners-up, in front of 22,000 fans. The Blues had defeated Essendon in eleven of the fourteen encounters before 1922; from 1922 the tables were turned – Essendon won its first five matches at Windy Hill against Carlton. Essendon clung to the top of the ladder and finished the season in second place – a significant improvement on ninth position in 1921. It was a season of champion forwards – the erratic Robert Merrick for the Maroons, who kicked nine against St Kilda, Roy Cazaly at South, and Dick Lee, who kicked his 700th goal in his final year at Collingwood. Unfortunately Lee missed some chances in the Grand Final, and the Magpies went down to Fitzroy, 9.14 (68) to 11.13 (79). There was a new star at Victoria Park named Gordon Coventry, who booted 42 goals, only 14 fewer than the leader, the high-marking Horrie Clover at Carlton.

Essendon continued to do well in the 1923 season, thanks largely to its 'Mosquito Fleet', eight senior players 5 feet 6 inches or shorter in height. On the last Saturday of the home-and-away fixtures, six of the VFL's nine clubs still believed they could win the flag. Behind Essendon and Fitzroy, three teams were tied on eight wins – South, St Kilda and Geelong – with Collingwood only half a game behind and favoured by a good percentage. So the 15 September Lakeside Derby at Albert Park was vital to the shape of the final four: Cazaly was now playing for South, and Dave McNamara was playing his last season as captain-coach for the Saints. Fans broke down the fence to squeeze in, and the final crowd was about 49,000, despite rain. South led by a few points at every change, and won, 8.20 (68) to 7.6 (48). At Corio Oval, Geelong made no mistake with Carlton to stay in the finals (the Blues missed the finals for the first time in nine seasons). Collingwood had needed either a Geelong loss or a Lakeside draw, but got neither, so it too missed the finals. The Grand Final was delayed until 20 October owing to heavy rain, and was won by Essendon over Fitzroy. The 1923 season was also the first since 1901 that the Same Olds topped the goalkicking list, with 68 goals to the dashing left-footer Greg Stockdale.

Nineteen twenty-four will be remembered as the year in which the VFL first awarded the Brownlow Medal, struck to commemorate the Geelong administrator Charles Brownlow. Happily for Geelong, the first Brownlow was won by one of its players, 'Carji' Greeves. Geelong finished 1924 in fifth spot – it was almost a necessary consequence of the Brownlow voting system that the medallion often went to the best player in an average team. Football was increasingly popular with Victorians; crowd sizes were growing so greatly that from this season on the VFL arranged the fixtures so that Melbourne and Richmond did not play home games on the same Saturday, nor St Kilda and South Melbourne. This policy was designed to ease traffic congestion around Yarra Park and Albert Park respectively. Traffic flow was one of the myriad ways football was starting to affect the culture of Melbourne and other cities. Collingwood and Carlton started the 1924 season well, with their full-forwards Gordon Coventry and Clover both kicking good scores. Richmond was winless by Round 5 but then recovered and had ten wins to its name by the end of the season, making it into fourth place. Collingwood lost six in a row in the latter half of the home-and-away season, thanks largely to injuries. Fitzroy, which had not lost a match by the time the clubs had played each other once, tried a new human pyramid method when standing the mark. Melbourne's season petered out, but its discovery of a new full-forward in the lightly-framed Harry Davie kept it off the bottom rung; St Kilda also had managed only four wins, but had a weaker percentage. The finals system used in 1924 was the same as that used in 1897, and equally flawed. Because Essendon won its first two finals matches convincingly, it did not need to win the

Grand Final (against Richmond) and proceeded not to. That evening the Windy Hill premiership celebrations turned sour when some players quarrelled with team-mates who had not tried their hardest. The VFL abandoned the round-robin finals system after 1924.

At last, in 1925, the dreaded bye was removed from the VFL competition, and it would not reappear until 1942. The plan had been to admit just one new team, and at least eight VFA clubs had applied during 1924 to move across to the VFL. Following an all-night meeting of the VFL, Footscray, Hawthorn and North Melbourne were all invited to join the League. North, which was making its third attempt (the others were in 1907 and 1921) only just eased out Prahran. (Rivalry with cricket clubs at football clubs like Collingwood was so bitter that aspirants who did not share control of their ground with a cricket club were more welcome in VFL ranks.)[14] North was the only one of the newcomers to win its first VFL match, in a thrilling encounter at Corio Oval, but it finished the 1925 season with merely five wins and languished at tenth position on the League ladder. Footscray managed just five wins and Hawthorn three. Hawthorn's first VFL win did not happen until Round 5 when it defeated fellow newcomer Footscray at Glenferrie. North continued to play tough football – in a match against Geelong in Round 12 there were six players reported on seventeen charges. During 1925, 1926 and 1927, the new clubs – Footscray, North Melbourne and Hawthorn – made up the tenth, eleventh and twelfth places on the ladder. In fact it would take almost three decades (1954) before the bottom three clubs on the final ladder did not include at least one of these three new clubs, and another two decades (1974) before all three reached the finals in the same season. This suggests the extent of the gap between VFA and VFL standards in the 1920s.

The reigning Premiers Essendon continued to do well in 1925, and won thirteen of the seventeen home-and-away matches, only to be defeated by Collingwood in the First Semi-Final. Fitzroy narrowly missed the finals on percentage points to Collingwood, and was not to make the finals again until 1943. Melbourne improved on its 1924 performance, finishing third with twelve wins and a draw. More significantly, its defence conceded less than 1000 points for the entire season, the second-last team to do so. Geelong was having a brilliant season in 1925. Against South in Round 10 it kicked 11.4 (70) to nil, a first-quarter record not bettered until 1972. Geelong lost only two matches in the season and slipped in the Second Semi-Final, but defeated Collingwood to claim its first VFL flag, a quarter of a century after being instrumental in creating the League in the first place. Geelong's aerialist Lloyd Hagger was leading goalkicker, but only 10 goals behind him with 68 for the season was young Gordon Coventry.

Nineteen twenty-six was only the third VFL season (after 1922 and 1924) during which all competing clubs kicked 1000 points or more for the season. It would take another five decades before tallies of 2000 points became commonplace. After 1926, with only five exceptions (North Melbourne in 1930, St Kilda in 1943, Hawthorn in 1953, St Kilda in 1955, Fitzroy in 1963) no VFL team finished below 1000 points in total. The basic reason for this sudden jump in the scoring was a seemingly innocuous rule introduced in 1922 which penalised players who forced the ball out of bounds; the rule was strengthened in 1924 to include any kind of kicking the ball across the line, whether deliberate or on the full. This rule, which lasted until the 1939 season, greatly helped offensive teams like Collingwood in the 1920s and Melbourne in the 1930s which had strong forward lines. Strong, direct football was the result. Australian Rules thus tended in a different direction from English football, where clean possession was not rewarded in this manner.

The 1926 season was more interesting than the shape of the final four would suggest. Collingwood, Geelong, Melbourne and Essendon finished on top – the same four as in 1925. North slumped and did not win any matches, though it drew with Hawthorn, 10.10 (70) to 10.10 (70) at Glenferrie in Round 13. The Northerners lost five games by less than a kick. South Melbourne also suffered a cruel season, defeating Geelong at Albert Park as it had done every year since 1905. The following round, Round 12 at Punt Road, South was trailing 8.8 to 9.14 at lemons (three-quarter time) but rattled on 8 goals in the last quarter with good linking play from ex-Magpie Charlie Pannam to captain Paddy Scanlan to Edward Johnson and won convincingly. But in Round 17 at home South lost to Collingwood by 1 goal and missed the finals on percentage. Essendon stayed ahead of South because in the last match South won by only 3 points. In the famous finals match between Melbourne and Essendon the Redlegs won by 3 points thanks to the courage of Bob Corbett, who defied doctor's orders to run back onto the field with his bandaged head and inspire his team-mates. Essendon did not recover from this loss; its next finals appearance was not until 1940. The following week Melbourne astounded its critics by defeating Collingwood 17.17 (119) to 9.8 (62), a record which would stand until the 1946 Grand Final. To cap off Melbourne's year, Ivor Warne-Smith won his first Brownlow and the two Redlegs wins against Collingwood in the finals campaign were the only Melbourne wins against McHale between 1922 and 1937. 'The spirit of 'twenty-six' was so important to Melbourne that it became a line in the club song. They had earned their new nickname, Redlegs, a reference to their red socks. But an indication of what lay in store was Gordon Coventry's effort in kicking 83 goals for the season.

Melbourne's 1926 triumph over Collingwood was a false dawn, for 1927 and the subsequent seasons belonged to the black-and-white army. In fact Melbourne lost every game to Collingwood from 1927 to 1937. Melbourne and Essendon slipped out of the four; they were replaced by Richmond and Carlton. The Collingwood team in 1927 discovered that it could win without relying on Gordon Coventry; he was goalless against the Tigers at Punt Road, yet the Magpies won comfortably. At Victoria Park on the blustery Saturday 3 September against Essendon, McHale instructed Coventry to play out from the goals, and the full-forward's team-mates took advantage of the open forward line. Geelong overcame its Albert Park hoodoo and finished the year third, with fourteen wins. The Grand Final was so wet it might well have been postponed. Coventry kicked Collingwood's only 2 goals in the second quarter to ensure a sluggish win over Richmond, 2.13 (25) to 1.7 (13). Collingwood became the first club in 1927 to take all three major prizes: the premiership, the Brownlow (Syd Coventry) and the leading goalkicker honour, to younger brother Gordon 'Nuts' Coventry, with 97 goals.

As with 1927, so with 1928. Collingwood met an improved North after the Shinboners defeated Carlton for the first time in VFL history (in Round 5 at Arden Street), and was more than a match for them. Similarly it withstood Melbourne in Round 9. Melbourne took Geelong's place in the final four, drew with Collingwood in the Second Semi-Final, and then lost by four points in the replay. In the Grand Final, Coventry sealed Richmond's fate with a record 9 goals and led the goalkicking again, this time with 89 goals. Melbourne's Warne-Smith became the first player to win a second Brownlow.

The glamour team continued to win in 1929, and would again play off against Richmond. The other finalists were Carlton and St Kilda, but since the Magpies won all eighteen of their home-and-away games, losing only the Second Semi-Final, the result was never really in doubt. Their percentage was a very impressive 172 per cent. The opening game against Richmond was ominous, with Collingwood kicking 13 goals straight (no behinds), a record not equalled until the 1970s. The 1929 Magpies became the first team to kick 2000 points in a season, with 1918 points scored in their home-and-away season. Again they also won the goalkicking tally ('Nuts' Coventry) and the Brownlow (Albert 'Leeter' Collier). Coventry set a new record for goals in a match (16 against Hawthorn in Round 13) and was the first VFL player to boot 100 goals in a season – in fact he kicked 124, an extraordinary improvement upon his 89 for the previous year, and not equalled until Pratt's 150 in 1934.

In 1930 Collingwood won its fourth premiership in a row, a feat unsurpassed in VFL history. Naturally, Carlton did not want to have its three-in-a-row effort of 1906, 1907 and 1908 eclipsed, so provided real opposition to the Magpies. In a thriller at Princes Park in Round 10, 40,000 fans saw the Blues come from an 11-point deficit at the nineteen-minute mark to win 16.20 (116) to 16.12 (112). Clover finished with eight and Vallence chipped in when it mattered. Melbourne began the season well, the smooth George Margitich kicking 11 against Essendon, then lost to Collingwood (which had the wood on it), and defeated Carlton in Round 15 by 6 points. But in one of the VFL's great boilovers, the lowly Mayblooms knocked Melbourne out of the final four with a stunning win in Round 18. Hawthorn put on 5 goals 8 behinds in the third quarter to win 12.18 (90) to 10.17 (77). Collingwood lost the final to Geelong, but exercised its right as the minor Premiers to play a Grand Final, and won convincingly, 14.16 (100) to 9.16 (70). Once again Coventry was the League's leading goalkicker.[15]

The Association was still a major force in Victorian football. When it lost the three teams to the VFL in 1925, the VFA was keen to build its numbers again and so admitted Coburg, Preston and Camberwell. Camberwell had dominated the Melbourne Districts Association, now renamed the League Sub-Districts, with teams such as Fairfield and Public Service. Oakleigh had prevented Camberwell from winning four Districts flags in a row by the last kick of the day in the 1924 Grand Final. In 1929 the VFA decided to expand to twelve teams, and took in Oakleigh and Sandringham, so as to capitalise on Melbourne's eastward suburban growth. Oakleigh, administered by publican Bill Wilkins and the sharp

Harry Wilkins, was led on the field by Frank Maher (ex-Essendon), Eric Fleming (ex-Geelong) and George Rudolph (ex-Richmond, and Jack Dyer's boyhood idol). With these three stalwarts and a stream of other handsomely paid ex-VFL players – such as Ted Thomas, part of Melbourne's 1926 premiership side – Oakleigh was a popular and successful club, boasting 1500 members. Oakleigh won its first three VFA games and finished the 1929 season in fifth spot. In only its second year Oakleigh won the first of two back-to-back VFA flags (1930, 1931). These were tough days in Association football – a brawl at the 1930 Grand Final led to five umpires being suspended and several players and officials being censured.[16] (Oakleigh became a consistent VFA performer, winning more flags in 1950, 1952, 1960 and 1972.) The VFA introduced several innovations during the 1920s, including a free kick for out-of-bounds play, two interchange players, and medical attendants at matches.[17]

In South Australia, the competition revived after the war. In 1921, Glenelg was admitted to the competition. In this first side was C. L. Stopford, who later became a local turf journalist under the byline 'Aintree'. That year's Premiers were Port Adelaide, led by star centre half-forward Harold Oliver; he was a great favourite with Port fans, who used to chant OL-I-VER as he flew for marks. South Adelaide's Don Moriarty won three successive Magarey medals in 1919, 1920 and 1921, playing at centre half-back.

West Adelaide, after a number of disappointing postwar years, improved to finish second in the 1923 season. Two individuals played a large part in this success – coach 'Shine' Hosking and ruckman-cum-captain Vic Peters. The eventual Premiers were Norwood, fighting off a persistent but inaccurate West Adelaide, which kicked 2.16.

Bruce McGregor, who had joined West Adelaide in 1923, was appointed captain-coach in 1926 and finished the year with the Magarey medal. In McGregor's second year, 1927, West Adelaide finished as minor Premiers for the first time, but had to play a challenge final against North Adelaide for the the flag, which it won.

In 1930, Percy Lewis coached North Adelaide to a premiership, and Farmer kicked his first ton of goals, 105 in all.

By the end of the 1920s, football had made it to the silver screen. A film survives of 'Pictures and personalities of the Melbourne football scene in the late 1920s or early 1930s'. The personalities are shown in training on their respective grounds: Fitzroy's Col Niven and Cecil Kerr, both from Maryborough, and Charles Chapman, 'Fitzroy's popular Captain'; Essendon's coach Charles Hardy and captain Norm Beckton, vice-captain Jack Vosti, players Keith Forbes and Gregory Johnston; from Hawthorn – Albert Hyde, Ted Pool, Albert Chadwick, Bob Sellers; from St Kilda – Barney Carr, William Cubbins, Stan Hepburn, Angus Mason and William Roberts; South Melbourne's J. H. Petchell (captain), Edward Johnson; Footscray's Arthur Stevens, Albert Outen, Alan Hopkins, and club secretary, V. Samson and coach Alex Eason (these players are shown on the Footscray field with their grandstand still under construction); and from Melbourne, Ivor Warne-Smith (Brownlow medal winner in 1926 and 1928), H. J. White, Robert Johnson, William Tymms, Dick Taylor and Bob Corbett. A match is shown between Essendon and Melbourne, which also includes shots of the spectators.[18] At the start of the game, players jog out on to the ground and are evidently fitter than their 1909 predecessors. Their country-town origins are noted in the commentary. Umpires now wear white and use recognisably modern signals to indicate aspects of play.

This documentary presents the quiet strength idealised as Australian manhood in the interwar era. The players smile ironically for the camera, and demonstrate their ability to run in packs. This 'rushing' is a new feature of the game, and reflects the new military discipline of the Anzac period. Play still depends basically on the kick and mark, but there is more emphasis on the modern handball, with a pair of players showing it as a sideways manoeuvre. It is not yet truly an offensive movement, rather a tactic for changing the corridor of attack or a device for getting out of trouble when opponents are closing in. The ratio of kicks to handballs is about ten to one. The quiet determination of the Australian footballer was about to become a familiar sight in the 1930s Depression.

part three
The 1930s
to the 1960s

Depression
Football

The 1930s Depression affected people in all parts of Australia, and Saturday afternoons at the football became a major recreation. Men were desperate to play professional football, as it was one of the few enterprises which guaranteed a job in those years. This was the context in which the Coulter Law was introduced, during the 1930 season, a clumsy attempt to keep players' wages down by striking a basic wage for them of 30 shillings per match. (A labourer earned 4 pounds a week.) What was good for a highly-regulated labour market across Australia was of less value in professional sport, however, and the Coulter Law remained a dead letter – it faded out at some forgotten moment in the 1960s.[1] Money was useful in buying flags – South's 1933 premiership side had so many expensive imports it was nicknamed the 'Foreign Legion'! The VFL clubs paid their players quite differently, owing to their very different financial positions. Dyer received from Richmond supporters twice as much again as he earned from the Coulter payment; Carlton paid a bonus for finals matches; Essendon paid 2 pounds for a win, 30 shillings for a loss. South Melbourne could not pay its players at all at the end of the 1930 season, but embarked on a fund-raising drive and turned its finances around. Melbourne continued its amateur tradition during the 1930s (but continued to find jobs for its players), while St Kilda and the new VFL clubs of 1925 were caught in the downward spiral of insufficient finances and poor performance on field.[2]

Collingwood still refused to pay its stars additional money. It was over one such pay dispute that Albert 'Leeter' Collier, an ardent advocate for the players' interest, spent two seasons playing for Cananore in the Tasmanian Football League, helping them to their 1931 flag. Jobs were found for players, particularly at the Carlton and United Brewery, on the tramways ·and with Collingwood Council. (Jobs for the boys was not considered poor form in those days!) This was not new – most of Melbourne's 1926 side had won employment with Vacuum Oil (Mobil) – and in the 1930s Depression jobs were a more powerful inducement than match payments. In 1932 the Collingwood players took another 10-shilling cut in wages which was to be recovered if they got into the finals (they got to the Preliminary Final). Jock McHale assisted the principle of wage equality by accepting the same salary as the players.[3]

The 1930s Depression brought clubs closer to their communities, as players were more likely to be locals (recruiting was cut back) and a night at the cinema or an afternoon at the football was a popular distraction. In 1933, with the legal assistance of first-year player Jack Galbally, Collingwood reached a new agreement with the local council which tilted the balance of control over Victoria Park away from the local cricket club.[4] One consequence was the end of baseball games as curtain-raisers before the football. Baseball had been played at some VFL grounds since 1897, managed by the suburb's cricket club; it had been played at Victoria Park since 1910. From 1934 baseball was replaced by junior football – teams were made up from local state primary schools, and Catholic schools followed in 1935. Apart from the war, the scheme ran until 1955 (when Under-Nineteens matches came to Victoria Park) and helped promote Australian Rules in local schoolyards.[5]

Membership increased, and recovered the levels lost in the early 1920s. Ticket agencies were now established outside the municipality, going northwards to Heidelberg and Northcote, and by the mid-1930s only one-third of Collingwood's members lived locally.[6] Collingwood admitted the unemployed free of charge to Victoria Park during the Depression. Collingwood's style of play in the 1930s became more physical – the crowd was now better separated from the players and the field was a theatre for more vigorous play.[7]

The Carlton crowd in those days was made up of everyday people. 'Mum says you'd take your hat and gloves, and take your tea-basket along. It was more like a picnic! Once the crowd dispersed at half-time – the men'd go down for a drink – the thermoses came out, and it was

(above)
MFC champion ruck, c. 1895.
Back row: Fred McGinis, George Moodie.
Front row: 'Dolly' Christie, George Moysey,
Herbert Fry. (Melbourne Cricket Club)

(left)
Peter Burns played in the Geelong team
which won premierships in 1882, 1883 and
1884. He then transferred to South
Melbourne, and played with that club from
1885 to 1891. He then returned to Geelong
and played a further eleven seasons, leading
the team in 1896 and 1900. (*Football and the
Clubs That Make It*, p. 22)

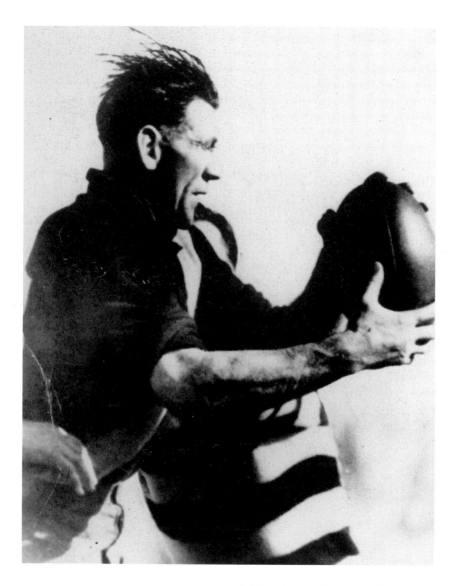

Jack Dyer bursting through a pack.
(Courtesy of Richmond Football Club)

(top)
Richmond's 1921 premiership side.
Back row: George Bayliss, Ernest Taylor, James Smith, George Weatherill, Robert Weatherill,
Mel Morris, Frank Harley, Vic Thorp.
Middle row: Frank Hughes, Hugh James, Max Hislop, Dan Minogue (captain/coach), Barnie
Herbert, Donald Don, Norman McIntosh.
Front row: Robert Carew, Clarrie Hall, Norman Turnbull. (Courtesy of Richmond Football Club)

(bottom)
Jack Dyer being chaired off the ground after his last game as a player for Richmond, in 1949.
Dyer played 312 games for the Tigers, and continued as a non-playing coach until 1952.
(Courtesy of Richmond Football Club)

(above)
The fearless Francis Bourke taking on the opposition. (Courtesy of Richmond Football Club)

(top right)
Collingwood's all-conquering side of the late 1920s. (*Football and the Clubs That Make It*, p. 7)

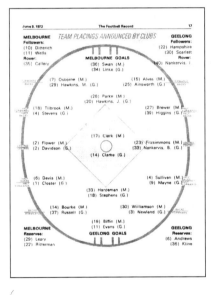

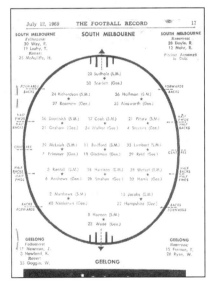

This diagram shows the expected positions of the players and the diamond which was introduced to reduce congestion at centre square bounces. The diamond was replaced by the larger centre square. (*Football Record*, 9 June 1973, p. 17. Just Collectables!)

The *Football Record* has been a crucial part of football watching, giving the teams and guernsey numbers, and providing half-time reading material. For the more statistically inclined, it also gives the opportunity to record the goals and behinds kicked by each player. (*Football Record*, 12 July 1969, pp. 16-17. Just Collectables!)

Peter Hudson was Hawthorn's star Tasmanian full forward. This photo captures Hudson's fluid grace as he soars above the pack. (Courtesy of *Hawks Forever*, Hawthorn Football Club)

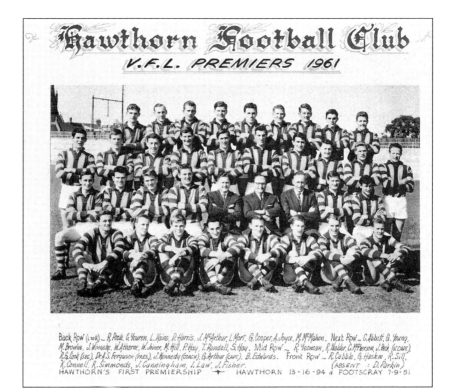

Hawthorn Football Club
V.F.L. PREMIERS 1961

Back Row (L to R) ~ R. Peck, G. Youren, L. Haine, D. Harris, J. McArthur, L. Mort, G. Cooper, A. Joyce, M. McMahon. Next Row ~ C. Abbott, G. Young, M. Browne, J. Winneke, W. Athroe, W. Joiner, M. Hill, P. Hay, T. Randall, S. Hay. Mid Row ~ R. Yeoman, R. Nalder, C. McPherson, J. Peck (V.CAPT.), R.G. Cook (SEC.), Dr.A.S. Ferguson (PRES.), J. Kennedy (COACH), G. Arthur (CAPT.), B. Edwards. Front Row ~ R. Cabble, G. Haskins, R. Sill, K. Connell, R. Simmonds, J. Cunningham, I. Law, J. Fisher. (ABSENT : D. Parkin)
HAWTHORN'S FIRST PREMIERSHIP ✛ HAWTHORN 13-16-94 d FOOTSCRAY 7-9-51

(above)
Hawthorn joined the VFL in 1925 and had to wait until 1961 to bask in the glory of a premiership. This was the team. (Courtesy of *Hawks Forever,* Hawthorn Football Club)

(left)
Neil Balme launches himself at the football, displaying all the vigour crucial to Richmond's successes in the 1970s. (Courtesy of Richmond Football Club)

Hawthorn star full-forward Peter Hudson usually kicks the simple flat punt when shooting for goal. His hands are evenly placed at the same level on each side of the ball and he runs in a straight line towards the goal. The right hand controls the drop while the left hand controls balance.

Footscray captain-coach Ted Whitten is a master of the torpedo punt kick. The spiralling effect of the ball is achieved by placing the left hand forward and the right hand back at the same level on the ball. Whitten runs in a straight line towards his target and allows his kicking leg to swing through straight.

Essendon half-back Barry Davis is a brilliant exponent of the drop kick. As with the ordinary punt kick, his hands are evenly placed and he runs in a straight line towards the target. The ball should hit the ground at an angle of about 45 degrees. Davis achieves distances up to 70 yds. with perfect timing and follow-through.

(left)
The various kicking styles which have been developed over the years in Australian Rules football. (*Football '70: The Royal Year*, pp. 62–3. Just Collectables!)

(top)
Dave McNamara is best remembered for his prodigious place kicking. (*Football and the Clubs That Make It*, p. 38)

(above)
The beginning of the game, as Collingwood crashes through the banner. (Mike Martin)

(above)
Bill Morris, Richmond's champion ruckman, prospered under the guidance of Jack Dyer, winning the 1948 Brownlow Medal. This photo shows him in a typical pose, palming the ball straight to the rover. (Courtesy of Richmond Football Club)

(right)
The public face of Gary Ablett, quiet and unassuming. On the field he is one of the most highly skilled and acrobatic players ever to have played the game. (Mike Martin)

The *Herald* supplement commemorating Carlton's 1982 premiership. The grinning Blue is Mike Fitzpatrick. (Just Collectables!)

The *Herald Sun* prints two versions of the Weg premiership lift-out poster, and discards the one not needed after the game. This is a rare copy of the unreleased Cats 1989 premiership souvenir. (Just Collectables!)

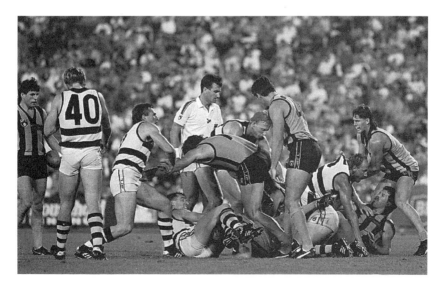

Australian Rules occasionally lapses into skirmishes such as this. (Mike Martin)

John Coleman was one of the most lethal
goalkickers to play Australian Rules football,
in a short career ended by serious knee
injury. Coleman kicked 537 goals in only 98
games. (*Football Life*, May 1973, p. 26. Just
Collectables!)

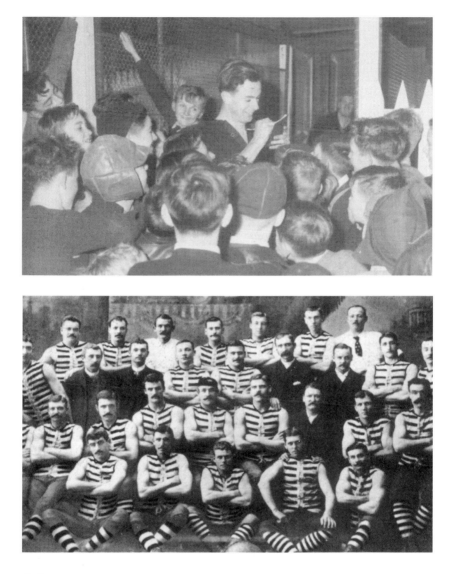

(top)
John Coleman swamped by young admirers
after a game. (*How to Play Aussie Rules*, p. 13.
Just Collectables!)

(bottom)
Moustaches and stripes were a feature of this
early South Melbourne side. (*Football and the
Clubs That Make It*, p. 42)

(*top*)
Alistair Lord kicking long in front of an
adoring home crowd at Kardinia Park. (*How
to Play Aussie Rules*, p. 20. Just Collectables!)

(*above*)
Football inspires faith and devotion. These
Hawthorn supporters are sporting a whole
range of Hawk paraphernalia typical of
cheersquad members. (*Football '70: The Royal
Year*, p. 7. Just Collectables!)

(top)
Geoff Tunbridge was an effective half
forward flanker for Melbourne. This photo
shows him under pressure from his pupils at
lunchtime kick-to-kick at Ballarat Grammar
School. (*How to Play Aussie Rules*, p. 9. Just
Collectables!)

(left)
Verdun Howell was an attacking full
back. This photo shows him defying the
conventional wisdom of punching from
behind, and outmarking North Melbourne's
John Dugdale. (*How to Play Aussie Rules*, p. 23.
Just Collectables!)

(above)
Jack Worrall coached Carlton to premierships in 1906, 1907 and 1908. This is the
1906 side. Worrall stands in the back row,
wearing a collar and tie. He preached a
work ethic and dicta such as 'booze and
football don't mix'. (*Footy and the Clubs That
Make It*, p. 4)

(above)
Ted Whitten became captain/coach of
Footscray at 23. This photo, taken at
training, shows in the background the
empty terraces of the Western Oval. (*How
to Play Aussie Rules*, p. 24. Just Collectables!)

(left)
Jack Collins (left) and Ted Whitten (right)
watch as Jack and Ted Jnr run down the
race. (*How to Play Aussie Rules*, p. 71. Just
Collectables!)

a very friendly crowd. It was a place you could take your wife or girl-friend.' In those days Princes Park was largely ringed by grass. Carlton was by now an immigrant suburb, and the newcomers felt welcome to wander in. The same was true of North Melbourne.[8]

In Victoria alone there were 1500 football clubs in operation during this decade, mostly in country leagues. They included the Metropolitan Amateurs, the Saturday-morning Industrial Football League, the Wednesday Football League, and the Protestant Churches Association. The Industrial League, formed in 1927, comprised ten clubs: Abbotsford Brewery, Carlton Brewery, Dunlop, Goodchilds, Harold Shoes, Havelock, Laygols, Miro, Raymonds, and Victoria Brewery. On Wednesday after-noons, approximately 11,000 fans watched a contest among eight clubs: Fire Brigade, Post and Telegraphs, Press, Railways, Telephone Exchange, Victoria Market, Waterside Workers, and Yellow Cabs. Most urban foot-ballers were working-class in social background (except those at Mel-bourne and certain of the Amateur clubs) as is suggested by these teams. (Banks and other commercial enterprises were to sponsor football teams only after World War II, a period of increased social mobility for Vic-torians.) Policemen such as Jack Dyer and Laurie Nash were also a sig-nificant group of footballers (although they were banned at Port Melbourne for three decades after the 1928 waterfront strike). More than half a million Victorians played, officiated at or watched the 750 games of football contested in Victoria each week during the season. It was now a significant industry. An estimated 105,000 barrackers followed one VFL team or another, while 25,000 attended VFA matches. Even the average country match attracted 200 fans.[9]

Country football had a popular appeal, as suggested by this doggerel from the town of Kilmore in 1929:

> *Football is a grand old game which everyone enjoys,*
> *And Kilmore's team at present has some very nifty boys . . .*
> *Dot Moore he is the captain — one of the very best,*
> *And Hussy and Tom Harrington have always stood the test.*
> *There is good old Murray Figgins, also Kenny Moore,*
> *Who always do their best to put up a winning score.*
> *Jim Pelly and Herb Collard always play the game,*
> *Our centreman is hard to beat, Tony Collard is his name . . .*[10]
> [And so on, through the team.]

Country football was enlivened also by occasional visits from the 'big smoke'. In October 1924 Leongatha played host to a friendly contest with VFA Premiers Footscray and defeated them by 5 points. It was a grand moment in the life of a country football team.[11]

The clubs which dominated in the 1930s were Launceston (1933–40), the VFA club Northcote (1929–36) and Melbourne (1939–41). Launceston is renowned for its football. It has been both a fertile nursery for VFL/AFL footballers as well as a place for retired professional legs to gambol around the ovals. In the North Tasmanian Football Association (the NFTA), Launceston had finished last in 1931 and 1932, and had then gone on to win the next six flags in a row (1933–38). One of the Cahill brothers in the team, Bill, played fifteen games for Essendon; Trevor Ranson played two senior games for St Kilda. And there were others – there was plenty of VFL experience in the area. The derby between North Launceston and South Launceston (then called City South) is a highlight of the local sporting year. It was 25 kilometres south of here, at Longford, that writer Martin Flanagan first fell in love with the game:

> When I was four years old, I slipped beneath the white wooden railing
> that circled the oval and wandered onto the football field. The heavy
> earth smelt rich and dank, and the afternoon sun was a flaming
> orange ball in the tall gums on the far side of the ground. I walked
> towards the home team's gathering; the players were in the middle of
> the group, their skin pink and steaming, sucking pieces of orange,
> holding the peel in their gritty fingers. A man with a red face and oiled
> hair was bending over, speaking in surging rhythms and sharp
> crescendos, smacking his fist into the palm of his hand.[12]

Uncle Tom Flanagan played with City, another Launceston club, alongside Laurie Nash and Roy Cazaly. City's glory days were in the early 1950s – the club won twenty-two flags before being amalgamated with South Launceston.

Meanwhile, the champion Melbourne side of the late 1930s was built on solid foundations, for the Melbourne Seconds won every Reserves flag from 1931 to 1935, a record-breaking effort never equalled.

The year 1931 saw the introduction of the McIntyre final four system, which provided consistency where there had been none in the past. Now the minor Premiers had to prove themselves by winning one or other of the semi-finals (and so retain an advantage in the double chance). The final four system was so successful that it remained in place until 1971. Another measure of young Kenneth McIntyre's success in devising the final four was that whenever the VFL decided to expand the finals (to five in 1972, to six in 1991 and to eight in 1994) it was to this man that they turned. The final four was immediately successful, even though the same four teams finished as finalists in 1931 as had in 1930. Once Carlton had defeated Melbourne in Round 8, none of the other clubs broke into the top group of Geelong, Richmond, Carlton and Collingwood. Footscray, only six years into the competition, made a concerted effort but was hamstrung by a lack of good forwards. During the finals, Geelong lost to Richmond in the Second Semi-Final and was downcast – until the club remembered that under the new rules it had the double chance! Geelong met Richmond again in the Grand Final and this time defeated it 9.14 (68) to 7.6 (48). The year was capped off by Fitzroy's Haydn Bunton winning his first Brownlow. Many pundits regard Bunton Snr as the game's greatest player ever – even though the tough men like Dyer thought he was too obsequious to umpires![13]

Geelong faded after a bright start in 1932 and the new glamour team was South Melbourne. South won ten games in a row. St Kilda battled along wracked by internal club wrangles, and had an up-and-down year on the field as a consequence. Melbourne started the season at the Motordrome (later re-named Olympic Park) while the MCG surface was being reconstructed, and ingloriously lost every game there. The 1932 Richmond–Carlton Grand Final is regarded as one of the best in the history of the VFL (alongside 1937, 1967 and 1972), with the Tigers winning 13.14 (92) to 12.11 (83) in front of 70,000 people. Haydn Bunton won the second of his three Brownlows (1931, 1932, 1935).

With the likes of Bunton, 'Chicken' Smallhorn (the 1933 Brownlow medallist), and the champion full-forward Jack Moriarty, Fitzroy was promising its fans to do better, and did so the following season. In Round 13 Smallhorn ran in from the centre, side-stepped four Magpies and put through the winning behind; Collingwood lost 7.21 (63) to 9.10 (64). The following week Collingwood lost again, this time to South, when the umpire did not hear the bell over the roar of the crowd. Now Collingwood, the champion team of the 1920s, missed the finals for the first time since 1924. Fitzroy's run of wins ended when Essendon bolted past with 5 goals straight in the last quarter of Round 17, the Dons winning their first game in fifteen outings. The Maroons slipped from second to fifth and would not make the finals again until 1944. St Kilda took a battering from North in Round 5, but won the game with fifteen players – the officials were so delighted they pinned badges of appreciation on these men's chests, the origins of the club's guernsey crest. South Melbourne timed its finals run well and defeated Richmond easily in the Grand Final. Pratt topped the year's scoring for the first time, with 109 goals.

When Pratt's 150 came in 1934, it was a highlight of the season, and remained an untouchable record (only equalled in 1971). Pratt kicked 8 goals in twelve minutes of the last quarter in a game against Essendon in Round 15. Overall, the South Melbourne 'Foreign Legion' team kicked a massive 2187 points for the eighteen home-and-away games of 1934. Nothing like this would be seen until Geelong's prodigious effort of 1989. Collingwood also played well in 1934, although a spiteful clash against Carlton in Round 10 brought the police onto the oval. Gordon Coventry was second highest goal-scorer, with 105 for the season, and also reached his 1000th goal during 1934. Geelong made it into the finals, but lost both finals matches in wet weather. The Grand Final was a showdown between the tough defence of Richmond (the best in the League that year) and South's great attack. The Tigers' forwards lifted for the occasion, and Richmond claimed its fourth VFL flag.

The 1935 season featured four draws and many close games, owing to the depth of the teams competing in the VFL. Exhibition games interstate also took their toll, and some clubs were affected by internal wrangling. Hawthorn won its only match ever at Corio Oval (in front of a mere 2500 spectators). Melbourne won the Reserves flag for the fifth year in a row (every year without making it to the seniors' final four); it was a portent of what was to come. Minor Premiers South Melbourne were defeated in the Grand Final by Collingwood.[14]

Collingwood's two flags, in 1935 and 1936, were the apex of its second good decade – it was runner-up in 1937, 1938 and 1939, going down in successive Grand Finals to Geelong, Carlton, and Melbourne. The Collingwood golden era ended in 1939: it would then miss the finals every season until 1945. Collingwood felt in the late 1930s that it was being punished by the other clubs and by the League for having been too successful, especially as controversial suspensions were handed out to its stars. The gentle full-forward Gordon Coventry got eight weeks in 1936, Albert Collier lost eight weeks in 1937, and his brother Harry received a fourteen-week suspension in 1938. Each of the incidents was relatively trivial, and the severity of the suspensions called into question the club's famous morale.[15]

Team fortunes come in distinct phases, however, and require clubs to experiment with new strategies and team combinations. Collingwood's McHale era had run its course by 1939, but there was no fresh infusion of ideas at Victoria Park until the 1950s. The club had an impressive administration in Curtis, Rush and Wraith. Wraith also rose in the ranks of Melbourne's Tramways to become general manager. Wraith arranged the sacking of the Seconds coach Thomas in 1939 when the Seconds team showed signs of being independent.[16]

Collingwood marched confidently into 1936, sweeping all before it. In the opening quarter of Round 2 against Richmond's 2.4, the team managed 8 goals straight, adding 6.1 in the second quarter. Melbourne showed definite signs of its re-emergence, including a 10-goal last quarter against the Southerners in Round 12. Richmond slipped, and was even beaten by North and Hawthorn for the first time ever. Collingwood defeated South Melbourne in the Grand Final, but it was the end of an era for both clubs. South never regained this form before going to Sydney in 1982, and Collingwood, with eleven premierships to its name barely three decades into the VFL's history, was destined to win only three more in the next six decades. In other words, it went from being a team which could guarantee its supporters a moment of glory once every three years to a club which would take twenty years on average to grab a flag.

Nineteen thirty-six was the year Jack Wrout started at Carlton. Jack Wrout was one of three brothers from the West Melbourne area who came across from North Melbourne Football Club that year. Wrout Snr was a postal engineer, and for a while the family rented a bluestone house in Chetwynd Street around the corner from their local church, St Mary's Roman Catholic. The three brothers (Jack, Des and Archie) set up a butchery engineering business in Racecourse Road, providing knives and other equipment to the trade. Football and other sporting connections helped the family business, although the only footballer to get a job with the Wrouts was Brent Crosswell, decades later. Jack Wrout was a small centre half-forward, kicking 256 goals for Carlton over 130 senior games. The legend has him pricking a wet ball with a safety-pin before passing it back to the umpire because he did not like playing with a heavy ball! The story is also part of family folklore.[17]

The VFL worked hard on the fixtures for the first time in 1937. The four clubs which met each other only once in the eighteen-match home-and-away series were rostered to meet each other twice the following season. South's decline began in 1937. At Glenferrie in Round 2, Hawthorn led St Kilda 8.7 to nil in the first quarter, but still managed to lose the match! (Players from this period claim that no-one really exerted themselves when playing against Hawthorn until the last quarter.) Collingwood, Geelong and Melbourne led the ladder early and were two games ahead of Richmond and the rest of the competition at the end of the year. In Round 16 Melbourne defeated Collingwood at Victoria Park for the first time since 1921, following a 6.6 burst in the last ten minutes. The Grand Final was Gordon Coventry's swan song: scores were tied at three-quarter time but Geelong kicked away in the last term to win by 5 goals. Dick Reynolds won the second of his three Brownlows (1934, 1937, 1938), Herbie Matthews came in second, and Jack Mueller third.

The new order of football announced its arrival at the start of the 1938 season. Round 2 was the first occasion on which all three new clubs of 1925 won their match on the same day. Footscray, now usually known as the Bulldogs rather than the Tricolours, was the best of the three, getting as far as the First Semi-Final before going down to Collingwood. The year 1938 was to end Carlton's longest premiership drought: finishing on top of the ladder, it defeated Collingwood. The Magpies were the side which had threatened all year, having immediately replaced the great Syd Coventry with Ron Todd at full-forward. Todd kicked 120 goals, his nearest rival being 'Soapy' Vallence of Carlton, who managed eighty. However, Collingwood seemed to have lost the knack of winning the big games, the very attribute which had brought it success in the 1920s. Geelong finished second on the ladder but was eliminated in the finals by losses to Carlton and Collingwood. Nineteen thirty-eight is also notable for the first celebrated final-quarter revival. Collingwood trailed Geelong by 16 points at three-quarter time, prompting eleven positional changes from Jock McHale; the reshuffle appeared to work and Collingwood kicked the winning goal in time-on to score what was in those times an innovative victory. Round 13 saw four 1-point results, and Reynolds won his third Brownlow medal.

The next season, 1939, following Melbourne's steady improvement in the latter half of the thirties, saw the 'Red Demons' grab the first of three premierships. It was a combination which had talent backed up by consistency, including players such as Barassi senior, Jack Mueller and Ray Emselle, drilled by 'Checker' Hughes.

The Barassi ancestry in Australia went back to 1854. Ron senior's grandfather Mario Barassi was one of two thousand Swiss–Italians and Northern Italians who had come to gold-crazy Victoria in the 1850s. These Italian-speaking people were flint-faced labourers who farmed the land around Daylesford in the central Victorian goldfields area. Some of the stone houses they built in the old Italian manner still stand as monuments to their doggedness. Around his house (today in ruins, a mile down the road) Mario ('Carlo') Barassi owned 2.5 acres of vineyards on either side of the gravelly Shicer Gully Road, surrounded by other Italian families. (These Italian men became self-sufficient without becoming wealthy; their wives were Italian or Irish. The locality was not very different from the little Swiss–Italian village of Semione from which this rugged first Barassi emigrated. Judging by the ship manifest, Mario Barassi migrated alone, without friends or family. This was extremely unusual, and suggests a strong individualism.) At nearby Guildford there is an Anzac obelisk just up the road from Delmenico's Family Hotel. Chiselled into this memorial are several local Italian names, including those of Ron senior and his brother Cliff. A few weeks after his well-known son was born on 27 February 1936, the elder Ron, a farm worker, got his first senior game with Melbourne. Also wearing guernsey No. 31, Ron senior roved for the Redlegs in their glory days of the late 1930s; he advanced as far as Nineteenth Man in the 1940 premiership side. His surname earned him the friendly nickname 'Musso', after the Italian dictator. Then he enlisted on 15 July 1940; a year later he died of shrapnel wounds at Tobruk when his truck ran over a landmine. It was 31 July 1941, and his only son hardly knew him. Ron senior was the first VFL player to die in World War II. (Turner's famous lecture at Monash was named after him, not his son.)

The 1939 Grand Final was to be Jock McHale's last, although of course he was kept on as Collingwood's coach for another decade. Footscray's premiership ambitions faded with a record eleven consecutive losses. St Kilda started the season brightly and eventually finished fourth, enjoying its first finals win since 1915, against Richmond. Ron

Todd kicked 120 goals to lead the goalkicking for the second year running.

By the 1940 season, the war's effects were obvious. Players left to enlist – of course some clubs suffered more than others. St Kilda started well but faded badly. Collingwood had its worst season for years and dropped to eighth – it was also damaged by Ron Todd crossing to Williamstown. Geelong appeared to be a much improved side, winning six in a row including a 3-point win against eventual Premiers Melbourne. But the Cats barely scraped into the four as injuries and sickness took their toll, and they were eliminated in their first final. Essendon made it through to the Preliminary Final under the guidance of new coach Dick Reynolds, which was a sign of better days ahead. Melbourne beat Richmond in the Grand Final. The enigmatic Des Fothergill defied Collingwood's change in fortune to share the Brownlow with Herbie Matthews (South Melbourne) and also kicked 56 goals in a season led by Jack Titus with 100.

Melbourne's attacking style brought it a third premiership in 1941. Its scores for the period were remarkably high, for it had a number of capable goalkickers, led by Norm Smith, who kicked 89 of his career 546 in 1941. Smith was supported by Ron Baggott (310 career goals), the rookie Fred Fanning (411 goals), and Percy Beames (323 goals). Another of Melbourne's strengths was a large lad from Echuca named Mueller. Jack Mueller was a champion; despite his having lost two fingers in an industrial accident in 1934, his marking was exceptional: 'I used to come in from the side and this made it difficult for my opponents to counter, particularly as I was tall.' Melbourne was a well-administered club under Hughes and Percy Page, and he made friendships, many of which lasted all his life. 'I particularly enjoyed the comradeship with team-mates and opponents over a drink after a game, the fact that I am still welcomed into any league club, and that even now [in 1993] people I meet, particularly at bowls, talk to me about my football career.'[18]

In 1941, Perc Bentley left Richmond for Carlton, and Jack Dyer took over as coach at Tigerland. When Carlton and Richmond clashed at Punt Road in Round 2, eighteen players were injured in a spiteful match. Geelong moved to its new home, Kardinia Park, after the military requisitioned Corio Oval. Essendon and Richmond both made the finals – they had lost fewer players to the war than Collingwood and Melbourne. Carlton finished on top of the ladder, showing dramatic improvement under its new coach, but became the first side since 1901 to miss the Grand Final after finishing on top. Melbourne, despite having twelve players injured or serving in the armed forces on Grand Final day – and facing an improving and full-strength Essendon – scored a courageous victory, winning 19.13 (127) to Essendon's 13.20 (98). The 1941 Brownlow was won by N. Ware (Footscray), ahead of the unlucky South Melbourne captain-coach Herbie Matthews. Norm Smith, while directing traffic at Melbourne, still managed to win the VFL's goalkicking.

In Western Australia in 1938, Claremont won its first premiership, beating East Fremantle in a replay Grand Final, the second in the history of the WAFL. (Claremont had changed its name from Claremont–Cottesloe in 1935.) Johnny Leonard had crossed from West Perth in 1938 and led Claremont to three premierships in his four years as coach. The Claremont club boasted a strong spine of key position players including Grieve, O'Neil, dual Sandover medallist Sammy Clark, Heusler, J. Compton and the versatile George Moloney. That year triple Brownlow medallist Haydn Bunton Snr won the first of his three Sandover medals with South Fremantle. The leading goalkicker, E. Tyson (West Perth), notched up 126 goals, including 17 in a match against Swan Districts.

The next season, 1939, Claremont won a second premiership, after finishing the home-and-away season on top of the ladder. The ever-strong East Fremantle side threatened Claremont's premiership ambitions by winning the Second Semi-Final by 6 goals. Claremont went into the Grand Final underdogs but got up to score a good 3-goal win. Bunton again took the Sandover.

By 1940 Western Australian clubs were beginning to feel the effects of wartime recruiting, though the standard of competition did not appear to fall away dramatically. In an open season, the contenders appeared to be East Fremantle, Claremont and South Fremantle. South Fremantle became stronger favourites for the flag after beating Claremont in the Second Semi; however Claremont, in its customary role of 'underdog', beat East Fremantle in the next final, and upset an inaccurate South Fremantle side, 13.13 (91) to 9.20 (74), in the decider. To add to Claremont's achievements, George Moloney took the rare double of both the goalkicking award and the Sandover. His 113 goals included 19 against South Fremantle.

West Perth defeated East Fremantle in the 1941 Grand Final to win the premiership; it was helped by the efforts of full-forward E. Tyson and captain J. Pola. The season was also marked by Bunton's third Sandover and George Doig's sixth year topping the competition's goalkicking, with 132 goals. By the time East Fremantle's champion had finished his career with 1111 goals, he was dubbed 'the Bradman of Western Australian full-forwards'.

In South Australia in 1931, North Adelaide won another premiership. The club expected to win its third premiership in a row in 1932, and won through to the Grand Final comfortably. On the day, however, Sturt outplayed North and won by 41 points.

Glenelg beat Port Adelaide in the 1933 Grand Final, using a number of unique tactical moves, spelled out in an individual briefing for each player. Apparently the celebrations that followed the win are still talked of 'with a reminiscent shudder'.

In 1940, North Adelaide's Ken Farmer kicked a match record of 23 goals (against West Torrens). Farmer retired the following year, having kicked a career total of 1419 goals, and having topped the goalkicking for eleven successive years.

Football also started in Darwin schools during this decade, taken by the Catholic Marist Brother Pye, who introduced the game as part of his idea of 'muscular Christianity'. (The first clubs had formed in 1917.)

For many Australians the 1930s depression did not completely finish until the onset of war. The war and its immediate aftermath signalled a new phase in football's development. By 1940 players were beginning to reflect a wider range of social backgrounds, and most VFL clubs were recruiting from well outside their districts. Collingwood, Geelong and North Melbourne still had a majority of local lads in their sides, but this was exceptional. Teachers, clerks, wool classers and other white-collar occupations were now more common among players.[19] This trend toward social mobility would increase after World War II.

Social Mobility

The 1940s was characterised by war, which again interrupted the competitions, and by the success of two clubs which emerged after the war with strong teams. These two clubs were South Fremantle, which rivalled East Fremantle in the late 1940s, particularly from 1947 to 1954, and Essendon, whose period of dominance from 1946 to 1951 stands out in VFL history. However, some of the best football seen in the 1942–1951 period was actually in army camps, played between scratch teams in khaki, cheered on by their adoring comrades.

Back home, Collingwood became in 1941 the first VFL club to hold a liquor licence, following a long-drawn-out campaign culminating in the capture of the licence held by the German Tivoli Club in Abbotsford when World War II started.[1] On the field Collingwood was depleted by the war, with dozens of players serving as soldiers. Two players, Norm Le Brun and Norm Oliver, were killed.[2] Few Collingwood players were in protected industries once conscription began to make inroads during the 1942 season. But a major factor was the departure of Seconds coach Hugh Thomas in 1939, and the defection of star full-forward Ron Todd to Williamstown in 1940, followed by the departure of the gifted Des Fothergill to Williamstown in 1941.[3]

The war affected how football would be analysed. The Anzac theme had permeated reportage in the interwar period – during World War II the Anzac idea became sufficiently commonplace as to provide the structure for the reporting of the 1945 'Bloodbath' Grand Final. This epic clash certainly ranks as a physically willing encounter, but its nickname owed a great deal to the hyperbole of sports journalists at the *Truth* and the *Sun*. The event's reporting also marked a key turning point in the literary history of Australian football, a moment of new possibilities. From this season onwards, a richer vocabulary of images would be used in the game's reportage.

Essendon's return to the winner's table was not altogether surprising. Essendon has been one of the most consistent clubs in the history of Australian Rules. After all, not only had Essendon dominated the VFA in the 1891–94 period, helping to hasten the development of professional football, its 'Mosquito Fleet' had been a force in the 1920s. Now, in the 1940s, the director of the Melbourne Fire Brigade was a devout supporter, and took on Essendon players. Because many of its players were firemen during their workaday week, the club retained a core of 'man-powered' men during the war. Indeed, Essendon featured in every VFL Grand Final from 1946 to 1951. Essendon's coach of the 1940s and 1950s, Dick Reynolds, had a success rate of 61 per cent. There was continuity in the Reynolds' appointment as coach, as 'King Richard' had played 320 games from 1933 to 1951, and coached the side from 1939 to 1960 (twenty-two seasons). The continuity of players becoming captains and then coaches of the same team was fundamental to certain VFL clubs.

Essendon has been called a 'conservative' club, a club of wowsers who saw football as a means of teaching young men – especially Protestant men – the virtues of self-control. One black-and-red fanatic remembers boyhood idols like Reynolds and Bill Hutchinson (1942–57, 290 games) coming to his school to preach against drinking and smoking. This was Moonee Ponds West Primary School in the 1940s. Essendon secretary Bill Cookson told journalist Alf Brown that Essendon's bill for soft drinks far exceeded the amount it spent on beer.[4] Eric Lund's father, a Swedish immigrant, could see no virtue in the game: 'Thirty-six fools kicking a bag of wind around is not my idea of a Saturday afternoon,' he would say. The immigrant son found the Windy Hill football ground – 20 minutes' walk away to the north – a place of cheap entertainment on Saturday afternoons, and somewhere to pick up pocket money. Like other Essendon lads he started selling food off a tray, and then graduated at the age of thirteen to operating his own kiosk. This was 1951, Essendon's sixth good year in a row – football grounds were still the province of suburban operators, small-time shysters with minuscule catering empires.[5] Some were loners, selling chestnuts over a hot stove outside the ground, or flinging small hand-made packets of peanuts into the crowd in exchange for 'a shillin' a bag'. Windy Hill was a regular beat for Johnnie Boyd, the Peanut Man, a famous figure in his brown jumper and flannelette shirt shouting out what sounded like 'perna pernoots' at various grounds from 1940 to 1991.[6]

The move to Windy Hill later lent the club its postwar nickname, the Bombers, owing to the new association with Essendon Airport. When things went poorly for the club in the late 1950s, *Herald* journalist Alf Brown cheekily renamed it 'The Gliders'. Essendon won its way into the heart of long-time supporter Harvey Reese because of the Bombers nickname, growing up as he did under the shadow of the Moorabbin airport.[7] Between the nicknames 'Same Olds' and 'Bombers' were two other nicknames, one a racist reference to the Aborigines, the other, 'the Dons', an old-fashioned English nickname for Spanish gentlemen.

Part of Essendon's stability lay in its regional location, especially after 1922. As the only VFL club north of Fitzroy and Footscray, Essendon dominated the north-western suburbs of Melbourne. It also had a handy rural zone in the Wimmera, from where it recruited Reg Burgess (1954–60, 124 games) who later captain-coached Casterton. Its local talent in the interwar period would fill any team, and, as already explained, a large number were employed as firemen. Among this group were Syd Barker, a fireman from Abbotsford, who captained the premiership teams of 1923–1924, Norman Beckton (Essendon Association), Dick Reynolds (Woodlands, also a local team), Jack Vosti (Brunswick, also a fireman), and 'Garney' Campbell (another fireman, who captain-coached Essendon from 1931 to 1933).

After World War II, the theme continued. Not only was Hutchinson a local (Essendon Stars), but so too were Harold Lambert (La Mascotte in the Essendon District League), Gordon 'Whoppa' Lane (another fireman, from Essendon United), Hugh Torney (a country fireman), Jack Clarkson (from North Essendon Methodists), Ken Fraser and Ron Evans (from Essendon Baptists–St Johns), and Raymond Martini (Flemington YCW).[8]

Another successful VFL club with strong community links was Carlton. There is a Grade One class photograph which includes young Fred Morton, aged six, taken in 1936 at the Faraday Street Primary School, dressed in his Carlton Football Club guernsey. He lived in a two-roomed house in Little Palmerston Street, right in the heart of Carlton, a working-class suburb full of Jews, Lebanese, Italians and other immigrants. From here he could walk to Princes Park, the sylvan glade which had been the Carlton club's home for two generations of followers. Football belonged to the community – there was little newspaper hype associated with the game when Fred was a boy and support for each club was word-of-mouth and communal. The caricatures of the leading players by cartoonist Dick Ovenden were memorable. The VFA competition enjoyed as much newspaper publicity as the VFL.

Fred Morton and the other urchins of Carlton played at being their heroes. 'I'm Micky Crisp!', one would yell; another would be Harry Vallence. In 1938 Carlton won its first flag for twenty-three years with players like 'Soapy' Vallence. Players such as Ken 'Solvol' Hands, only a teenager in the infamous 1945 Bloodbath Grand Final, were the models for Fred Morton's generation. Hands had come up through amateur Geelong ranks – his manliness was a pure ideal for the youngsters of Carlton. Many of these players were veterans of either war. Micky Crisp had his scalp shot off, and played with a tin-plate covering his skull. Much of the imagery of football was actually military in origin. Bluey Truscott was undoubtedly a great fighter-pilot, but his football service for Melbourne was exaggerated in retrospect.

In 1944 a leg injury finished Jack Wrout's career, after ninety-seven consecutive games, but he stayed close to the club, and remained good friends with 'Mocha' Johnson, Bertie Deacon and 'Soapy' Vallence.[9]

In the 1940s, Princes Park was surrounded by the smoking fires of braziers on which food vendors cooked saveloys. Through the fallen leaves of autumn and the slosh of winter, groups of local people made their way on foot toward the turnstiles. The corrugated-iron fences, despite their barbed-wire tops, made it easy for nimble local children to get in free of charge. Men selling packets of peanuts from burlap sacks moved among the crowd. Local boys collected empty beer bottles for pocket money. The ground's conditions were not glamorous – spectators on the terraces stood at an acute angle, ankle-deep in mire, exposed to all the elements. Fred, who was of a West Indian background, went to the football on his own and ignored the taunts of 'Nigger' from opposing supporters in the crowd. The taunts about 'Dagoes' and Jews, even in immigrant Carlton, suggested that the bigots did not particularly single out the dark-skinned.

Fred's own dark skin put him in the Koori camp. Out on the emerald-green field there were very few Aborigines playing football at that time. When Fred Morton went to Salesian College in Sunbury he played in scratch teams with Collingwood – the Collingwood club had a tradition of mixing it with Catholic schoolboy teams. So Fred had the distinction of playing against Collingwood's Jack Regan, the 197-game 'prince of full-backs'. Collingwood Football Club had the dubious distinction of never having fielded an Aboriginal player in its entire history, until it drafted Wally Lovett in 1982.

Later in life Fred Morton popularised the situation of Aboriginal footballers with articles and short stories such as his 'Saturday Afternoon Hero' published in the *Bulletin* in 1961. This particular story was based on a gun full-forward playing for Orbost Football Club. There is some dispute about whether the Lake Tyers club had difficulties winning entry into a league, such as the East Gippsland Football League; certainly some Victorian country leagues are accused of keeping out Aboriginal teams. One of the interesting pieces of football mythology is the allegation that no white team wanted to play a black team, especially in mid-winter mud when players become unrecognisable: there was always the tribal white fear that a different and fresher eighteen Aboriginal players would run out onto the field after half-time! There were several Victorian bush teams in those days which had Aboriginal players, including Orbost, Buchan, Bruthen and Eumeralla. Cummeragunja in the Murray Valley League produced several fine Aboriginal players, such as the expert ball-handler Eddie Jackson, who played eighty-four games for Melbourne between 1947 and 1952. Jackson was Nineteenth Man in Melbourne's 1948 premiership side.

As a young man, Fred Morton played country football and enjoyed the social cachet it brought, the doors it opened. He discovered this when as a young teacher he had to front up to the Bairnsdale district inspector. The older man was approving: 'I saw you playing at Lakes Entrance. Good to see you playing a body contact sport. Not like golf; that's a poofter's game!' Indeed, teaching and football went together well – at Carlton it was a good combination for John James and for Mike Fitzpatrick.

Carlton in Fred's youth did not suffer from its later image as a silvertail club – it was merely a good, clean club, unlike the hated and dirty arch-rivals Collingwood. Collingwood's ground, also within walking distance for Fred, was surrounded by factories; the location of Carlton's ground enabled its followers to step outside the grimy reality of Monday to Saturday work. When Carlton became gentrified later in his life, Fred Morton was less likely to attend its matches, and would more often go elsewhere in search of the real football he knew as an urchin on the mean streets of inner-urban Melbourne.[10]

Collingwood's poor record during the 1940s led to internal discontent, including rumours of a player rebellion led by 'Mac' Holten (later to become a federal parliamentarian). The discontent climaxed at the start of the 1950 season, with McHale's end as a coach, the short-lived appointment of Bervyn Woods, the sacking of Frank Wraith and the old guard, and the appointment of Phonse Kyne.[11]

In 1945, when the VFA had lost some players to the VFL owing to the Association's wartime shut-down, the two organisations met and discussed a better rationalisation of senior football. The concept of divisions was broached, or geographical sections. But once again in the sorry history of VFL–VFA relations, no realignment was reached.[12] With the creation of the Under-Nineteens competition in 1946, football in Victoria fell into a shape which would remain familiar for many decades. It was a hierarchy of four competitions:

The VFL competition: world-class professional football, the peak to which the ambitious player might aspire; professionally managed on business principles.

VFA competition: for the large numbers of men who would like to participate in professional-standard football but without the pressure (and commercialism?) of the top national competition; organised on a local basis, and strongly identifying with local areas; professionally managed.

Amateur football: for the far greater numbers who would like to participate in recreational football. The largest share of this category is country football.

Junior football: essentially for school-aged children; organised on a local basis, and identifying with local areas; co-operatively and voluntarily managed; dependent on some external funding.[13]

There are some curious features to this arrangement. The continuing lack of co-operation between the League and the Association was set in train by the acrimony of 1897, and peace has never been declared. It was the VFL rather than the VFA which took responsibility for junior football. Neither the VFL nor the VFA retained the style of close relationship with schools and universities typical of American sport – this remained the province of the amateurs.

By the 1942 season, the war had resulted in a gradual loss of players throughout the competition. It is a testament to the game's community importance that the VFL competition continued despite the world war. The VFA went into recess, and the better VFA players joined VFL clubs for the duration. The season was shortened from eighteen to sixteen games. Collingwood and Melbourne were amongst the clubs hardest hit by the war, because their players were less likely to be in 'manpowered' industries whose employees could not be drafted. Once the war had shifted the status quo within the competition, some interesting results were produced. Hawthorn beat Collingwood for the very first time, breaking a sequence of twenty-nine losses, and Richmond beat Collingwood by a record margin of 138 points in Round 3. Both Collingwood and Melbourne missed the finals and their places were filled by South Melbourne and Footscray. The Richmond versus Essendon contest of Round 6 degenerated into a near-riot after the three-quarter-time bell did not sound and an Essendon player kicked an opportunistic goal. The match was decided by a point, and Richmond supporters and players demonstrated their frustration. Carlton charged towards the finals in the last eight rounds, winning several games from behind in the last quarter. However, it had left its run too late and missed the finals on percentage: this was doubly unfortunate for the Blues as the final was to be played at Princes Park, where top side Essendon had not won for seventeen years. Richmond and Essendon dominated the finals series, killing off the challenges of Footscray and South, and then clashed in the Grand Final at Princes Park. Essendon's rebuilding process (attributed to the appointment of Dick Reynolds as coach) culminated in a premiership win over the Tigers.

In 1943 Geelong was forced to withdraw from the competition due to travel restrictions. This resulted in a bye for the other clubs, and a temporary clearance for Geelong players to other teams. Many clubs had to relocate during the 1943 season because their grounds were taken over by the military. The changes were as follows: Footscray to Yarraville Oval, St Kilda to Toorak Park, Melbourne to Punt Road, and South to Princes Park. Essendon dominated the season again, and Richmond remained near the top for most of 1943. The surprise packet was the recently renamed and rejuvenated Hawthorn. Roy Cazaly changed its nickname from the 'Mayblooms' to the more ferocious 'Hawks', and Hawthorn came in fifth, an achievement it would not better until 1957. By the final round Essendon was the only team certain to finish in the four: four other teams were on ten wins – Carlton, Richmond, Fitzroy and Hawthorn. Hawthorn missed out on the finals campaign, losing to lowly North Melbourne after its star forward Culpitt was called to the RAAF. The score was North Melbourne 8.11 (59) to Hawthorn 7.16 (58). The Tigers reversed the result of 1942, beating Essendon in a close Grand Final by 5 points. R. Harris kicked 63 goals for the Premiers, followed by Fred Fanning of Melbourne who kicked 62.

By 1944, the effects of the war were easing. Geelong rejoined the competition, but struggled to field a competitive side and finished last. Footscray and Carlton clashed in the final round for fourth position, which was decided on the last kick of the day – Harry Hickey of Footscray just made the distance from 50 yards out on the siren. The strong Richmond side led by Jack Dyer again was near the top of the ladder. Fitzroy finished second on the ladder and won both its finals to take the 1944 premiership, defeating the consistent Richmond. The Tigers were appearing in their third successive Grand Final. Melbourne's Fred Fanning led the goalkicking with 87 goals.

The 1945 season saw a lengthened draw to compensate for the shortened seasons of the war years. There was also a break that year in the pattern of Essendon's and Richmond's dominance, with the finalists of 1945 all different from those of the preceding year. South Melbourne, Collingwood, North Melbourne and Carlton made the finals. Carlton took until the last round to consolidate its place in the finals, and went on to win the premiership from fourth, the first side to do so without the double chance. The 'Bloodbath' Grand Final took its name from the number of violent clashes which occurred in front of a packed Princes Park, bursting its seams with a record 62,986 fans. Violent episodes have always stood out more at smaller venues like Windy Hill and Princes Park, where the spectators are offered a closer view of all the action than at the larger MCG. In 1945, Fanning led the VFL's goalkicking again, posting 67, just in front of the 66 kicked by Hawthorn's Alec Albiston.

The following year, 1946, saw the reintroduction of the Brownlow medal, the beginning of the Under-Nineteens competition, and the introduction of the Twentieth Man. Essendon got back on track, grabbing the lead from Footscray which set a still-standing club record of nine wins in a row. Collingwood and Melbourne, both sides ravaged by the war, began to rebuild and made the finals. The Demons surged into the finals with a thirteen-game winning streak that only ended in the Grand Final where they lost 22.18 (150) to 13.9 (87) to the powerful Essendon side. Bill Brittingham kicked 66 goals for the Premiers, followed by the 63 tallied by Des Fothergill back at Collingwood. Don Cordner, medical doctor and Melbourne champion, won the Brownlow.

In 1947, Melbourne's burly Fred Fanning kicked 18 against St Kilda in Round 19 in his memorable day out at the Junction Oval. Fanning's tally, from twenty kicks, was virtually the red-and-navy team's winning margin: it shattered Gordon Coventry's 1930 effort of 17 and set a record which still stands. Fanning, in this his best year, went on to kick 97 goals for the season. Carlton gained top position in Round 5 and went on to win a premiership. The Blues of 1947 were hailed as the most consistent side in the competition. Bert Deacon, Carlton's vice-captain and champion centre half-back, won the club's first Brownlow. Geelong put in its best year since the war and was described as 'the best side out of the finals', a regular honour which chills Cats supporters to this day.

If the 1947 season produced a clear winner, 1948 produced a series of dramatic fluctuations in form. Fitzroy started the year well, reaching the top of the ladder at the half-way mark of the season; however, what was expected to be a routine win over St Kilda – which had managed just one draw from its previous thirty-one matches – turned into a nightmare loss and Fitzroy never really recovered. The Lions missed the finals and finished seventh. Geelong appeared to have improved but couldn't string two wins together during 1947. Melbourne took second place after a number of scares during the season and looked nowhere near as impressive as first-placed Essendon. In a fitting finale to a close and confusing season, Essendon kicked its way to a draw against Melbourne, having fifteen more scoring shots: the score was 7.27 (69) to 10.9 (69). After throwing away the first final, the Dons could never get back into the replay and Melbourne ran out comfortable winners. The 1948

Brownlow was won by Richmond's William Morris, a ruckman renowned for being so fair that he would pick up opponents after knocking them down.

Nineteen forty-nine was another open season, with a number of clubs making a run at a finals berth. North Melbourne had grown into a tough and resilient side, finishing the home-and-away matches on top of the ladder. Carlton played well all year but ran out of momentum with injuries to Howell and Henfry, key players in their side. Melbourne made a charge to the four in the middle part of the season, winning eight in a row, but dropped vital games at the end of the season and missed the finals. Though it was to be Essendon's year, that team struggled and only gained momentum after Round 14. Once it got moving it had a trump card in a first-year player called Coleman, who appeared to be the answer to the goalkicking woes of the year before. Coleman kicked 100 goals in his first season in League football. Bill Brittingham, who had played at full-forward the year before, was relieved to move to full-back, where he went on to serve Essendon with great distinction. Essendon finished fourth and played a powerful brand of football to take the flag and exorcise the demons of the previous season. This season was also Jack Dyer's last.

The 1950 season began a flurry of activity in the Magpie nest; when Jock McHale retired after thirty-seven years at Collingwood, the committee's mistake in making the short-lived Bervyn Woods appointment instead of the more popular Phonse Kyne seemed to unsettle the black-and-white army. It finished seventh. St Kilda started the 1950 year well, but faded badly in the second half of the season. Geelong strung enough wins together in its best year since the war to finish fourth after the home-and-away games. The Cats met defeat in the Preliminary Final against the improving North Melbourne, a side which had captured the imagination of the footballing world as it challenged for its first premiership. Unfortunately for the Shinboners, Essendon had carried its finals form of the previous year right through the season, losing only one game, and winning the premiership. Essendon's dominance was highlighted by the fact that it won all three grades of competition, a first in the VFL competition. John Coleman, without a hint of the second year blues, kicked 120 goals for the Bombers.

The 1950 finals series appeared to take a heavy toll on its participants. Melbourne struggled and suffered what has been described as the club's worst defeat in its history against Footscray; North Melbourne failed to capture the form that had taken it so close the previous year; and perhaps the most dramatic slump was at Essendon, the side that had so completely dominated the competition the year before. Curiously, Essendon had won thirty-two of its last thirty-three matches, and then opened its 1951 ledger with four losses in five weeks. As these dominant teams stumbled, out of the pack came Fitzroy, Richmond, Collingwood, Footscray and Geelong. Fitzroy and Geelong played for top position in Round 13 at Kardinia Park, and Geelong won well, which appeared to kill off Fitzroy's challenge; Fitzroy eventually slipped to fourth after a promising first half of the season. Richmond also started well, winning its first six games, but followed up with a six-game losing streak. The Tigers, despite having the most statistically potent forward line, appeared to be struggling at the other end of the ground. Collingwood and Footscray were well placed behind Geelong on the ladder near the end of the season. However, the dangerous Essendon had recovered from a poor start to the season and was pushing for a place in the four. A vital encounter in the final round against Carlton saw the Bombers overcome a determined Carlton and cement a place in the four. This match came at a cost, for, in a controversial finding, Coleman was reported for striking Carlton's dependable Harry Caspar and suspended for four weeks.

The Bombers nonetheless continued their charge during the finals, beating Footscray in the elimination final by 9 points, and then defeating Collingwood by 2 points in the Preliminary Final. Geelong won its Second Semi easily against Collingwood and moved into its first postwar Grand Final. Essendon played its third close game in three weeks, but trailed at every change, resulting in an 11-point win to the Cats. To cap off Geelong's best year in over a decade, the VFL's goalkicking was led by Cat George Goninon, the full-forward wooed from Essendon when Coleman arrived at Windy Hill. Goninon kicked 86 to Coleman's 75, including a bag of 11 against Collingwood in the Second Semi, a new finals record. The final Geelong triumph for 1951 was the Brownlow won by Bernie Smith, the first back-pocket player to win the best and fairest medal.

Meanwhile, the senior Western Australian competition was disrupted by the war, and an under-age competition was set up for the 1942, 1943 and 1944 seasons. Clearance conditions were relaxed during these years. In this period many of WA's finest players played for service teams. Swan Districts stood out of the competition in 1942. The first year of under-age competition saw a clearly superior West Perth side finish three games clear on top of the ladder, and go on to defeat Claremont in the Grand Final. In 1943, East Fremantle (including a young Jack Sheedy) defeated Swan Districts in the Grand Final. Having not competed the year before, Swans Districts did well to finish the season in fourth place and battle through to make the Grand Final. East Perth went through the 1944 season undefeated, winning all nineteen matches. The finals produced some good games between the other sides, including a draw between West Perth and Perth; however, East Perth appeared to be unstoppable as it continued its winning run to claim the premiership over East Fremantle.

A senior competition in the WAFL was resumed in 1945 and, not surprisingly, the start of the season generated immense excitement and anticipation. This year saw the introduction of a relayed free kick paid when an infringement occurred after a player had disposed of the ball. As the 1945 season unfolded, it did not disappoint football fans in the West, for the co-tenants of Fremantle Oval, South Fremantle and East Fremantle, emerged as the main contenders for the flag. It was a particularly exciting year for South, which had not enjoyed success since its distant 1917 premiership. The Bulldogs were led by players such as captain Neil Lewington, Frank Jenkins and Bernie Naylor. They were also favoured by a most fortuitous recruiting coup when the brilliant rover Steve Marsh, who had turned up to Fremantle Oval intending to train for Easts, found South's door open early and wandered in. East Fremantle's track record was in almost complete contrast to South's, as it had won nineteen premierships and did not intend to surrender to its lowly co-tenants. After a slight hiccup in the middle of the year, East Fremantle won its last ten games in a row to finish on top of the ladder. In the Second Semi, East Fremantle met West Perth, which had also had a good year, splitting the two Fremantle sides by finishing second. East Fremantle won convincingly. South, having finished third, defeated Swan Districts in the First Semi. Swan Districts were only making their fourth appearance in the finals since joining the competition in 1934. South's success continued during the next week when it defeated West Perth. This paved the way for a derby Grand Final. East Fremantle took out its twentieth premiership convincingly, but South had begun a golden period. The 1945 Grand Final was the first where the Simpson medal was awarded to the best on ground, the inaugural winner being East

Fremantle ruckman, Alan Ebbs. The Grand Final was the culmination of the career of East Fremantle's hero and goalkicker George Doig.

The following year, 1946, saw perhaps one of the most awesome, albeit one-sided, seasons in the history of the WAFL competition. East Fremantle won all nineteen of its home-and-away games, to finish six games clear of second-placed West Perth. The finals series, however, did not prove to be the formality many expected, as East Fremantle became locked in a close struggle with West Perth in the Second Semi. Easts were 2 points down, with thirty seconds on the clock, when 'Runty' McDonald, roving on the forward line, swooped on a crumb and put East Fremantle back in front. The disappointed West Perth side regrouped to defeat Subiaco the following week, and earned a second crack at East Fremantle. The Grand Final produced another close game, which again East Fremantle won by a goal, notching up its thirty-first consecutive win! Something of the relative strengths of each competition can be seen from the fact that Collingwood, third-placed in the VFL, played a friendly game against East Fremantle that year. Collingwood won the match, 11.16 (82) to 9.10 (64).

The 1947 season started with good news for the South Fremantle side, as Ross Hutchinson, who had led East Fremantle and West Perth to premierships before the war, joined the club as captain-coach. Meanwhile, East Fremantle had started the season winning, adding to its winning streak. The Fremantle sides met undefeated, and a record crowd of 17,538 watched South Fremantle finally end the unprecedented dominance of East Fremantle. South came from behind in the last quarter to win by a mere 4 points. West Perth again finished second at the end of the home-and-away season; it was led by captain-coach 'Popsy' Heal, who had already enjoyed success as a player, was rated as one of the best post-war wingers in the West, and was to prove an astute and inspiring coach. (Heal later became a Labor parliamentarian.) South went on to finish on top of the ladder, and entered the finals confident of ending its premiership drought. South met and beat West Perth in the Second Semi. As in the previous year West Perth won through to the Grand Final, defeating the improving Perth side. The Grand Final was an intense and controversial battle. When 'Scranno' Jenkins decked a West Perth player behind play, the ball was taken off a West Perth player shooting for goal and taken to the site of the incident, which was further out from goal: South cleared the ball and captain Hutchinson slotted home 2 goals to give South Fremantle its third premiership. The 1947 flag added extra fuel to the rivalry between the two Fremantle clubs. The South side included Bernie Naylor, its champion full-forward, Clive Lewington, possibly the competition's best centre, and a capable defence led by F. Jenkins, a talented and hard-running centre half-back. Lewington took the Sandover that year, and Naylor topped the goalkicking with 96. In 1947, players began receiving a weekly payment of 15 shillings in a new WAFL provident scheme.

Nineteen forty-eight appeared to be the year when West Perth might take the next step, winning sixteen out of nineteen games for the season, winning one and losing one against the WAFL benchmark team, South Fremantle, and finishing the season on top of the ladder. The contenders were clearly defined as West Perth, South Fremantle, East Fremantle and Perth. The competition at this point had developed into two groups, with these four sides regularly playing off in the finals up until 1955. Claremont, East Perth, Swan Districts and Subiaco all endured lean times during these years. West Perth's hopes were dashed by the South Fremantle side, which narrowly defeated West Perth in the Second Semi, and went on to win back-to-back premierships by repeating the dose a fortnight later. Perth's star ruckman Merv McIntosh won his first Sandover medal. (McIntosh's daughters became prominent netballers.) Naylor continued his domination of the goalkicking award, kicking 89 for the season, including a 13-goal haul against Subiaco.

In 1949 South was favoured to win its third premiership in a row. However, in an injury-ridden season the Bulldogs could rarely put their best combination on the field. Nevertheless, the crowds were still coming to South Fremantle–West Perth matches, with 26,740 watching the South win at Subiaco Oval. Perth finished on top of the ladder in the 1949 season, followed by West Perth, desperate for a premiership, South Fremantle third, and East Fremantle lying fourth. After coming close in the previous three years, West Perth advanced to the Grand Final with a solid win over Perth. South Fremantle could not repeat the magic of the previous two years, losing to a talented Perth line-up in its final. Then captain-coach Heal led his team to victory, beating Perth by 30 points.

For the 1950 Western Australian season, star centreman Clive Lewington took over as coach from Ross Hutchinson. Hutchinson retired from football to pursue a career in politics, was elected the Liberal member for Cottesloe in 1950, and held this blue-ribbon seat for twenty-seven years. Meanwhile, Jerry Dolan, the East Fremantle captain-coach, returned for his last season. Dolan coached East Fremantle to four flags in twelve seasons. (He later became a Labor Parliamentarian.) Overall, the 1949 season appeared to be a cakewalk, for South won nineteen games out of twenty-one for the home-and-away contest. The four maintained its familiar configuration, with South Fremantle finishing first, followed by West Perth, Perth, and East Fremantle. Lewington led his team to its third premiership in four years, with South beating West Perth in the second semi, 15.17 (107) to 11.14 (80). South then met the Perth side in the Grand Final in a close game, caused partly by South's inaccuracy, the scores being 12.23 (95) to 13.11 (89).

The year 1951 was West Perth's, with the club winning the premiership, the Sandover medal (Fred Buttsworth) and the goalkicking. The vital players in this powerful side were Fred Buttsworth, centre half-back; full-forward Ray Scott, who kicked 127 goals to lead the table at the end of the year; together with utilities Don Porter and Jack Larcombe. The season itself gives a slightly different picture, as West Perth started slowly, losing both to the two strong Fremantle sides and to the improving Claremont side, and at one stage dropping out of the four. Then West Perth, with a powerful burst at the end of the season, secured second position. South Fremantle threatened to continue its habit of winning the big games as it beat West Perth in the Second Semi by 8 points. West Perth defeated Perth convincingly the next week, and faced the side which had frustrated many of its premiership campaigns, South Fremantle. The intense rivalry of these two clubs did on this occasion translate into one of the closest Grand Finals seen in the WAFL. West Perth eventually triumphed, winning by only 3 points: the score was West Perth 13.10 (88) to South Fremantle 12.13 (85).

The 1942–44 period in South Australia was not notable for its football. Football was played in response to an appeal by the military to provide some entertainment for the the public and for troops on leave. But there was a shortage of players and the clubs were amalgamated on geographic lines as follows: Norwood–North Adelaide, Sturt–South Adelaide, West Adelaide–Glenelg, and Port Adelaide–West Torrens. The crowds, though confused at times by these temporary wartime alliances, supported these matches in good number. Indeed, the 1942 Grand Final attracted 35,000 people.

Port–Torrens won the first wartime premiership in 1942, but all the next three flags were taken by the North–Norwood combination. As well as this combined competition, there was a series of other matches involving combined services teams versus SANFL combined sides. The services sides included VFL players such as Ron Todd and Des Fothergill, and local goalkicking ace Ken Farmer.

The players played for free during this period, and only played if available on Saturday afternoons, because no special leave was given to footballers. This patriotic spirit was carried on in the dispersal of gate-takings, of which 50 per cent were given to charity. The 1945 Grand Final was a contest between West Torrens and Port Adelaide. West Torrens won the premiership by 13 points, but it had first to survive nervous moments in the First Semi Final, where it beat North Adelaide after the bell rang unheard owing to the noise of the crowd. This was also the year Jack Oatey was appointed playing coach of Norwood. During his reign, from 1945 to 1956, Norwood would only miss the finals once. In 1946, Norwood won the first of its three premierships in five years under Oatey's leadership. Norwood's P. A. Dalwood topped the goalkicking with 70 goals, while R. W. Hanks (West Torrens) won the Magarey medal.

After a slow start to the 1947 season, West Adelaide won its first premiership in twenty years. The Blood and Tars won ten out of the last eleven games, including the Grand Final. They won the Grand Final without suspended star centre half-forward Jack Broadstock. Hanks took the Magarey for the second year, while Port's A. R. McLean booted 80 goals.

After Norwood took the 1948 flag, in 1949 North Adelaide won its first premiership in eighteen years, guided by the clever tactician Ken Farmer. North's H. R. Phillips won the Magarey for the second year running.

The consistent Norwood won the flag in 1950, but in 1951 Port Adelaide won the first of many premierships under the leadership of Fos Williams, who instilled a ferocity and fanaticism into the club. His was a results-oriented style of football, which he described in his own words as 'minimum approach to goal with the maximum body power'.

Williams emphasised quick and direct disposal for driving the ball forward. Norwood's talented ruckman J. E. Marriott earned the Magarey that year, while Glenelg's C. J. Churchett was the top SANFL goalkicker for the fourth season in a row.

The 1940s had begun with war and ended with the promise of prosperity. Affluent clubs Essendon and East Fremantle were the two strongest teams of this decade; others like Carlton were also doing well. As the 1930s Depression and World War II receded, football was coasting on the new tide of prosperity. The superstars of the day, such as John Coleman and Jack Sheedy, represented an affluence which stood in marked contrast to the heroes of the 1930s Depression, typified by Jack Dyer and Lou Richards. Football was less about the gritty determination of Anzacs and battlers, and rather more about glamour and success. In the 1950s the road to winning was mapped out by means of The Golden Rules.

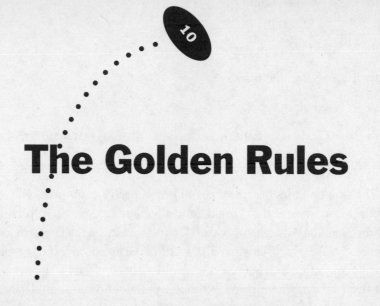

The Golden Rules

The 1950s were a decade in which the game's rules and conventions changed again. Football was now more fluid and less territorial. Rugby and other football codes do not emphasise attacking play until the ball is in the offensive half; Australian Rules players from the 1950s were taught to start an attack the moment possession was gained, anywhere on the field. This strategy was formalised at the end of the 1950s by the game's most astute tactician, Len Smith, in his famous document, entitled 'The Golden Rules'.

Rule 1   Get the ball through the goals in the quickest possible manner, but remember that kicking the ball into an opponent is a football sin. (Attacks should be started from the half-back line, and the quickest route to goal employed.)

Rule 2   Two men together at all times.

Rule 3   No packs or crushes.

Rule 4   Crumbs, crumbs, crumbs. (Three out of four possessions are gained by the ball spilling from a pack.)

Rule 5   Play close to opponent (backmen).

Rule 6   Team spirit, intelligent talking. (Call specific instructions to your team-mates.)

Rule 7   Mind your opponent.

Rule 8   Stand on the mark.

Rule 9   Stop your opponent from playing on.

Rule 10   Tackle opponent in possession of ball. (Legitimate tackling is the only way to take a ball from an opponent.)

The Golden Rules became a key to every coach's team plan. The skills thought important in 1951 are demonstrated in a training film produced by the National Australian Football Council. Thirty years later, the comparable NAFC video illustrated only three kicks (drop punt, torpedo, checkside), with no reference to the older styles of kick. The handball was explained in more detail, although the around-the-shoulder handball was not mentioned. Possession and defensive skills were emphasised in a way not evident in the 1951 film.[1] The team game which had developed after 1951, based on Len Smith's Golden Rules, was a way of reconciling the individualism inherent in Australian football with the military model popular between the wars. The fluid team game of the postwar period relied greatly on a new style of on-ball player called the ruck-rover. He epitomised the new notion of masculine hero appropriate to the age: the ruck-rover was as rugged as the old heroes like Jack Dyer or Syd Coventry, but possessed the speed and skills of Harry Collier or Haydn Bunton Snr. The ruck-rover was an individual hero, but he brought his team-mates into the game.

Success belonged in the 1952–60 period to Melbourne (1954–60), coached by Smith's brother Norm, and to Williamstown, which dominated the VFA from 1954 to 1959. Port Melbourne was a strong VFA team from 1950 to 1957. Port Adelaide loomed large in the South Australian competition from 1953 to 1959. Willie and Port Melbourne in the VFA were as British as Footscray in the VFL. Indeed, Port styled itself by the very British nickname of 'the Boroughs' (not the 'Burras'), so as to distinguish itself from the hated 'city' of South Melbourne.

Of these powerful 1950s teams, the best was the VFL side Melbourne, led by Barassi. In the eleventh round of 1953, Ronald Dale Barassi's ample chest sucked in the perfumed Junction Oval air as, aged seventeen, he galloped out for the first of his 263 senior games; remarkably, he was destined to play in six Grand Final wins. After a few matches in

No. 2, he made the No. 31 guernsey famous at Melbourne. Captain of Melbourne at the age of twenty-four, Barassi was one of the first true ruck-rovers and a specialist in the art of busting through packs. His football career would contain a curious paradox – it seemed to most of the football fraternity that he was the rugged individualist. In classic photographs he is the man whose fierce kicks goalward win the match, despite the efforts of his opponents to pin back his arms. So he stands as a potent symbol of postwar Australian masculinity. But Barassi had also learned well the Golden Rules enunciated by Len Smith, and was wedded to the discipline of the team plan. This paradox would be evident throughout his playing and coaching career. Off the field he was a cadet executive at Millers Rope Works and he had boarded with coach Norm Smith in Coburg since coming down from Castlemaine in 1949. Parenthood coincided with his assumption of football leadership, for Barassi became a father in the same year he became captain of Melbourne, with the birth of the first of three children to his first wife.

By one of the great ironies in Australian sporting history a man who was to help shape modern Australian notions of masculinity himself grew up fatherless. After his father died in 1941, Ron junior's mother, Elza Barassi, stayed on in Melbourne, living with her brother Allan Ray in Coral Avenue, West Footscray. Of mixed English and Irish descent, her father had been a mine manager.[2] Elza managed the canteen at the nearby Kinnears Rope Works by day and by night sold Hilliers chocolates at the State Theatre in Flinders Street. She travelled up to Guildford at least once a month to see her son, who was living with his grandfather and Aunt Mary. By now Ron's favourite reading was the English boys' weekly, *Champion*, featuring his fictional hero Rockfist Rogan. Barassi completed primary school in 1947 and spent the next year at Castlemaine Technical School. The following year, 1949, Barassi was down in Melbourne, living in West Preston, studying first at Preston Technical School, and then at Footscray Technical School. That year, 1949, Ron played the first of his three seasons of football with the Under-Sixteen Preston Scouts in the Preston District Junior Football Association. On Sunday mornings he would cycle across to Norm Smith's house in Coburg and socialise with Fitzroy players like Butch Gale; Smith was then coaching Fitzroy. In 1952 Smith landed the coaching job at Melbourne, and Barassi started in the Melbourne Under-Nineteens. At the end of that year, Elza remarried and moved to Hobart; she decided to leave Ron in

Melbourne with Smith. Smith, who had been a close friend of Ron's father, could from then on be described as a foster father, standing in for the man Ron never knew.

In some ways it was a strange relationship. Even though he lived in the coach's house, the lodger received no special treatment. Smith also had a son, Peter, eleven years younger than Ron (and who later played for Melbourne and Carlton). Ron had to look in the Friday morning newspaper to see if he had a senior game that week; if anything, Smith was harder on him than necessary so as to avoid any invidious comparisons by other Demons. Barassi, Smith, Fred Fanning and others had jobs at Millers Rope Works in Brunswick, as the firm's managing director, Bruce Hogg, was a committee member at Melbourne. After breaking into the seniors in 1953, Ron and several other young Melbourne players were blooded in the 1954 Grand Final at the hands of a better and much tougher Footscray side. This prepared them well for subsequent years. In 1955 Denis Cordner rucked and Barassi roved. Magnificent seasons in 1956 and 1957 followed, and the 1958 flag would also have been theirs had it not been for Collingwood's clever ploy of putting Barry 'Hooker' Harrison on to Barassi. Melbourne won the fights, but Collingwood the premiership.

Norm Smith's aggressive style of coaching is evident in the films of the period. The red-headed Smith believed that hypnosis was an essential tool of the coach. The Movietone version of the 1956 Grand Final between Melbourne and Collingwood shows the size of the crowd, the use of Olympic insignia, and some interesting passages of play. The spoken commentary is, however, poorly synchronised with the actual play.[3]

Footscray's moment of fame came and went. In the 1954 Grand Final the Bulldogs doubled the score of the young Melbourne side, 15.12 (102) to 7.9 (51). Charlie Sutton, the rugged captain-coach, told his team-mates to concentrate on the football while he would personally deal with the Demons, knocking over three of them in the opening minutes. 'Beware the Dogs' appeared over the players' race at the Western Oval. The postwar Footscray club has been renowned for its fighting qualities on and off the field; to many people in Melbourne's West it has symbolised their own plight. Life is a dour struggle, and like the club they must live on to fight another day. Ted Whitten, 'Mr Football', was born in West Footscray, son of a hard-drinking quarry worker. He played

321 games for Footscray, and twenty-nine for Victoria. He was one of several St Augustine's boys who started with the club in the 1950s, part of a sudden inrush of young Catholic men to what had been a Protestant club. The club's mentality was grim and purposeful.

The famous story of Whitten's first game as coach sums up this mentality. Nineteen fifty-seven was Mr Football's seventh season of playing, aged twenty-three: the club had sacked Sutton and installed him as coach. He was giving his pre-match address, all stutters and stammers, anxious about how his team-mates viewed his usurpment of Sutton, but unable to articulate this fear. The door swung open and the room fell silent; there was the little man himself, the legendary captain of the '54 premiership side! Without any ado, Charlie ambled over and wished Whitten the best of luck.

The old Catholic clubs like Collingwood were also changing. At Collingwood in 1950, the sixty-year-old McHale was sacked without warning. The club then botched the replacing of McHale – his successor, 110-gamer Bervyn Woods, lasted only five days in the position, such was the outcry from the supporters. The entire committee – including Bob Rush and secretary Frank Wraith – was thrown out for making a bungle of things. Under new leadership the 1950s were much better years for Collingwood. When Collingwood won the 1953 flag, it had built its membership to 11,500. This was more than the hated Carlton, which had momentarily eclipsed Collingwood in popularity during the last of McHale's years. The excitement of the 1953 Grand Final gave both Jock McHale and John Wren fatal heart attacks. The club's faithful servant Bob Rose was runner-up in the Brownlow that year. Now the Melbourne–Collingwood rivalry began. Norm Smith told his players: 'You're not a footballer until you've played Collingwood at Victoria Park. If you could hold your head high after a match there – you would be a man!' Collingwood's win over Melbourne in the 1958 Grand Final underlined its desperation to prevent its four-flags-in-a-row record being equalled, and was all the more impressive since Melbourne had defeated Collingwood on the ten previous occasions. Kyne told his players at the 1958 Grand Final that the eyes of previous generations of Magpies were on them that day – the legends of the past would be 'feeling every bump, contesting every mark, booting every kick'. It was not just present-day players out there on the MCG turf that afternoon, but the ghosts of players long dead, summoned up to help. 'Hooker' Harrison harassed

Barassi constantly during the game, Bill Serong broke Ian Ridley's nose, and Murray Weidemann lined up several Melbourne players. The Demons retaliated and won the ensuing fight, but lost the match.[4]

By the early 1950s Carlton had momentarily outstripped the arch-enemy Collingwood in signing up subscription-paying members. It was an indication that postwar social mobility was having its effect on the old immigrant suburb and its residents, past and present. Tribalism was portable: as they moved out to leafier suburbs, Carlton's old Jewish, Lebanese and Italian families remained true to the Blues. Jews did not play senior football, but on Sundays in the 1950s there was a revival of the scratch matches between the old Carlton Jewish families (called North of the Yarra) and families who had settled in the postwar Elsternwick–St Kilda enclave (South of the Yarra). This ritual contest usually took place on a picnic ground in the outer northern suburbs, and prefigured the formation of the Jewish amateur club, Ajax. (The one or two Jewish men who made it to professional ranks in fact usually played for St Kilda. But, just as there were few Jews in American major league baseball, playing professional Australian football did not particularly appeal to young Melbourne Jews.)[5]

The larger religious issue was sectarian Christian. Resolving the Catholic–Protestant tension was important to any club's success because it opened the way for recuits from many backgrounds. In those days Hawthorn patterned itself on Collingwood – John Kennedy had been a Magpie supporter in his youth, and McHale was his model. The sectarian conflict at Hawthorn did not erupt until the late 1940s – until then it had been a harmonious suburban club. In 1950 Hawthorn adopted brown-and-gold stripes, and during the 1950s its Protestant–Catholic rivalry was resolved under the firm leadership of Kennedy, a devout Catholic. Ironically, the time would later come when Collingwood tried to emulate Hawthorn.[6]

The emergence of Catholic schools in Australian Rules football was an important development of this decade, and formed an essential part of this story. Catholics were enjoying the first fruits of social mobility, and school football was a rite of social passage. Schools like De La Salle in Malvern, St Patrick's in Ballarat and Assumption College in Kyneton could claim dozens of VFL and AFL stars over the next few decades.

The 1952 season kicked off with Geelong and Collingwood starting strongly, winning their first six games; South Melbourne also started well, winning five out of the first six. This year had a unique round, known as the 'National Day' round, where VFL clubs competed for premiership points at country and interstate venues. Five decades had elapsed since the last time this had been tried. The reports suggest that despite an absence of state players and poor weather these games were well received in both Brisbane and Sydney. However, interstate home-and-away games were not organised again until 1979. Overall, the 1952 season was plagued by poor weather and this is reflected in the year's low scores. Essendon for the first time in some years missed the finals, only producing patches of form. Coleman continued to dominate, kicking 13 goals against Geelong at Kardinia Park and finishing the season with 103 goals. The next best was George Goninon's 59 for the Cats. Geelong established itself at the top of the ladder, followed by Collingwood. After these two followed a tight battle among Fitzroy, Carlton and South Melbourne for the remaining two places. Fitzroy held off a tiring South Melbourne to consolidate its place in the final four. As for South, it would have to wait until 1970 for its next finals appearance. The 1952 finals series was a statement of Geelong's dominance, as it beat Collingwood easily in the Second Semi, and then repeated the dose in the Grand Final, winning the club's only back-to-back VFL premiership. Geelong was nicknamed the 'tearaway' side for its famous attack-at-all costs strategy. The half-back line of Hyde, Middlemiss and Williams drove the ball forward with repeated fast 'dashes'.[7] That season Richmond's 'gentle giant', Roy Wright, won the Brownlow, a triumph for a player who had contended with injury and a lack of opportunity behind Richmond's powerful ruck division of Dyer, Morris and Jones, not to mention Dyer's amazement that a man of sixteen stone could not inflict more pain upon the opposition!

Geelong's winning streak continued into the next year, for it won every match until Round 14, when it was stopped in a physical contest by Collingwood. This loss ended Geelong's record winning streak of twenty-six games. It is interesting to note that winning sequences in Australian football are relatively short compared to those in other codes of football and other team sports. The four in this year took shape early, with Geelong, Footscray, Collingwood and Essendon all remaining in the four after Round 10, with Geelong remaining on top of the ladder all year and the other three locked in a close battle for the other positions. Footscray showed the big improvement, basing its play around a strong backline, and making it through to the preliminary final. After its shock absence in 1952, Essendon enjoyed a return to finals football. Buoyed by the psychological ascendancy gained by its mid-season win over the Cats and by continuing good form, Collingwood went on to win the 1953 premiership, beating Geelong in both the Second Semi and in the Grand Final. In goalkicking, John Coleman eclipsed the field, kicking 97 to Goninon's 65. Coleman started the year with bags of 10, 11, and 10 goals in consecutive weeks. Essendon's brilliant but unlucky rover, William Hutchinson, won his first Brownlow at the age of thirty. He had lost the previous year on a countback, and had been third in 1948 and in 1951. Hutchinson possessed damaging pace and was a brilliant kick at goal; he also teamed well with 'Bluey' McClure, the Bomber ruckman.

As so often happens, the season-long certainty of the eventual finalists in 1953 was in direct contrast to the following season. Nineteen fifty-four was an open and exciting contest, with seven clubs having finals aspirations. Early in the season, John Coleman received a serious knee injury in what was to be his last match for the Bombers; he was leading the goalkicking with 42 goals at Round 6, and he had kicked a club record of 14 the week before. (This record still stands at Essendon four decades later.) Despite its finals disappointment of the year before, Geelong started the year well, and its form looked good leading up to the finals, where it won the last eight games in a row. North Melbourne enjoyed a much-improved season, finishing in the finals, beating Geelong, Collingwood and Carlton, and drawing with Footscray at Arden Street. A relatively young Melbourne side, under Norm Smith, improved to finish fourth at the end of the home-and-away games. Essendon, Richmond and Collingwood all finished a game outside the finals. The Bombers played good football but could only miss Coleman, while Richmond threatened but lost some close games which proved costly. Collingwood appeared to struggle all year to find its premiership touch and finished a disappointing seventh. The finals saw Geelong, from first place, lose all its finals and be bundled out of the finals. The form sides were Footscray and the young Melbourne side, which disposed of North. These sides met in the Grand Final, and the more experienced and tougher Footscray won its first and only VFL premiership. Richmond ruckman Roy Wright won his second Brownlow, and Jack Collins chipped in to help Footscray to the flag with his 84 goals, including 7 in the Grand Final.

The improvement and potential within the Melbourne club of the previous year were quickly converted into a premiership under the guidance of Norm Smith in 1955. Collingwood appeared to have had the measure of the Demons during the year, beating them in their Round 11 struggle. Geelong was prominent during the season but dropped its last game to finish third. The shock of the season was the form of reigning Premiers Footscray; the Dogs had stayed in the four for most of the season. But with losses to Geelong, Melbourne and Essendon in the later stages of the season, the triumphant Bulldogs of 1954 missed out on the four to Essendon by half a percentage point. The finals series saw Melbourne and Collingwood clash twice – in the Second Semi and in the Grand Final. The Melbourne combination was too strong for the Magpies. The 1955 Brownlow went to Fred Goldsmith, full-back for South Melbourne and Victoria, while the consistent Bill Hutchinson ran second. Noel Rayson topped the goal kicking with 80 goals for Geelong.

The Olympic year, 1956, in many ways continued the pattern set in the previous year. Melbourne emerged as the team to beat, with its strong complement of ruck-rovers and rovers. Collingwood and Geelong pursued Melbourne throughout the year, and the battle for the double chance between these two sides came down to the last two rounds. Geelong lost at home for the first time in two seasons to Collingwood, and then to the unpredictable Essendon in the final round. The Cats lost the second chance for the second year running to Collingwood. Footscray made the finals, finishing fourth, and then defeated Geelong in the First Semi-Final. Collingwood and Melbourne clashed twice, and Melbourne ran out convincing Premiers, beating Collingwood 17.19 (121) to 6.12 (48) in front of a massive crowd of 115,802 people. St Kilda enjoyed a more successful year, partly due to the form of first-year full-forward William Young, a lightly-built forward who kicked 56 goals for the Saints. Peter Box of Footscray won the Brownlow, becoming the only Footscray player to win the medal and also play in a premiership side.

The 1957 season was an exciting one which remained open for much of the year. This was the year Ted Whitten, aged twenty-three, was named captain-coach of Footscray in place of the successful and popular Charlie Sutton. Melbourne would go on to win its second hat-trick premiership, but not without some scares along the way. Geelong's appearances in the finals came to a dramatic and emphatic end when the blue-and-whites dropped to last at the end of the season. Hawthorn improved dramatically and made the finals for the first time, making the Preliminary Final in which it met Melbourne. Melbourne's game had began to flow at the right end of the season, and it ended Hawthorn's first finals campaign, winning 22.12 (144) to 11.10 (76). Essendon faced Melbourne with some optimism, having beaten the Demons in the Second Semi; however, Melbourne carried on from the Preliminary Final and beat Essendon well. The 1957 Brownlow was claimed by Brian Gleeson, the high-marking St Kilda centre half-forward and ruckman. Sadly, because he injured his knee right at the start of the 1958 season, 1957 turned out to be Gleeson's last complete year of football. Footscray's Jack Collins topped the goalkicking for the second time.

Football's centenary year, 1958, was the stage for Melbourne's attempt to equal Collingwood's record of four premierships in a row. Throughout the season it appeared that the Demons were destined to achieve this feat. The Demons remained on top of the ladder after Round 8 and only lost three games for the season. The Lions had good wins over Collingwood and Melbourne at the picturesque Brunswick Street Oval and enjoyed a good year after threatening to win the wooden spoon the year before. Collingwood seemed to be Melbourne's major threat throughout the 1958 season, but almost lost the vital double chance in the last round to Fitzroy when the Magpies were defeated by the Roos at Victoria Park: they were saved only by Hawthorn beating Fitzroy in the same round. The finals shaped then as a battle royal between Melbourne and Collingwood. Melbourne defeated Collingwood easily in the Second Semi, 11.12 (78) to 4.9 (33), but the Magpies fought off the honest North Melbourne in the Preliminary Final and went into the Grand Final as underdogs. On the day itself, Collingwood triumphed, winning a tight Grand Final 12.10 (82) to 9.10 (64). (The black-and-white horde would look back fondly to 1958 for many years – until their next flag in 1990.) St Kilda's Neil Roberts won the 1958 Brownlow. His career had taken off once he was moved from the forward line to the centre half-back position. Talented Magpie full-forward Ian Brewer kicked 73 goals to lead the season's goalkicking.

The Magpies seemed to have exerted so much effort in defending their record against Melbourne that a premiership hangover was inevitable in 1959. After losing games early in the new season, they notched a good win over Essendon at Windy Hill, their first victory at that ground in seven years. Melbourne was still the dominant side in the competition, and it appeared that its Grand Final defeat had merely been an aberration. The Demons finished the season on top of the ladder, losing four games and drawing one. Ron Barassi had one of his best years at the club, and was inspirational as a pack-breaking ruck-rover who kicked 46 goals for the year. Carlton moved back into finals football, finishing a consistent second at the end of the home-and-away season. Essendon slipped into the four after North faltered against the rejuvenated South Melbourne. The Bloods (a nickname suggested by their red sash) were inspired by their newly-appointed captain, Bob Skilton. Skilton, a South Melbourne local, went on to win the Brownlow medal in this year. The finals series was an exciting one, for Collingwood had won its last ten games and the club and its fans expected success. Essendon was also finding form at the right end of the year. These two sides met in the First Semi, and the Bombers stopped the Magpies' winning run, beating the reigning Premiers by 6 goals. The Dons went on to defeat Carlton in the Preliminary Final, and faced the ever-powerful Melbourne in the Grand Final. The Bombers' effort in making the Grand Final from fourth is noteworthy in itself, and they hung on until three-quarter time. Then Melbourne unleashed a 6-goal burst in the last quarter to beat the tiring Essendon side. Ron Evans of Essendon topped the 1959 goalkicking with 79 goals, in front of the Brownlow medallist Skilton who kicked 60 goals as a rover.

In 1960 Melbourne and Essendon both established themselves at the top of the ladder early in the season. Fitzroy played a consistent year of football to finish second on the ladder. Perhaps one of the major events of the 1960 season was Hawthorn's final defeat of Collingwood at Victoria Park in Round 13, a feat that had taken thirty-five years. Perhaps more importantly, it was a sign of the more competitive spirit being instilled into the brown-and-golds. Hawthorn missed out on the finals only on percentage to the improving Collingwood side. The finals series produced close games between Essendon and Collingwood, the Magpies winning by 9 points, and between old rivals Collingwood and Fitzroy, where the Pies denied Fitzroy a Grand Final appearance by a mere 5 points. In direct contrast, Melbourne let no side near it in the Second Semi, where it held Fitzroy to 4.16 (40) to 14.18 (102), and in the Grand Final in heavy conditions, where the Melbourne side outscored

Collingwood in every quarter to score a convincing win, 18.14 (122) to
2.2 (14). John Schultz, the Footscray ruckman, won the Brownlow medal.
Schultz had been recruited from Boort and represented Victoria twenty-
four times, and he was recognised as an awkward but fair player. Ron
Evans followed up the previous season's success with 67 goals, including
a bag of 10 in Round 11 against Hawthorn, to win the goalkicking.

The VFL story in the 1950s is a history of changing club fortunes. In
the meantime, some things had not changed since the prewar days.
Conditions at the grounds around Melbourne were unhygienic. Terraces
bulged with overcrowding, toilet and other facilities were woeful; the
profits at the MCG merely helped subsidise cricket and were not put
back into football.[8] The admission price was still very low – by tradition
it was kept at about the price of a glass of beer. Ninepence before the
war, it was one shilling and threepence during the 1950s, rising only to
5 shillings (50 cents) in 1966 and 3 dollars in 1980.[9] These prices have
always been considerably below the cost of equivalent professional sporting contests in the United States. Country leagues continued to com-
plain that their best players were poached by the VFL, with no return to
the rural competitions. (When Victorian zoning was finally introduced
in 1967, this brought country clubs no financial reward, but at least
prompted some VFL clubs to sponsor developmental work in their particular zones.)[10]

Newspaper reporting was another constant, especially the use of the
game's four quarters as an organising device for journalists. This continued into the 1960s, particularly in the prose of Alf Brown. The narrative had a strong beginning, middle and end.

> The narrative is carefully located within a landscape: the arena, the
> breezy or 'greasy' conditions and the ground filled to capacity. The
> game itself comprises the most visible actions of players, umpires,
> trainers and fans told as an unravelling string of exploits: marks, goals,
> tackles, free kicks, incidents, intervals, duels and drives. The way these
> moments are made visible within the narrative is also the strategy by
> which a good story was made of the game.[11]

The discourses of the football print journalist and of the coach were
eventually to become closer to each other than they were in the Alf
Brown days. In print, analysis would take the place of description, while

the continuous narrative style of Alf Brown would later be found in the instantaneous radio version. Brown's retelling followed close on the heels of the action itself, communicated by telephone for the final edition of the evening *Herald*, together with its bright pink companion, the *Sporting Globe*, and thrown off the backs of the delivery trucks by 6.30 p.m., right throughout Melbourne's inner suburbs, merely ninety minutes after the game was done.

St Kilda fan Brian Matthews evokes this period and place well:

> They're crowding for a beer at inner suburban pubs after Hawthorn or Carlton or Fitzroy have scraped in or gone down just up the road at Princes Park, with the rain starting [to fall] on the smoky windows and the homeward traffic idling past in silver lines. And they're straggling away from the MCG, hunched down in their coats, scuffling swirls of abandoned streamers, *Footy Records* and pie bags; and they're buying their *Heralds* and turning to the back page on the trams; and they're winding home sadly home from Moorabbin where the Saints have just proved yet again that this isn't the year . . . The temperate, dry, brilliantly lit winters of Perth and Adelaide . . . just don't breed an atmosphere like that; they'll be in it – but they'll never be of it.[12]

Obsolescent too would become the metaphors of yesteryear. Images of war or of class struggle would be replaced by accounts of sharemarket-like rises and falls on the League ladder. Club fortunes would later wax or wane, much like the varying indicators of corporate performance. But Alf Brown's readership was male and blue-collar, and his words were devoured just like the pies and the beer. This readership was distant from the boardrooms of corporate Australia in the 1960s, and these sturdy proletarians certainly had no interest in overall club performance. They were mainly concerned to learn week by week, quarter by quarter, how individual players were travelling – and to some extent how the team was going. To be concerned about the club overall would have required a peek into the finances and business practices of their beloved Magpies or Tigers – and this was unthinkable in old class-ridden Australia.

The journalists catered to this 'six o'clock swill' readership. Before the pubs stopped serving beer at six ('Time gentlemen, time!'), the paper-boys slid between the jostle of men, hawking the penultimate edition of the Saturday *Herald*, which contained Alf Brown's narrative as far as the three-quarter-time scores. Typically Alf Brown's descriptions followed an opening summary paragraph (which could be rewritten if the game swung the other way) followed by the scorelines and the team line-ups (which in those days hardly differed from the published line-ups):

> At Essendon: Estimated 25,000.
> The ground was heavy in the centre and towards the members' goal.
> Umpire Woolfe took a mark off Gallagher but evened up a minute
> later with a charity free. Gallagher, deadly last week, missed a 'sitter'.
> Essendon, faster, had all the play but their forwards would not get in
> front. In addition they played the wrong wing and attacked into the
> wind.
> After 19 minutes hammering at the favored outer goal Essendon had
> four points.
> Hawthorn full-forward Ingersoll leading out fast, flattened Hutchinson.
> Hutchinson and the Essendon grandstand were furious about it.
> Hawthorn, on one of their few visits forward, took the lead when
> Morrie Young goaled. They led 1.0 to 0.4.
> After 22 minutes, Birt goaled for Essendon. Then Gallagher kicked his
> third successive behind. It was a poor game and the many scrambles
> favored rugged Hawthorn.
> Quarter-time scores –
> ESSENDON . . . 1 5 11
> HAWTHORN . . . 1 2 8
> First quarter goalkickers – Essendon: Birt. Hawthorn: Young.[13]

Meanwhile, over in Western Australia, the 1950s began well for South Fremantle and ended well for East Perth. Subiaco won the Reserves flags in 1958 and 1959, and it looked as if its time was coming again. The 1959 senior team was the best to represent Subiaco for a decade or more, finishing second to East Perth after a strong run home. Charlie Tyson had come down from South Fremantle to coach Subiaco in 1956. In this team were many Subiaco legends, including champion utility Laurie Kettlewell, and half-forwards Kevin Merifield and Merv Screaigh.

South Fremantle finished the 1952 season with seventeen wins and three losses to finish on top of the ladder, followed by West Perth on fifteen wins and five losses, setting up another clash between these fierce rivals. More suprisingly, East Fremantle missed the finals for the first time since 1915, making way for Claremont (under the leadership of first year captain-coach 'Sonny' Maffina) and for East Perth, making their first appearances in the finals since 1942 and 1944 respectively. Neither of these sides could break the stranglehold of West Perth and South Fremantle, however, and it was these two sides which met in the Grand Final yet again. West Perth went into the game the warm favourite, having beaten South Fremantle in a high-scoring Second Semi-Final, 19.16 to 17.13. West Perth appeared to have the premiership well within its grasp, holding a 5-goal lead at half-time. The normally calm and cool Clive Lewington, in his first year as non-playing coach, blasted his players, and South responded, particularly ruck-rover Des Kelly. His game was so inspired that the contest is remembered as 'Kelly's match'. Other crucial members of South's 1952 premiership combination included the long-kicking Bernie Naylor – who won the goalkicking with an impressive total of 132 goals for the season, including a bag of nineteen versus East Fremantle – and the Sandover medallist Steve Marsh, a quick and dangerous rover.

In 1953, South established a record-breaking dominance in the competition: the highlight was a home game against Subiaco, in which South Fremantle kicked a record 35.18 (228). Bernie Naylor's tally that afternoon was 23 goals, easily a Western Australian record. South lost just two games in this season, and capped off this remarkable year with a record margin victory in the Grand Final, walloping West Perth 18.12 (120) to 8.13 (61). Not surprisingly, Bernie Naylor topped the 1953 goalkicking, kicking 156 goals during the home-and-away season, and another 11 in the finals series, to finish the year with 167 goals. The Sandover that year was taken by Perth's Merv McIntosh. Also in 1953, Graham Farmer made his senior debut for East Perth, fresh from Sister Kate's Home (now Manguri), and East Fremantle moved to the East Fremantle Oval.

The next year, 1954, was the climax of South Fremantle's dominance; it won another premiership in a local derby against East Fremantle, and smashed its own winning margin in the Grand Final, winning 21.14 (140) to 9.8 (62). East Fremantle had a greatly improved year, despite this crushing loss to South in the Grand Final. West Perth finished second on the ladder, but was disappointing in the finals, losing to both the Fremantle sides; West missed the retired Buttsworth. In what would be his last year, Bernie Naylor (South) topped the goalkicking again, with

133 goals. Merv McIntosh won his second Sandover medal.

Nineteen fifty-five saw a change in the pattern of South's dominance, since Perth, which had finished in the four many times since 1945, was able to go on in the finals, with the perennially strong South Fremantle, West Perth, and the revived East Fremantle. This year also saw the introduction of a 15-yard penalty paid against players who wasted time. The season progressed as though the two Fremantle sides would be the main contenders for the flag. South Fremantle finished on top, in front of East Fremantle on percentage; the other positions were filled by Perth and West Perth. Perth won its way into the Grand Final by beating West Perth and South Fremantle, setting up a meeting with East Fremantle in the Grand Final. The game itself produced a remarkable comeback victory for Perth which was trailing 2.2 (14) to 8.5 (53) at half time and 2 points down at three-quarter time, kicking into a strong breeze in the last quarter. Perth, inspired by ruckman Merv McIntosh who was playing his last game for the club, outscored East Fremantle, and won by 2 points in front of a record crowd of 41,962. This was Perth's first premiership since 1907. Ern Henfry, who played in Carlton's 1947 premiership side, coached Perth from 1953 to 1959 and from 1962 to 1965. The precocious John Todd won the Sandover medal for South Fremantle in his first year. Ray Scott (later an umpire) kicked 83 goals for West Perth to win the goalkicking. South Fremantle, East Fremantle, West Perth and Perth had made up the four eight times in the seasons from 1945 to 1955.

The following season, 1956, Jack Sheedy moved to East Perth as captain-coach and developed a handball-oriented style of play which worked well with the young but talented East Perth side, which included Graham Farmer and Ted Kilmurray. East Perth beat South Fremantle twice in the season, and finished the home-and-away series on top of the ladder. East Perth met South Fremantle in the Second Semi and defeated South, and repeated the dose in the Grand Final, winning by 13 points to claim its first premiership since 1944. Aptly, Graham Farmer won the Sandover medal, while John Gerovich of South Fremantle kicked 74 goals to win the goalkicking.

The pre-season move of South Fremantle's premiership rover Steve Marsh to East Fremantle as captain-coach was bound to have an immediate impact on the 1957 season. (It was the first time that East Fremantle had recruited a coach from outside the club.) His success matched that of Jack Sheedy's the year before, with East Fremantle having a much-improved season. Meanwhile, East Perth continued its success under Sheedy, finishing on top of the ladder, followed by Perth, then East Fremantle, and West Perth making up the four. South Fremantle missed the four for the first time in twelve years. The finals series produced a mixture of predictable results. East Perth went straight into the Grand Final, winning its Second Semi against Perth easily, and a titantic struggle between East Fremantle and Perth ensued. East Fremantle's celebration of its Diamond Jubilee season appeared to be heading to an untimely end when, at three-quarter time in the Preliminary Final against Perth, it was 55 points down, 16.17 (113) to 9.6 (60). East Fremantle had the breeze in the last quarter, and with the introduction of Nugent into the ruck pulled off an extraordinary win, kicking 10 goals in the last quarter, with rover Ray Howard putting them 4 points in front in the last minute of the game. The game almost degenerated into farce when a supporter (presumably from East) imitated the siren with such accuracy that the crowd ran onto the field thinking the game was over. The match was held up for five minutes as the ground was cleared; the game started again but Perth was unable to add to its score, and when the siren rang a second time East Fremantle was into another Grand Final. The Grand Final shaped as a battle between two of the newer coaches in the competition, and East Fremantle again fell behind, trailing by 24 points at half-time, and again showed its ability to come from behind, eventually beating the East Perth side 10.18 (78) to 9.8 (62). Jack Clarke won the Sandover medal for the Premiers, while Don Glass (Subiaco) won the goalkicking, kicking 83 goals.

The centenary year of Australian football, 1958, was celebrated in Western Australia by a lightning premiership. Ray Schofield, a 277-game full-back remembered for his contests with the great Bernie Naylor, took over as captain-coach of West Perth. Schofield replaced Frank Sparrow, who moved into radio commentary and became one of Western Australia's best-known voices, as well as a television identity. East Fremantle and East Perth set the early pace in the competition, followed by West Perth. The genuine contenders for the premiership shaped as East Perth and East Fremantle. In the Second Semi they clashed and East Fremantle won well, taking the week's rest; however, the win came at a cost, with East Fremantle's captain-coach being suspended for four weeks for striking East Perth rover Ron Lawrence. East Perth was then forced to play in the Preliminary Final against Perth. By Western Australian standards it was a low-scoring affair, with East Perth winning 6.13 (61) to 4.9 (33). The Grand Final was a return match between East Fremantle and East Perth, and East Perth turned the tables on East Fremantle, winning 8.17 (65) to 8.15 (63) in a pressure-filled match.

In 1959 Perth moved from the WACA to Lathlain Park. Don Marinko junior was appointed captain-coach in place of Ray Schofield. East Perth won its first seventeen games of the season, before losing three at the end of the year. West Perth missed the finals, losing its crucial last game, and Claremont beat Perth, which put it into the First Semi and elevated East Fremantle to the Second Semi. Subiaco made the finals for the first time since 1946 and continued its success in the finals, walloping Perth in the First Semi 26.23 (179) to 7.8 (50). Subiaco then met East Fremantle in the Preliminary Final, beating East also, to make its first Grand Final appearance since 1935. East Perth went straight into the Grand Final after beating East Fremantle in the Second Semi. The final generated considerable interest, particularly the emergence of Subiaco, which was attempting to win its first premiership since 1935. A record crowd of 45,325 turned out. Unfortunately for Subiaco, East Perth proved too steady and won its third premiership in four years. Graham Farmer won the best-on-ground award, the Simpson medal. That year the Sandover went to West Perth's B. Foley, while Neil Hawke (East Perth) topped the season's goalkicking. (The latter was a cousin of the future Prime Minister and later played cricket for Australia.)

In 1960, Footscray star Arthur Olliver was appointed to coach West Perth. At South Fremantle John Todd was replaced by ex-Footscray and Victorian centre half-back Marty McDonnell. Steve Marsh regained the coaching position at East Fremantle. The 1960 season was an open one, with the top four clubs – West Perth, East Perth, South Fremantle, and East Fremantle – all locked together on thirteen wins, separated only by the number of draws each team had played. Subiaco finished fifth with twelve wins to its name. West Perth, finishing on top of the ladder, won through to the Grand Final by defeating East Perth in the Second Semi. East Perth bounced back the following week to beat East Fremantle and take its place in the Grand Final. West Perth enjoyed instant success under its new coach to take the premiership at the expense of East Perth,

17.13 (115) to 12.11 (83). Graham Farmer (East Perth) won the Sandover, and the celebrated John Gerovich (South Fremantle) topped the
scoring list with 101 goals.[14]

The 1950s was a halcyon period in Western Australian football, and
the size of the crowd grew accordingly. Total attendances rose from just
under 600,000 in each of the three seasons 1956, 1957 and 1958 to
just over 700,000 in 1959, and more than 750,000 during the 1960s.
This increased interest in local football was partly due to the leadership
provided by the greater number of expatriate Victorians playing and
coaching in the West. But it also had a lot to do with the ability of young
Western Australians to employ their natural talents in the better-coached
sides.

In South Australia the 1950s belonged to Port Adelaide. In 1952,
North Adelaide won the flag after finishing minor Premiers. After Norwood defeated Port in a close Preliminary Final, the Grand Final was
expected to be close and tough; instead, North Adelaide produced an
explosive display and won by 18 goals. The following season West Torrens took the premiership after playing and beating Port Adelaide in what
was rated as one of the best Grand Finals played in South Australia. The
game was only settled by Ray Hanks' last-minute goal. However, this
was a false dawn, for it was to be the Eagles' only premiership prior to
merging with Woodville.

And Port was about to win six flags in a row. Nineteen fifty-four was
the first of these. Laurie Cahill was appointed coach of West Adelaide,
and the Blood and Tars finished runners-up to Port. Glenelg appointed
its first full-time coach in ex-Essendon player Charles 'Chooka' May.
May was responsible not only for the senior side but also for the club's
juniors and for visiting schools. The next two years, 1955 and 1956,
were Port years. Port's D. E. Boyd won the Magarey in 1956. Nineteen
fifty-seven was a close call. Replacing Jack Oatey, Haydn Bunton Jr took
over as coach of Norwood at the age of nineteen, leading it to second
place, only losing to Port by 11 points in the Grand Final. Port now
began to pull away from Norwood as South Australia's most successful
flag-winner.

Port Adelaide, the wealthiest of the South Australian clubs thanks to
its social facilities, was led for three decades by Fos Williams from 1950.
The celebrated rover was captain-coach during the 1950–58 period,
which included the first five of the six flags in a row. Those who played

in all six premierships were John Abley, Dave Boyd, Neville Hayes, Geoff Motley, Ted Whelan and Lloyd Zucker. Port also continued to enjoy stable administration under the secretaryship of Bob McLean, who took the post in 1949 and, like Williams, stayed for three decades.

In 1958 Port Adelaide became Premiers yet again. A firebrand coach, North Melbourne's Alan Killigrew, was appointed at Norwood, and brought with him a number of seasoned VFL players to supplement Norwood's side. The following year, 1959, was Port's sixth flag in a row, while North Adelaide took the 1960 premiership.

The systematic coaching inspired by Len Smith's 'Golden Rules' is the dominant theme of the 1950s. The game reflected the new social mobility of postwar Australia and was becoming increasingly distant from its inner-urban industrial roots. The presidency of the VFL passed in the 1950s to Kenneth Luke, a self-made businessman whose dream was to develop VFL Park. Sir Kenneth was quite different from McClelland, and presaged a new kind of VFL presidency.[15] Styles of play were now fluid and more team-oriented. However, all attempts to promote the game in the Rugby states and outside Australia were fruitless. The National Day experiment of 1952 was not repeated. Fanciful ideas of exporting Australian football to the United States led nowhere; only one Queenslander, Irwin Dornau, made it to VFL ranks in this period; the match of the day in Sydney's local competition attracted merely 5000 spectators on average. However, the interstate carnivals started again and were a sign of the closer links across the footballing states.[16] Australian football was stronger than ever in Victoria, South Australia, and the West.

New Skills

The 1960s was the first televised decade in Australian football. Television had arrived in Melbourne for the 1956 Olympics, and within a few years the traditional style of humour favoured by barrackers in the Outer had begun to inform the way the game was presented on the 'idiot box'. 'World of Sport' became the standard method for describing football on the new medium. Former players without even basic media skills such as voice training were made to sit as a panel of supposed experts, like judges sitting at a bench, and to ridicule each other's views of this or next week's players and teams. So overnight the traditional humour of football was translated successfully into TV. 'World of Sport' indeed earned the (dubious) distinction of becoming one of the world's longest-running television shows. 'World of Sport' was one of several TV programs covering the period from Thursday evening right through to Sunday afternoon and the VFL replays were slotted into the Saturday evening. The conventions of filming the game on TV were to remain fixed for four decades. Quite simply, cameras went wherever the ball went. There were no aerial shots or more elaborate camera angles, and this remained the pattern of televised football. A match televised in 1995 looks much like it did in 1965 – except it became colour from 1975. A highlight of Thursday night television was 'League Teams', with Bobby Davis, Lou Richards and Jack Dyer parading as the three wise monkeys. 'League Teams' disappeared in about 1980, about the same time as the arrival of the new intellectualising implicit in radio comedy. Newspaper

159

commentary began to be analytical rather than descriptive at roughly the same time.[1] This was because television took over the narrative function, with commentators inanely telling viewers what they were seeing!

The game was undergoing its own changes. The 1960s were the decade of new skills in Australian Rules. The dropkick and the defensive handball disappeared, and were replaced by new ways of playing attacking football. But in other ways it was still a simple time: young people wore duffle-coats to the match and older people rugged up.

The 1961 season was to signal the end of the Melbourne hegemony, and also the beginning of a decade not dominated by any one single VFL club. Hawthorn moved up the ladder to finish the 1961 season on top. St Kilda also ended a long absence from finals football: the Saints had to defeat North Melbourne on the Junction Oval. In a tense finish, the Saints overturned a three-quarter-time deficit, kicking 4 goals in the last quarter to ensure their place in the finals. After the siren there were chaotic scenes as players and fans celebrated this victory of the St Kilda Football Club. Footscray also made its return to finals football. Melbourne finished in the four, but appeared to lack the spark of its glory years, and lost narrowly in the Second Semi to Hawthorn, and then lost to Footscray in the Preliminary Final. These two clubs were the eventual Grand Finalists. In front of 107,935 people these two 'battling' clubs played an entertaining final. Footscray was leading at half-time, only to be overrun in the second half by the 'commando'-style Hawks. The popular Johnny James won the 1961 Brownlow for Carlton, also winning his club's best and fairest. His team-mate Tom Carroll, in his first year of senior football, kicked 54 goals, 4 goals better than another impressive youngster, Cat Doug Wade, also playing his first year.

Melbourne started the 1962 season seemingly intent on revenge, winning six straight and thrashing their Preliminary Final opponents Footscray in Round 3. However, just as in the previous year, other contenders came out of the pack. Essendon played strongly all year, beating all of the other eventual finalists. Geelong continued on its gradual improvement, though its star recruit Graham 'Polly' Farmer injured himself early in his debut game and missed the season. Nonetheless, the increasingly burly Wade continued to kick goals – in fact, 68 in all to lead the goalkicking – and the stylish Alistair Lord won the Brownlow despite almost being suspended in a case of mistaken identity with his twin brother, Stewart Lord. Carlton that season played a dour style of football, concentrating on defence rather than high scoring, and it too enjoyed a good year, finishing third at the end of the home-and-away season. The finals series again showed that the easiest path to a premiership was victory in the Second Semi. Essendon defeated Geelong 14.21 (105) to 7.17 (59) in a display of inaccuracy from both sides. Carlton played Melbourne, winning by just 2 points, and starting a thrilling passage to the Grand Final. The next week in the Preliminary Final Carlton kicked 4.4 in the last quarter to force a draw with Geelong. The replay was almost as close but Carlton sqeezed in front to win by 5 points. Essendon, after two weeks' rest, went on to record its third win for the year over the weary Blues.

Hawthorn returned to form in 1963, recapturing the form of its premiership year. Its stumbling block throughout the year was another improved Geelong side, which played one draw with the Hawks and also outscored them. Essendon fell victim to the increasingly potent premiership hangover, and in the last round percentage match with the Saints was denied a place in the finals. Melbourne again made the finals, but this was the year it was hampered by the suspension of the brilliant and sometimes fiery Barassi. The finals series saw Geelong inflict two further defeats upon Hawthorn in both the Second Semi and the Grand Final to win the flag. These matches were of particular interest, for the two sides played such different styles of football. Geelong attacked through the vision of Farmer, Goggin, and Lord, while Hawthorn played a cruder but effective style of football, heavily reliant on the leading goalkicker of the competition, John 'Elvis' Peck, who kicked 75 goals for the season. Bob Skilton won his second Brownlow in a stand-out individual performance in a struggling side. Graham Farmer finished equal second with Daryl Baldock, a measure of the impact he had had in his first full year of VFL football.

The 1963 Premiers took their winning style into the new season, winning ten of their first eleven contests. In one memorable match at Kardinia Park, Geelong met North's physicality head on: North's ruckman Ken Dean was told at half-time he would be facing police charges owing to an incident with Geelong's Denis Marshall, and the ill-feeling continued after the final siren. Players and officials clashed in the race – North's fiery coach Alan Killigrew had his nose broken in the skirmish. Geelong was displaced from top position by Melbourne, who defeated the Cats at Kardinia Park in Round 11. Melbourne also accounted for

Collingwood in Round 8 in front of a crowd of 86,000 at the MCG. Melbourne defeated Hawthorn with a last-minute running goal by Hassa Mann at Glenferrie in Round 17. This defeated the brown-and-gold hopes for a finals berth, despite Hawthorn having won every other game at its swampy home ground during the 1964 season. Fitzroy had a terrible year, failing to win a match, while Carlton started well but finished down the ladder. Geelong paid dearly for resting Doug Wade in the final round, losing to St Kilda and conceding the double chance to the Magpies. Top-placed Melbourne flogged Collingwood in the Second Semi-Final, 19.20 (134) to 6.9 (45). In the First Semi, Geelong overcame an early Bomber lead to triumph by 9 points, but then lost to Collingwood in a joyless and low-scoring Preliminary Final, 5.14 (44) to 7.6 (48). The 1964 Grand Final was a classic struggle, until Demon back pocket 'Froggy' Compton kicked his first goal for the entire season to clinch the flag by 4 points. No-one could have predicted it would be Melbourne's last premiership for more than three decades. Hawthorn's John Peck kicked 68 goals to lead the scoring in 1964, while Carlton's Gordon Collis won the Brownlow.

The popular saying now became 'No Barassi, no Melbourne' – the mystique which grew around Barassi was so powerful that people began to believe in the match-winning agency of one great individual. Budgies were taught to recite his name.[2] Matches it seemed could be won or lost on the valour of one player, especially in such a key position as ruck-rover. Barassi played the game like Rockfist Rogan. In 1963 he missed the finals owing to a striking charge involving Richmond's Roger Dean; the Tribunal refused to view a still photograph and a piece of television footage which would have cleared him!

Then, at the end of the 1964 season which Melbourne won in sensa-tional fashion, came the event for which Barassi will always be remem-bered – he accepted a payment of $20,000 over three years to go to Carlton as playing captain-coach. Young Demon supporters everywhere tore the 31 off their guernseys in disgust – it was regarded as a great betrayal. (Smith even offered to step down as coach in Barassi's favour.) Barassi disappointed young Melbourne fans precisely because he had found his way into their hearts: he had come to represent everything that was good about father-figures. He had been reliable in every crisis; he had been brave and dependable in a pivotal role; he had been loyal to the navy-and-red tribe. Barassi's move to the Blues was masterminded by the shrewd George Harris. Carlton had uncharacteristically been out of finals contention since 1947; now it was Melbourne's turn. Melbourne was the only VFL club not to feature in any finals campaign during the rest of the 1960s, the entire 1970s decade, and most of the 1980s. The captain's departure had ripped something out of the club – he was the first captain in the history of the VFL to go straight to another club. (Gary Dempsey did likewise in 1979.)

Once Barassi had left, Melbourne fell away in the 1965 season. The club lost a match to Richmond for the first time since 1951 (the Tigers now shared the MCG with them) and suffered a 10-goal trouncing at the hands of St Kilda. Smith was sacked, replaced by Checker Hughes for a week, and then restored to his position in an extraordinary about-face. Collingwood put Melbourne out of its misery in Round 17. St Kilda, playing out of its new home at Moorabbin, surged to first place and finished the season on top. North spent the 1965 season at Coburg, but returned to Arden Street in 1966. Hawthorn fell from fifth in 1964 to wooden-spooners in 1965. Fitzroy looked on the verge of extinction, but did well to win four matches during the season. Essendon suddenly appeared as the form side of the finals, defeating Geelong in the First Semi by 52 points and Collingwood in the Preliminary Final by 55 points. St Kilda in the meantime defeated Collingwood by 1 point, 13.24 (102) to 14.17 (101), and faced Essendon in the Grand Final. However, the Bombers continued on their way, kicked clear in the third quarter and won their eleventh VFL flag by 35 points in front of an MCG crowd of 104,846. John Peck again led the goalkicking, for the third year in a row, while St Kilda's Ian Stewart won the first of his three Brownlows.

Nineteen sixty-six witnessed some unusual fortunes, in an erratic and closely-fought season. Melbourne fell away completely; it was now obvious their golden era was over. Richmond improved steadily, and threatened to join the finalists. Collingwood finished on top for the first time since its heyday in the 1920s. Geelong won ten matches in a row to finish third, but then fell down to Essendon by 10 points. Collingwood defeated St Kilda in the Second Semi, but the Saints won their way back into the Grand Final by beating Essendon. Finally, in a result which would haunt Magpie fans for a quarter of a century, the Saints pipped Collingwood by just 1 point, a behind kicked by Barry Breen. To make matters even better at Moorabbin, Ian Stewart won his second Brownlow. Essendon's Ted Fordham won the goalkicking prize.

In 1967 Fitzroy quit Brunswick Street for Princes Park. Hawthorn threatened to improve with a new player named Peter Hudson, who kicked 57 goals in his first year. Carlton and Richmond were beginning to build new attacking sides, and to develop the all-out style which would become the hallmark of the 1970s. Richmond's potency was boosted by the arrival of Royce Hart, who booted 55 majors in his debut season. Richmond and Carlton finished the home-and-away fixtures on top of the ladder. Essendon started 1967 poorly, losing to Geelong at Windy Hill for the first time in thirteen years. St Kilda lost its winning way early in the season and conceded too much ground to the other teams, ending up fifth. Collingwood took fourth spot, but its best football was at the start of the season. Third-placed Geelong enjoyed two good wins in the finals campaign, defeating the Magpies in the First Semi, and then Carlton in the Preliminary. Richmond moved into the Grand Final with an impressive display of attacking firepower not seen since the high-scoring Essendon side of the 1950s, kicking 20.21 (141) to 14.17 (101). Richmond overcame Geelong in the Grand Final by 9 points. Years later this defeat still rankled with Polly Farmer, but it was a portent of 1970s-style football. Doug Wade was the years's top scorer, with 96 goals, and Saint Ross Smith won the 1967 Brownlow.

For the 1968 season the VFL introduced twenty rounds to the home-and-away competition, paving the way for the longer seasons of subsequent decades. Richmond suffered a premiership hangover – after losing to Essendon in Round 7, the Tigers were trapped in fifth spot for the rest of the season. The Dons improved markedly to vie with Geelong, St Kilda and Carlton for top places. Playing an iron-clad defensive style, the Blues opened their 1968 account with ten wins, before going down to Essendon at Windy Hill. These two eventual Grand Finalists played a much more defensive style of football than had been their game plan in the previous seasons. Geelong had a patchy year in 1968, sometimes brilliant and at other times dropping the easy ones. In the last Round the Cats lost their double chance at the hands of St Kilda, which in turn secured its own place in the finals and kept Richmond out. Hawthorn improved to sixth position, with Hudson kicking 125 goals for the season. In the First Semi Geelong overturned the previous week's result, defeating St Kilda 19.13 (127) to 11.17 (83), while Carlton defeated Essendon in the Second Semi, 13.17 (95) to 8.11 (59). Essendon was too strong for the enigmatic Cats in the Preliminary Final, 11.25 (91) to

9.13 (67). As the finals campaign ground on, the defensive game plans improved: in the Grand Final, Carlton defeated Essendon in a slugged-out battle, 7.14 (56) to 8.5 (53). Swan Bob Skilton won the last of his three Brownlows in 1968.

The trend toward an increased scoring rate was quickened in 1969 by the re-introduction of the out-of-bounds rule. Negative tactics became less effective and some of the weaker sides became more competitive. North Melbourne improved, winning its first four matches. Hawthorn continued to improve, building a more balanced side around Hudson (who topped the year with 120 goals). When the reigning Premiers were showing early-season staggers, coach Barassi came back onto the field for a one-match comeback and helped remotivate the Blues. Carlton played consistently for the remainder of 1969 and finished second Collingwood was playing tough and resilient football, coming from behind on several occasions to win games during the season and finishing on top of the ladder. Richmond again started slowly – at one point in the season the Tigers lost six out of seven games – and were once more in danger of missing the finals. Not surprisingly, especially when one considers the talent in this side, the Tigers lifted their form, beating Carlton and the improved Hawthorn to squeeze into the four. Geelong finished third and met the resurgent Tigers in the First Semi. What followed can be best described as a rout, as the Tigers did as they pleased, winning 25.17 (167) to 7.7 (49). The Second Semi saw Carlton kick away in the third quarter and account for Collingwood by 36 points. The Preliminary Final saw Collingwood and Richmond level at half time, but Richmond gained the ascendancy in the third quarter, kicking 7.2, and then held on to win by 26 points. Richmond defeated Carlton in the Grand Final 12.13 (85) to 8.12 (60).

Barassi coached Carlton with a discipline rarely seen. He became the authoritarian father-figure. Around this time he grew the trademark moustache which became a symbol of masculinity in the late 1960s. (The sportsman's moustache had fallen out of favour during the clean-cut 1950s.) One veteran player, Billy Barrot, the ex-Tiger, was so daunted by the coach's half-time dressing down that he immediately left the ground, went out to his car, drove away, and never came back.[3] The most-quoted example of this match-winning discipline, of course, came in the 1970 Grand Final against Collingwood. Since Carlton was losing badly at half-time, Barassi gave the instructions which reflected how completely the game had changed, how much it had become a game of athletic speed rather than brute strength. This is how one player remembered Barassi's famous speech: 'Well, that game's over. Now we begin another with a new team. Forget that first half. Go handball happy. The first player who hangs his head in shame will be taken from the field. We can peg them back four goals in a quarter. Go out there and don't disgrace Carlton. Even if we lose, be proud of yourselves.'[4] Of course these were not his exact words, but roughly the true content.[5]

The plan almost fell apart near the start of the last term, when Magpie Des Tuddenham intercepted a handball on the Carlton backline. Blues ruckman Peter 'Percy' Jones ran hard and tackled him, earning a free kick right in the Collingwood goal square. 'It was speed born of desperation,' said Barassi. 'And what did Perce do with the free? Without even hesitating he hand-balled to a running teammate. It was football discipline at its best.'[6]

The VFL introduced a twenty-two-round competition in 1970 and matches began at VFL park. Collingwood moved to top place after the third round and remained in top place for the rest of the home-and-away competition. South Melbourne made the finals for the first time since 1945, finishing fourth. It was Norm Smith's second year with the Swans. At one stage of the season only two wins separated third club St Kilda and Fitzroy in eleventh place. The Swans beat Geelong at Kardinia Park for the first time in twelve years to cement their place in the four and the Cats missed out on the finals for the first time since 1961. The finals appeared to be a formality after Collingwood beat all comers in the second half of the season by increasingly large margins, and beat its nearest rival Carlton by 73 points at Princes Park. After making the finals South Melbourne was beaten soundly by St Kilda in the First Semi, and Collingwood and Carlton played a close Second Semi, with Collingwood overcoming a third-quarter deficit to defeat the Blues by 10 points. Carlton proved to be too good for St Kilda in the Preliminary Final, setting up another Carlton–Collingwood epic. The Grand Final which followed in front of a record 121,696 people has been described as perhaps the best ever in the VFL/AFL. Collingwood appeared to have the game under control and the premiership in its grasp, leading 10.13 (73) to 4.5 (29) at half-time. Under instructions from coach Barassi to handball constantly, the Carlton players kicked 13.4 to Collingwood's 4.4 in the second half to win a stunning victory, a loss which was to haunt the Collingwood psyche until the final siren of the 1990 premiership. P. Bedford of South Melbourne won the Brownlow Medal and Peter Hudson again won the goalkicking with 146 goals.

Melbourne and Hawthorn both enjoyed good starts in 1971. Carlton appeared to struggle, and only spent one week of the season in the four. Melbourne's charge ended with defeat at the hands of Footscray at the MCG. St Kilda and Richmond maintained a consistent level of performance throughout the year, finishing second and third respectively. Hawthorn had a successful home-and-away season, finishing on top of the ladder, with full-forward Peter Hudson equalling Bob Pratt's goal-kicking record by kicking 150 goals. Hawthorn had the edge over St Kilda in the finals, hanging on to win narrowly in the Second Semi, and in the Grand Final Hawthorn unleashed a withering comeback in the last quarter, kicking 7.2 to win 12.10 (82) to 11.9 (75). Richmond eliminated Collingwood in the First Semi, but was knocked out of contention by St Kilda in the Preliminary Final. I. Stewart (Richmond) took the Brownlow.

When Barassi got too old to play at Carlton, in the 1968 season, John Nicholls took the captaincy. Nicholls thought Barassi's main contribution to the game was his emphasis on smothering and tackling, particularly to break up the pretty kicking of teams like Collingwood,[7] but this was probably less important than the underlying team discipline which provided the logic for such physicality. Rockfist Rogan understood that he needed mates on the field to win. Under Barassi Carlton's edge in the titanic struggle with the hated Collingwood was a respectable 9–7. Against his old team, the balance sheet read Carlton 9, Melbourne 3. But in the very first encounter against his former teammates, a match with some feeling in Round 8 of 1965, the lowly Demons got up by 37 points.

Carlton was not a ritzy club until Menzies came along. 'I can remember meeting Menzies and having to bow and scrape,' recalled Jack Wrout's niece, thinking back to the 1960s. The social club was built in that period, an all-male and working-class fraternity where the ex-players liked to meet before a match. Once Malcolm Fraser also joined Carlton, attracting the same reverence as the other Prime Minister, Carlton became a mecca for silvertails. Half the top deck was turned into corporate boxes. Barassi was wooed from Melbourne, 'a real coup', and the club's prestige soared. Although the younger players bemoaned Barassi's disciplinarian methods, the new coach was good for the club's playing success.[8] One adoring fan penned a long poem for her heroes:

> *Serg. Silvagni is the Blues' ruckrover,*
> *He never stops trying till the match is over;*
> *Though now he's in the veteran stage;*
> *His ability isn't marred by age.*
>
> *For John Nicholls no introduction's required;*
> *His great skill and strength must be admired;*
> *He's very fair and his strength he'll use*
> *Whenever he's needed to bolster the Blues.*
>
> *Two handy second ruckmen are Hall and Greenwood;*
> *Second only to Nicholls, at throw-ins they're good . . .*

And so on through the Carlton stars of the 1966 season.[9]

Exhibition Street, West Footscray was home in the 1960s to Ted Whitten and Doug Hawkins. (They both moved further out later.) 'Mr Football' and 'The Hawk' have been tangible symbols for the club and its history. Their names have been lent to the two main stands on either side of the Western Oval. On EJ's last day, a match against Hawthorn in Round 5 of 1970, there was no commemorative club event, no show of emotion about the Braybrook boy who had played a then-record 321 games for the Bulldogs. The rain camouflaged Whitten's tears as he left the ground choked by a mob of well-wishers, including a ten-year-old boy named Doug Hawkins. There is a quiet shyness about such men, a turning-in which marks the Bulldogs. It is a key aspect of the club's character, and can be traced sociologically back to the suburb's Protestant working-class and lower-middle-class roots. Footscray's supporters, club officials and totemic players have these attitudes and values in common: 'You had to be tough in our day. We were brought up never to show that you are hurt . . . I never showed any emotion in football . . . In our day, we played for the love of the club and the jumper. We played for virtually nothing.'[10]

The social base of the old Footscray was tough: the residents worked in the foundries, railways, glassworks and the local Angliss meatworks. Footscray had only one great rival in the old days, and that was Geelong.

'Footscray have never done well at Kardinia Park. Each year, E.J. Whitten had driven to Geelong, jaw set, intent on victory; the best result he had managed in twenty years was a single draw.'[11] The reason possibly was that Footscray knew its place in the meat industry: the club represented the slaughtermen who owed their jobs to the graziers of the Western District for whom Geelong played.

Collingwood blossomed as a club after 1958, with a sumptuous social club built in 1959, palatial clubrooms and two new grandstands built in the late 1960s from liquor profits. It was already a big-business club in the 1960s at a time when other clubs were still modest suburban concerns. It was not obvious at the time, however, that Collingwood was entering three decades without a premiership, a drought which would not be broken until 1990. By 1967 Collingwood had 16,000 social and football members and was still growing.[12] In 1961 Floreat was formed at Collingwood; this was a club for elite supporters, based on the Coterie at Melbourne, the Confreres at Hawthorn, and similar ginger groups in at least four other clubs. Anxiety about the elitism of Floreat was one of the factors which counted against Jack Galbally in the watershed election for club president in 1963. Tom Sherrin, scion of the famed local sports-goods manufacturing family, came out decisively on top in that contest, and Floreat disbanded. However, the disunity reflected in this battle between the Catholic and the Masonic halves of the club told on the field, for 1963 was a dismal season.[13]

In other states, new developments in football were occurring. Bassendean in the 1950s was a respectable, church-going, working-class community in Perth's northern suburbs. Its team, the Swan Districts Football Club, was named to represent the chain of localities stretching along the Swan River between Guildford and Maylands. It was the eighth and last of the WAFL clubs to be established, and was formed in 1934. There are local families who in the 1990s can claim to have attended regularly since the first ball was bounced at Bassendean Oval in that distant autumn. SDFC won its first seven matches in 1934 – a record which still stands for a club entering senior ranks – but did not win a flag during the next three decades. The team has always played in black-and-white stripes. Swan Districts played an honest, rough-hewn style of football, recruiting mostly local young men. One such was Tom Stannage, son of the Anglican minister appointed to Bassendean's St Mark the Evangelist church in 1950 (when Tom was five-and-a-half years old). The Reverend James Eakins-Stannage had migrated to Australia from Ireland in 1910 and was sixty-four when Tom was born. He had been a gymnast as a young man and was a strong believer in the 'Four Square' philosophy – one of the sides to life's ideal square being sporting endeavour. Although he was too old to kick a football to young Tom, the Rev. Stannage nonetheless cheerfully allowed his barefooted son to practise kicking and receiving a ball off the wall at the back of the church. (A stone church wall, with its various corrugations, sends a football back to the kicker in a variety of loops, twists and turns.) This helped Tom Stannage in his playing days to read the travel of a ball coming off a pack, or off the miskick of the opposing full-back.

Stannage's nickname was 'the Prof', owing to his academic inclination. (True to his sobriquet, Stannage went on to take his PhD at Cambridge and to lecture in Australian history at the University of Western Australia.) Sport was central to the Bassendean of his childhood; children preferred to receive sporting gear above all other Christmas presents – they would then run triumphantly down to 'the Bic' (the local Bassendean Improvement Committee recreation reserve) and show the equipment off to their mates. The player Stannage most admired was Swan Districts full-back Tim Barker, a fine-looking fireman who represented the state and wore the No. 19 guernsey. Stannage admired Barker for the elegance of his play, and began as a backman in junior football but was directed out of the backline by successive coaches, and developed into a winger. Left-footed, he played on the left wing, and earned a reputation as a good defensive player. One trademark was an uncanny ability to capture the full-back's miskick: Stannage could see the wobble in the backman's hand as he prepared to roost it long in the fashion of the time, and he knew enough about the wind eddies at Bassendean to reckon where the ball would drop. This was an early example of rebound football.

These were good years for Swan Districts. This was a team which swept all before it during the halcyon seasons of the early 1960s. In one outing against South Fremantle in 1962, Haydn Bunton junior amassed more than a hundred kicks – easily the best statistic of any senior player.[14] Kicks far outnumbered handballs in this style of game. The club's video history illustrates that the Swans relied strongly on mark-and-kick tactics. 'Bunt' and his players made good use of long, slow dropkicks. Haydn Bunton coached Swan Districts to its first three flags, in 1961,

1962, and 1963. Stannage, then a nineteen-year-old university student, was playing B-grade Amateurs and learning how to overcome his fears, up against 'red-eyed lunatic men from Fremantle, teams where half the men were in gaol the next season!' Stannage played fifty-five games for Swan Districts from 1964 to 1967, and was selected to represent Western Australia at Hobart in 1966. (The carnival clashed with Stannage's studies and to his later regret he withdrew from the team which defeated all comers except the Victorians.)

Stannage's premiership team-mates graduated from Swan Districts Football Club to good local businesses. Keith Slater set up a sports store at Midland; Billy Walker became the licensee of the North Beach Hotel; Colin Reynolds and others became local property owners; Ken Bagley became a printer; Fred Castledine went from being from the wrong side of the tracks to being one of Perth's better-known horse trainers; Colin Maynard tried out in the VFL and then returned to Perth to establish a hardware business. Full-back Joe Lawson went into insurance sales and others followed him into St George's Terrace, but for the most part Haydn Bunton junior's charges won economic independence in local networks. Peter Manning, who took the wing opposite Stannage, became an accountant, but this was rare; social mobility for WAFL footballers then did not mean a professional career, let alone getting into university. Almost all married locally and stayed in the area. Most players continued to be involved in the club's fortunes after their playing days were over. Bill Walker, regarded as one of WA's finest players, won three Sandovers, played in the 1961, 1962, and 1963 premiership teams, and helped administer the club during its 1982, 1983, and 1984 flags; he is honoured in the name of a stand at Bassendean Oval. Tom Stannage came back as chairman of selectors and helped secure John Todd as coach in 1977. Todd was a coach of pure poetry: he conducted not so much coaching sessions as open learning seminars, and he inspired his charges with epic stories of endeavour. One week they were to play a big game against South Fremantle; a large WA crowd of 21,000 had gathered to watch their favourite son Stephen Michael play his two hundredth game. Undaunted by the occasion, Todd told his players the story of Leonidas and Xerxes; the Swans went on to beat South Fremantle by 5 goals.[15] (The Spartan king Leonidas died at Thermopylae in 480 BC, but only after he and three hundred companions held back a massive Persian army led by Xerxes for two days.)

In 1961, Dan Murray (ex-Fitzroy, and father of Kevin) took over as coach of Subiaco. Geelong and Victorian rover Peter Pianto joined Claremont as captain-coach. Haydn Bunton was appointed captain-coach of Swan Districts after his stint at Norwood. It was a period of increased player talent and interstate movements among the VFL, SANFL, and WAFL. Magpie Ray Gabelich played a year with West Perth, while Hawthorn's fiery ruckman Maurie Young pulled on the East Perth colours. A combination of good recruiting and the footballing savvy of Haydn Bunton saw Swan Districts improve from last to second on the ladder at the end of the home-and-away games, a year which included the club's still-standing record score against South Fremantle of 28.20 (188) to 13.15 (93). East Perth continued its good form, finishing on top of the ladder, winning nineteen games and losing only two. Subiaco and West Perth made up the four. Swan Districts met East Perth in the Second Semi and were beaten by the reigning Premiers 14.22 (106) to 7.16 (58). The East Perth machine appeared to be unstoppable. Swan Districts went into their Preliminary Final clash the underdogs against Subiaco, which had beaten East Perth during the year. The Swans survived a close finish, winning 16.19 (115) to 15.9 (99), going through to their second Grand Final appearance. The Swans appeared to have little chance, having lost eighteen out of the previous nineteen games against East Perth. But Swan Districts jumped to an early lead at quarter-time and remained in front the rest of the day, winning their first premiership. The 1961 flag was a triumph for Bunton and for ruckman Keith Slater, who won his duel with Graham Farmer in this Grand Final.

In 1962 Melbourne's Bob Johnson was appointed to captain-coach East Fremantle. Graham Farmer left East Perth to play with Geelong. Jack Sheedy retired as a player. Barry Cable played his first game for Perth. Subiaco appointed Richmond's Dave Cuzens (originally from the West) as captain-coach and recruited Austin Robertson junior as a full-forward. John McIntosh made his debut for Claremont. The Swans started the season slowly, but soon threatened to win back-to-back premierships, finishing the year on top of the ladder. East Perth appeared to struggle with the loss of Farmer, and of Sheedy, who missed most of the year only to come out of retirement for the last match in a bid to make the finals. Unfortunately, East Perth lost and missed the finals. East Fremantle had an improved year and finished second, followed by South Fremantle, and then West Perth. Swan Districts appeared to have the answers to all challenges in the final series, beating East Fremantle twice to win its second flag. To cap off the year, the Sandover medal went to Bunton.

The next season, 1963, East Fremantle's ruckman Jack Clarke retired. East Perth started without John Watts, Don Langdon, and wingman Paul Seal. Peter Tannock joined the club. The season was one of two parts for the Royals: they lost seven out of their first ten games, and won ten out of their last eleven. Perth finished on top of the ladder, and Swan Districts finished fourth, after having a less convincing year than the previous two years. East Fremantle finished second on the ladder. The finals saw the East Perth side's winning streak come to an end at the hands of Swan Districts in the First Semi, 15.11 (101) to 7.11 (53). Perth and East Fremantle played off in the Second Semi, with East Fremantle winning. Perth met the Swans, with two interesting selections: Bob Coleman, Perth's full forward, who had not played since the halfway point of the season; and reserves player Ray Lawrence. These selection gambles almost paid off, as Perth, facing a 43-point deficit at half-time, clawed its way back to 8 points. It lost the game only through inaccuracy, kicking 1.8 in the third quarter and 5.12 in the last. The Swans met a confident East Fremantle in the Grand Final, and the game was close until Swan Districts were able to kick away in the last quarter, winning by 22 points. The Swan Eric Gorman's 9.1 was a highlight of the game. The 1963 goalkicking chart was headed by ex-Essendon Ron Evans, who booted 97 for the season.

Swan Districts started the 1964 season as favourites. Subiaco appointed Swan Districts ruckman Keith Slater as coach. South Fremantle set a new precedent for transfer fees, paying $2500 for East Fremantle centreman Ray Sorrell (the 1963 Sandover medallist). Claremont improved to finish fourth and play in the finals for the first time since 1952. In the first live telecast of the Sandover medal on Channel 7, twenty-year-old Barry Cable won the award. Swan Districts missed the finals as did East Perth. The finals took on a different form which included Claremont, Subiaco, Perth, and East Fremantle. East Fremantle finished the season on top of the ladder. Perth's temperate weather produced an improbably wet First Semi-Final. While Claremont prospered in the heavy going, Subiaco appeared unable to come to terms with the conditions, and Claremont won by 12 points. East Fremantle brushed aside Perth in the other semi-final in a 53-point victory, including 8.5 from captain-coach Bob Johnson, to advance into the Grand Final. Claremont continued its drive to the premiership by beating Perth in a close Preliminary Final, winning by 10 points. Claremont went into the Grand Final as the rank outsider, with the powerful East Fremantle side expected to win comfortably. The game developed into a close affair, with East Fremantle kicking away to an 8-point lead with only two minutes of play remaining. Then Claremont's Brewer kicked 2 goals in the remaining two minutes, and Claremont hung on in a thrilling last thirty seconds to win its first premiership since 1940.

In 1965, West Perth appointed ex-Footscray rover Bob Spargo as their captain-coach. Haydn Bunton was replaced after the Swans' disappointing year by Fred Castledine. Jack Sheedy was replaced at East Perth by ex-Fitzroy Kevin Murray. Mal Brown made his debut for East Perth. Swan Districts recovered during this season to finish on top of the ladder, ahead of Claremont, which was enjoying another good year, West Perth and East Fremantle. The First Semi-Final was a tough game, as West Perth lost Spargo and forward Evans early in the match, and East Fremantle finished full of running to win 16.15 (111) to 13.14 (92). Swan Districts moved into the Grand Final after defeating Claremont in the rain, 9.14 (68) to 8.8 (56). This set up a Claremont–East Fremantle clash in the Preliminary Final and East Fremantle, hungry for revenge after the Grand Final loss of 1964, beat the Tigers more convincingly than the scoreboard suggests, 9.15 (69) to 8.8 (56). East Fremantle kicked an appalling 1.12 in the last quarter. The Swans suffered the fate of other favourites in the Grand Final. They had worked their way to a 21-point lead at three-quarter-time, only to see it evaporate as East Fremantle produced an inspired final term into the breeze, kicking 9.4 to run out Premiers by 21 points. The consolation for the Swans was that local favourite Bill Walker took the Sandover.

Nineteen sixty-six was a watershed year in the WAFL, for Claremont, East Fremantle and Swan Districts entered a decline which would last until the 1970s. Perth was one of the clubs that stepped up to fill the void under the direction of ex-East Perth player Mal Atwell, who was appointed captain-coach. Perth won eleven straight in the middle of the season. South Fremantle finished last for the second year running, despite replacing the costly Sorrell with John Todd as captain-coach. The positions at the start of the finals were Perth, East Perth, West Perth, and East Fremantle, all of which enjoyed a sizeable break on the rest of the competition. East Fremantle was eliminated by West Perth in the First Semi. Perth advanced into the Grand Final, meeting East Perth captain-coach Atwell's old club. In a close, bruising and unyielding game, the Atwell combination, fired by the brilliance of Barry Cable, won by 16 points. Bill Walker won his second Sandover, while Bob Johnson was top goalscorer with 89 goals.

In 1967 Subiaco imported Alan Killigrew from Victoria as its coach, and regained the services of Austin Robertson (after his year with South Melbourne). Kevin Murray (who returned to Fitzroy) was replaced as East Perth's captain-coach by Derek Chadwick. East Perth dominated the qualifying rounds, winning seventeen out of the twenty-one games. South Fremantle improved under Todd, defeating East Perth during the season, finishing in third place, and making a welcome return to the finals. Perth made the finals also, finishing second behind East Perth, and then picked up form dramatically. It beat East Perth in the Second Semi, following a last-quarter burst led by Cable, winning 9.9 to 8.10, and went into the Grand Final. In the other final, between South Fremantle and East Perth, the Bulldogs appeared to be heading to a Grand Final berth. Then a withering burst of football by East Perth, led by Syd Jackson, produced a 9-goal final term which sealed the game. East Perth's impressive finish prompted innovation from Perth coach Atwell, who carefully guarded his plan to switch himself from the back-line to full-forward. The ploy worked: he kicked 6 goals, helping Perth to a 3-goal win. Many said he deserved the Simpson medal, which was awarded to Barry Cable. That year Bill Walker shared his third Sandover with John Parkinson (Claremont).

The following year Subiaco replaced Killigrew with Haydn Bunton after only one year. South Fremantle gained the services of Tom Grljusich, who returned from three years with Central Districts. Perth retained its winning combination virtually intact. It continued to win, losing only two games in the qualifying rounds. Austin Robertson enjoyed his most productive season, kicking a record-breaking 157 goals for the season, including 13.2 against Swan Districts and 15.11 against East Fremantle. The final four comprised Perth, West Perth, East Perth, and Subiaco. It was the first time since 1931 that neither Fremantle side qualified for the finals. Subiaco appeared to benefit from Haydn Bunton's coaching and contested the First Semi against East Perth. The Lions seemed to be gone at the start of the last quarter, as East Perth goaled again, and stretched its lead to 45 points. Subiaco rallied and kicked 8 out of the next 9 goals, to be 4 points up with a minute to play. Fate then swung finally in East Perth's favour: its interchange player Vic Evans kicked what was the winning goal with sixteen seconds on the clock. (Evans went on to become very senior in the insurance industry.) Perth ground its way to victory in the Second Semi over West Perth. The next final saw a fast-finishing West Perth leave its run too late; East Perth hung on to qualify for another attempt at beating Perth. But again the Atwell–Cable combination proved too strong, and Perth won happily, 16.14 (110) to 13.8 (86). Perth also won the reserves competition. The San-dover went to Perth's Barry Cable.

Perth started the next year with the slogan 'Four in a line in 1969'. Meanwhile Hassa Mann took over at South Fremantle as captain-coach. Denis Marshall returned from Geelong to start his career as a playing coach at Claremont. Jack Sheedy returned for his last season as coach of East Perth. East Perth seemed to benefit from Sheedy's return, winning seventeen games and drawing one for the season to finish 10 points clear on top of the ladder. Perth lost a vital last-round game against bottom-of-the-ladder Claremont, and missed second place on the ladder and consequently the double chance. This was taken by West Perth, which was enjoying a good year in captain-coach Graham Farmer's second season. When Perth finished third on the ladder, its golden run of premierships appeared to be at an end. This became even more apparent when it scraped home against Subiaco in the First Semi-Final by 6 points. The Second Semi saw West Perth clash with East Perth, in front of a record crowd of 35,740. The game's intensity and heavy clashes left this one of the most talked-about finals in WAFL history. West Perth won both the fights and the game, 12.11 (83) to 7.15 (57), and set about preparing for its first Grand Final appearance since 1960. East Perth faced Perth in the final, with a no-win record in six attempts in finals. Fortunately it was able to stop this losing streak, and went on to win impressively, 19.8 (122) to 9.22 (76). The Grand Final saw an eagerly anticipated rematch between East and West Perth. However, rather than the tough and tight physical contest of the Second Semi, what now developed was a rout. West Perth kicked away from East Perth, leading at one stage 18.19 to 4.6, before East Perth rallied in the last quarter, making the final score 21.21 (147) to 10.14 (74). East Perth's Mal Brown took that year's Sandover, while Subiaco's Austin Robertson again led the goalkicking.

As in Victoria, a free kick was introduced in 1970 for kicking the ball out on the full. The R & I Bank Little League competition was inaugurated. Twenty-three-year-old Mal Brown replaced Jack Sheedy as coach of East Fremantle. After Round 6, Eric Sarich was replaced by Harry Neesham as captain-coach of East Fremantle. Having made only one finals appearance in the entire decade, South Fremantle now underwent a remarkable transformation for a club which had finished last in the 1969 season. West Perth lost a number of key players to other clubs, including centre half-forward John Wynne to Norwood, Bill Valli to Collingwood, and ruckmen Brian Sampson and Neil Evans. As a consequence, the club struggled, dropping from first to sixth. Barry Cable went to North Melbourne for one year. Subiaco blooded a number of players who were to have substantial Western Australian or Victorian careers, such as Mike Fitzpatrick, Peter Featherby, Keith Watt, and Mick Malone. These players, coupled with Austin Robertson's goalkicking flair, made a significant improvement to the Subiaco side. Subiaco finished third after the qualifying rounds. Claremont had a much improved year, only missing out on a finals appearance on percentage. Following a solid season under its youthful captain-coach Mal Brown, East Perth finished fourth and played Subiaco in the First Semi-Final. Subiaco was expected to win, but East Perth put on a faultless display of finals football and won 17.14 (116) to 10.6 (76), quelling the running game of Subiaco and the goalkicking talents of Austin Robertson. In the other semi Perth, which had finished on top of the ladder, met South Fremantle, making its first Second Semi-Final appearance since 1956. South Fremantle appeared to have squandered too many opportunities in the first quarter, kicking 2.12, but was able to kick 10.4 in the remaining three quarters, and held on against a persistent Perth side to win by 4 points. East Perth met traditional rivals Perth the following week, but despite a stirring last quarter was unable to advance to the Grand Final, losing by 4 points to the steady Perth combination. The Grand Final was played in wet and windy conditions which were expected to favour Perth. However, the Bulldogs, led by Hassa Mann, appeared to revel in the conditions, winning 15.7 (97) to 6.18 (54). The 1970 goalkicking tally was led once more by Austin Roberson, with 113 goals.

Nineteen seventy-one was Graham Farmer's last year of competitive football. Peter Steward returned from Victoria to West Perth, while Cable returned to Perth. East Fremantle appointed Alan Joyce as coach, the seventh East Fremantle coach since 1960. East Fremantle went on to finish third after a good season, and played Claremont in the First Semi. West Perth enjoyed a solid season under Farmer, and won a vital game in the last round to qualify for the Second Semi against the odds-on favourites for the flag, East Perth, which had won sixteen out of twenty-one games during the season. Not surprisingly, East Perth won the Second Semi against West Perth 9.8 (62) to 7.10 (52). Meanwhile, East Fremantle proved too strong for Claremont, winning 18.21 (129) to 11.16 (82). The final between West Perth and East Fremantle went to the last minute, as East Fremantle's Gary Fenner lined up a set shot for goal in the dying moments of the game, 4 points down. The kick missed and West Perth moved into the Grand Final. Inspired by Farmer's pre-match address and artistry in the ruck, West Perth scored an emphatic victory over East Perth 14.17 (101) to 9.15 (69). This was Graham Farmer's last game in the WAFL.

Farmer's last game was a fitting symbol of the important theme of the 1960s. Polly Farmer brought from Western Australia a new style of ruck-work and an accurate long handball which would expand the game's repertoire.

Similar developments were taking place in South Australia, especially at Sturt under the leadership of the famous coach Jack Oatey. Sturt dominated the South Australian competition from 1965 to 1970. The new skills of the period being tried out in the minor football states would later influence the style of play in the heartland of Australian football, the VFL.

Developments in Western Australian and South Australian football went largely unnoticed in Victoria. When Scanlen's decided to produce football cards in 1963, nineteen of the twenty cards featured VFL stars. There were no VFA stars, no South Australians, and only one Western Australian, Haydn Bunton of Swan Districts. The 1966 Scanlen's series included several Western Australian players but that was the end of interstate players. No series until the entry of the Eagles in 1987 included any non-VFL players (although in 1982 a separate Western Australian series was produced by Scanlen's for sale in Perth).

In the South Australian competition, 1961 was West Adelaide's year. The Premiers, led by Kerley, won in a game played in gruelling conditions of 95 degrees. The following year, 1962, Port Adelaide took the premiership, on the boot of the leading goalkicker in the state, R. F. Johns (76 goals). That was the season lowly Sturt appointed Jack Oatey as its coach. In 1963 Port Adelaide won back-to-back flags, again with R. F. Johns in the goalkicking van. In 1964, Woodville and Central District joined the competition (the latter is often pronounced 'Central Districts'). Ken Eustice joined Central District as captain-coach. Bob Simunson was appointed captain for his first game in the league. Neil 'Iron' Kerley took South Adelaide to a flag in 1964 after it had been wooden-spooner the season before.

Oatey's methods of precision football began to pay dividends in 1965: Sturt reached the Grand Final for the first time since 1941. Although Sturt was the highest-scoring side in the minor round, due in many ways to the revolutionary possession-style game taught by Oatey, the doubters still wondered whether it had the necessary toughness to win in the conditions of a finals campaign. Sturt answered its critics well, coming from behind in the Preliminary Final against South Adelaide, and only just failing against Port Adelaide in the Grand Final. After being 33 points down at the start of the last quarter, Sturt got within 3 points of the perennially strong Port side.

Sturt began winning its flags, five in all, in 1966. The team's first three Grand Finals were against Port, the last two against Glenelg. Neil Kerley joined Glenelg as playing coach in 1967, lifting the side into fourth position and changing the fortunes of a club which had only won three games the year before. In 1969, Glenelg continued to improve steadily under Kerley and won the minor premiership for the first time. But Sturt proved to be too strong and took its fourth premiership.

In 1970 Lindsay Head retired from West Torrens, having played 327 games and won three Magarey medals. Don Lindner, remembered for his 'freakish high marking', retired that year from North Adelaide after 284 games. Meanwhile, Port Adelaide marked its centenary with a celebratory game between the Channel 7 All Stars and the Port Adelaide champions. The match attracted 17,000 spectators and ended in a draw.

(The All Stars wore the company logo of a 7 inside a circle on their guernsey, a bizarre sight.)

In 1971, at North Adelaide, Mike Patterson became the first Victorian to coach a South Australian side to a premiership. Barrie Robran was universally judged best on ground. Newly appointed captain-coach Tony Casserly took Central close to its first Grand Final, after it just failed to beat Port Adelaide in the Preliminary Final.

Oatey's death in 1993 went unreported in the Victorian media, but he had revolutionised the game at Sturt in the 1960s. He had taken a team which missed the finals for several decades to the pinnacle of success, and his ideas became a standard feature of play. A Jack Oatey Medal was inaugurated in 1981 for the best player in the South Australian Grand Final.

The 1960s was the decade the other footballing states began to catch up to Victoria. Since 1908 there had been fifteen carnivals – the Victorians had won all but three. In 1960, however, South Australia defeated the mighty Vics by 69 points, and then in 1963 defeated them again on the MCG. It was an indication of the success of new styles of team play.

In the 1965 carnival match at Adelaide the South Australians convincingly defeated the Victorians, 12.11 (83) to 3.1 (19). North Adelaide's Don Lindner continued during the 1960s to demonstrate through his spectacular marking the new skill level evident in South Australia. His team-mate Barnie Robran even won the grudging praise of Lou Richards and other Victorian pundits. Lindsay Head, the 'golden boy' of South Australian football, complained that Victorian clubs were milking South Australia of its talent: although it would be another two decades before Adelaide entered the national competition in its own right, the pride in the state's players was evident even then.

part four

The 1970s to the 1990s

'Going the Long Bomb'

The 1970s, the seasons from 1972 to 1980, were the decade in which the VFL began to reform the game's overall administration, to take it out of the hands of so-called amateurs and put it more on what was regarded as a desirable business footing. Luke was replaced in 1971 as VFL president by another businessman, Sir Maurice Nathan, who in turn passed the presidency to Dr Allen Aylett in 1977. Aylett reflected this same brash businessman outlook, as he candidly revealed in his autobiography.[1] Their new corporate ideas began to take effect in this decade: the game was about to move inexorably away from its suburban base, and the first two clubs to recognise and react to the new business mentality were Carlton and North Melbourne. Increasingly, American ideas were to be influential in the game. However, Richmond resisted this corporate style and won success as an old-fashioned them-against-us club, much to Aylett's chagrin. Richmond made an art form of 'going the long bomb' – putting pressure on the opposition's backline with persistent long torpedo punts goalward. What the tactic lacked in finesse it made up in results for a side which had not tasted success since the days of Captain Blood.

There were several signs of the new corporate mentality in the VFL. From 1968 club members were no longer admitted free to away games; a proportion of club revenues and gate receipts were pooled among clubs to equalise the competition and to help pay for Waverley, which hosted its first match in 1970. Waverley Park was built in the hope of freeing the VFL from the grip of the cricket authorities who controlled the MCG. The clubs reacted by introducing new mechanisms for raising revenue, including reserved seating and private boxes (even at proletarian Victoria Park, where they were installed in 1975). Clubs also started hunting for sponsorships: sponsorship started at Collingwood in 1977 with $40,000 from Yakka.[2] (One unfortunate consequence of this rush for sponsors was that product names now took over the signage space at grounds where once the fans had put up team banners.) The new corporate leadership of the VFL decided that the competition could be better equalised; their first experiment was with zoning – it was introduced supposedly to help all clubs, weak or strong. Victorian country zoning was introduced at the end of 1967, and produced an outcry from Collingwood when it was allocated the Western District. The twelve zones, based on the country football leagues, were supposedly chosen by lot. Collingwood had always opposed zoning and felt cheated when it was allotted the area around Hamilton, now far more thinly populated than in its glory days. Besides, this allocation meant that only half of the Western Border League became Magpie territory, for that league spilled over into South Australia.[3]

Richmond's rise under Tom Hafey predated the effect of these broad reforms. Neil Balme was a product of this Hafey era. Balme was born in Perth and grew up in Mt Pleasant and then Wembley. His father was a sales manager with Nestles. After Balme's first-year apprenticeship with Subiaco in 1968, the family moved to Melbourne and Balme was free to choose to try out for any VFL club. He chose Richmond. Balme played 159 senior games for Richmond between 1969 and 1979, kicking 230 goals. He played his first senior game in 1970, a year which went badly for the 1969 Premiers. In the 1971 team Balme was part of a strong forward line with Kevin Bartlett and Royce Hart. The 1970s were years of strong camaraderie at Richmond, coached by Tom Hafey and administered by Graeme Richmond and Alan Schwab. One of Balme's mentors was Ray 'Slug' Jordon, the club's junior coach. Balme found he had joined a club where he had team-mates who looked after him as a young man. Without exaggeration, Richmond in the 1970s was probably the best-administered club in the history of the VFL. The officials allowed the players to organise the social life of the club. 'They also encouraged the players to get involved in the Richmond community – none of us came from Richmond, but we all belonged to it!', remembered Balme two decades later.[4] There were still traces of the club's Irish Catholic heritage, and the players were constantly reminded that although they were elite professionals they were nonetheless playing on behalf of a specific community, with its own values and traditions. (Whenever Richmond veterans meet socially, even years later, they perform a ritual tiger-pawing greeting, such is the camaraderie of this group.)

In the Richmond seniors Balme was second ruck, changing in the forward pocket. Richmond defeated Collingwood in the 1972 Qualifying Final – Balme kicked 4 goals from the pocket. Balme was Richmond's top scorer and one of the better players in its losing Grand Final team of that year. His tally for the year was 55 goals. A strong mark, he also earned a reputation for toughness, and is remembered particularly for an incident with Geoff Southby, when the Carlton full-back was knocked unconscious by Balme in Richmond's 1973 Grand Final win. The Southby incident rankled with supporters of other clubs because it occurred in the broader context of a them-against-us philosophy which set Richmond apart. On Grand Final day in 1973 Richmond won every flag in the VFL – the seniors, the reserves, the Under-Nineteens, and even the Under-Seventeens. The order of the day was tough them-against-us speeches from coach Tom Hafey and from club officials, especially Graeme Richmond, who had presided at Richmond from 1962 to 1968. Richmond's toughness produced fireworks: in Round 7 of 1974, an away game against Essendon erupted into the so-called Windy Hill Riot, a half-time fracas involving players and officials, discussion of which got as far as State Cabinet. This episode and the failure of Brownlow favourite Kevin Bartlett to win the best-and-fairest award provided rich motivational material to Hafey. Richmond finished at the top of the ladder that year and convincingly defeated North Melbourne in both the Second Semi-Final and the Grand Final.

This proved to be a high spot in the history of the club. It took several years for Richmond to win the flag again after the triumph of 1973–74. It finished third in 1975, seventh in 1976, fourth in 1977, seventh in 1978, and eighth in 1979 before winning its next premiership in 1980. It was a period when players were first packaged and commodified by the media. In the words of Richmond supporter Ian Turner: 'The players become pop stars. John Goold designs gear and Don Scott used to model it. Royce Hart and Neil Balme look more and more like [the international soccer players] Charlie George and Georgie Best, who in turn look more and like the Beatles and the Stones.'[5]

Balme went to South Australia after Richmond. As coach at Norwood, Neil Balme helped foster a new coaching style, building up an affinity with players. Norwood became a regular SANFL finalist and won the flag in 1982 and 1984. Balme was also thrown the great challenge of coaching the South Australian Eagles, the first blended team in senior football history since the Melbourne–University merger. Balme's successful decade in South Australia was based on a possession-at-all-costs philosophy, and was influenced by local conditions. The South Australians were playing a wholly different style of football, largely under the guidance of Sturt coach Jack Oatey. The SANFL teams developed a possession game which concentrated on quick-hands disposal, wide-angle vision and pin-point kicking. Except for Port Adelaide, the South Australian clubs eschewed what they saw as the Victorian culture of 'Rip, shit or bust!' football. The Victorian game of the 1970s emphasised maximum penetration, with long probing kicks which were calculated to put pressure on the other team's defence. This was very much the style favoured at Richmond during Balme's period.

Twenty-two-game Melbourne veteran Paul O'Brien recalls this period from the other side of the fence:

> I was a Richmond supporter in that era. I remember they always had
> those long kicks – they would run it from the backline and they
> would kick over the line in the centre zone to create the pressure.
> There was that sheer movement, and then the Bartletts and the
> Sproules were just crumbing. I remember they had a lot of support
> from that half-back line.[6]

Even the VFL power teams of the 1980s – Hawthorn and Essendon – continued to use much of Richmond's 1970s style of football. After all, many of Hafey's players went on to become senior coaches – notably Kevin Sheedy, Mick Malthouse and John Northey – and took his ideas further. Balme sees the values of the greedy 1980s exemplified in this aggressive style of play. At the end of the decade the West Coast Eagles introduced a hybrid style which offered a portent of the quicker 1990s.

North Melbourne also became a force in the 1970s, with players like the big-hearted ruckman, Peter Keenan. 'Crackers' Keenan grew up in a large Catholic farming family at Yarrawonga and went to the local parish school. His coach was a nun who barracked for North Melbourne because blue and white are the colours of Our Lady. Keenan's mother was a cousin of Dave McNamara. Like his father and his uncle, Keenan went to Assumption and, like several of his classmates, graduated from the famous footballing school directly into VFL ranks. Keenan had cheekily written to Jim Cardwell, the Melbourne administrator, recommending himself for the Demons. Cardwell went to see Keenan and asked Brother Domnus for advice. Starting with Melbourne in 1970, Keenan fell out with the club hierarchy and went to North Melbourne, then Essendon, and then back to Melbourne with Barassi at the end of the decade.[7] Meanwhile, retiring from football at the age of thirty-five, Barassi ran a furniture business for eight years, and then, after playing a few games for Port Melbourne in the VFA, was enticed to coach North Melbourne for the 1973 season. Norm Smith was his right-hand man. The VFL had relaxed the rules on player transfer – now any ten-season veteran could change clubs, and Barassi picked up John Rantall, Doug Wade, and Barry Davis. It is commonly believed in football folklore that this rule change was brought about specifically to help Barassi; in fact the Kangaroos, who opposed this change in the laws, were simply quicker than the other clubs, interviewing twenty-two eligible players within forty-eight hours of the rule change.

The new rule of 1973, that ten-year veterans could become free agents, was bitterly opposed by most clubs, including Collingwood, which believed it merely added to wage inflation. Collingwood was not as successful as North Melbourne, but did acquire George Bisset (Footscray) and John Williams (Essendon).[8] The ten-year rule was one the players themselves wanted – they were not pleased when it disappeared only a year later. At North Melbourne Barassi's disciplined approach to coaching was given as the main reason for North's flags in 1975 and 1977.[9] But in actuality the game had changed, and no longer could a single individual direct an entire team. Now the coach was in fact assisted by a large staff, even including a hypnotherapist, the celebrated Lee Saxon, as well as Andrew Taggart and 'Slug' Jordon. Clubs were by now more corporate enterprises, and team success depended on good management skills. The players were now almost young enough to be Barassi's sons. Indeed, the younger North Melbourne players had been born around the time Barassi first played senior football: Malcolm Blight and Brent

Crosswell were born in 1950, 'Crackers' Keenan in 1952, and Wayne Schimmelbusch in 1953. There was still a fair bit of Rockfist Rogan in the man. Barassi continued to blast these young men in the old-fashioned way. His speech to the losing team after the 1974 Grand Final was absolutely damning.[10] On one infamous occasion, Blight was dragged for kicking a deft goal from the boundary line when the team plan called for him to centre the ball!

Collingwood was not travelling as well as North Melbourne in the corporate 1970s. In 1970 the ingrained tradition of wage equality at Collingwood came to an end. The matter was brought to a head because of a strike by two of the club's champions, Des Tuddenham and Len Thompson. Tuddy and Thommo were unhappy that Collingwood was paying extra money to bring over the gun Subiaco player Peter Eakins, and their rebellion led to a new pay scale at the club. They lost their positions as captain and vice-captain, but from the 1970 season onwards Collingwood players were paid according to the number of matches they had played.[11] This militancy was reflected elsewhere – much to the chagrin of president Alan Hird, Essendon's top players followed up with a strike of their own which led to improved conditions and a players' association headed by Geoff Pryor.[12]

Sherrin resigned Collingwood's presidency when the club again failed to make headway in the 1974 season, and the job fell unwanted to an unknown local businessman, Ern Clarke. Clarke took the position only after Jock McHale Jr, Frank Galbally, Hector Crawford, Sir Edgar Coles and others had declined the doubtful honour. Clarke had Ken Billings and David Galbally on his ticket. Clarke attempted to free the players of the burden of tradition, for he attributed the Colliwobbles to this. One symbol was the removal of old photographs from the dressing rooms. Clarke established the club's first official coterie, the Woodsmen – once Floreat had been disbanded in 1963, Collingwood was the last VFL club to establish a formal network of wealthy supporters. Clarke began telling the coach how to do his job whenever Collingwood was doing poorly – naturally this strained relations between the president and Weidemann. Clarke's mentality was that of the modern professional – for one thing he wanted Weidemann to use statisticians, a radical notion at Collingwood in 1975. As the 1976 season opened, dissension within the club reached a new zenith, with players accused of not passing the ball to the over-paid 'Fabulous Phil' Carman. Clarke resigned in May 1976.[13]

John Hickey presided over Collingwood's improved position in the latter half of the 1970s. After the club's wooden spoon in 1976, the Magpies were able to secure the services of Tom Hafey himself as their coach, ahead of several other serious contenders; the former Tiger was installed as Collingwood's eleventh coach at the end of the 1976 season. Obsessed with football, Hafey earned the respect of the players and engineered a level of team spirit the club had not experienced for at least a decade. In just one season Collingwood shot to the top of the ladder and only missed the flag after the drawn Grand Final. But then the 1978 finals campaign also went poorly: Hafey's use of hypnotherapist Lee Saxon on the morning of the Preliminary Final seemed like a gimmick at pragmatic Victoria Park. A dozen senior players were immediately cleaned out, including Carman and Len Thompson. These players were not adequately replaced – even when players like Hawthorn's Leigh Matthews asked to sign up as Magpies! Hickey spent more lavishly on getting new players than was generally recognised, but failed to catch several key players on offer, including Bernie Quinlan at the moment 'Superboot' was sold by cash-starved Footscray to the Lions. Collingwood's second-rate players performed heroically in the 1979 and 1980 Grand Finals (against Carlton and then Richmond), but David Williamson's 1980 movie *The Club* correctly identified conflict between the president and the coach as endemic to a (fictional) Collingwood. The 1981 defeat in the Grand Final at the hands of Carlton hurt even more, because the Magpies managed only 2 behinds in the final term to 4.7 by the Blues. Hafey had lost the support of the players and of the captain Peter Moore (who crossed over to Melbourne) – and he was sacked after Collingwood lost the first eight games in 1982. The Hickey administration was ousted soon after.[14]

Carlton had adjusted better than Collingwood to the new corporate mentality. By the 1970s Carlton was the kind of place big deals could be done. Club president George Harris entertained the nation's Treasurer, Dr Jim Cairns, during the early part of the 1975 season, and offered to help the Australian government find money outside traditional borrowing sources. It was the disclosure of the letters of authority to Harris that caused Whitlam to dismiss Cairns in July. Cairns was only an occasional football-goer, but the lunches at Princes Park cost him dearly![15] One symbol of Carlton's stability was that former players like Jack Wrout still served on the club committee, and were still active: of all the players who served the Blue guernsey, one of those Wrout most admired was Syd Jackson (136 games, 1969–76). Even disasters were well-concealed at Princes Park: when Carlton's new coach for 1978, triple Brownlow medallist Ian Stewart, resigned after a few weeks in mysterious circumstances, the public explanation was that he was suffering from a 'minor heart ailment'. Yet Stewart went back to coaching the following season with South Melbourne (1979–81).

Television was one of the major forces in the corporate ethos of football. The VFA's fortunes revived during the 1970s, following Channel 10's decision to televise its games. Channel 10 was originally known as Channel 0 and began broadcasting games in 1967 as part of its strategy to compete against the three older television channels in Melbourne. Channels 2 and 9 withdrew from televising VFL football after being outbid by Channel 7. The VFL withdrew from the 1977 national carnival and with the support of Channel 7 started its own night competition in 1979.[16] Channel 7 supported the VFL's attempts to expand football into Sunday and evening broadcasts, beginning with the Sunday matches in Sydney in 1979.[17] The ABC's Channel 2 took over VFA games from Channel 0, so by 1977 only two channels were broadcasting senior football.[18] The VFA competition picked up some new support because of television. VFA side Oakleigh was invigorated by the arrival of Bob Johnson junior (ex-Melbourne and East Fremantle), who led the team to a flag in 1972, kicking a record 25.17 (167) to 18.15 (123) against Dandenong, – a record which stood until 1981.[19]

In the meantime, in Western Australia in 1972 Claremont selected Verdun Howell as its coach, while Denis Marshall remained as a player at the club. Barry Cable took over as coach of Perth from Mal Atwell. Atwell moved to South. Peter Steward took over as captain-coach of West Perth. Claremont's reorganisation appeared to have immediate results. Claremont won eighteen out of the twenty-one qualifying games to finish on top, followed by East Perth which was also a strong combination, winning fifteen of the twenty-one games. West Perth and Perth also made the finals but did not appear to threaten the two top-placed sides. In the First Semi Perth beat West Perth 12.18 (90) to 11.9 (75). The clash of the top two clubs produced what was described as an upset; however, East Perth had been prominent in the last few seasons. Ably led by Brown, in a close game East Perth won 12.14 (86) to 11.3 (69). Claremont won comfortably the next week against Perth, and moved into the Grand Final. The Grand Final of 1972 was relatively low scoring, 9.17 (71) to 8.8 (56). East Perth won its premiership with a side built around a strong defence which included Simpson medallist Ken McAullay, Gary Malarkey, and half-back Richard Michalczyk. Captain-coach Mal Brown was then aged twenty-five.

In 1973, the trend of recruiting Victorian coaches continued, as Subiaco recruited ex-Saint Ross Smith as captain-coach to succeed Haydn Bunton. West Perth replaced Peter Steward with ex-Melbourne player Dennis Jones, and East Fremantle again changed coaches, replacing Alan Joyce with John Todd. This season also saw a number of innovations; as in the VFL, the centre diamond was introduced (two seasons later it was changed to a square) and sponsorship was introduced to the league. But the major event was undoubtedly Subiaco winning its first premiership in forty-nine years over a West Perth side it had lost to four times during the year. Claremont experienced a disturbing loss of form, finishing last after heading the ladder in 1972. The Second Semi was one of the highlights of the year, for Subiaco and East Perth went goal for goal all afternoon; Subiaco won an exciting game 18.13 (121) to 17.9 (111) to advance to the Grand Final. Subiaco players also polled well in the Sandover medal, with Peter Featherby, Mike Fitzpatrick and Ross Smith finishing second, third, and fourth respectively. The Sandover was won for the third time by Perth's Barry Cable.

In 1974, Mal Brown left for Richmond, Barry Cable went to North Melbourne, and Bruce Duperouzel migrated to St Kilda, as the VFL offers became increasingly attractive. Ken Armstrong took over as coach of Perth. South Fremantle appointed Colin Beard to replace Mal Atwell. Full-back Ross Glendinning also made his debut at East Perth in 1974. East Perth, perhaps shaken by the loss of Mal Brown, dropped out of the four. Its spot was taken by Swan Districts, which was making another of its lightning raids on a premiership. Swan Districts advanced to the Final, where it met a strong Perth side. Perth beat Swan Districts 12.12 (84) to 9.15 (69) and moved into a Grand Final against a motivated and consistent East Fremantle, which appeared once again to find the winning formula in Todd's second year as coach. East Fremantle had the edge on Perth, having beaten it during the year on four occasions. The Grand Final proved to be no exception as East Fremantle kicked away to win a high scoring game, 17.20 (122) to 15.10 (100). The leading goalkicking for 1974 was Max George (Swan Districts), whose 89-goal haul included 14 against West Perth.

Mal Brown returned to Western Australian football in 1975, after a year with Richmond. He joined Claremont as captain-coach, only to be suspended in a practice match for fifteen weeks, thus delaying his return until well into the season, at which point he was again suspended, this time for six weeks. Subiaco lost its champion full-forward Austin Robertson to retirement, and also lost Mike Fitzpatrick to Carlton. David Parkin was appointed as coach of Subiaco. South Fremantle ended a thirteen-year hoodoo when it defeated East Perth at Perth Oval. During the 1975 season, South Fremantle improved to finish fourth and beat East Perth in the First Semi by 65 points. The other final was even more one-sided, between top-placed West Perth and Swan Districts. Swan Districts had walloped West Perth by 105 points in its last encounter; in the finals, however, West Perth ran all over the Swans to win 20.22 (142) to 8.16 (64). South defeated Swan Districts in the Final, and met West Perth in the Grand Final. The bitter rivalry between these sides in the 1950s promised a spirited struggle. The result in a finals series of one-sided games was perhaps not that surprising. A huge crowd of 52,322 watched West Perth in the second half surge to a 104-point victory, 23.17 (155) to 7.9 (51). Barry Day kicked 7 goals in the last quarter for West Perth.

The headlines for 1976 were: Graham Farmer was installed as coach of East Perth. Swan Districts appointed ex-Footscray rover Stewart Magee as its captain-coach. The first Sunday game was held, a match played between West Perth and Claremont at Leederville Oval. The two-umpire system was introduced in Round 2. Mal Brown resigned from Claremont in August, after the notorious John Colreavy affair. (Brown had sent Colreavy back on the ground after he had been replaced by the Nine-teenth Man, a breach of rules before the invention of the interchange system.) Brown was suspended by the League for twelve months as an official, so he continued his playing career the next year with South Fremantle. East Perth, Perth, South Fremantle, and West Perth emerged as the contenders for the 1976 flag. The competition was tight until the last round, when Perth dropped back to fourth, with South taking a place in the Second Semi. West Perth and Perth played off in the First Semi: the game started at a breakneck pace with West Perth leading early, and then Perth caught up and kicked away to win 20.18 to 13.4. The Second Semi featured heroics from East Perth as it held off South with only sixteen fit players in the second half to win by 23 points. South disappointed its fans again the next week when it was beaten convincingly by Perth in the Final. The Grand Final saw Perth beat East Perth, 13.14 (92) to 11.3 (69).

Nineteen seventy-seven saw Graham Moss return from the VFL to coach Claremont. John Todd was appointed coach of Swan Districts. Alan Joyce returned to East Fremantle. Perth always appeared to be a chance to win back-to-back premierships, finishing the season on top of the ladder, followed by East Fremantle, West Perth and East Perth. South Fremantle missed the four by a game. From the first final it appeared the battle would be to decide who would get to play Perth in the Grand Final. Perth won easily against East Fremantle and went into the Grand Final. The final between East Fremantle and West Perth was won by the Old Easts despite the absence of their local star, Brian Peake. But Perth's aggressive, high-scoring style of football continued in the Grand Final, and it beat East Fremantle 26.13 (169) to 14.12 (96). The consolation prize for East Fremantle was that Peake took the 1977 Sandover.

The following year, 1978, Barry Cable returned from North Melbourne and was appointed captain-coach of East Perth. Ian Miller returned from Fitzroy and joined Cable at East Perth. Graham Campbell, the West Perth premiership coach, returned to his home state of Victoria to coach Fitzroy. Mal Brown began his seven-year stint as coach at South Fremantle, and won new respect for his skill in encouraging all kinds of players. At the start of the 1978 season it appeared that Perth was likely to win a third premiership and, as the home-and-way matches progressed, the Demons cemented a position at the top of the ladder. Beneath them there was a five-way struggle for the remaining three places between West Perth, South Fremantle, Claremont, East Fremantle and Cable's new club East Perth. East Perth's chances at the start of the year looked good, as it had signed Cable and Miller, but at the halfway point of the season it was struggling in sixth place, needing to win all of the remaining seven games to finish in the finals. East Perth accomplished this task, though only just tweaking Perth by 5 points and South Fremantle by 2. East Perth's charge displaced the unlucky Claremont which missed the finals by a tenth of one per cent. West Perth, Perth and South Fremantle made up the final four. West Perth and South Fremantle played off in the First Semi-Final. Both sides had showed good form thoughout the year with South Fremantle playing consistent football under Brown, and

West Perth enjoying a ten-game winning sequence during the year. The Final saw South Fremantle win 13.17 (95) to 12.10 (82). The Second Semi pitted Perth against East Perth; Perth established its place as favourites by beating East Perth 13.8 (86) to 8.9 (57). The win came at a cost when full-forward Murray Couper was reported and suspended for throwing the ball at an umpire. East Perth hit back in the Final against South Fremantle, kicking an impressive 27.15 (177) to South's 9.11 (65). East Perth's full-forward Paul Arnold kicked 9.1. The Grand Final was played in driving rain, and East Perth was able to carry into the match the momentum it had generated, winning by a slender margin of 2 points, 11.15 (81) to 12.7 (79). To add to celebrations among the Royals, the 1978 Sandover went to Phil Kelly.

The following year opened in sensational fashion, for the League narrowly averted an umpires' strike at the start of the 1979 season. The controversy continued in the pre-season campaign. A practice match between Perth and East Fremantle disintegrated as players and a boundary umpire were felled, causing Perth coach Ken Armstrong to lead his side from the field. East Perth ruckman B. Smith was appointed coach of East Fremantle, taking over from Alan Joyce. The Fremantle sides started the year strongly, attracting record crowds to their local Derbies at East Fremantle Oval and at Fremantle Oval. Another highlight was Barry Cable's four-hundredth senior appearance, embracing a career that included 225 games for Perth, 116 for North Melbourne, thirty-six for East Perth, sixteen for Western Australia, and one for Victoria. This was the year Swan Districts and Subiaco indulged in a scoring feast, with Swan Districts kicking a massive 40.11 (251) to Subiaco's 20.7 (127), producing the highest aggregate score in the WAFL. Two players made large contributions: Swan Mark Olsen kicked 13.3 and Subiaco's Gary Buckenara kicked 9.1, playing in the centre. Amid the frenzy of record breaking, Claremont moved to the top of the ladder, winning sixteen of its twenty-two games. It was followed by the two Fremantle sides, and then East Perth. In another high-scoring contest, the First Semi saw East Fremantle squeeze home against East Perth 19.14 (128) to 18.18 (126). Meanwhile, Claremont's solid season was to end in disappointment, starting with a loss in the Second Semi against South Fremantle, and another, the next week to East Fremantle in the final. An all-Fremantle Grand Final attracted an over-capacity crowd of 52,781, more than Subiaco Oval could comfortably handle. The barrackers witnessed another high-scoring affair, typical of the 1979 season. East Fremantle kicked away in the last quarter to win 21.19 (145) to 16.16 (112). East's Kevin Taylor kicked 7.3 and became the first rover to kick a hundred goals in a season. He also won the League's top goalkicking honour, with a haul of 86. (In determining this honour, Western Australia does not follow the Victorian convention of adding goals kicked in the finals to the year's official total.) East Perth's Kelly won his second Sandover. Off the field, Barry Cable suffered a severe injury to his leg after being pinned by a tractor on his farm. He was able to continue to coach East Perth in 1980.

Nineteen eighty was the year the WANFL took the National from its name to become the West Australian Football League (WAFL). (At the end of the 1980s it was briefly called the State League.) South Fremantle became involved in a clearance wrangle in obtaining Collingwood ruckman Derek Shaw. Shaw gained a Supreme Court injunction in lieu of the clearance from Collingwood and played for his new club. Subiaco sacked coach Peter Burton after its first-round defeat. Swan Districts added increased defensive intensity to its football but its place on the top of the ladder at the end of the qualifying rounds was still attributable to its ability to kick large scores. South Fremantle finished second for the second year running, helped by the brilliant Maurice Rioli and Stephen Michael, as the Bulldogs surged into the finals by winning twelve games in a row. Claremont again played in the finals but was unable to win a final, followed by East Perth which just held out West Perth to keep its place in the finals. The gap after the top two sides appeared to be large throughout the season and the finals series again highlighted this gap. South Fremantle defeated Swan Districts 11.22 (88) to 11.12 (78) in a close game, but the next week the Swans thrashed East Perth in the final, 28.13 (181) to 15.15 (105), and moved into the Grand Final. South was too strong in the Grand Final, with Rioli dominating out of the centre, and Joe McKay holding up the defence. South Fremantle won comfortably, 23.18 (156) to 15.8 (98). South's Stephen Michael won the 1980 Sandover.[20] The continuing gap between Victoria and the West was revealed in an interesting sidelight of the 1980 season: East Perth applied to join the VFL, and the application was rejected without even the courtesy of a comment.

The 1970s in South Australia were not dominated by any one team. Port continued to win flags, as did Norwood and Sturt. In 1973, Glenelg (coached by South Australian football icon Neil Kerley) lost only one game during the season, which included a winning streak fourteen games long. Despite Glenelg's dominance of the home-and-away season, the Grand Final produced a close contest, during which North Adelaide almost stole Glenelg's hat-trick premiership. Glenelg lost the lead at the start of the time-on period, then the side lifted, and a mark and kick from Graham Cornes put them 1 point in front. Another mark to forward John Sandland in the goal square sealed the game and gave Glenelg its second ever premiership. Meanwhile, Port legend Fos Williams retired as coach after twenty-one years, including nine years as playing coach (1950–58) and in a non-playing role from 1962 to 1973. This period yielded nine premierships, a record not equalled until 1994.

In Victoria, 1972 was an open and exciting season, with the introduction of the Final Five, devised by McIntyre to replace his 41-year-old Final Four system. Hawthorn lost Hudson to injury in Round 1 and gradually slipped out of contention. Essendon improved under Tuddenham's captaincy. But the ladder's top rungs were filled by the three teams which were destined to dominate the 1970s – Richmond, Carlton, and Collingwood. St Kilda kept up its form and finished the 1972 season in fourth spot by defeating Hawthorn in the last round at Glenferrie. The Hawks were pushed down to sixth and lost the opportunity to defend their premiership in the finals. The new attacking style of the 1970s was already evident in the high scores of 1972, and this trend continued in the finals. St Kilda ended the Bombers' promising season, 18.16 (124) to 10.11 (71). Collingwood went down in successive weeks to Richmond and St Kilda. After Richmond defeated Carlton in the replay of the drawn Second Semi, the Tigers had won twelve games in a row and looked unbeatable for the flag. But Carlton defeated St Kilda in the Preliminary Final and went on in the scoring-frenzy Grand Final to vanquish Richmond, 28.9 (177) to 22.18 (150). Meanwhile Collingwood took the year's other honours: Len Thompson won the Brownlow and Peter McKenna booted 130 goals.

Having signed Barassi on as coach and having recruited good players, North Melbourne entered 1973 with confidence. It had won only one match in 1972, but in 1973 it won ten, drew another, and finished the year just out of the Final Five. Once again the same teams took the top three spots: in order, Collingwood, Richmond and Carlton. Geelong crashed to eleventh. Essendon was again eliminated in the finals by St

Kilda; Collingwood stumbled in the finals once more, after winning nineteen games in the home-and-away series. Richmond lost the Qualifying Final to Carlton, but fought back to meet them in the Grand Final, and triumphed, 16.20 (116) to 12.14 (86). Bombing the forward line was a flag-winning strategy, even if it produced more behinds than goals. North's Keith Greig took the Brownlow that year, while Peter McKenna top-scored with 86 goals.

Hawthorn marked its move to Princes Park in 1974 with a finals appearance. Indeed, it was the first year all the new teams of 1925 made the finals together. Carlton slumped terribly at the start of the season, dropping to eleventh place and only towards the end of 1974 rising back to seventh. Richmond and North battled all season for top position; the Tigers moved a game clear of the Kangaroos with the ruthless perfection of their attacking team plan. The extent of their vigour was demonstrated by the notorious incident at Windy Hill this season, an all-in fracas involving players, officials and police. Not surprisingly, Richmond went on to win the Grand Final, pitted against the vastly improved North Melbourne, 18.20 (128) to 13.9 (87). Doug Wade, now playing for North, in 1974 became only the second VFL player to kick a thousand goals – and also topped the year's list. Keith Greig won his second Brownlow.

The Grand Finallists of 1974 took a while to get going in 1975 – Richmond did not win a match until Round 5, while North Melbourne did not enter the five until Round 14. Hawthorn and Carlton gained an early break on the rest of the VFL competition. Behind them were seven clubs locked in a battle for a finals berth. North came good at the right end of the season, fighting for a place in the finals, but went down to Hawthorn in the Second Semi by 11 points. Richmond made it through from the Elimination Final to the Preliminary, defeating Collingwood and Carlton along the way. But the Tigers then met their end at the hands of North, and the Northerners went on to lead Hawthorn at every change in the 1975 Grand Final and to win their first VFL flag by 55 points. Footscray's Gary Dempsey won the Brownlow and Hawthorn's Leigh Matthews led the goalkicking with 68 for the season.

In the VFL, 1976 was an even year. Collingwood was on the bottom of the ladder in Round 15, but was only two games out of the five. Again Hawthorn and Carlton moved up to the top of the ladder. Robert Walls kicked 10 goals in Carlton's Round 7 demolition of Richmond. After five years at the top, Richmond began to struggle; Collingwood likewise collected its first-ever wooden spoon in 1976. Geelong showed signs of improvement, finishing the year in fourth spot. North again started the season slowly, but improved to finish third. North and Hawthorn had developed a keen rivalry. Hawthorn finished the home-and-away matches in second position, went on to defeat the Kangaroos in the Qualifying Final, and then defeated the Blues in the Second Semi-Final to earn a week's rest. Carlton and North were left to battle out the Preliminary Final; North won it by merely 1 point, after Carlton squandered many opportunities in front of goal. In the 1976 Grand Final, not unexpectedly, Hawthorn led at every change to defeat North Melbourne 13.22 (100) to 10.10 (70). Graham Moss won the 1976 Brownlow, while Geelong's Larry Donohue topped the season with 105 goals kicked.

Stung into action by its dismal performance the preceding year, and led by new coach Tom Hafey, Collingwood was a new force in 1977. The Magpies moved to top position after Round 6. They crushed their arch-rivals Carlton, inflicting the worst defeat the Blues had ever suffered (a record which would stand for six years). Collingwood headed a group of the top six sides – along with Hawthorn, North, Richmond, South, and Carlton – which were a clear distance ahead of the rest. The 1977 season saw South Melbourne's first finals appearance in many years. As for Collingwood, it finally looked as if its atrocious September hoodoo was to be exorcised: its not-quite-successful finals performances had been christened 'the Colliwobbles'. North Melbourne won through from the First Semi-Final to play Collingwood in the 1977 Grand Final. North was down, 4.15 to 9.12, at three-quarter time, but came back and the match ended in a draw. The following Saturday North led all day and, although Collingwood got to within 11 points in the final term, the Kangaroos took out their second premiership. The Colliwobbles were still afflicting the Magpies! South Melbourne's Graeme Teasdale won the Brownlow that year, and Peter Hudson led the goal-kicking.

Hawthorn and North continued their rivalry into 1978. The Northerners looked good early in the season, winning their first eight games. Although Hawthorn finished the year in second place, it and North Melbourne began to drop games against lowly sides as the season wore on. After finishing last in 1977, St Kilda improved, missing the finals by only half a game. Richmond dropped out of the finals race in a disappointing year. Early in 1978, Carlton's field performance was affected by internal club wrangles – Robert Walls left the Blues for Fitzroy – but under new captain-coach Alex Jesaulenko, Carlton won thirteen out of its last fifteen matches and marched into the finals. It defeated Geelong in the Elimination Final, only to be beaten by the Magpies in the First Semi-Final by 15 points. Collingwood was then defeated convincingly in the Qualifying Final by Hawthorn, 23.16 (154) to 14.14 (98), and then by North Melbourne in the Preliminary Final, 14.12 (96) to 12.12 (84). The Hawthorn–North rivalry dominated the finals. Hawthorn won its Second Semi encounter by 14 points, and produced a 7-goal third quarter in the 1978 Grand Final to triumph, 18.13 (121) to 15.13 (103). North's Malcolm Blight won the Brownlow that year, while Bulldog Kelvin Templeton kicked 118 goals for the season.

A highlight of the 1979 season was the VFL's exhibition match at the Sydney Cricket Ground, the Round 10 contest between the 1978 champions, Hawthorn and North. The game drew a crowd of 31,391, and gave the League renewed hope of breaking into Sydney. But Hawthorn's successful run was over – in 1979 it fell to seventh spot on the ladder. North Melbourne, along with Carlton, started the new season more impressively. Both undefeated for six weeks, these two sides met in Round 7 at Princes Park. It was close all afternoon, but two late goals to Glendinning and Easton gave North a stirring victory. Fitzroy enjoyed a much-improved year, winning nine games, and at one stage of the 1979 season sat in second place. In a crucial last-round clash at Geelong, the Lions hoped to gain third place and the vital double chance. But on that day the Cats came from behind in the last quarter, kicking 6.2, and Fitzroy's third spot went to Collingwood. Undaunted, Fitzroy disposed of Essendon in the Elimination Final, while in the Qualifying Final North Melbourne beat Collingwood easily. The Magpies then rallied the following week and ended Fitzroy's flag ambitions, winning 16.20 (116) to 12.22 (94). Carlton in the meantime moved into the Grand Final by beating North in the Second Semi-Final. The Preliminary Final witnessed Collingwood reversing the result of the Qualifying Final – the Magpies led North all day and moved into the Grand Final for yet another tilt at that elusive premiership. Although Carlton had clearly emerged as the form team of 1979, Collingwood took it right up to the Blues, playing an inspired last quarter to falter by merely 5 points. Collingwood's tall blond Peter Moore won his first Brownlow that year, while Footscray's Kelvin Templeton again top-scored with 91 goals.

In 1980 Alex Jesaulenko retired as Carlton's captain-coach in a club upheaval, despite having led the Blues to thirty-five wins across forty-two matches. Carlton started the season well, continued strongly toward the end of the home-and-away series, and moved up the ladder into second place at the expense of the faltering Tigers. Richmond for its part started the 1980 year brilliantly, including an eleven-game winning streak only ended by Fitzroy in Round 15. At the end, however, Richmond dropped games late in the season to finish third. Geelong began the year steadily and moved up the ladder as the season wore on, claiming top position at the end of the home-and-away season for the first time since 1956. Collingwood won crucial games at the business end of the season to sneak into fifth spot. The finals series that followed was unique to the Final Five format. From fifth place Collingwood defeated North in the Elimination Final by just 8 points, and then walloped Carlton by 50 points in the First Semi. A miraculous last-minute snap from Rene Kink brought the Magpies to victory over Geelong in the Preliminary Final, and to a place in the Grand Final. Richmond's passage to the Grand Final was only slightly less spectacular. It defeated Carlton by an impressive 8 goals in the Qualifying Final, and then beat Geelong by 4 to move into the Grand Final. So the two top teams of 1980 actually both missed out on the Grand Final, which was fought out between the fifth and third sides. And then Collingwood's struggle to make it this far told on the day, while Richmond returned to its winning ways of the early season. Richmond won easily, 23.21 (159) to 9.24 (78), and its forward Michael Roach was the 1980 top goalkicker, posting 112 majors. Kelvin Templeton (Footscray) meanwhile won the Brownlow.[21]

So the 1970s decade closed as it had begun, with a top goalkicking score of more than a ton. In most years this had been the case, unlike the previous two decades. After John Coleman's 120 in 1950, it had been rare for the top scorer to kick more than a hundred goals until the arrival of the Hudsons, Wades, McKennas and others of the 1970s. This indicates the importance of all-out attack to the winning teams of the 1970s. The 1980s, however, would see a new balance between attack and defence.

Balanced Attack and Defence

The years 1981 to 1991 witnessed a deepening of the corporate culture in football, coinciding with the dominance of economic rationalism in national politics. The old League was replaced in 1985 by a commission, a move initiated by the outgoing president, Dr Allen Aylett, whose values were similar to those of Luke and Nathan before him. Former St Kilda player Ross Oakley then rose to the top job, and sought to put some of the new economic rationalist ideas into practice. The decade began with an omen of what was to come.

At the beginning of the 1980s, for reasons which suggested it was ignorant of the game's history, the VFL uprooted South Melbourne Football Club, sending the Bloods to Sydney. This policy decision revealed how little the factors underlying the game's success were understood at the highest level of its administration. Attempts to create a national competition were based on some doubtful assumptions, not the least of which was that Sydney should be the site of the game's initial expansion out of Victoria, instead of (say) Canberra. The VFL was unable to reconcile its differences with South Australia and Western Australia, which would have been far more logical avenues for expansion. The VFL was also saddled with the presumption that private clubs were the thing of the future, despite the game's strong record of public ownership, and the VFL was therefore susceptible to the siren calls of the entrepreneurs in other cities who knew virtually nothing about Australian Rules football and its traditional supporter base ('the market').

Meanwhile, as it is a dynamic game, the winning tactics continued to evolve, and the philosophy of constant pressure on the opposition's backline gave way to a radically new idea. Two clubs stood out in the 1980s as paragons of the decade's style. Both were VFL clubs and both worked hard to balance their attack with their defence: these clubs were Hawthorn and Essendon.

Hawthorn in the 1980s found the right balance between attack and defence. It was as if the brown-and-gold teams of the previous two decades had been reincarnated at the same moment in time. The late 1950s–early 1960s team had excelled at defence – where Phil and Sted Hay had stood, their places at Glenferrie were now taken by Langford and Ayres. The late 1960s–early 1970s forward line built around Hudson was now focused around Dermott Brereton, Leigh Matthews and Jason Dunstall. Geelong's Ablett might have been regarded as the most exciting player of the 1980s, but Dunstall was the most admired. Week after week, precise bullet-like passes were fired into Dunstall's supplicant arms. Dunstall was the centre of the famous Hawthorn trident formation advancing out of the forward line.

As with Hawthorn, so with Essendon. Good game plans are supported by good administrations and one of their signature features is good recruiting. In the 1980s and 1990s Essendon players were just as likely to be recruited locally; the national growth of the game has not affected this club's local content, even though Essendon is regarded as one of the AFL's most imaginative recruiters. On the 1987 player list the locals were Ed Considine (Strathmore), Alan Ezard (Coburg), Gary Foulds (West Essendon), Paul Hamilton (St Bernard's), Mark Harvey (Keilor), David Johnston (Doutta Stars), Gavin Keane (St Bernard's), Simon Madden (St Christopher's), Gary O'Donnell (Essendon Under-Nineteens), Paul Salmon (Essendon Under-Nineteens), Peter Somerville (Essendon Reserves), Mark Thompson (Airport West), and Michael Thomson (Aberfeldie). The Wimmera connection continued to bring rich rewards, with Tim Watson and Merv Neagle from Dimboola, Glenn Hawker and Roger Merrett from Kaniva, David Flood and Dean Wallis from Nhill, Shane Heard from Horsham, and Graham Schultz from Warracknabeal. The five Daniher boys from Ungarie in southern NSW were vital to Essendon in the 1980s, as were some interstate recruits, particularly Bill Duckworth from West Perth, the much-unsung Leon

Baker (from Avenel via Swan Districts), Paul Weston (ex-Glenelg) and Anthony Buhagiar from East Fremantle.

The value of Aboriginal players had been recognised for some time at Essendon, beginning in the early 1950s with Norm McDonald. The turning point came with Michael Long, whose brother followed him to the club. The Kicketts, Wanganeen and Che Cockatoo-Collins were sought subsequently. Once a tolerant milieu was created in the 1980s, the ex-Carlton player Syd Jackson also became involved in the social life of the club. Essendon was among the first VFL clubs to recognise that Aboriginal players have a grace and agility for which white players are not as often noted. In one memorable incident, Michael Long trapped the ball just inside the boundary line, kept his hand on the Sherrin's apex as he pirouetted around the boundary to avoid his opponent, and then in the same motion took the ball up and booted it on.[1]

Flags in 1962, 1965, 1984–85 and 1993 brought Essendon's tally to fifteen (equal with Carlton, ironically the team they defeated in 1993). In the history of the VFL/AFL, the team has won 58 per cent of its games (a percentage bettered only by Collingwood, Carlton and the West Coast Eagles). Its coach since 1981 has been Kevin Sheedy, whose success rate as a coach is 65 per cent (equal with Jock McHale and Checker Hughes, and slightly better than Sheedy's mentor, Tom Hafey). Sheedy barracked for Essendon as a boy, but lived in Prahran and was tied by residential rules to Richmond (1967–79, 251 games). (His report card from St Ignatius school in Richmond said of him: 'Good at sport, good at religion but not very good at science.') Sheedy understands that some kind of stability is needed in a club, and only within that is innovation possible. 'Sheedy believes football must be studied and nurtured from the toddler's first kick to the bounce of the ball in the Grand Final.' Success starts with the club, not the team: '"Not many players leave Essendon because of turmoil in the club," is his boast.'[2] Essendon remained a district rich in sporting venues, with facilities for baseball, soccer, croquet, and the rest. Even after the club moved to the MCG in 1993, Windy Hill, where the players still trained, became a major recreational centre for Essendon supporters looking for poker machines, a social life and good meals.

While Essendon and Hawthorn in the 1980s were well administered and played this balanced style of football to perfection, Melbourne re-emerged as a football force in the late 1980s with a gritty defensive style which did not produce a flag, while Geelong took the older idea of constant attack to new heights, but also failed to win a premiership. At Geelong they believe in the health-giving powers of country life; the Cats administration looks for the gun player from the bush just waiting to be discovered; and at Geelong coaches like Hafey who insist that individual champions play as part of a champion team will have their hearts broken. These are the three elements of modern Geelong mythology.

The mythologising about country life was part of Geelong's pastoral background: 'God made the country, and man made the town.' Geelong's character as a football club and the supposed therapeutic value of country life are closely intertwined. Cats supporters nodded knowingly when ruck-rover Mark Bairstow returned to captain-coach Lake Grace in the Western Australian wheatbelt for the 1990 season; his batteries replenished, Bairstow came back to 'the bright lights' of Geelong for the 1991 year. Geelong is perceived, mythically, to recruit exclusively from St Patrick's Ballarat, Geelong Grammar and Geelong College. No doubt rural Victoria supplies modern Geelong with some talent. The Hockings and John Barnes kicked footies to each other in the back streets of Cobram. Gavin Exell hailed from Northern United, via the Carlton Reserves. Billy Brownless' connections with rustic Jerilderie are more easily recalled than his descent from an illustrious ancestor who helped create the medical school at Melbourne University. And so on. But Australian country towns perhaps have few avenues to fame apart from sport and popular entertainment. No-one challenges the right of a town's young men to express themselves through football; big-city players often have a business or professional interest, thanks to the greater social pressure placed on them. No citizen of Geelong expects their footballers to do more than produce match-winning efforts at Kardinia Park. Perspective is quickly lost.

Closely associated with the standing of the country-town footballer is another myth: that somewhere in the bush is the gun player, largely untutored, possessing natural skills, who will turn around the big-League team's fortunes. Luckily for the myth, such players do occasionally appear. Bruce Lindner from the Barossa and Gary Ablett from Drouin helped restore Geelong's confidence in the surprise-packet bush miracle-worker during the 1980s. In this period, when Geelong was racking up higher and higher scores than had ever been seen in the VFL, perhaps half the senior team were individual champions. Brian Peake's dramatic arrival at

Kardinia Park by helicopter one Thursday afternoon in June 1981 typified this recruiting mentality. (Curiously, Aboriginal players were not part
of this thinking – Peake's Aboriginality was never discussed, nor had
Polly Farmer's ever been. Rod Waddell, who played twenty games as a
Cat in 1982–84, is the only exception to the rule.)

The greatest attacking team of all time had a third and final characteristic: no coach succeeded in melding these champions into a team! The
1980s Geelong side was uncoachable. Under rover Bill Goggin (1980–82)
the Cats lost two Preliminary Finals one year after the other, and then
played an entire season without winning any away matches. Tom Hafey,
whose greatness as a coach can be measured by the number of his
protégés, tried to bring order at Geelong from 1983 to 1985. When he
left, he took with him to Sydney those Cats like Greg Williams who were
clubbable. John Devine brought his personal discipline from years as a
half-back flanker to the coaching job in 1986–88, but the players resisted
his concept of a team plan. Malcolm Blight tried a more subtle approach,
but it was still a defeatist club, trapped in its own history, which could
immortalise Blight's first year with a video entitled *One Kick from Glory*.[3]
After three Grand Final defeats, Blight walked away from the job.

If Geelong was offence writ large, the Demons of the 1980s specialised
in defensive play. On 1 October 1980 Barassi dramatically announced
he was going 'home', to coach Melbourne. The game, however, had
changed since 1964, and his return was not enough to change Melbourne's fortunes overnight. In short, it was no longer an individual's
game. Many Melbourne players simply felt intimidated by Barassi, and
not at all encouraged. Even his favourites, such as Brent Crosswell, say
that he only knew Genghis Khan tactics. Crosswell says this was also
how Barassi played chess. Nor was buying star players for the Demons
enough; as soon as they broke down, the team's fortunes slumped again.
Melbourne commenced the 1980s still in abysmal form. In the 1981
season, Footscray conceded Melbourne's only win for the entire year
when the Demon champion Robbie Flower kicked a goal after the siren.
Barassi introduced some talented youngsters to the game, including some
Irish recruits who had grown up on Gaelic football, but he was not to
reap the benefits John Northey would when 'Swooper' took over the
coaching job at Melbourne in the latter half of the decade. By then,
however, Barassi had left the football scene, and appeared to have given
up the game for good. (One journalist presciently predicted: 'Barass will

be back. Maybe Dr Edelsten's magic chequebook will do the trick.'[4])

Collingwood did not adjust well to the balanced team game of the 1980s. In September 1982 the entire Collingwood committee was thrown out of office for the first time in the club's history, following rallies and mass meetings convened by the New Magpies (Alan McAlister, Ranald Macdonald, and the rest). The New Magpies invested lavishly in new players and engaged the South Australian John Cahill to coach the team. In 1984 the team was thrashed by Essendon in the Preliminary Final, losing by a record 123 points. Collingwood's only saving grace was that it could still claim 16,000 season ticket-holders, down from 19,000 in 1982 but at the time the League's greatest number.[5]

Collingwood's traditional support remained, despite pessimistic accounts of the demise of inner-suburban loyalties.[6] As working-class families left the Magpie turf for the northern suburbs they simply took their black-and-white allegiance with them. As for ex-Richmondites, their old haunts were still only a train ride away from the eastern suburbs. Take the London Tavern Hotel, at the corner of Lennox Street and Richmond Terrace. This was owned by Graeme Richmond, long-time servant of the Football Club – and in later years managed by John ('Swooper') Northey, the dour sheepfarmer from Derrinallum who played for the club in the 1970s and coached it in the 1990s. The back bar of the hotel might have been taken over in the 1980s by the yuppies who represent the gentrification of the suburb, but in the front bar – it's the same old story, older Tigers drawing back on their roll-yer-owns who remember every detail of the club's finer moments.

Cheer squads became better organised in the 1980s. Modest displays of club colours were first started in the 1950s, but VFL cheer squads in the 1980s began to produce huge and colourful banners, often with a sharp critique of what was happening. In 1988 the VFL House switchboard was jammed when the Magpies cheer squad warned supporters the League was planning to move Collingwood from Victoria Park. Robert Flower's last home-and-away match at Western Oval in 1987 inspired a huge portrait, with the simple inscription JUST FOR YOU. Menzies' death produced a Carlton banner, A TRIBUTE TO SIR ROBERT. R.I.P. Wry comments include: SUPPORTING GEELONG IS LIKE BEING ON THE DOLE. THERE AREN'T MANY BENEFITS. Hawthorn's cheer squad proved to be particularly literary, with gems such as the 1985 Grand Final banner, in gothic script, FOR WHAT WE ARE ABOUT TO

RECEIVE MAY THE LORD MAKE US TRULY THANKFUL. Or the 1988 Grand Final, showing a woman with premiership guernseys on a Hill's Hoist, and the line BRING 'EM HOME TO MAMA.

The 1980s was the decade senior football ceased to be confined to Saturday afternoons. This was the first indication that it was broadening commercially. In 1981, senior professional football consisted of six games across suburban Melbourne and Geelong played on Saturday afternoons and administered by the VFL. By 1991, it was nation-wide, played in Sydney, Brisbane, Adelaide and Perth, with televised games across the weekend, and administered by the AFL. The relationship between the League and the Victorian State Government changed during the 1980s, with interesting consequences. At the beginning of the decade, with a Liberal government in power, the relationship was cosy. This was revealed by the Sunday fixturing controversy. One context for the 1981 campaign by the VFL to introduce Sunday football games was Melbourne's proposed Olympics bid for the 1988 Games. The public's tolerance of traffic chaos occasioned by sporting events had to be tested. Another context was planning ahead for CHOGM, the Commonwealth Heads of Government Meeting, nicknamed Closing Half of Greater Melbourne.

So it came to pass that on two Sundays, 2 and 9 August 1981, VFL football was played on the MCG and the effects of these matches on other activities, including VFA matches, was measured. There would have been perhaps 30,000 patrons at Windy Hill if the match against Collingwood had been played there as fixtured. In fact 64,000 attended the MCG, almost 60 per cent of the total attendance for that round; the $194,000 in gate receipts was more than 70 per cent of the VFL's total takings that weekend. The University of Melbourne researchers commissioned to survey these Sunday matches found that although police reports suggested a greater proportion of family groups than usual, the turnstile records revealed no significant increase in the proportion of children entering the ground. Older residents of neighbouring suburbs were more likely to oppose the introduction of Sunday football, although naturally there was some support for Sunday matches to be played out at VFL Park. The authors of the report speculated that the residential areas around the MCG might decline in popularity – the opposite in fact occurred. It was thus necessary to improve the overall amenities around the ground – Punt Road was finally widened (this had been initially proposed in 1965) and local residents were given parking permits designed to protect their parking spaces. (In the Richmond of old, no-one used to have cars anyway, so this had not been an issue.) Sunday football was one part of the liberalisation of the Sabbath, a day which in this very Protestant city had traditionally been an occasion for family functions, church worship, the notorious 'Sunday drive', and little else. Four separate opinion polls conducted in 1981 found that only about 20 per cent of Melburnians supported the introduction of Sunday football. It was not clear how vigorously Sunday football was opposed by the majority.[7] As the practice became more commonplace during the 1980s, there was little organised opposition to it.

VFA attendances were adversely affected by the VFL hosting Sunday football. At Coburg only 2000 attended a match that would usually have attracted 5000. The Players Association was also opposed to Sunday games, as professional footballers still relied financially on Monday-to-Friday jobs and needed the Sunday to recover. Earlier in 1981 the VFL had put to the VFA a plan for co-operation which the Association viewed as a blatant attempt at a take-over.[8] When Labor came to power in 1982, its initial assumption had been that it would have less difficulty dealing with the VFL than with that powerful symbol of the local Establishment, the Melbourne Cricket Club (MCC), which owned the MCG. In fact Premier John Cain found that on issues such as whether the Grand Final should be moved to Waverley, the MCC was easier to negotiate with than the representatives of the people's game. Following much negotiation, the League in fact made peace with the Cricket Club and moved into the Great Southern Stand at the MCG at the end of the decade.[9] (By 1995, the AFL was even on good terms with the cricket authorities in Adelaide, much to the annoyance of the SANFL.)

There was still a place for amateur football in Victoria, however. The Metropolitan Junior Football Association, founded in 1892, had become the Victorian Amateur Football Association (VAFA), better known as 'the Amateurs'. From 1896 to 1932 its president was the redoubtable 'Dicky' Adamson, who campaigned tirelessly against the greed of professionalism. The VAFA was dominated at first by Old Scotch, which won the A Grade regularly from 1923 to 1934, then by University Blacks, which won every year from 1938 to 1949. Reflecting the rise of the Catholic schools, Old Paradians began to win flags, taking six in the 1960s decade. 'The Amateurs' retained their deep-seated colonial traditionalism, as hinted in the song Adamson wrote for the Collegians team from Wesley:

When all the turf is gleaming with dewy rains of May,
Between the goal posts tall and grim, we sally forth to play;
For we're a band of brothers – Collegians gay we are,
Who rally round the Gold and Purple Flag we love – Hurrah!

A group of former De La Salle students formed their own amateur club in 1955, winning the E Grade flag in their very first season and moving up the ranks. By 1980 De La had won three A Grade premierships in the space of four years. In the 1980s, Ormond took its turn, winning every year from 1987 to 1990, under coach Mike McArthur-Allen. In 1994, Old Melburnians defeated Collegians in the VAFA Grand Final. Across the eight grades of VAFA competition (from A to H), approximately two hundred clubs have existed. Many have been schools-based (Peninsula Old Boys; St Patrick's (Ballarat) OC, 1939–40, 1951–55, 1964–75) while others have been youth groups, such as the YMCA (Young Men's Christian Association, 1892–93). Several have been made up of workmates and friends, such as Commonwealth Bank (1947–90), Myer (1937–54), GTV9 (1986), and Naval Base Flinders (1927–28). The Jewish club Ajax (1957–) and Celtic (1900–02) have represented ethnic communities. Many are suburban, such as East Malvern (1929–64) and Coolaroo Rovers (1980).[10]

In Western Australia, the decade opened with new coaching staff. For the 1981 season, East Fremantle appointed Ken Smith as coach. Grant Dorrington took over from Barry Cable at East Perth. Bruce Monteath returned to South Fremantle after six years at Richmond. Barry Cable became coach of North Melbourne after the resignation of Malcolm Blight. A draft system was introduced which limited the Victorian competition to taking twenty-four interstate players. Mal Brown was once again involved in a dispute with the League, this time because of a brawl in a pre-season game. Brown took his players from the field and was fined by the League. On the field, once the 1981 season got underway, Claremont streaked in front of the rest of the competition, winning 19 out of 21 games. Swan Districts and South Fremantle were again prominent. The Second Semi saw Claremont beat Swan Districts for the fourth time that year, 14.24 (108) to 12.9 (81). The Swans played South Fremantle in the Final, and South demolished the Swans in the second half, winning 28.10 (178) to 15.15 (105). Now having a taste of finals success, Claremont took the game up to South Fremantle in the second half, coming from behind in the last quarter to win 16.25 (121) to 12.24 (96). This was a triumph for a club which had previously only won four premierships. South's Stephen Michael won the Sandover for the second year in a row, while Claremont's Warren Ralph bagged 120 goals.

In 1982, Denis Cometti (later better-known as a Channel 7 commentator) was appointed coach of West Perth, the first ex-West Perth player to be appointed since 1959. The exodus of Western Australian talent to Victoria continued in 1982: Maurice Rioli to Richmond, Simon Beasley to Footscray, Gary Buckenara to Hawthorn, Jim and Phil Krakouer to North Melbourne, and Alan Johnson to Melbourne. Despite the ebb and flow of football talent, the 1982 season proved to be one of the closest on record. Swan Districts, Claremont and West Perth all finished the home-and-away matches on fifteen wins, separated only by percentage, before the last round. Claremont and West Perth played in the last round, with the winner guaranteed a spot in the Second Semi-Final. Claremont won and finished the season on top of the ladder. Swan Districts also had to beat South Fremantle to play off in the Second Semi-Final, which it did. Swan Districts then defeated Claremont in the Second Semi, 14.26 (110) to 12.10 (82). Claremont beat West Perth in the Final easily, 18.23 (131) to 13.15 (93), setting up a rematch with Swan Districts. Led by the successful combination of John Todd as coach and Graham Melrose as captain, Swan Districts romped away in the Grand Final, winning 18.19 (127) to 11.12 (78). Swan Districts' popular Phil Narkle took the Sandover, while Claremont's Warren Ralph again topped the goalkicking.

The next year, 1983, Greg Brehaut, arguably the finest wingman produced in Western Australia, was appointed to coach East Perth. Peter Daniel was involved in a coaching merry-go-round at Subiaco: he replaced Ken Armstrong but after only eleven games he himself was replaced by Brian Fairclough. As a sign of the corporate era, East Fremantle officially changed from Old Easts to the 'Sharks', though the grizzled men in the stand kept the faith with the traditional nickname. South Fremantle enjoyed a better year, finishing the qualifying round on top of the ladder. However, its success during the year was marred by a last-game loss to Claremont. It met Claremont again in the Second Semi and lost again, and was bundled out of the finals the following week by Swan Districts. Again Claremont and Swan Districts met in the Grand Final, and though Claremont went closer, Swan Districts won its second consecutive premiership, 15.14 (104) to 12.11 (83). Graham Moss retired after playing as captain-coach of Claremont. Claremont's Warren Ralph again topped the scoring list, with 123 goals, while East Perth's John Ironmonger won the Sandover.

The headlines of 1984 were numerous: Moss continued as non-playing coach of Claremont. Claremont lost Warren Ralph and Wayne Blackwell to Carlton. The Swans lost Phil Narkle, Mike Smith, Leon Baker and Peter Kenny to Victoria, and Stan Nowotny, Graham Melrose, and Alan Cransberg to retirement. Robert Wiley and Peter Bosustow returned to WA football and were signed by Perth. Subiaco appointed Haydn Bunton as coach. The League experimented with live telecasts and country games, with a match fixtured in Bunbury. East Fremantle had a good qualifying round, finishing second and qualifying for the Second Semi-Final for the first time since 1977. Despite the loss of good players, Swan Districts still finished on top of the ladder. Claremont finished third, followed by East Perth. Perth finished on the bottom of the ladder for the second year running. The Swan Districts' winning streak was ended by East Fremantle in the Second Semi, 15.12 (102) to 10.16 (76). In the other semi, Claremont beat East Perth in an all-out attacking game, 23.10 (148) to 19.12 (126). The final between Claremont and Swan Districts saw Claremont get away to an early lead before the Tigers were reeled in by the Swans, who went on to win by 21 points. The Swans were aiming for a hat-trick flag on Grand Final day, and in the first quarter they kicked 10.7 to 0.3, which was answered by an equally impressive 9.3 by East Fremantle in the second quarter. The Swans kicked away in the second half to win again.

In 1985, the centenary year of the Western Australian competition, Mal Brown was appointed as coach of Perth for three years. Stephen Michael played his last season for Claremont after recurring knee problems. East Fremantle avenged its Grand Final loss in the opening round, shellacking Swan Districts 20.23 (143) to 9.10 (64). This game was the first of a twelve-game winning sequence, and East Fremantle grabbed top place. Subiaco made a welcome return to the finals, finishing second. Swan Districts faded slightly, but still made the finals, eventually bowing out to Subiaco in the Preliminary Final. Subiaco emerged as the genuine challenger to the dominant East Fremantle, playing in its first Grand Final since 1973. The contest was close, with Subiaco almost toppling East Fremantle. The scores were 15.12 (102) to 14.13 (97), and East Fremantle had secured its twenty-sixth premiership. This was also the year Murray Wrensted won the Sandover.

The following year, 1986, Subiaco and East Fremantle continued to dominate the competition, setting up another confrontation in the finals, finishing four games clear of the other finalists, Perth and Claremont. The Second Semi resulted in a drubbing for Subiaco, which lost 20.13 (133) to 12.11 (83). The Lions entered the Preliminary Final chastened, and dished out similar treatment to Perth, winning 26.12 (168) to 15.7 (97). Then the Grand Final saw Subiaco defeat the Sharks surprisingly easily, with the scoreboard reading 19.16 (130) to 8.13 (61). In only his second year of football, South Fremantle's Mark Bairstow took out the Sandover.

Although dominated by the formation of the West Coast Eagles, 1987 was also the year Gerard Neesham was appointed to coach Claremont, and in his first year coached the side to nineteen wins, one loss, and one draw. The Tigers outclassed Subiaco in the Second Semi and the Grand Final to win the club's sixth premiership. Neesham's record in coaching Claremont was to prove quite extraordinary, with flags in 1987, 1989, 1991 and 1993. More than thirty of his players went on to careers in AFL football. Perth's Mark Watson won the 1987 Sandover, but Claremont's Derek Kickett (who was ineligible owing to suspension) polled sixteen more votes. The goalkicking list that year was led by Todd Breman (Subiaco) with a haul of 101.

The West Coast Eagles entered the VFL competition in the same season as the Brisbane Bears and at a time when the Sydney Swans was a private company. The introduction of these clubs was popularly seen as a means of carrying out a financial rescue of the VFL. (It is still not clear whether the VFL was as insolvent in the mid-1980s as was made out by the AFL ten years later when justifying their much-vaunted Five Year Plan of 1994.) Thus the Eagles were introduced into the main competition in unfortunate circumstances; they were seen as a parvenu club which was being brought into the national League for its dowry rather than for its talent. This perception was strengthened by the clean-cut and sun-drenched image of the West Coast players promoted by the new club. Their club song sounded like a jingle rather than a traditional anthem. Their occupational backgrounds certainly did not convey the traditional image of footballers, either: a pharmacist half-back flanker who rose to captaincy, sundry investment advisors, a publican with a shock of blond hair, and a conspicuous lack of working-class types.[11] The Eagles were the first VFL team to be named after something other than a suburb, since the demise of University long before present memory. This added to the feeling among Victorians that the new club represented a break with tradition, that it helped symbolise the 1980s in Australian football. The Eagles seemed to stand for everything about the Me Decade which traditionalists detested.

For Western Australian football fans, the creation of the Eagles was a landmark occasion. No longer would the state's best players be poached by VFL clubs in the dreaded eastern states; now they had a local team to aspire to play in. These fans had won a moral victory with the formation of state-of-origin football in 1977 – these were contests which Western Australians were more likely to win. Visiting Victorian teams had always assumed that the standard was so much lower that only a minimal effort was required of them. (Of the thirteen interstate matches from 1966 to 1977, Victoria defeated Western Australia every time; in a stunning reversal of fortunes, under the new rules, from 1977 to 1988, Victoria won only eight, conceding six to the Sandgropers.) The West Coast Eagles gave Western Australians a new opportunity to prove themselves. At first, coached by local men Ron Alexander and then John Todd, the Eagles did not play the balanced football required of the 1980s. Their offensive style was well-suited to the open grounds of the west, but less adaptable to the confined ovals in Melbourne. Subiaco is longer even than Waverley, by a good 5 metres. The Eagles were perceived by Victorian clubs as relying on pace and running, to the detriment of other aspects of a well-rounded team plan. But big things were in store for the Eagles in the 1990s.

The 1980s decade started well for Essendon, with fifteen wins in a row early in the 1981 season. (This was the best effort by a VFL side since Collingwood's winning streak of eighteen games in 1929.) Unfortunately the Bombers were defeated by Geelong at Kardinia Park in the last round, and went down to Fitzroy in the Elimination Final. Hawthorn had an even worse year, fading to finish in sixth spot. Richmond was unable to capture its premiership form of 1980, while Geelong played a very defensive style all year, which was to be its undoing in the finals. It was beaten first by Collingwood in the Qualifying Final and then by Carlton in the Second Semi-Final. It came down to a Grand Final between Carlton and Collingwood. The Magpies held a 21-point lead in the third quarter, but slipped in the finish.

In 1982, South Melbourne's move to Sydney saw some immediate results, winning the pre-season competition and stringing together seven wins in the season proper, its best result since 1936. The Swans did not have the staying power necessary to get into the finals, however. Geelong did not win any games away from Kardinia Park for the entire season. Collingwood stumbled and Tom Hafey was sacked. Melbourne showed some good form, winning eight games for the year. The finalists were a rejuvenated Richmond and North Melbourne, the hardy perennial Carlton, and the two glamour sides of the decade, Hawthorn and Essendon. When Essendon was knocked out of contention by North and Hawthorn by Carlton, the way was clear for the Blues to take back-to-back flags. Melbourne's Brian Wilson won the club its first Brownlow since 1946, while Malcolm Blight kicked 103 goals for the year.

Richmond slumped in 1983, losing the first five games, which signalled the end of its golden period. North Melbourne looked good in the middle of the season, but fell away in the finals. Footscray and Geelong made promising starts to 1983, but then drifted out of contention. Fitzroy survived a mid-season slump to finish third, but was defeated in the finals, first by Hawthorn when Richard Loveridge kicked a last-minute goal and then by Essendon with a brilliant last quarter. Essendon had defeated Carlton in the Elimination Final and then thrashed North in the Preliminary Final. The Grand Final, however, was typical of 1980s football, for it was a devastating exhibition of disciplined play. Gone were the all-out attacks of the 1970s, which usually produced big but close score-lines. Now the form teams were more likely to break through opposition defences with powerful advances that began with a rebound attack from the half-back line. In the 1983 example, Hawthorn not only piled on 20.20 (140) but also held Essendon to 8.9 (57).

The following season saw the Victorian competition dominated by the 1983 Grand Finalists: Essendon recorded eighteen wins and only four losses, Hawthorn eighteen wins and five defeats. The next closest team was Carlton, with thirteen wins for the home-and-away season. North Melbourne fell away, while Geelong and Footscray were edged out of the finals by Fitzroy. Fitzroy provided the 1984 season with real excitement:

the Lions were perched on the bottom of the ladder in Round 9, with only one win, and then moved steadily up into fifth position and a finals berth. Essendon destroyed Collingwood in the Preliminary Final, 28.6 (174) to 5.11 (41) and so the contestants in the Grand Final were predictably Hawthorn and Essendon. The Hawks had won every encounter with Essendon during the 1984 year and at three-quarter time held a handy four-goal lead. But then in a blistering last quarter the Bombers kicked 9.6 to win easily. Peter Moore, now playing for Melbourne, won the Brownlow, while 'Superboot' Quinlan for the second year running topped the League's goalkicking.

Footscray was the surprise packet in 1985, finishing the season in second place by playing the solid unspectacular game favoured by coach Mick Malthouse. The Bulldogs pushed Hawthorn in the Preliminary Final but did not have an answer for Leigh Matthews, who kicked two important goals. However, Footscray had the pleasure of Brad Hardie winning the Brownlow and Simon Beasley topping the goalkicking for 1985. The Round 12 clash between Hawthorn and Geelong ended in assault charges being laid by the police against Matthews for striking Neville Bruns. Hawthorn's team plan was still imperfect and its form patchy; the Hawks played well at the business end of the season, however. In the Grand Final Hawthorn went down to Essendon nonetheless, with the last quarter turning into an 11-goal rout.

Leigh Matthews moved to Collingwood as coach in 1986 and the Magpies began their storm into the finals. Their full-forward Brian Taylor topped the League's scoring, with 100 goals for the season. Essendon suffered from injuries to several key players and was not a serious proposition. Sydney bought several big-name players and finished second on the ladder. The Swans still struggled on Melbourne grounds, however, and lost both finals matches. The disciplined team plan at Hawthorn now fell into place: the team moved into top position halfway through 1986 and stayed there. Hawthorn lost to Carlton in the Second Semi-Final, but regrouped and walloped Fitzroy by 56 points in the Preliminary Final. Hawthorn then outplayed Carlton in all four quarters of the Grand Final.

The League expanded to fourteen teams in 1987, with the addition of the Bears and the West Coast Eagles. The Bears won only six games, just ahead of trouble-torn Richmond, while the Eagles enjoyed a good start in the VFL with eleven wins. Melbourne was the surprise of 1987, getting to the finals for the first time since 1964 after a stirring win at Western Oval over Footscray in the last round. The Demons then demolished North Melbourne and the Sydney Swans in successive weeks, but ran up against Hawthorn in the famous Preliminary Final. Melbourne led all day but Hawthorn was dogged and deserved to be close at the end. The infamous 15-metre penalty conceded by Jim Stynes after the siren made Gary Buckenara's kick for goal quite easy – but 'Bucky' was a cool customer who would probably have made the distance anyway. With South Australians Stephen Kernahan and Craig Bradley added to its playing list in 1987, Carlton waited in the wings and after a week's rest would have defeated either Melbourne or Hawthorn in the Grand Final, played in very hot conditions. Tony Lockett both topped the 1987 goalkicking and shared the Brownlow with Hawthorn's John Platten.

Collingwood did better in 1988 and went into the finals, playing a robust and defensive style of football; Carlton likewise put in a very consistent year. The Eagles made the finals in only their second year. All three contenders were, however, knocked out by Melbourne, which under John Northey had perfected its defensive game. Starting with the tough backline of Alan Johnson, Danny Hughes and Sean Wight, the Demons got used to having the lowest score kicked against them year in, year out. Even fast-flowing teams like the Eagles ran hard up against Melbourne's wall-like defence. The only real threat to Melbourne, because the Bombers again failed to make the finals, was Hawthorn, which had lost only three games in the entire season. The Grand Final was predictably a bloodbath, with Melbourne having no answer to the waves of brown-and-gold attackers streaming through its shattered defences. It was little wonder that Jason Dunstall was the top-scoring forward, with 132 goals.

Hawthorn was once more the benchmark team of the Victorian competition in 1989, again losing only three matches for the entire year. Under new coach Malcolm Blight, Geelong showed some extraordinary fluctuations in form during the course of the season. Melbourne lost five of its last six home-and-away games but found form in the Elimination Final against Collingwood, with a blistering 9-goal third quarter. Essendon defeated Geelong at its own high-scoring game in the Qualifying Final by tagging its on-ballers Paul Couch and Mark Bairstow. Because Northey used taggers in the same way, Blight benched these two the next week and bamboozled Melbourne. Hawthorn's Dermott Brereton usually saved his best football for the finals and this year knocked out Essendon's Paul Van Der Haar. Essendon was shellshocked and lost the following week to Geelong. In the Grand Final Mark Yeates attempted to deal with Brereton, but Hawthorn, reduced to sixteen players at the end, held off by a goal against the fast-finishing Cats. Gary Ablett that day kicked 9 brilliant goals. The other spoils of the year were shared between the Grand Finalists, with Dunstall again leading the goalkicking and Paul Couch taking the Brownlow.

Geelong and Hawthorn both struggled in 1990. The Cats dropped down the ladder and Hawthorn had to face Melbourne two weeks in a row, in both the last round and the Elimination Final. Melbourne's gritty game came good and it won both encounters, a milestone in the club's history. It was the first time since 1982 that Hawthorn had not made the Grand Final, and this opened the way for the Collingwood–Essendon clash. In this willing encounter a freakish goal by Peter Daicos midway through the first quarter gave the Magpies the confidence they needed to end the club's thirty-two-year Grand Final hoodoo.

The highlight of 1991 was Adelaide's dramatic entry into what was now called the AFL. The Adelaide Crows were given several goals head-start every time they played in front of their parochial one-eyed supporters at Football Park, but were less successful on other grounds. St Kilda won through to its first finals appearance for two decades. Hawthorn recovered its poise and defeated the West Coast Eagles in the Grand Final.[12]

The success of Adelaide and the West Coast in 1991 suggested how much the gap with Victorian teams had now narrowed. Interstate influences on the Victorian game were now evident. There was a productive diversity of styles across state lines. Moving to South Australia in the late 1980s after a career commenced in Victoria earlier that decade convinced ex-Melbourne player Paul O'Brien of the difference in style between the states. South Australian conditions emphasised precision ahead of aggression. 'The best 5 per cent of South Australian players would not score better than the top 5 per cent of Victorians on a skills test – but overall it is true.' 'Chris McDermott is thought of as aggressive, but his skill level is very high.' This became an important consideration as O'Brien got older. When he turned thirty-two, he reflected that 'my precision has become better in later years; I can no longer rely on raw aggression and naked athleticism.' At one stage he gave up football and went to Europe, but found that he was more deeply committed to the game than he realised. 'The adrenalin of that contact is quite amazing really. I went through a stage where I couldn't get footy out of my system. I was in Yugoslavia and I kept having these recurring dreams – about my boots being polished! It was really wild. So it's been good to get back and play!'[13]

From 1987 the interstate games and carnivals dramatised the differences in playing style between Victoria and its western neighbours. For writer Martin Flanagan, who had recently moved to Melbourne from Tasmania, the differences were striking:

> It seemed to me that the Victorians were more practised, more rigid in their ways. They prided themselves on the physicality of their game, but in successive matches the South Australians defeated them with, I thought, skill and imagination. The Victorians seemed to have dug themselves into the sort of hole English professional cricket has become. At the time, all the best rovers in the game originated from outside Victoria. I thought that was significant because the game has to be essentially skill-based for the little man to have a chance. The more overtly physical the game becomes, the more it degenerates into a litany of bruising encounters, the less chance rovers have. I also thought the Krakouers (from Mount Barker WA) played less creative footy the longer they were in Victoria, and they were the most creative players I've seen. West Australian footy has tended to be different again – theirs is an agile, long-running game which has presumably has a lot to do with their larger ovals and their greater proportion of Aboriginal players.[14]

The development of a national competition in the 1980s produced more change than any other decade since the creation of the VFL in the 1890s. The VFL, having embarked on a corporate agenda, set the conditions in which several clubs almost went bankrupt in the mid-1980s, and by the end of the decade had metamorphosed into a national body, the AFL, which was chastened by a major episode right at the end of the decade. This episode began innocently enough with secret discussions between the VFL hierarchy and the Footscray club administration, but it would lead to a surprising conclusion.

Possession
at All Costs

At the cusp of the 1990s there occurred a battle with far-reaching significance for national football. The VFL, in the process of becoming the
AFL, had worked with the then administration of Footscray Football
Club to broker an amalgamation with Fitzroy. But as things turned out,
the battles of the 1980s – South Melbourne in 1981, Fitzroy in 1986 –
were still fresh in people's minds, and community leaders in Melbourne's west were able to wage war quite successfully. A new club
president, local lawyer Peter Gordon, formed a new board of directors.
A new coach was found in an ex-player, Terry Wheeler. The players were
kept out of the limelight (at South Melbourne they had panicked and
gone on strike). Energetic supporters rattled tins on street corners, sold
bumper stickers with provocative slogans such as MERGE OAKLEY INTO
OUTER SPACE, and managed to raise the necessary funds. A book was
produced detailing the story, *Too Tough to Die*.[1]

The Footscray Fightback campaign, as it became known, had several
important implications. One was that it inspired other clubs in the Melbourne area not to go meekly down the South Melbourne path, but to
resist amalgamation or forced relocation, and to raise funds from the
public by appealing directly to tradition in mass campaigns. Richmond
and Fitzroy in particular found some backbone in their dealings with the
AFL. Fitzroy's television advertisements showed Lions trophies and team
photographs of yesteryear being unceremoniously dumped into a freshly-
dug grave at the Brunswick Street Oval: the voice-over claimed that no

League club had ever before had its life extinguished – which shows just how completely University's existence has been forgotten! (Fitzroy's salvation would not come until the end of the 1994 season.)

Another implication of the Footscray episode was its endorsement of tribalism as the underlying logic of football support, despite the apparent domination of Australian Rules football by commercial interests; without community support, the private companies running the new Sydney and Brisbane clubs struggled to keep afloat, while at Footscray a financially weak public entity flourished on an extraordinary swell of popular sentiment. Local builder Cec Sergeant, whose father had worn the Bulldogs guernsey back in '07, quietly explained to an *Age* reporter why his winter Saturdays were spent staring out into the middle of the Western Oval: 'When I look out there, I see him . . .'[2] With that kind of personal identification made public on the front page of the morning newspaper, it was difficult to go wrong. The new Footscray administration also wisely elected to diversify the enterprise, particularly by opening up the Western Oval to a range of sports, including soccer and baseball. The board was expanded to add expertise in these other sports and included local veteran baseballer, Robert Hayes.

In a surprising way, however, the Footscray saga revealed how thoroughly clubs are confined by tradition as well as how they draw strength from their past. Footscray remained a big-hearted battlers' club, reflecting a hard-headed, pragmatic working-class view of the world. Unlike North Melbourne, it was also a decidedly Protestant club. The Protestant working-class way is unornamental, close-lipped, modest. 'It's bad manners in working-class culture to project an image', mused Martin Flanagan when reflecting on the 1993 season, as he followed the Footscray club from one week to the next for a book he was writing. Flanagan was forcibly struck by how unnervingly quiet these Footscray players were. The Choco incident was particularly revealing; but for an injury, Round 21 would have been Brian Royal's two hundredth game, so the cheer squad prepared a suitable banner anyway. However, 'Choco' on crutches and in civvies had to be cajoled to come out of the race and acknowledge the crowd's cheers – it does not do to have tickets on oneself in this culture.[3]

The men who have made up the Footscray board have been cut from the same cloth. The observation is important because it helps explain much about the club's outlook and characteristic response to change.

Footscray's nickname and guernsey colours reflect just how British Prot-estant the community saw itself. The strength of the Footscray Board lies in its homogeneity. Its members reflect the traditional elite of the region – resilient business and civic leaders buoyed by strong religious convic-tions who value persistence and honesty above all else.[4] Before 1989, the strength of this group was also its weakness – it was socially and culturally so homogeneous as to have difficulty in broadening support for the club beyond those barrackers who shared the core values of the Bulldogs. The new elements coming into Melbourne's west during the postwar period were less and less likely to support Australian football. By 1987 only six of the thirty-nine players on Footscray's senior list were from western suburbs backgrounds. The 1989 crisis had the positive benefit of obliging the club to broaden its appeal, to widen its supporter base and local networks. In casting their net wider, they were rewarded; for example, Footscray's champion ruckman Ilija Grgic, from a Croatian background, who was the club's main find of the 1993 season, had grown up not far from the Western Oval without even knowing of the club.

Another consequence of the Footscray episode was that some media commentary has become far more overtly political and critical. This meant a healthy diversity of views. In the 1990s the radio narratives of Tim Lane or Rex Hunt came to replace the continuous print discourse, and the Saturday-night *Herald* slipped from view, closed down even before the *Herald* was amalgamated with Melbourne's morning tabloid, the *Sun*. The print journalists were now writing for a wider variety of readers, male and female, and were more inclined to comment on a club's financial position or corporate morale. Historian Ian Turner was in the vanguard of this trend with a series of articles he wrote for the *Australian* in the late 1970s. Fans were encouraged to think of their team not so much as an assortment of individuals, winning and losing from week to week, as a club which embodied certain values and aspirations. From this point it was a short step to the critique of the Victorian Football League itself (coinciding with the South Melbourne decision of 1982), a trend which broadened with the Footscray events.

However, certain topics still remained taboo, as journalist Gerard Wright explained in 1993; these included the private life of the coaches, and the 'doubtful' decisions of umpires.[5] Gerard Wright's natural habitat is the press box. The modern press box at the Melbourne Cricket Ground overlooks the Members wing; a large low-ceilinged room, its terraced desk-benches can accommodate about fifty journalists. Trained pairs of eyes watch the game through the glass window in unblinking gaze. Quips are despatched like effortless handballs around the room. At each turning point in the game, appreciative cries break the cool professional veneer of these scribes. There is a studied objectivity about their gaze, even though most of these writers barrack for a team themselves. Jack Dyer, whose allegiance is taken for granted, sits near the timekeepers. Stephen Reilly and Rohan Connolly, both black-and-red inside, quietly confide that, five weeks before the 1993 Grand Final, already 'Essendon are the moral Premiers!' Gerard Wright is unusual in that he follows no particular team – rather the game itself. He writes for 'the reasonably football-literate reader, one who can take a few jokes about the game', and believes 'the assumption must be that one is writing for people who weren't there.'[6] There are plenty of journalists who cannot write good football stories; the famous example is Graham Perkin, the legendary chain-smoking editor of the *Age*, who so badly wanted to write football stories that he adopted a pseudonymous by-line and did it anyway. It is a definite advantage to have played the game – Wright ruck-roved at different times for VFA team Werribee, for Shepparton and for Walla Walla (in the Hume League).

Much the same system of notation is used by each of the journalists. As the eighteen players take up position at the start of the game, the names of the remaining pair in each team are noted – these are 'sitting on the bench', that is, the initial interchange players. Then the manning-ups are quickly noted, a process which takes several minutes. Since the published team lists rarely approximate the actual playing positions in modern football, this documentation needs to be rapidly assembled. It looks like this, scribbled across the page:

SMITH	MANN	MARTYN
SEXTON	GRGIC	GRANT

and so on down the page. Each time a goal is kicked, a notation is made, such as

(2.05) Grgic 45 m from mark 6.6.–42

which translates as: 'Two minutes and five seconds into the [second] quarter, Grgic marked and then kicked a goal from 45 metres out, taking Footscray's score to 6.6 (42).'

A perfect example of palming the ball out of
the ruck. The player is Roy Wright, dual
Brownlow Medal winner. (*How to Play Aussie
Rules*, p. 66. Just Collectables!)

(*top*)
Alan Killigrew was renowned for his fiery oratory. The player just to his right is a young Alan Jeans. (*How to Play Aussie Rules*, p. 110. Just Collectables!)

(*bottom left*)
Journalists feed people's enormous interest in football. (Mike Martin)

(*right*)
1990s football: disciplined Eagle Ashley McIntosh clearing the ball. A sparse Melbourne crowd looks on in dismay. (Mike Martin)

The 1962 South Melbourne side.
Back row: R. Kingston, C. Deacon, K. Colvin, N. Forge, J. Trethowan, R. Burke, M. Oaten, D. Howland, K. Mithen, J. Heriot.
Middle row: A. Goodall (secretary), G. Crough, R. Munn, F. Johnson (vice captain), N. McMahen (coach), R. Skilton (captain), H. McLaughlin, R. W. Tait (president).
Front row: B. Bennett, B. McGowan, H. Alexander, A. Dunn, G. Heyme.
(Just Collectables!)

Australian Rules football involves a number of rituals. One of these is the series of signals used by goal umpires to indicate a score has been made. (Mike Martin)

The Foster's Cup, now the Ansett Cup, is the night competition that acts as the final pre-season tune-up for AFL clubs. Here, Tim Darcy launches himself skyward to take a spectacular mark. Robert Scott (no 8) waits as a good rover should, at the front of the pack. (Mike Martin)

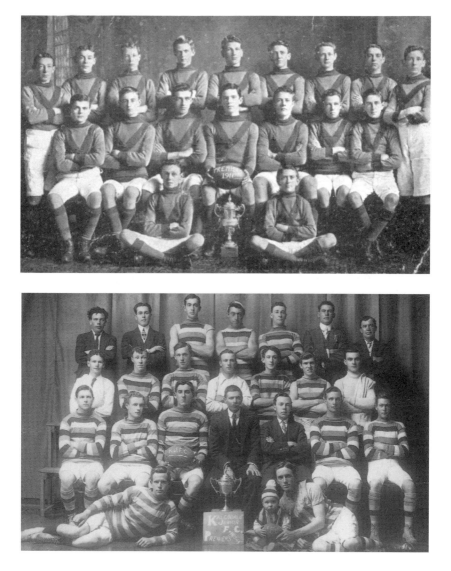

(top)
The Christian Brothers' College, Victoria
Parade, Junior 18 premiership side of 1911.
Catholic schools have produced many
Australian Rules footballers in all states.

(bottom)
The Kalgoorlie Junior Football Club in
1914. (*In Old Kalgoorlie*, by Robert Pascoe
and Frances Thomson, Western Australian
Museum, 1989, p. 162)

(top)
Victorian state training. State of Origin clashes are still an important part of Australian Rules football. (Mike Martin)

(bottom left)
David Parkin fulfilling the 'teacher' role at Carlton during training. (Mike Martin)

(above)
Many clubs produce a newsletter for members and diehard fans. This is a Carlton publication of 1967, showing a Carlton player in a dominant position against archrival Collingwood. (*The Blues*, 1967, front cover. Just Collectables!)

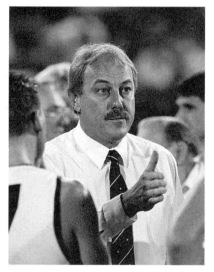

(top)
The St Kilda football team in their pre-war guernseys, with Aboriginal 'mascot'.

(bottom left)
Malcolm Blight encouraged an attacking style of football at Geelong. The style took Geelong to three Grand Finals in Blight's five years as coach. (Mike Martin)

(above)
Alan Joyce is a coach who emphasises discipline and cohesion within a team. (Mike Martin)

Bruce Doull, one of Carlton's best players of recent years, attempting to evade Hawthorn's Jason Dunstall. (Mike Martin)

A selection of club membership passes.
(Just Collectables!)

Kevin Sheedy dishing out another of his
patented backspin handballs to send
Richmond into attack. (Courtesy of
Richmond Football Club)

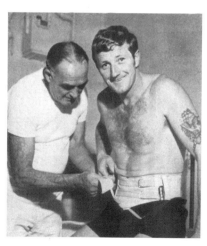

Fitzroy's Kevin Murray has his back brace
fitted by one of every club's most important
people, the trainer. (*Football '70: The Royal
Year*, p. 25. Just Collectables!)

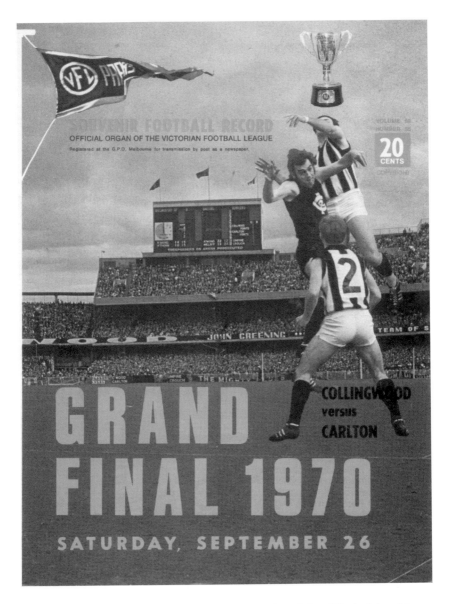

A special 1970 Grand Final edition of the
Football Record, for the match between
Collingwood and Carlton. (*Football Record*,
26 September 1970. Just Collectables!)

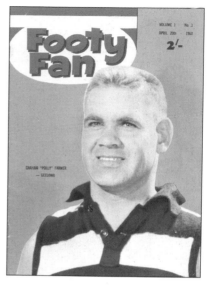

Bernie Smith, the first specialist back pocket player to win the Brownlow. (Just Collectables!)

Graham Farmer on the front cover of *Footy Fan*. In his second year at Geelong he was to play a large part in the Cats' successful premiership campaign. (*Footy Fan*, 20 April 1963, front cover. Just Collectables!)

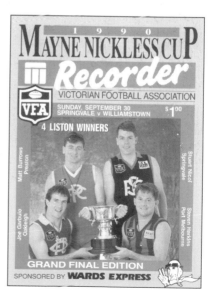

Sam Kekovich appears focussed during this three-quarter time break. (*Football Record*, 12 June 1969, front cover. Just Collectables!)

The VFA is in many ways the 'community code' of Melbourne football. (*VFA Recorder*, Grand Final edition, 1990. Just Collectables!)

Ivor Warne-Smith, c. 1928.
(Melbourne Cricket Club)

Jack Sheedy, a symbol of masculinity, began the tradition of players and ex-players releasing books about their careers and their contemporaries. (*My Football Life*, by Jack Sheedy and Darcy Farrell, front cover)

While newspapers have traditionally been the mainstay of football news, magazines such as *Footy Fan* have played a part in football culture. This edition shows the boom recruit Ray Gabelich in a contemplative pose. (*Footy Fan*, 6 June 1964, front cover. Just Collectables!)

Les Foote was one of North Melbourne's finest players. He was a talented and highly adaptable footballer who could play anywhere on the field.

The 1949 Geelong side.
Back row: D. Brown, B. Morrison, A. Monahan, J. Condon, F. Flanagan (vice captain), J. Hyde, R. Davis, I. Toyne.
Middle row: D. Bauer, B. Smith, L. Turner, J. Fitzgerald, T. Morrow (captain), P. Hunt, R. Renfrey.
Front row: A. Irvine, W. Russell, S. Tate.
(Just Collectables!)

Leigh Matthews addressing Collingwood players during a break in the game. (Mike Martin)

Mick Malthouse has turned the West Coast Eagles into a highly disciplined and skilled side. (Mike Martin)

Dermott Brereton at the peak of his powers.
(Mike Martin)

The 1949 Hawthorn side, in their old guernsey.
Back row: E. Fletcher, M. Williams, C. Philip, A. Prior, R. Boys, V. McKinnon, F. Prowse, K. Hopper.
Middle row: J. Robison, A. Le Nepveu, K. Curran (vice captain), A. Albiston (captain), N. Pearson, C. Austen, G. Anderson.
Front row: J. O'Donohue, R. Fisher, N. Black.
(Just Collectables!)

Hawthorn captain Michael Tuck holding aloft the 1986 premiership cup. (Mike Martin)

Alan 'Yabbie' Jeans was crucial to Hawthorn's success in the 1980s. (Mike Martin)

(above)
Norm Smith and players after the 1957
Grand Final. (Melbourne Cricket Club)

(right)
Ron Barassi, c. 1956.
(Melbourne Cricket Club)

The goals kicked and the other key moments are noted, and any inferences about the direction of attack, or the tactics used by either team, come later. (When the umpires do not hear the half-time siren, and Footscray scores an extra goal, the timekeepers and the journalists are sanguine – they can recall other examples of this happening.) At the end of the match, the journalists make a hurried scrutiny of the match statistics made by officials in the press box. This helps form their judgements about the game, and prepares them for the next stage, the traditional post-match interviews with the coaches. On this occasion the losing coach, Denis Pagan, has a new statistic ready to help explain North Melbourne's predicament: his team had the ball inside its 50-metre scoring end a total of thirty-nine times during the latter half of the game (but only scored twenty-one times). Although no journalist took up this point in his story the next day, all of them (except Jack Dyer) attended the interviews and made some reference to either coach's opinion.

The stories reflect the readership of each newspaper. *Truth* emphasises the individual aspect: because John Longmire was injured in this match, North Melbourne now has no chance to progress in the finals. The *Herald-Sun* account contrasts the earlier match between these teams at the Western Oval, and argues that now the wrong match-ups were used by North Melbourne. Again, individual players are emphasised. In the *Sunday Age*, Wright's version contains a mix of explanations: a plethora of images and metaphors makes up the 1990s account. In Gerard Wright's terms, football is variously a performance ('stage fright'), a comic moment ('the usual Western Oval suspects'), a visual display ('a sea of desperately flailing arms') and at times even a reference to other sports ('the Roos back-pedalled'). The account refers endlessly backwards (to earlier matches or occasions) and also forwards in time.[7]

If newspaper versions alter over time, television coverage hardly changed at all between its beginnings in the late 1950s and the 1990s. The visual techniques employed by the television stations took no advantage of the possibilities of the medium. The closed-circuit version live to air which could be seen in the super-boxes found its way hardly re-edited for the evening public broadcast. None of the techniques favoured by American broadcasters had found their way into the Australian game. Yet the coaches, particularly Kevin Sheedy, had built up libraries of video which enabled them to call up a sample of the most common moves of next week's opponents, and to plan the attack accordingly.

Just as there was now a wide range of views about the game, the diversity of coaching styles was far more obvious. Ex-Tiger Neil Balme took the coaching position at Melbourne in 1993 and put into practice what he had learned about 1990s coaching. His ideas on coaching developed in combination with his management experience. After his playing days, like many other ex-footballers Balme was taken up by Doug Heywood into the packaging industry, and rose through the ranks at Renown & Pearlite (later part of Amcor). His management philosophy is one of 'empowerment', giving players or employees the opportunity to take initiatives, rather than the old-style top-down approach. This means encouraging each player to take responsibility for the club's performance in the act of playing: 'After all, he is the managing director when the ball is in his area!'[8] The secret of good coaching in the 1990s came down to encouraging players to seize the initiative: 'When the Golden Rules metabolise under pressure, the initiative will be spontaneous', according to one young coach. This man had played in a VFL team in the early 1980s; his coach then, who was a strong father-figure, appeared in retrospect to be guilty of over-coaching. Even the most skilled players on that team used to make 'stupid mistakes' under this coach's authoritarian pressure.

Getting the player to think about the club ahead of himself has a number of consequences. One is the importance of general fitness and all-round skills, rather than the old adaptability to one position or another on the field; this has been the contribution of fitness specialists such as Chris Jones. Another is the increased use of set plays, such as the kick-out huddle, developed by Robert Walls at Fitzroy in the early 1980s. A third consequence is helping players deal with the inevitable end of their playing careers; a team-oriented person will accept what is best for the group. Finally, reflex handballs and short passes work best when the receiving player takes responsibility for putting himself in the angle of vision of the team-mate with the ball; the loud and clear calling in Len Smith's sixth Golden Rule is no longer sufficient.

The changes at Melbourne between Northey in the late 1980s and Balme in the 1990s are considerable. Northey favoured long bombs, except when the team was ahead on the scoreboard; Balme calls for greater use of handball. Northey required his full-back to kick out wide to increase the rebound angle; Balme wants an attack set up directly from the backline. Northey emphasised tagging the best opponents and sharking around the packs; Balme deploys the aggressive players up the ground, including Rod Grinter and Peter Rohde in the forward line. Under Northey, Kevin Dyson was a fixed pivot in the centre; under Balme's instructions, Glenn Lovett is a mobile centreman who plays half-a-kick ahead of the game. The finest moment for Northey's defensive style was the gritty pair of back-to-back wins against Hawthorn in the last home-and-away match of 1990 and the Elimination Final of the following week. Balme's free-form style resulted in a purple patch of wins against all the top teams, including Essendon, in the middle of the 1993 season. It also meant that in 1994, Melbourne could twice defeat Hawthorn, its bogey team of the 1980s.

The movement of senior coaches across state lines became less un-usual as the game's national development gathered pace. Malthouse's 'defection' to the West was a symbolic moment. So too was Barassi's move in 1993. When he had finished coaching, Barassi turned to his hotel interests – the upstairs bar at his Mountain View Hotel in Richmond was refurbished as a mock changing room, while the downstairs bar was decorated with a scale model of the MCG on its ceiling. But he was about to become a coach again. In April 1993, at the age of fifty-seven, ironically just three weeks after an April Fool's Day joke about the subject on ABC Radio 3LO, Barassi took over the Swans coaching job. The AFL continued to put a lot of money in to the Sydney venture, which was rapidly becoming its equivalent of Napoleon's march on Moscow, and was visibly relieved when Barassi took up the challenge of coaching what was now officially called the Sydney Football Club (instead of the Sydney Swans). Barassi was sanguine about the Sydney experiment. He admitted the original launch of the Sydney Swans in 1982 had been undertaken for the wrong reason – to save South Melbourne in some form, rather than to create a national competition.[9] There was a further curious irony in his appointment, since South Melbourne had been Norm Smith's last (and futile) coaching effort – Barassi's foster father had gone to try to save South in 1969. It remained to be seen whether Rockfist Rogan could do better.

The appointment of Mick Malthouse as coach to the West Coast Eagles was an interesting example of the new diversity in coaching styles, for the teak-tough Malthouse brought a new discipline to their team plan. The backline became a very stable feature of their play. From 1991 to 1994, across four entire seasons, the defensive sextet (Hart, Brennan, McIntosh, Worsfold, Jakovich and McKenna) played 407 out of 498 possible matches. This is an extraordinary statistic in modern football.[10] Together these backmen conceded only 1572 points for the entire home-and-away season; the average across the AFL that year was 2077 – in short, the Eagles began with an average advantage of almost 4 goals every match! This backline was reminiscent of Melbourne in the 1950s or Essendon in the 1960s. The Malthouse game-plan was simple and effective. Relying on a half-back line which was stronger than any opposing half-forward line in the competition, the Eagles' centre line fell back whenever centre clearance was not achieved; the combined centre and half-backs then worked the ball forward to an open forward set-up from which opponents had been artfully drawn. This basic game plan suited the team well, building on its great running and other strengths, and covering its essential weakness – a lack of firepower up forward. Despite finishing the 1994 home-and-away season on top of the AFL ladder, and winning the flag, the team ranked seventh in scoring.

Burdened by the same one-team baggage which also affects Geelong and Adelaide, the Eagles are subjected to an unhealthy degree of local scrutiny. In fact the mere appointment of a Victorian, Malthouse, as coach in 1990 helped provide an external point of reference for the team. Gradually too there was a mixing of players with other AFL clubs – Paul Peos to Brisbane, Peter Wilson from Richmond, Darren Bennett and, later, Dean Irving to Melbourne. Malthouse developed the more determined defensive play which became an essential feature of the West Coast game plan. Then in 1994 came the long-awaited announcement of a second Western Australian team, based in Fremantle and called (improbably) the Dockers. (An unkind nickname incorporating the team's anchor design followed soon after.) The cynics in Fremantle announced that their community had already provided a football team – called the Eagles! And there is little doubt that the core players of the Eagles mostly have a Fremantle pedigree. (Those not from South Fremantle or East Fremantle come from neighbouring Claremont.) Nicknamed the 'Magnificent Seven', these players were team-mates in the 1985 Teal Cup, won by Western Australia. Two club publications celebrate these seven men.[11] The 'Magnificent Seven' are: John Worsfold (South Fremantle), Guy McKenna (Claremont), Paul Peos (East Perth), Scott Watters (South Fremantle), Chris Lewis (Claremont), Chris Waterman (East Fremantle) and Peter Sumich (South Fremantle). Fremantle's rich vein of football talent has been well-mined by the Eagles. Of the forty-two players on the 1992 team list, twenty-one came from South Fremantle, East Fremantle, or Claremont. Of the 1985 Teal Cup champion team from the West, interestingly, no other players have stepped up into AFL ranks, except the renegade Allen Jakovich. Fremantle selected the Claremont coach Gerard Neesham as its inaugural coach in preparation for the 1995 season. Neesham's 'chip and draw' style is in keeping with the possession game of the 1990s.

The introduction of more systematic training was another feature of the 1990s. The development of traineeships in AFL is connected with the pattern of coaching in the game. Coaches and their assistants are responsible for the apprenticeship of players, but are themselves subject to the whims and opportunities of club politics. Kevin Sheedy has long been an advocate of introducing some kind of traineeship system, and instructed David Wheadon to investigate the British soccer traineeship. The British system gives players skills in first-aid and pulling a beer, but apparently little else. Enlisting the support of coaches and other club officials who were ex-teachers, a TAFE system of professional development was started in 1992. It was one factor in Essendon's premiership win in 1993. In 1994 the AFL joined the scheme (after some reluctance) and 200 traineeships were established. The basic idea is that players work three days at the club, and two days at the Footscray campus of the Western Metropolitan College of TAFE. At the club they are rotated around various tasks and acquire a wide range of skills. Most clubs have enough business interests and connections to develop these skills. Most importantly, however, the players are available on club premises for regular training drills during the working week. Three days a week at 11:30, for instance, the Essendon trainees concentrate on their 'quick-hands' handball disposal, practising this skill over and over.

Traineeships guarantee players a base income while providing them with some job-related skills. Federal funding for Australian football has been poor, because the game is not international. The traineeship scheme (funded to $12m) represents an important breakthrough. There are several issues to be resolved, such as the idea of a training academy at Waverley, which would be the AFL's preference. Players still rely on the generosity of supporters to get employment, but such jobs do not always lead to a career. Players are therefore encouraged to enter tertiary studies, as the hours of university study can be renegotiated to fit training schedules and other club demands.

On reflection, the teaching of Australian football has been very poor, especially in comparison to golf or tennis. With exceptions like Walls, Parkin and Wheeler, coaches have generally been unhelpful in assisting players to analyse and correct errors in skill or match tactics. Essendon during 1993 learned to take a more theoretical approach to the game. The better the team, the less guesswork involved. At Windy Hill on training nights the most common angles from which goals are scored in regular play are marked out on the oval using witches hats. Analysing the statistical basis of a team's success and loss is essential to knowing how to beat it: North Melbourne, for example, is very predictable from a statistical point of view. The future of Australian football relies on footballers and coaches learning from other codes. Each club must become a learning organisation, to acquire concepts and ideas from hockey, soccer and other team sports. North Melbourne's 'front and square' game relies on the hockey principle that players line up for the opportunity to try for goal. Soccer's ideas of space and time, depth and width can be used to reduce the tendency of packs to form at centre half-forward and cenre half-back on the Australian ground. American football carefully measures the scoring ratio of the opposing teams; although the average AFL team kicks an average score of 52 goals, 48 behinds, Footscray kicks only 49 goals from every 100 scoring shots. Goal-scoring can be improved by using the 60-degree angle in front of goal. This is the basketball principle of using the area under the ring to wait for the second chance. Waiting for the second chance in front of the goal is the North Melbourne principle. Melbourne, on the other hand, has now copied Adelaide in over-handling the ball. According to some critics, its style is exposed wherever a weaker player has responsibility for moving the ball on, and can be put under pressure.

Great coaches, like Neesham, Hafey and Pagan, have their protégés all over Australia. Sheedy is rather more of an isolate, but a Sheedy school will develop in time. He is a most positive loser, someone who can conjure up a win from defeat. With the development of coaching, good sports writing and other theorising, Australian football becomes more diverse and more interesting.[12] Writing about football is now not only the province of ex-players, journalists and coaches, but also academic and literary authors.

Much of what was written about the game until the 1990s had a desperate tone to it, a cringe about whether this indigenous game was fit to earn the attention of serious writers. Indeed, very few intellectuals admitted to enjoying the game; fewer still incorporated football into their writing and social theorising. In 1985 one Australian literary encyclopaedia could only admit to there being one poet, two playwrights and two historians writing about the game. This is a serious understatement.[13] For example, the doyen of Australian Rules football was an academic, Ian Turner, a professor of history at Melbourne's Monash University. The day after Turner's sudden death in 1978, the city's morning tabloid honoured him with the placard FOOTY PROF DIES. Turner would have liked that, although an obituary writer could have summed up his career in other ways – Turner achieved much else in his life. The significance of the poster was that Turner was the first academic to take seriously a game which had been so central to the lives of his fellow Melburnians during the previous 120 winters that it was, ironically enough, very much taken for granted.

Turner's mentor Manning Clark also loved football, and the Carlton Football Club in particular. But the game does not figure prominently in his magnificent six-volume epic, *A History of Australia*. The line dividing aesthetes from athletes was so strong in Australian universities that Australian football did not enjoy the respectability of English cricket as a topic for the academic common room. The turning point came in 1988 with the publication of an anthology, *The Greatest Game*, in which the football thoughts of two dozen writers were collected. Among these was Martin Flanagan.

Born in Tasmania in 1955, Flanagan grew up on a healthy diet of the satirical weekly *Nation Review*, English sports writers, and contemporary poets like Phillip Larkin. Although often thought of as a sports writer himself, Flanagan's own work encompasses poetry and human-interest journalism, as well as fiction. While posted to a Burnie boarding school for his adolescence, Flanagan learned a great truth about Australian life: 'Sport was the one place which had imagination and passion and feeling.' He invested his imaginative self during those years in sport: 'I think if you invest that much of yourself in it at that particular time then in a sense that's everything you need to know about sport!' Flanagan continued to play football at the University of Tasmania while studying law; in the university team he had a role as its chronicler and court jester.

Two years after graduation he went to live in Glasgow; there he discovered that writers could find a social role for themselves in describing everyday life. When he came to Melbourne in 1985, all he knew were the suburbs which had lent their names to the great football teams of the VFL. He knew of Footscray, for instance, but he knew little of Melbourne's west.[14]

Throughout the 1993 season, Flanagan followed the Footscray team week in and week out. The book which resulted, *Southern Sky, Western Oval* belongs to the same genre as *The Coach*, a match-by-match account of North Melbourne under coach Barassi in 1977. In retrospect, *The Coach* was football seen through the thick coating of media gloss. Its photographs were televisual trick-shots; its description was newspaper-style; its analysis was as circumstantial as a coach's post-match address. *Southern Sky, Western Oval* could not be more different; it eloquently captures the cadence and rhythm of the game. Indeed, it is told from right inside the game. The mass media are absent. The unblinking eye of the television, the bloodless prose of the mass-circulation press, the insubstantial commentary of commercial radio, none of these artificial spectators can get a word in edgeways. Clichés have not been allowed to intrude; not one player is described as 'flamboyant'; there is not one 'living legend'; and no match 'goes down to the wire'.

Instead this account is a direct transposition onto the printed page of the cries and whispers of the crowd, the odd faces and gesticulations of the anonymous barracker – 'the man with the red face and small black eyes' you see once and never again – and the momentary flash of insight from the player Flanagan sits alongside during the long plane ride to Perth. The thumbnail sketches in this book are dazzling. Port Melbourne identity Tommy Lahiff has come to help Footscray – Tommy looks 'like an army biscuit on legs'. The coach is excited at the start of the season – 'Wheeler was bouncing on his toes, chest full of air, liquid brown eyes alive with good humour.' Brave little rover Tony Liberatore shrugged his tag in Round 22, 'like a man ridding himself of an overcoat in hot weather'.[15] The clue to Flanagan's style is that when interviewed he sounds just as he reads. All the hallmarks of orality are there in the text – transitions back and forward in time as smooth as they are in conversation; pithy aphorisms ornamental to the prose; and the agonistic qualities of a surging crowd mid-way through a game.

Finally, the book ends with Wheeler's controversial sacking a few

games into the 1994 season. Wheeler is the charismatic coach the club needed during its moment of crisis in 1989. Four seasons later, just as Max Weber would have predicted, the forces of rationality require a stricter disciplinarian, and the job is given to the hard-headed Alan Joyce. Wheeler is a genuine visionary, a natural orator and an inspiring teacher; his philosophy of coaching reflected his professional background. He did not impose his own style of play as a backman onto the players; rather, he sought to create the conditions of team structure where each Bulldog could express his own individuality and skills. His favourite pupil was 'The Axe', Simon Atkins. Playing in the pivotal centre, Atkins was one of the AFL's top possession getters in 1992 – he embodied the creative spark of Wheeler's ideal team. But when The Axe was tagged out of contention in 1993, this revealed the essential vulnerability of Wheeler's style.[16] (Atkins left the Bulldogs at the end of 1994.)

Writing about football improved during the 1990s; so did the comedy. The game's traditional inner-suburban larrikinism was successfully translated into a mass media product. The essence of this new comedy was its disarming frankness, its subversive search for a 'truth' about the game. It was expository, revealing, investigatory; when the journalists were not prepared to talk about what went on behind the closed doors of clubs, the comedians did. People in the street felt just as cut off from the wheeling and dealing of the big rich football clubs as they did from the company boardrooms and political party rooms. Dark forces lurk behind the game, just as in real life: 'And they know who *they* are!' is the catchcry of the Coodabeen Champions on Saturday morning radio. We cannot name the evil that stalks our everyday existence, but football comedy makes us feel better because we can easily describe the game's wreckers.

Comedy in football is of various kinds. One is the parody of the aggrandisement of the game, poking fun at those who make large claims about particular players or clubs. (Every second player is so talented he must be in line to win the Brownlow.) Another is a muted critique of the business aspects of the game. ('How much did they pay you for that goal, Umpire?') Another may be called the variety-club style of humour. (Lou Richards dresses up in vaudeville costume.) All these kinds of comedy work best in ensemble form, not as individual stand-up, precisely because the game's humour originates in the crowd. Hence the need for three or more characters in a panel, a tradition which continued

into the 1994 season and Channel 9's 'The Footy Show'. This program reverted to the panel format for the accidental reason that Channel 7 refused to provide them with footage, and the result was striking. The program immediately attracted a huge following – largely because it resonated, perhaps unwittingly, with some very deeply set characteristics of football humour. For example, the traditional role of the footy pub in transmitting the game's humour was illustrated by one of the program's regulars, the comedian Trevor Marmalade, who was portrayed as the know-all barman.

Comedy, then, derives its power from the nostalgic roots of the game, and sets the observer in a position of opposition to the changes being brought wilfully into the game. Even something as innocuous as the match ratio device used to determine ladder position, when it was introduced in 1991, was successfully lampooned as a symbol of the new-fangled changes being foisted onto the game. Humour can hardly be brought to bear against the game – Keith Dunstan's Anti Football League is odd precisely because it is such a rarity. However, since football went national, the television audiences barrack in the privacy of their own lounge rooms; no longer are there two adversarial groups at every match. Curiously, Australian Rules has failed to produce fan magazines like the British football publication, *Foul.* Yet it is still true that the barrackers want to resist the industrialisation of the game, especially at times when their own lives are being thoroughly modernised.[17]

Comedians found it easy to defend a club like Footscray from the clutches of the AFL, because it stood for an inner-suburban innocence to which everyone could relate. Here is one example from the Coodabeen Champions in 1991:

TONY LEONARD:	Wasn't it good last Saturday driving through the back streets of Footscray? Past old Dr Con's surgery on Commercial Rd, up Shepherd St, past the high-rise flats, outside Charlie Sutton's old pub.
IAN COVER:	One of the great disappointments of my life last Saturday was actually, Tony, getting out of the car, because to that stage I'd had a half-hour trip around Footscray, having all the landmarks pointed out to me: 'Yeah, used to go to that shop . . . Yeah, great burgers there . . . Yes, good betting there . . .'

TONY LEONARD: Yes, it's just wonderful.

IAN COVER: And as we were driving around the streets of Footscray we saw the people on foot making their way to the Western Oval to see Footscray play Essendon and Tony said to me in the car . . . I said, 'It's pretty big out here, you know, Footscray and Essendon.'

TONY LEONARD: You know, there was a bloke standing behind me and he obviously does not like the suburb of Essendon, not necessarily the team. He started barracking for Footscray. Knows nothing about it. He says, 'Ah, got the ball, he's my man Atkinson, he's my man Atkinson!' Another bloke says, 'You moron, his name's Atkins', and the bloke turns around and says, 'I'm using my Japanese, mate!' Which I thought was a very snappy answer.[18]

The maturing of the national competition in the 1990s had different consequences for local and state leagues across Australia. Country football was in a poor state generally, and mergers were common in some regions as clubs struggled to cope with population shifts and the decline of industry. More hours of televised AFL football kept at home people who would otherwise be out watching their local club. The Amateurs and the VFA continued, but their crowds did not grow in size. Western Australian football was certainly not as popular in the 1990s, thanks to the effect of the national competition. Only 18,000 people attended the 1994 Grand Final, a contest between East Fremantle and Claremont. The Tasmanian league was also struggling in the 1990s against televised AFL games. The 1994 Grand Final played at North Hobart attracted a crowd of only 14,000. Clarence won its first back-to-back flag in a good contest with New Norfolk. In the Northern Tasmanian Football League Grand Final, Ulverstone defeated Latrobe in front of 6000 spectators. Ulverstone has been invited to join the TFL.

North Launceston, which joined the Tasmanian Football League in 1986, is coached by David Rhys-Jones (South Melbourne, Carlton, 1980–92). 'The Robins' have come close to a flag for several seasons. South Launceston (1986) is coached by Dale Weightman (Richmond, 1978–93), who has given 'the Bulldogs' new bite. Burnie (1987) is coached by another VFL veteran, Mark Lee (Richmond, 1977–91) and combines the Burnie Hawks and Burnie Tigers. Launceston (1994) was the only other North Tasmanian club to join the TFL and is still finding its feet. New Norfolk (1986), nicknamed 'the Eagles' are financially strong and have attracted good players. Glenorchy (1986) won the flag in its first TFL year, but 'the Magpies' have struggled in recent seasons. 'The Seagulls', Sandy Bay (1986) play out of North Hobart Oval, along with Hobart (1986), 'the Tigers', and North Hobart (1986), 'the Demons'. The Demons have won half the TFL flags (1987, 1989, 1991, 1992). Clarence, led by talented Stevie Wright (South Melbourne/Sydney, 1979–92), plays out of Bellerive Oval as the Roos. Finally, the eleventh current TFL team is the Devonport Blues, now coached by big Andy Goodwin (Richmond, Melbourne, 1987–93). In this restructured format, Tasmanian football has a chance of surviving as a serious competition.

Canberra football has also survived. In 1923 the ACT Australian Football League was formed, then called the Canberra Football League. The first teams were Acton (nicknamed the 'Jackaroos'), Canberra (made up of tradesmen and builders), Federals (labourers, miners, sewer-workers) and Duntroon (mostly civilians). There were many changes in teams, and by 1930 the sides were Eastlake, Ainslie, Queanbeyan, Acton and Manaka. Acton was replaced in 1974 by West Canberra, and teams from Belconnen (1971) and Sutherland (1979) entered the competition.

Football also continued to flourish in the Northern Territory, where the season runs over the summer months. Teams such as St Mary's (the Saints, in green and gold), the Darwin Buffaloes, the Wanderers, North Darwin, Northcliff and Waratah/Palmerston make up a vigorous competition. Exhibition matches involving a composite Northern Territory side have been played against teams from all around Australia, including South Fremantle (1973), the Australian Amateurs (1979), won by the visitors; Queensland (1974), Glenelg (1985), Essendon (1986) and the Swans (1987), won by the locals. The first organised clubs in the Northern Territory were the Waratahs and the Wanderers, who played off at Darwin in January 1917. A third team, the Warriors, comprising employees of the Vestey Meatworks, formed soon after.

South Australian football continued to flourish in Adelaide in the 1990s. The 1994 Grand Final was won by Port Adelaide (its thirty-second premiership) coached by John Cahill. It was Cahill's five hundredth match and his ninth flag, equalling the record of Fos Williams. The 1994 runners-up were the newly amalgamated side, Woodville–

West Torrens. The match was attended by a respectable-sized crowd of 41,000. From 1995 South Adelaide (the Panthers) will relocate further south, to Noarlunga. In 1993 Glenelg moved back to its traditional oval on the bay. The South Adelaide move parallels the decision in 1964 to take football north to Elizabeth, when Central District entered the senior competition. There are now nine teams in the state competition: the black-and-white Magpies, Port Adelaide (1870), based traditionally at Alberton Oval, but happy to move to Adelaide Oval if that is the price for joining the AFL; Glenelg (1921) at Glenelg Oval, in black and gold (the Tigers); Woodville–West Torrens (1990) playing out of Woodville Oval in green and blue, with a gold eagle (the Eagles); North Adelaide (1883), the Roosters attired in red and white, based at Prospect Oval; South Adelaide (1877), the Panthers in navy blue and white, previously based at Adelaide Oval; West Adelaide (1897) in black with a red sash, based at Richmond Oval (the Bloods); Norwood (1878) at Norwood Oval in navy and red, nicknamed the Redlegs; Central District (1964), better known as the Bulldogs, in red, white and blue, based at Elizabeth Oval; and Sturt (1901), whose guernsey lends the nickname Double Blues, based at Adelaide Oval.

The South Australians kept the Victorians at a safe distance for many years – their suspicion of the AFL's motives would be confirmed by the events of 1995. Instead of relying on cricket grounds such as Adelaide Oval, the South Australian league was keen, like the then VFL, to develop its own ground. Their own oval, Football Park, opened in May 1974, quickly became the state's premier football facility, and superseded Adelaide Oval as a place where finals could be played. Thus the SANFL was more successful than the VFL had been in the development of Waverley. By 1993 the eleven millionth fan walked through the turnstiles at Football Park. But in 1995 the AFL announced a deal with the Adelaide Oval cricket authorities for an upgrade of that facility which would permit the second South Australian club, Port Adelaide, to use it as a home base. So the political battles between football authorities which have bedevilled the game in the past will continue in the future.

What else is there to say about the future of the game?

Future Prospects

Zones and
Set Plays

What does the immediate future hold for the game? Set plays and zonal strategies are part of a growing interest in ritualised recreation. As the world around football becomes more chaotic, new patterns and formalities will emerge within the game itself. Will the game become more commercialised? Australian football is not merely commercialised – according to Bob Stewart, it has recently moved into a new stage of hyper-commercialisation. Football's commercial development can be measured by the dramatic increase in the operating expenses of each club in the 1990s compared to what was the common pattern, say, three decades ago.

'I played a few games on the wing at Melbourne in the mid-1960s,' explained Stewart. 'When I went looking for the administration of the Melbourne Football Club, what I found was the secretary, Jim Cardwell, and a part-time typist. That was the sum total of the administration!' Thirty years on, any senior club typically has about a dozen staff forming its administration. A club's annual turnover has increased in the meantime from approximately $65,000 in the mid-1960s to more than $5 million in the mid-1990s. Inflation notwithstanding, that represents a significant widening of the game's commercial base. Bob Stewart's thesis is that this commercialisation has increased in direct proportion with what in marketing jargon is called 'product innovation'. In other words, rule changes in football can be explained largely as a means of increasing the gate takings from a public which wants to be entertained by a faster and more skilful game.

'The game was not very attractive on a wet Saturday afternoon in July in the 1960s.' It is contestable whether rule changes can be summed up by a term such as 'product innovation'. Many changes to the game's laws owed their origin to the wish of administrators to even out the competition. Changes in the 1960s, for instance, were partly designed to answer the challenge posed by John Kennedy's commando-style strategies at Hawthorn.

There are definite limits to the game's commercialisation. Unlike American baseball, for example, Australian clubs have remained public entities. All attempts at creating privately owned clubs (in Sydney and in Brisbane) have failed, despite the AFL's best efforts. Football is a subsidised industry, like Australian manufacturing. The entrance price for adults was traditionally about the cost of a beer. Even in the 1990s, the ticket to a game cost less than a bottle of good chardonnay. The public accepted that the real cost of its attendance was three times that amount, and was happy to accept some signage, free tickets for local worthies, and the modest style of commercialisation which indicated local business support for the suburban club.

Over time, the club tribalisms spilled across the artificial boundaries on the map. The 1994 round of council amalgamations in Melbourne did not diminish tribal support for Richmond, Collingwood, or any of the other old municipalities. If undertaken much earlier, such reforms might have had a dramatic effect. Local government support was important in fostering the first clubs; these clubs then won a level of support which transcended municipal borders.

As for the future of the game, Barassi has been one of its great visionaries. He was wrong to predict in 1977 that private ownership of clubs would supersede the traditional, members-based system so peculiar to Australian football. But he did say: 'A decade from now, I would like to think I could be coaching a Sydney team' in a national competition. 'In my spare time, I will be sitting on my patio at Potts Point, overlooking Sydney Harbour, and wondering who will be spearheading the invasion of America!'[1]

Rugby League will not usurp Australian Rules football in Melbourne. The State of Origin match at the MCG on 8 June 1994 attracted a huge crowd, not because of any sudden interest in Rugby League, but because tens of thousands of Melburnians wanted to share in an event. It was 'a unique thing', 'worth looking at', with a strong novelty value: 'I wanted to be there on a historic occasion', as one MCC Member put it.

The MCG has always been an important place for people to meet. An estimated 130,000 people took part in the Billy Graham Crusade in 1959; 121,626 were there to watch the famous 1970 Grand Final; roughly 120,000 attended the finale of the Eucharist congress in 1973; and 107,700 patrons were at the opening ceremony of the Olympic Games in 1956. Indeed, the only disappointing crowd at this venue was for the Pope's visit, when one could tell by all the empty seats in the Members area that the MCC still did not have many Catholics in its ranks!

The 1994 Rugby League match was the third hosted at the MCG; the first was in 1878 between Carlton and the Waratahs; the second in 1914. On each occasion the crowd did not fully understand or appreciate what was happening on the field. The Barassi Line separating the two football codes was as rigid as ever.

The future of Australian football is tied to the political system. Australian football and political parties have a long connection, but it is not a simple relationship. Many parliamentarians, especially on the Labor side, have built a political career through sporting networks, especially Rules. The founding father of Collingwood was W. D. Beazley, who became Speaker of the House in the Victorian Parliament in the early years of this century. The socialist John Scaddan, nicknamed 'Happy Jack' for his extravagant public-sector spending while Premier of Western Australia, was an active president of Subiaco, going regularly to matches and sitting on the coach's bench. Several leading politicians have played senior football (Don Chipp played creditably for the VFA team Prahran, and three senior games with Fitzroy in 1947) and some have belonged to the 'hundred royal families' in Melbourne, Adelaide and Perth whose talented sons have dominated the game. Examples include Neil Tresize, Ray Groom and Brian Dixon. John Curtin's nephew played for Fitzroy during the Second World War. No senior politician on either side of politics has ever declined to be a ticket-holder of a club. Even Don Dunstan, a champion of new definitions of masculinity, was a strong supporter (Norwood).

The reason is very simple. Australian football has a tribal energy which politicians understand and respect. Phil Cleary, the federal independent who took Bob Hawke's seat from Labor, is a former footballer and coach who intuitively understood the power of this local energy. The suburban club is a powerful means of mobilising opinion on any issue, and as an organisational form is hard to beat. (Indeed, the local sporting club is the building block of the new Forza Italia movement.) The reasons for this renewed interest in sporting clubs are not difficult to identify. The collapse of Stalinist economies and the proliferation of international communication systems make it very difficult for political parties of either extreme. Political and cultural allegiances are far more contestable. Citizens are far more knowledgeable about political and cultural events occurring across national boundaries. Sport is an example of a cultural event which can be viewed from a distance – hence the fear that Victorian schoolchildren know more about American basketball than their own indigenous code of football. In popular culture there is the spectre of an Orwellian future (and a Roman past) where millions of spectators watch a blood-sport which has no grander purpose than to keep them entertained and distracted.

This scenario is mistaken. With the globalisation of culture, there has in fact been a process of retribalisation. Privately, people are more likely to respond to this shrinking of world distances by defining themselves more and more as members of closely-defined cliques or social groups. So, with every step in the process of European unification, for example, has come the local claims for sovereignty of the Welsh, the Sicilians, the Basques and the rest. Add to this mixture the new politics of the women's movement and the environmental lobby, and the result is a postmodern challenge for national political parties. Sport is important because at its best-managed it provides a means for these groups to find sources of cultural attachment. Within major sports, each club has a 'character' which helps define and sustain divergent blends of belief and hope. Sport is thus part of the agenda of 'communitarian politics', and this is clearly the immediate future of Labor Parties in Australia, Britain and elsewhere. Communitarian politics has at its core the notion that societies need to have their moral and ethical precepts carefully articulated, and that the role of the political class is not merely to argue over the division of the society's spoils (resource politics) but to debate these underlying normative issues (what sort of society we think we are). Sport takes centre stage precisely because it inculcates certain values (literally, that which is sporting).

Sport is therefore not merely a cultural sideshow. The claim that AFL players are entertainers, and therefore should be covered by the same terms and conditions as other workers in the entertainment industry, sounds intuitively right, but is actually quite wrong. The correct industry grouping is in fact the cultural industry. The popular conception of footballers would divide them off from members of Melbourne's artistic set, but Gary Ablett and John Brack have much more in common than either would probably recognise.

What will be the future governance of football? 'I love my football but I can't stand the League!' has long been a common cry of Victorians. The reasons are deeply embedded in the state's history, and can be traced back to a popular distaste for overbearing authority. Indeed, even governments of all hues have had difficulties with the League. In 1982 and 1983 the young Cain Government intended to view favourably the shifting of the Grand Final to Waverley, but the more that Cain's officials examined the issue, the more they found the stodgy tradition-bound MCC easier to deal with than the then VFL. The retention of the MCG as the venue for the Grand Final was the first step in the chain of events which led to the AFL co-operating with the MCC in the building of the Great Southern Stand. The Kennett Government has already had a private dispute with the AFL over the plans for a Museum of Sport to be built on the Jolimont Railyards site.

On the other side of the ledger, the AFL is in one sense the whipping-boy for the various clubs. The League can be used as an excuse for almost anything that goes wrong in the game. The League has also done more than any other peak football body to promote the development of junior football, especially since it created the Under-Nineteens competition in 1945.

The real issue is in fact the League's form and structure; instead of being a corporation or managing agent, it should be transformed into a regulatory body, with statutory powers and responsibilities. There is an implicit conflict in an AFL which sees itself as a private corporation dealing with sixteen clubs which are all public and voluntary associations. The failure of the private clubs (Brisbane, Sydney) during the 1980s was a major victory for the traditions of the game (and a victory for communitarian politics). The solution is to make the AFL a better regulator. Its problem is not that it should not regulate; its problem is that it does not know how to regulate. The Players' Association should have a representative on the Commission; there should be other community-derived representatives (playing the kind of role that the late Jack Hamilton was meant to play), and the restructured AFL should look beyond merely the USA for ideas on how to regulate sporting contests.

In the 1994 season it was the judiciously balanced fixtures much more than the salary cap or the draft system which ensured an even competition. So the poor aspects of the 1995 season's fixture, such as the timing of the interstate match, are a more glaring problem than ever.

So one prospect is a new role for the AFL as a regulator. At the same time, the clubs themselves need an injection of new talent and ideas. Footscray has only just begun to seek new ways of attracting Vietnamese and other immigrant supporters. Its star ruckman of 1993 and 1994, Ilija Grgic, grew up near the Western Oval in a Croatian subculture which did not even know that Australian Rules existed. More women should be drafted onto the club boards of management. Government should invest in training programs for the new boards, using sports academics as appropriate.

Clubs and the AFL have to learn more about their own supporters – where they live, what their demographics are, how far they would be prepared to travel to see their team, and so on. The glaring example of this blind-spot was the 1982 move of the Swans to Sydney. The group within South Melbourne which engineered the move assumed that real-life barrackers would be happy to become television spectators, and that the Sydney crowds would rapidly increase to more than 20,000 paid-up members. The Melbourne supporters of the Swans did indeed drop away, but the average crowd size at the SCG a decade later was only 12,000. South Melbourne would have done better to move to Moorabbin, as the Hennessey Report urged, where St Kilda had gone seventeen years earlier. The game's essential tribalism will be proven when, in the west, Fremantle will develop as a proletarian club, outdistancing the increasingly middle-class Eagles.

Political parties have a role in the future of the game. The future of the game in Victoria is too important for economic and cultural reasons for the Government and the Opposition to ignore. Yet sport has such a taken-for-granted quality in our culture that it does not get the attention from the political parties that it deserves. One of the interesting ironies in the late Ian Turner's life was that he did more than any other academic to promote a debate about football, and he did more than anyone else to help Labor rewrite its platform for the 1972 election, but he never linked the two projects.

For Turner and for most Australians, the gap between the aesthetes and the athletes remained unbridgeable. One had to make a choice between a football match and an art gallery opening – the two were mutually exclusive. People lost sight of the fact that Victorians could indeed excel both in football and in art: two-thirds of all Australian art resides in Victoria, yet no-one has ever suggested moving a Victorian art gallery to Sydney.

Football clubs deserve the same attention we give to the preservation and restoration of National Trust buildings. Not only do they have an intrinsic cultural value, they also generate tourism and other economic benefits. There should be more books of interpretation, including translations for foreign visitors, and more effort put into linking tourism publicity with the season's fixtures. American baseball fixtures are known more than a year in advance, and calendars and other promotional materials are prepared accordingly.

What will be the industrial status of players in the future? Players should be protected by the same conditions which apply to other workers in the cultural industries. The father-son rule and other regulations which safeguard the traditions of the game should be continued. The free-agent rules which apply to European soccer should be trialled. The salary cap exists less to protect the game and more to help clubs bargain with players; it should be raised and set against a reasonable benchmark (such as a percentage of gross takings). Zoning cannot be reintroduced as it probably constitutes a restraint of trade, and the draft may not survive legal challenge. Hence the clubs should be given new responsibilities for developing district football, and first-refusal of players coming up through those local ranks. The new traineeships for AFL players financed by the Federal Government should be supported by state initiatives.[2]

Australian football has a centrality in the national culture equivalent to baseball in America. The questions about its origins, successes and future are also asked about baseball in the United States, particularly in the aftermath of the 1994 players' strike.

The Victorian market can be developed further. The future of the eleven Victorian clubs is no longer a real issue, as long as a finite amount of funding is made available to develop young players from all parts of the state. Even the weakest AFL club, Fitzroy, on its best day can take in $15,500 in gate receipts. The main reason people attend a match is to experience once more the sense of excitement of a closely fought contest. Television does not provide this; the nuances of play are not captured and textual intrusions such as the time-clock detract from the game's immediacy.

There will always need to be a minimum-sized crowd, and the challenge for the five weak clubs (Fitzroy, Footscray, Richmond, North Melbourne and Melbourne) is to ensure that at least 15,000 or so people actually attend their matches. Within an evenly fixtured competition, this requires each team to have a 'character' which is appropriate to the team's history, traditions, current game plan, and leading personalities. The history of the game is littered with mistakes by club managements which went against this principle. (To cite one embarrassing example: in about 1938 the Fitzroy Football Club decided to adopt the nickname, the Gorillas, an idea which lasted only until 1957.) Another option is the novelty approach – such as having Fitzroy play one or two home games each season in a country town such as Ballarat or Albury. Trains and coaches could take the faithful from Melbourne's suburbs (which was not possible when the idea was tried in Tasmania several seasons ago). No Victorian country town has enough commerce to sustain an AFL club, but one-off crowds of 15,000 could be mustered for such events. The better weather of northern Victoria would be attractive in mid-July when the Western Oval becomes unfriendly, and Ballarat could host a Lions match in the early spring. The Nauru Government, looking at football from a distance, understands enough about the benefits of identity to invest in Fitzroy during 1994.

The game will be exported into Asia, in the same way that American baseball has its Asian equivalent (and has been improved upon in Taiwan, Japan and elsewhere).

When will women join AFL ranks? Women's football is healthy in South Australia and Victoria; competitive football in the Victorian Women's League was by the mid-1990s a contest among seven clubs, including Ballarat and Bendigo. Some suburban clubs, such as Northcote Park, fielded both male and female teams. Women's role as supporters is now recognised by two AFL clubs which have women on their boards. Women have been senior umpires in Western Australia since 1989 and at junior levels elsewhere.

Clubs should be encouraged by the Victorian Government to recognise and promote their distinctive character. The market is bigger than they know, and their own club histories are more interesting than the public is allowed to know.

Finally there is no doubt about the future of black football. Australian Aborigines were playing *marn-grook* before Tommy Wills went to Rugby school; they adapted well to the white rules after the 1930s; and from the 1960s they brought new skills and ideas into the game. In the 1990s, Martin Flanagan commented: 'The people who have added the most to it in recent times have been the Aboriginal players, with just the odd exception, such as Ablett and maybe Carey. Some say Williams has Aboriginal blood and doesn't care to admit it. But all the other talents have been Aboriginal players, especially the Krakouers, Lewis (a classic footballer), Michael Long (entirely unorthodox), Maurice Rioli . . . In Yuendumu, I was told that Australian football has real affinities with the corroboree – real flight and grace.'[3]

Writing Your Own Club History

Look at good models. Find a club history which is similar to the one you would want to write. Consider factors such as the character of your club, its age, and whether your readers would be more interested in an emphasis on match results, individual personalities of the past, or the club's administration. Once you have found a club history similar to the one you are contemplating, read it carefully and critically.

Identify your sources. Survey what is readily available; make lists of the kinds of materials to which you can get access. Are there older players still living in the district you can meet? Has someone kept the old club records in their attic? Do local newspapers contain match descriptions? Does the town library have a vertical file system with newspaper cuttings? After all this searching, there will be gaps. How can you cover these absences in the formal record?

Interview and triangulate with documents. Begin by interviewing the oldest informants first, partly as a mark of respect to veteran players and administrators, but also because they are more likely to die first and take valuable memories with them. When interviewing, use a tape recorder and have your questions written out in advance. Develop a worksheet with much the same questions and blank spaces where you can enter extracts of their answers. Using much the same questions means you will be able to generalise later. Ask to borrow photographs and newspaper clippings, as these will aid your informant's memory and prove useful when designing your book. With each answer, think about the documentary materials which would support or modify what you are being told, and how you might go about getting them. For instance, someone's residential address in a particular year can be checked through the Post Office Directories in Western Australia or the **Sands and MacDougall's** listings in Victoria. One informant's memory can be checked by asking the right question of another informant: this process is called 'triangulation'.

Statistics

Premiers, Runners-up, Medallists and Leading Goalkickers

Victorian Football Association, Victorian Football League and Australian Football League

	Premiers	Runners-up	Brownlow medallist or Champion of the Colony	Leading goalkicker
1877	Carlton	Melbourne	G. Coulthard (Carlton)	C. Baker (Melbourne) 12 goals
1878	Geelong	Melbourne	H. P. Douglass (Geelong)	G. Coulthard (Melbourne) A. Christie (Geelong) 15 goals
1879	Geelong	Carlton	G. Coulthard (Carlton)	G. Coulthard (Melbourne) 19 goals
1880	Geelong	South Melbourne	James Wilson (Geelong)	H. P. Douglass (Geelong) 33 goals
1881	South Melbourne	Geelong	James Wilson (Geelong)	E. Brooks (Carlton) 25 goals

	Premiers	*Runners-up*	*Brownlow medallist or Champion of the Colony*	*Leading goalkicker*
1882	Geelong	Essendon	James Wilson (Geelong)	H. McLean (Geelong) 29 goals
1883	Geelong	South Melbourne	John Baker (Carlton)	Phil McShane (Geelong) 29 goals
1884	Geelong	Essendon	J. T. Kerley (Geelong)	Phil McShane (Geelong) 33 goals
1885	South Melbourne	Essendon	Peter Burns (South Melbourne)	G. Houston (Hotham) 38 goals
1886	Geelong	South Melbourne	J. C. Pearson (Essendon)	Phil McShane (Geelong) 51 goals
1887	Carlton	Geelong	John Worrall (Fitzroy)	T. McShane (Geelong) 36 goals
1888	South Melbourne	Geelong	D. D. McKay (South Melbourne)	D. D. McKay (South Melbourne) 50 goals
1889	South Melbourne	Carlton	W. J. Hannaysee (Port Melbourne)	J. E. Barratt (South Melbourne) 40 goals
1890	South Melbourne	Carlton	John Worrall (Fitzroy)	J. Grace (Fitzroy) 49 goals
1891	Essendon	Carlton	Peter Burns (South Melbourne)	J. Grace (Fitzroy) 37 goals
1892	Essendon	Fitzroy	Charles Forbes (Essendon)	Albert J. Thurgood (Essendon) 56 goals
1893	Essendon	Melbourne	Albert J. Thurgood (Essendon)	Albert J. Thurgood (Essendon) 64 goals
1894	Essendon	Melbourne	Albert J. Thurgood (Essendon)	Albert J. Thurgood (Essendon) 63 goals

	Premiers	Runners-up	Brownlow medallist or Champion of the Colony	Leading goalkicker
1895	Fitzroy	Geelong	George S. Vautin (Essendon)	D. de Coite (Geelong) 42 goals
1896	Collingwood	South Melbourne	Bill Strickland (Collingwood)	N. Waugh (Essendon) 29 goals
1897*	Essendon	Geelong	Fred McGinis (Melbourne)	Eddy James (Geelong) 27 goals
1898	Fitzroy	Essendon	R. P. J. Condon (Collingwood)	Archie Smith (Collingwood) 31 goals
1899	Fitzroy	South Melbourne	Michael Grace (Fitzroy)	Eddy James (Geelong) 32 goals
1900	Melbourne	Fitzroy	Fred E. Leach (Collingwood)	Albert J. Thurgood (Essendon) 26 goals
1901	Essendon	Collingwood	Albert J. Thurgood (Essendon)	Fred Hiskins (Essendon) 34 goals
1902	Collingwood	Essendon	Ted Rowell (Collingwood)	Ted Rowell (Collingwood) Albert J. Thurgood (Essendon) 33 goals
1903	Collingwood	Fitzroy	Hugh Gavin (Essendon)	Edward Lockwood (Collingwood) 35 goals
1904	Fitzroy	Carlton	Vic Cumberland (St Kilda)	Vince Coutie (Melbourne) 39 goals
1905	Fitzroy	Collingwood	Percy Trotter (Fitzroy)	Charles Pannam (Collingwood) 38 goals
1906	Carlton	Fitzroy	'Dookie' McKenzie (Essendon)	Michael Grace (Carlton) 50 goals

	Premiers	*Runners-up*	*Brownlow medallist or Champion of the Colony*	*Leading goalkicker*
1907	Carlton	South Melbourne	Dave McNamara (St Kilda)	Dick Lee (Collingwood) 47 goals
1908	Carlton	Essendon	Bill Busbridge (Essendon)	Dick Lee (Collingwood) 54 goals
1909	South Melbourne	Carlton	Bill Busbridge (Essendon)	Dick Lee (Collingwood) 58 goals
1910	Collingwood	Carlton	Dick Lee (Collingwood)	Dick Lee (Collingwood) 58 goals
1911	Essendon	Collingwood	Bruce R. Sloss (South Melbourne)	Vince Gardiner (Carlton) 47 goals
1912	Essendon	South Melbourne	Ernie J. Cameron (Essendon)	Harry Brereton (Melbourne) 56 goals
1913	Fitzroy	St Kilda	Vic Cumberland (St Kilda)	Jim Freake (Fitzroy) 56 goals
1914	Carlton	South Melbourne	David J. McNamara (St Kilda)	Dick Lee (Collingwood) 54 goals
1915	Carlton	Collingwood	Dick Lee (Collingwood)	Dick Lee (Collingwood) 66 goals
1916	Fitzroy	Carlton	Vic Thorp (Richmond)	Dick Lee (Collingwood) 48 goals
1917	Collingwood	Fitzroy	Paddy O'Brien (Carlton)	Dick Lee (Collingwood) 54 goals
1918	South Melbourne	Collingwood	Jack E. Howell (South Melbourne)	Ern Cowley (Carlton) 34 goals
1919	Collingwood	Richmond	Vic Thorp (Richmond)	Dick Lee (Collingwood) 56 goals

	Premiers	Runners-up	Brownlow medallist or Champion of the Colony	Leading goalkicker
1920	Richmond	Collingwood	Roy Cazaly (South Melbourne)	Gordon Bayliss (Richmond) 63 goals
1921	Richmond	Carlton	Horrie Clover (Carlton)	Dick Lee (Collingwood) Cliff Rankin (Geelong) 64 goals
1922	Fitzroy	Collingwood	Goldie Collins (Fitzroy)	Horrie Clover (Carlton) 56 goals
1923	Essendon	Fitzroy	T. J. Fitzmaurice (Essendon)	Greg Stockdale (Essendon) 68 goals
1924*	Essendon	Richmond	'Carji' Greeves (Geelong)	Jack Moriarty (Fitzroy) 82 goals
1925	Geelong	Collingwood	Colin Watson (St Kilda)	Lloyd Hagger (Geelong) 78 goals
1926	Melbourne	Collingwood	Ivor Warne-Smith (Melbourne)	Gordon Coventry (Collingwood) 83 goals
1927	Collingwood	Richmond	Syd Coventry (Collingwood)	Gordon Coventry (Collingwood) 97 goals
1928	Collingwood	Richmond	Ivor Warne-Smith (Melbourne)	Gordon Coventry (Collingwood) 89 goals
1929	Collingwood	Richmond	Albert Collier (Collingwood)	Gordon Coventry (Collingwood) 124 goals
1930	Collingwood	Geelong	Stan Judkins (Richmond) Alan Hopkins (Footscray) Harry Collier (Collingwood)	Gordon Coventry (Collingwood) 118 goals
1931	Geelong	Richmond	Haydn Bunton (Fitzroy)	Harry Vallence (Carlton) 86 goals

	Premiers	Runners-up	Brownlow medallist or Champion of the Colony	Leading goalkicker
1932	Richmond	Carlton	Haydn Bunton (Fitzroy)	George Moloney (Geelong) 109 goals
1933	South Melbourne	Richmond	'Chicken' Smallhorn (Fitzroy)	Bob Pratt (South Melbourne) 109 goals
1934	Richmond	South Melbourne	Dick Reynolds (Essendon)	Bob Pratt (South Melbourne) 150 goals
1935	Collingwood	South Melbourne	Haydn Bunton (Fitzroy)	Bob Pratt (South Melbourne) 103 goals
1936	Collingwood	South Melbourne	Dinny Ryan (Fitzroy)	Bill Mohr (St Kilda) 101 goals
1937	Geelong	Collingwood	Dick Reynolds (Essendon)	Gordon Coventry (Collingwood) 72 goals
1938	Carlton	Collingwood	Dick Reynolds (Essendon)	Ron Todd (Collingwood) 120 goals
1939	Melbourne	Collingwood	Marcus Whelan (Collingwood)	Ron Todd (Collingwood) 121 goals
1940	Melbourne	Richmond	Des Fothergill (Collingwood) Herb Matthews (South Melbourne)	Jack Titus (Richmond) 100 goals
1941	Melbourne	Essendon	Norm Ware (Footscray)	Norm Smith (Melbourne) 88 goals
1942	Essendon	Richmond	Medal suspended during WWII	Lindsay White (South Melbourne) 80 goals
1943	Richmond	Essendon	—	Dick Harris (Richmond) 63 goals
1944	Fitzroy	Richmond	—	Fred Fanning (Melbourne) 87 goals

	Premiers	Runners-up	Brownlow medallist or Champion of the Colony	Leading goalkicker
1945	Carlton	South Melbourne	—	Fred Fanning (Melbourne) 67 goals
1946	Essendon	Melbourne	Don Cordner (Melbourne)	Bill Brittingham (Essendon) 66 goals
1947	Carlton	Essendon	Bert Deacon (Carlton)	Fred Fanning (Melbourne) 97 goals
1948	Melbourne	Essendon	Bill Morris (Richmond)	Lindsay White (Geelong) 86 goals
1949	Essendon	Carlton	Ron Clegg (South Melbourne) Col Austen (Hawthorn)	John Coleman (Essendon) 100 goals
1950	Essendon	North Melbourne	Alan Ruthven (Fitzroy)	John Coleman (Essendon) 120 goals
1951	Geelong	Essendon	Bernie Smith (Geelong)	George Goninon (Geelong) 86 goals
1952	Geelong	Collingwood	Roy Wright (Richmond) Bill Hutchinson (Essendon)	John Coleman (Essendon) 103 goals
1953	Collingwood	Geelong	Bill Hutchinson (Essendon)	John Coleman (Essendon) 97 goals
1954	Footscray	Melbourne	Roy Wright (Richmond)	Jack Collins (Footscray) 84 goals
1955	Melbourne	Collingwood	Fred Goldsmith (South Melbourne)	Noel Rayson (Geelong) 80 goals
1956	Melbourne	Collingwood	Peter Box (Footscray)	Bill Young (St Kilda) 56 goals

	Premiers	Runners-up	Brownlow medallist or Champion of the Colony	Leading goalkicker
1957	Melbourne	Essendon	Brian Gleeson (St Kilda)	Jack Collins (Footscray) 74 goals
1958	Collingwood	Melbourne	Neil Roberts (St Kilda)	Ian Brewer (Collingwood) 73 goals
1959	Melbourne	Essendon	Bob Skilton (South Melbourne) Verdun Howell (St Kilda)	Ron Evans (Essendon) 79 goals
1960	Melbourne	Collingwood	John Schultz (Footscray)	Ron Evans (Essendon) 67 goals
1961	Hawthorn	Footscray	John James (Carlton)	Tom Carroll (Carlton) 54 goals
1962	Essendon	Carlton	Alistair Lord (Geelong)	Doug Wade (Geelong) 68 goals
1963	Geelong	Hawthorn	Bob Skilton (South Melbourne)	John Peck (Hawthorn) 75 goals
1964	Melbourne	Collingwood	Gordon Collis (Carlton)	John Peck (Hawthorn) 68 goals
1965	Essendon	St Kilda	Ian Stewart (St Kilda) Noel Teasdale (North Melbourne)	John Peck (Hawthorn) 56 goals
1966	St Kilda	Collingwood	Ian Stewart (St Kilda)	Ted Fordham (Essendon) 76 goals
1967	Richmond	Geelong	Ross Smith (St Kilda)	Doug Wade (Geelong) 96 goals
1968	Carlton	Essendon	Bob Skilton (South Melbourne)	Peter Hudson (Hawthorn) 125 goals

	Premiers	Runners-up	Brownlow medallist or Champion of the Colony	Leading goalkicker
1969	Richmond	Carlton	Kevin Murray (Fitzroy)	Doug Wade (Geelong) 127 goals
1970	Carlton	Collingwood	Peter Bedford (South Melbourne)	Peter Hudson (Hawthorn) 146 goals
1971	Hawthorn	St Kilda	Ian Stewart (Richmond)	Peter Hudson (Hawthorn) 150 goals
1972	Carlton	Richmond	Len Thompson (Collingwood)	Peter McKenna (Collingwood) 130 goals
1973	Richmond	Carlton	Keith Greig (North Melbourne)	Peter McKenna (Collingwood) 84 goals
1974	Richmond	North Melbourne	Keith Greig (North Melbourne)	Doug Wade (North Melbourne) 103 goals
1975	North Melbourne	Hawthorn	Gary Dempsey (Footscray)	Leigh Matthews (Hawthorn) 68 goals
1976	Hawthorn	North Melbourne	Graham Moss (Essendon)	Larry Donohue (Geelong) 105 goals
1977	North Melbourne	Collingwood	Graeme Teasdale (South Melbourne)	Peter Hudson (Hawthorn) 110 goals
1978	Hawthorn	North Melbourne	Malcolm Blight (North Melbourne)	Kelvin Templeton (Footscray) 118 goals
1979	Carlton	Collingwood	Peter Moore (Collingwood)	Kelvin Templeton (Footscray) 91 goals
1980	Richmond	Collingwood	Kelvin Templeton (Footscray)	Michael Roach (Richmond) 112 goals
1981	Carlton	Collingwood	Bernie Quinlan (Fitzroy) Barry Round (South Melbourne)	Michael Roach (Richmond) 86 goals

	Premiers	Runners-up	Brownlow medallist or Champion of the Colony	Leading goalkicker
1982	Carlton	Richmond	Brian Wilson (Melbourne)	Malcolm Blight (North Melbourne) 103 goals
1983	Hawthorn	Essendon	Ross Glendenning (North Melbourne)	Bernie Quinlan (Fitzroy) 116 goals
1984	Essendon	Hawthorn	Peter Moore (Melbourne)	Bernie Quinlan (Fitzroy) 105 goals
1985	Essendon	Hawthorn	Brad Hardie (Footscray)	Simon Beasley (Footscray) 105 goals
1986	Hawthorn	Carlton	Robert DiPierdomenico (Hawthorn) Greg Williams (Sydney)	Brian Taylor (Collingwood) 100 goals
1987	Carlton	Hawthorn	Tony Lockett (St Kilda) John Platten (Hawthorn)	Tony Lockett (St Kilda) 117 goals
1988	Hawthorn	Melbourne	Gerard Healy (Sydney)	Jason Dunstall (Hawthorn) 132 goals
1989	Hawthorn	Geelong	Paul Couch (Geelong)	Jason Dunstall (Hawthorn) 138 goals
1990	Collingwood	Essendon	Tony Liberatore (Footscray)	John Longmire (North Melbourne) 98 goals
1991	Hawthorn	West Coast	Jim Stynes (Melbourne)	Tony Lockett (St Kilda) 127 goals
1992	West Coast	Geelong	Scott Wynd (Footscray)	Jason Dunstall (Hawthorn) 145 goals
1993	Essendon	Carlton	Gavin Wanganeen (Essendon)	Tony Modra (Adelaide) 129 goals

	Premiers	Runners-up	Brownlow medallist or Champion of the Colony	Leading goalkicker
1994	West Coast	Geelong	Greg Williams (Carlton)	Gary Ablett (Geelong) 120 goals

*First year of VFL competition
**First year Brownlow medal awarded. In 1981 retrospective medals were awarded for dual winners of the past.

Victorian Goal Aggregates (to end of 1994)

Player	Goals	Matches	Average goals per match
Gordon Coventry (Collingwood)	1299	300	4.25
Doug Wade (Geelong, North Melbourne)	1057	267	3.96
Jason Dunstall (Hawthorn)	1011	208	4.86
Jack Titus (Richmond)	970	294	3.30
Leigh Matthews (Hawthorn)	915	332	2.76
Tony Lockett (St Kilda)	898	183	4.90
Peter McKenna (Collingwood, Carlton)	874	191	4.58
Gary Ablett (Geelong)	839	209	4.01
Bernie Quinlan (Footscray, Fitzroy)	815	366	2.23
Kevin Bartlett (Richmond)	778	403	1.93

South Australian National Football League

	Premiers	Runners-up	Magarey medallist	Leading goalkicker
1877	South Adelaide	—	—	J. Young (Adelaide) 14 goals
1878	Norwood	—	—	W. Dedman (Norwood) 12 goals
1879	Norwood	—	—	W. Dedman (Norwood) 12 goals
1880	Norwood	—	—	J. Traynor (Norwood) 7 goals
1881	Norwood	—	—	E. Pollock W. Duffy (Norwood) 7 goals
1882	Norwood	—	—	H. Wardrop (South Adelaide) 14 goals
1883	Norwood	—	—	J. Litchfield (Port Adelaide) 13 goals
1884	Port Adelaide	—	—	R. Roy (Port Adelaide) 22 goals
1885	South Adelaide	—	—	H. Hill (South Adelaide) 19 goals
1886	Adelaide	—	—	R. Stephens (Adelaide) 17 goals
1887	Norwood	—	—	A. Bushby (South Adelaide) 25 goals
1888	Norwood	—	—	C. Woods (Norwood) 29 goals

	Premiers	Runners-up	Magarey medallist	Leading goalkicker
1889	Norwood	—	—	C. Fry (Port Adelaide) 32 goals
1890	Port Adelaide	—	—	J. McKenzie (Port Adelaide) 54 goals
1891	Norwood	—	—	C. Woods (Norwood) 55 goals
1892	South Adelaide	—	—	C. Woods (Norwood) 46 goals
1893	South Adelaide	—	—	A. Daly (Norwood) 88 goals
1894	Norwood	—	—	A. Daly (Norwood) 47 goals
1895	South Adelaide	—	—	A. Daly (Norwood) 46 goals
1896	South Adelaide	—	—	J. Kay (South Adelaide) 25 goals
1897	Port Adelaide	South Adelaide	—	J. Tompkins (Port Adelaide) 27 goals
1898	South Adelaide	Port Adelaide	A. Green (Norwood)	J. Kay (South Adelaide) 35 goals
1899	South Adelaide	Norwood	S. Malin (Port Adelaide)	A. Daly (South Adelaide) 32 goals
1900	North Adelaide	South Adelaide	—	A. Daly (South Adelaide) 27 goals
1901	Norwood	Port Adelaide	P. Sandland (North Adelaide)	W. Miller (Norwood) 44 goals

	Premiers	Runners-up	Magarey medallist	Leading goalkicker
1902	North Adelaide	South Adelaide	T. Mackenzie (West Torrens)	J. Kay (South Adelaide) 28 goals
1903	Port Adelaide	South Adelaide	S. Waye (Sturt)	A. Daly (North Adelaide) 54 goals
1904	Norwood	Port Adelaide	—	W. Miller (Norwood) 35 goals
1905	North Adelaide	Port Adelaide	T. Mackenzie (North Adelaide)	J. Mathieson (Port Adelaide) A. Daly (North Adelaide) 30 goals
1906	Port Adelaide	North Adelaide	T. Mackenzie (North Adelaide)	J. Mathieson (Port Adelaide) 42 goals
1907	Norwood	Port Adelaide	J. Mack (Port Adelaide)	J. Quinn (Port Adelaide) 32 goals
1908	West Adelaide	Norwood	J. Tierney (West Adelaide)	J. Mathieson (Port Adelaide) 33 goals
1909	West Adelaide	Port Adelaide	H. R. Head (West Adelaide)	R. Townsend (Norwood) 22 goals
1910	Port Adelaide	Sturt	S. Hosking (Port Adelaide)	F. Hansen (Port Adelaide) 46 goals
1911	West Adelaide	Port Adelaide	H. V. Cumberland (Sturt)	F. Hansen (Port Adelaide) 41 goals
1912	West Adelaide	Port Adelaide	D. Low (West Torrens)	F. Hansen (Port Adelaide) 37 goals
1913	Port Adelaide	North Adelaide	T. Leahy (North Adelaide)	F. Hansen (Port Adelaide) 39 goals
1914	Port Adelaide	North Adelaide	J. Ashley (Port Adelaide)	J. Dunn (Port Adelaide) 33 goals

	Premiers	Runners-up	Magarey medallist	Leading goalkicker
1915	Sturt	Port Adelaide	F. N. Barry (South Adelaide)	F. Fitzgerald (West Adelaide)
1916*	—	—	—	—
1917	—	—	—	—
1918	—	—	—	—
1919	Sturt	North Adelaide	D. Moriarty (South Adelaide)	L. Lackman (Port Adelaide) 26 goals
1920	North	Norwood	D. Moriarty (South Adelaide)	F. Golding (Sturt) 30 goals
1921	Port Adelaide	Norwood	D. Moriarty (South Adelaide)	R. Bent (Norwood) 42 goals
1922	Norwood	West Adelaide	R. Barnes (West Adelaide)	T. Hart (Norwood) 50 goals
1923	Norwood	Sturt	H. Riley (Sturt)	P. Lewis (North Adelaide) 58 goals
1924	West Torrens	Sturt	W. Scott (Norwood)	R. Bent (Norwood) 53 goals
1925	Norwood	Port Adelaide	A. G. Lill (Norwood)	R. Bent (Norwood) 59 goals
1926	Sturt	Port Adelaide	B. McGregor (West Adelaide)	R. Bent (Norwood) 65 goals
1927	West Adelaide	North Adelaide	B. McGregor (West Adelaide)	J. Owens (Glenelg) 80 goals
1928	Port Adelaide	Norwood	J. Handby (Glenelg)	J. Owens (Glenelg) 83 goals
1929	Norwood	Port Adelaide	R. Snell (West Adelaide)	L. Dayman (Port Adelaide) 86 goals

	Premiers	Runners-up	Magarey medallist	Leading goalkicker
1930	North Adelaide	Port Adelaide	W. Scott (Norwood)	K. Farmer (North Adelaide) 105 goals
1931	North Adelaide	Sturt	J. Sexton (West Adelaide)	K. Farmer (North Adelaide) 126 goals
1932	Sturt	North Adelaide	M. Pontifex (West Torrens)	K. Farmer (North Adelaide) J. Owens (Glenelg) 102 goals
1933	West Torrens	Norwood	W. Dunn (Sturt)	K. Farmer (North Adelaide) 112 goals
1934	Glenelg	Port Adelaide	G. Johnston (Glenelg)	K. Farmer (North Adelaide) 106 goals
1935	South Adelaide	Port Adelaide	J. Cockburn (South Adelaide)	K. Farmer (North Adelaide) 128 goals
1936	Port Adelaide	Sturt	W. McCallum (Norwood)	K. Farmer (North Adelaide) 134 goals
1937	Port Adelaide	South Adelaide	H. Hawke (North Adelaide)	K. Farmer (North Adelaide) 108 goals
1938	South Adelaide	Port Adelaide	R. Quinn (Port Adelaide)	K. Farmer (North Adelaide) 112 goals
1939	Port Adelaide	West Torrens	J. Pash (North Adelaide)	K. Farmer (North Adelaide) 113 goals
1940	Sturt	South Adelaide	M. Brock (Glenelg)	K. Farmer (North Adelaide) 125 goals
1941	Norwood	Sturt	M. Boyall (Glenelg)	B. Schultz (Norwood) 100 goals
1942	—	—	—	R. Reynolds (Sturt/South Adelaide) 45 goals

	Premiers	Runners-up	Magarey medallist	Leading goalkicker
1943	—	—	—	W. Isaac (Norwood/North Adelaide) 73 goals
1944	—	—	—	W. Isaac (Norwood/North Adelaide) 76 goals
1945	West Torrens	Port Adelaide	R. Quinn (Port Adelaide)	S. Scott (South Adelaide) 64 goals
1946	Norwood	Port Adelaide	R. Hanks (West Torrens)	P. Dalwood (Norwood) 70 goals
1947	West Adelaide	Norwood	R. Hanks (West Torrens)	A. R. McLean (Port Adelaide) 80 goals
1948	Norwood	West Torrens	H. Phillips (North Adelaide)	C. Churchett (Glenelg) 88 goals
1949	North Adelaide	West Torrens	H. Phillips (North Adelaide)	C. Churchett (Glenelg) 72 goals
1950	Norwood	Glenelg	I. McKay (North Adelaide)	C. Churchett (Glenelg) 105 goals
1951	Port Adelaide	North Adelaide	J. Marriott (Norwood)	C. Churchett (Glenelg) 102 goals
1952	North Adelaide	Norwood	L. Fitzgerald (Sturt)	J. Willis (West Torrens) 85 goals
1953	West Torrens	Port Adelaide	J. Deane (South Adelaide)	M. Mayo (Norwood) 78 goals
1954	Port Adelaide	West Adelaide	L. Fitzgerald (Sturt)	W. McKenzie (North Adelaide) 67 goals
1955	Port Adelaide	Norwood	L. Head (West Torrens)	P. Caust (Sturt) 57 goals

	Premiers	Runners-up	Magarey medallist	Leading goalkicker
1956	Port Adelaide	West Adelaide	D. Boyd (Port Adelaide)	R. Johns (Port Adelaide) 70 goals
1957	Port Adelaide	Norwood	R. Benton (West Adelaide)	P. Phipps (West Adelaide) 90 goals
1958	Port Adelaide	West Torrens	L. Head (West Torrens)	R. Johns (Port Adelaide) 55 goals
1959	Port Adelaide	West Adelaide	L. Fitzgerald (Sturt)	W. Dittmar (Port Adelaide) 74 goals
1960	North Adelaide	Norwood	B. Barbary (North Adelaide)	W. Dittmar (Port Adelaide) 69 goals
1961	West Adelaide	Norwood	J. Halbert (Sturt)	G. Kingston (West Torrens) 79 goals
1962	Port Adelaide	West Adelaide	K. Eustice (West Adelaide)	R. Johns (Port Adelaide) 76 goals
1963	Port Adelaide	North Adelaide	L. Head (West Torrens)	R. Johns (Port Adelaide) 54 goals
1964	South Adelaide	Port Adelaide	G. Motley (Port Adelaide)	R. Sawley (Sturt) 70 goals
1965	Port Adelaide	Sturt	G. Window (Central District)	I. Brewer (Norwood) 96 goals
1966	Sturt	Port Adelaide	R. Kneebone (Norwood)	E. Freeman (Port Adelaide) 81 goals
1967	Sturt	Port Adelaide	T. Obst (Port Adelaide)	D. Sachse (North Adelaide) 90 goals
1968	Sturt	Port Adelaide	B. Robran (North Adelaide)	R. Vidovich (Central District) 62 goals

	Premiers	*Runners-up*	*Magarey medallist*	*Leading goalkicker*
1969	Sturt	Glenelg	Fred Phillis (Glenelg)	Fred Phillis (Glenelg) 137 goals
1970	Sturt	Glenelg	Barry Robran (North Adelaide)	Fred Phillis (Glenelg) 107 goals
1971	North Adelaide	Port Adelaide	R. Ebert (Port Adelaide)	D. Phillis (Glenelg) 99 goals
1972	North Adelaide	Port Adelaide	Malcolm Blight (Woodville)	M. Coligan (Norwood) 81 goals
1973	Glenelg	North Adelaide	Barry Robran (North Adelaide)	K. Whelan (Sturt) 107 goals
1974	Sturt	Glenelg	R. Ebert (Port Adelaide)	K. Whelan (Sturt) 108 goals
1975	Norwood	Glenelg	P. Woite (Port Adelaide)	D. Phillis (Glenelg) 123 goals
1976	Sturt	Port Adelaide	R. Ebert (Port Adelaide)	D. Phillis (Glenelg) 98 goals
1977	Port Adelaide	Glenelg	T. Grimwood (West Adelaide)	Tim Evans (Port Adelaide) 87 goals
1978	Norwood	Sturt	Kym Hodgeman (Glenelg)	Tim Evans (Port Adelaide) 90 goals
1979	Port Adelaide	South Adelaide	J. Duckworth (Central Districts)	G. Hewitt (Woodville) 83 goals
1980	Port Adelaide	Norwood	R. Ebert (Port Adelaide)	Tim Evans (Port Adelaide) 146 goals
1981	Port Adelaide	Glenelg	M. Aish (Norwood)	Tim Evans (Port Adelaide) 98 goals

	Premiers	Runners-up	Magarey medallist	Leading goalkicker
1982	Norwood	Glenelg	Tony McGuiness (Glenelg)	Tim Evans (Port Adelaide) 125 goals
1983	West Adelaide	Sturt	A. Antrobus (North Adelaide)	Rich Davies (Sturt) 151 goals
1984	Norwood	Port Adelaide	John Platten (Central District)	Tim Evans (Port Adelaide) 127 goals
1985	Glenelg	North Adelaide	G. Fielke (West Adelaide)	Malcolm Blight (Woodville) 126 goals
1986	Glenelg	North Adelaide	Greg Anderson (Port Adelaide)	Stephen Nicholls (Woodville) 103 goals
1987	North Adelaide	Glenelg	Andrew Jarman (North Adelaide)	John Roberts (North Adelaide) 111 goals
1988	Port Adelaide	Glenelg	Greg Whittlesea (Sturt)	Stephen Nicholls (Woodville) 103 goals
1989	Port Adelaide	North Adelaide	Gilbert McAdam (Central District)	Rudi Mandebaker (Central District) 93 goals
1990	Port Adelaide	Glenelg	Scott Hodges (Port Adelaide)	Scott Hodges (Port Adelaide) 153 goals
1991	North Adelaide	West Adelaide	Mark Naley (South Adelaide)	Scott Morphett (Woodville-West Torrens) 99 goals
1992	Port Adelaide	Glenelg	Nathan Buckley (Port Adelaide)	Mark Tylor (Port Adelaide) 97 goals
1993	Woodville– West Torrens	Norwood	Brenton Phillips (North Adelaide)	Mark Tylor (Port Adelaide) 90 goals
1994	Port Adelaide	Woodville– West Torrens	Garry McIntosh (Norwood)	Scott Hodges (Port Adelaide) 129 goals

Top Ten Career Goalkickers

Player	Goals
K. Farmer (North Adelaide)	1410
T. Evans (Port Adelaide)	1042
D. K. Phillis (Glenelg)	884
J. Owens (Glenelg)	817
R. Davies (Sturt)	781
J. Roberts (Woodville/Torrens/North Adelaide)	618
M. Greenslade (Sturt/Glenelg)	615
N. Roberts (Torrens/Norwood)	613
D. Schultz (Norwood)	609
R. Woodcock (Norwood)	602

Western Australian Football League

	Premiers	Runners-up	Sandover medallist	Leading goalkicker
1885*	Rovers	—	—	—
1886	Fremantle	—	—	—
1887	Fremantle Unions	—	—	—
1888	Fremantle Unions	—	—	—
1889	Fremantle Unions	—	—	—
1890	Fremantle	Metro	—	—
1891	Rovers	—	—	—
1892	Fremantle	West Perth	—	—
1893	Fremantle	West Perth	—	F. Knox (Fremantle) 10 goals
1894	Fremantle	West Perth	—	J. Davies (West Perth) 20 goals
1895	Fremantle	Imperials	—	Albert Thurgood (Fremantle) 53 goals
1896	Fremantle	—	—	Albert Thurgood (Fremantle) 47 goals

	Premiers	Runners-up	Sandover medallist	Leading goalkicker
1897	West Perth	Fremantle	—	Albert Thurgood (Fremantle) 27 goals
1898	Fremantle	West Perth	—	H. Loel (Fremantle)
1899	West Perth	East Fremantle	—	H. Loel (Fremantle) 50 goals
1900	East Fremantle	South Fremantle	—	L. Daly (West Perth) 30 goals
1901	West Perth	East Fremantle	—	H. Loel (West Perth) 45 goals
1902	East Fremantle	West Perth	—	H. Loel (West Perth) 35 goals
1903	East Fremantle	West Perth	—	T. McNamara (West Perth) 32 goals
1904	East Fremantle	Perth	—	E. Kelly (East Fremantle) 25 goals
1905	West Perth	East Fremantle	—	H. Kelly (South Fremantle) H. Sharpe (East Fremantle) 50 goals
1906	East Fremantle	West Perth	—	H. Sharpe (East Fremantle) 34 goals
1907	Perth	East Fremantle	—	H. Sharpe (East Fremantle) 48 goals
1908	East Fremantle	Perth	—	H. Sharpe (East Fremantle) 22 goals
1909	East Fremantle	Perth	—	S. Sloss (East Perth) 30 goals

	Premiers	Runners-up	Sandover medallist	Leading goalkicker
1910	East Fremantle	East Perth	—	G. Thomas (South Fremantle) 31 goals
1911	East Fremantle	West Perth	—	E. Bellion (West Perth) 30 goals
1912	Subiaco	East Fremantle	—	H. Limb (Subiaco) 40 goals
1913	Subiaco	Perth	—	A. Halliday (Perth) 46 goals
1914	East Fremantle	South Fremantle	—	A. Halliday (Perth) 38 goals
1915	Subiaco	Perth	—	H. Limb (Subiaco) 46 goals
1916	South Fremantle	East Fremantle	—	A. Halliday (Perth) 38 goals
1917	South Fremantle	East Fremantle	—	A. Rawlinson (East Fremantle) 32 goals
1918	East Fremantle	East Perth	—	Samson (Subiaco) 29 goals
1919	East Perth	East Fremantle	—	J. Lawn (East Fremantle) 47 goals
1920	East Perth	East Fremantle	—	Pat Rodriguez (Subiaco) 36 goals
1921	East Perth	East Fremantle	T. Outridge (Subiaco)	Alan Evans (Perth) 64 goals
1922	East Perth	West Perth	H. Boyd (West Perth)	Bonny Campbell (South Fremantle) 42 goals

	Premiers	Runners-up	Sandover medallist	Leading goalkicker
1923	East Perth	East Fremantle	W. Thomas (East Perth)	Dinny Coffey (East Fremantle) 36 goals
1924	Subiaco	East Fremantle	J. Gosnell (West Perth)	Bonny Campbell (East Perth) 65 goals
1925	East Fremantle	Subiaco	G. Owens (East Perth)	Ted Flemming (West Perth) 50 goals
1926	East Perth	Subiaco	J. Leonard (Subiaco)	Bonny Campbell (East Perth) 82 goals
1927	East Perth	South Fremantle	J. Craig (West Perth)	Bonny Campbell (East Perth) 74 goals
1928	East Fremantle	East Perth	J. Rocchi (South Fremantle)	Sol Lawn (South Fremantle) 70 goals
1929	East Fremantle	South Fremantle	W. Thomas (East Perth)	Sol Lawn (South Fremantle) 96 goals
1930	East Fremantle	South Fremantle	E. Flemming (West Perth)	Frank Hopkins (West Perth) 79 goals
1931	East Fremantle	Subiaco	L. Richards (East Fremantle)	Doug Oliphant (Perth) 84 goals
1932	West Perth	East Perth	K. Hough (Claremont)	Ted Tyson (West Perth) 96 goals
1933	East Fremantle	Subiaco	S. Clarke (Claremont)	George Doig (East Fremantle) 106 goals
1934	West Perth	East Fremantle	S. Clarke (Claremont)	George Doig (East Fremantle) 152 goals
1935	West Perth	Subiaco	L. Daily (Subiaco) G. Krepp (Swan Districts)	George Doig (East Fremantle) 113 goals

	Premiers	Runners-up	Sandover medallist	Leading goalkicker
1936	East Perth	Claremont	G. Moloney (Claremont)	George Doig (East Fremantle) 109 goals
1937	East Fremantle	Claremont	Frank Jenkins (South Fremantle)	George Doig (East Fremantle) 144 goals
1938	Claremont	East Fremantle	Haydn Bunton Snr (Subiaco)	Ted Tyson (West Perth) 126 goals
1939	Claremont	East Fremantle	Haydn Bunton Snr (Subiaco)	Bert Gook (Perth) 102 goals
1940	Claremont	South Fremantle	E. O'Keefe (West Perth)	George Moloney (Claremont) 129 goals
1941	West Perth	East Fremantle	Haydn Bunton Snr (Subiaco)	George Doig (East Fremantle) 141 goals
1942	West Perth	Claremont	L. Bowen (West Perth)	Ted Brunton (West Perth) 94 goals
1943	East Fremantle	Swan Districts	T. Moriarty (Perth)	Robin Farmer (Claremont) 97 goals
1944	East Perth	East Fremantle	J. Davies (Swan Districts)	Alan Watts (East Perth) 101 goals
1945	East Fremantle	South Fremantle	G. Bailey (Perth)	Bill Baker (West Perth) 83 goals
1946	East Fremantle	West Perth	J. Loughridge (West Perth)	Bernie Naylor (South Fremantle) 131 goals
1947	South Fremantle	West Perth	Clive Lewington (South Fremantle)	Bernie Naylor (South Fremantle) 108 goals
1948	South Fremantle	West Perth	Merv McIntosh (Perth)	Bernie Naylor (South Fremantle) 91 goals

	Premiers	Runners-up	Sandover medallist	Leading goalkicker
1949	West Perth	Perth	G. Maffina (Claremont)	George Prince (East Fremantle) 81 goals
1950	South Fremantle	Perth	J. Conway (East Fremantle)	Ron Tucker (Perth) 115 goals
1951	West Perth	South Fremantle	F. Buttsworth (West Perth)	Ray Scott (West Perth) 141 goals
1952	South Fremantle	West Perth	Steve Marsh (South Fremantle)	Bernie Naylor (South Fremantle) 147 goals
1953	South Fremantle	West Perth	Merv McIntosh (Perth)	Bernie Naylor (South Fremantle) 167 goals
1954	South Fremantle	East Fremantle	Merv McIntosh (Perth)	Bernie Naylor (South Fremantle) 133 goals
1955	Perth	East Fremantle	John Todd (South Fremantle)	Ray Scott (West Perth) 83 goals
1956	East Perth	South Fremantle	Graham Farmer (East Perth)	John Gerovich (South Fremantle) 74 goals
1957	East Fremantle	East Perth	J. Clarke (East Fremantle)	Don Glass (Subiaco) 83 goals
1958	East Perth	East Fremantle	E. Kilmurray (East Perth)	Bill Mose (East Perth) 115 goals
1959	East Perth	Subiaco	Brian Foley (West Perth)	Neil Hawke (East Perth) 114 goals
1960	West Perth	East Perth	Graham Farmer (East Perth)	John Gerovich (South Fremantle) 101 goals
1961	Swan Districts	East Perth	N. Beard (Perth)	John Gerovich (South Fremantle) 74 goals

	Premiers	Runners-up	Sandover medallist	Leading goalkicker
1962	Swan Districts	East Fremantle	Haydn Bunton Jnr (Swan Districts)	Austin Robertson (Subiaco) 89 goals
1963	Swan Districts	East Fremantle	R. Sorrell (East Fremantle)	Ron Evans (West Perth) 97 goals
1964	Claremont	East Fremantle	Barry Cable (Perth)	Austin Robertson (Subiaco) 94 goals
1965	East Fremantle	Swan Districts	Bill Walker (Swan Districts)	Austin Robertson (Subiaco) 108 goals
1966	Perth	East Perth	Bill Walker (Swan Districts)	Bob Johnson (East Fremantle) 92 goals
1967	Perth	East Perth	Bill Walker (Swan Districts) J. Parkinson (Claremont)	Phil Tierney (East Perth) 119 goals
1968	Perth	East Perth	Barry Cable (Perth)	Austin Robertson (Subiaco) 162 goals
1969	West Perth	East Perth	Mal Brown (East Perth)	Austin Robertson (Subiaco) 116 goals
1970	South Fremantle	Perth	P. Dalton (Perth)	Austin Robertson (Subiaco) 116 goals
1971	West Perth	East Perth	D. Hollins (East Fremantle)	Austin Robertson (Subiaco) 111 goals
1972	East Perth	Claremont	I. Miller (Perth)	Austin Robertson (Subiaco) 98 goals
1973	Subiaco	West Perth	Barry Cable (Perth)	Phil Smith (West Perth) 84 goals
1974	East Fremantle	Perth	G. Melrose (East Fremantle)	Max George (Swan Districts) 90 goals

	Premiers	Runners-up	Sandover medallist	Leading goalkicker
1975	West Perth	South Fremantle	A. Quartermaine (East Perth)	Murray Couper (Perth) 63 goals
1976	Perth	East Perth	P. Spencer (East Perth)	Norm Uncle (Claremont) 91 goals
1977	Perth	East Fremantle	Brian Peake (East Fremantle)	Ray Bauskis (South Fremantle) 108 goals
1978	East Perth	Perth	P. Kelly (East Perth)	Ray Bauskis (South Fremantle) 82 goals
1979	East Fremantle	South Fremantle	P. Kelly (East Perth)	Kevin Taylor (East Fremantle) 102 goals
1980	South Fremantle	Swan Districts	S. Michael (South Fremantle)	Simon Beasley (Swan Districts) 97 goals
1981	Claremont	South Fremantle	S. Michael (South Fremantle)	Warren Ralph (Claremont) 127 goals
1982	Swan Districts	Claremont	P. Narkle (Swan Districts)	Warren Ralph (Claremont) 115 goals
1983	Swan Districts	Claremont	J. Ironmonger (East Perth)	Warren Ralph (Claremont) 128 goals
1984	Swan Districts	East Fremantle	Steve Malaxos (Claremont) Michael Mitchell (Claremont)	Brent Hutton (Swan Districts) 83 goals
1985	East Fremantle	Subiaco	Murray Wrensted (East Fremantle)	Mick Rea (Perth) 100 goals
1986	Subiaco	East Fremantle	Mark Bairstow (South Fremantle)	Mick Rea (Perth) 90 goals
1987	Claremont	Subiaco	Mark Watson (Perth)	Todd Breman (Subiaco) 111 goals

	Premiers	Runners-up	Sandover medallist	Leading goalkicker
1988	Subiaco	Claremont	David Bain (East Perth)	Todd Breman (Subiaco) 77 goals
1989	Claremont	South Fremantle	Craig Edwards (South Fremantle)	Neil Lester-Smith (East Fremantle) 90 goals
1990	Swan Districts	Claremont	Mick Grasso (Swan Districts)	Glen Bartlett (East Perth) 69 goals
1991	Claremont	Subiaco	Ian Dargie (Subiaco)	John Hutton (Claremont) 100 goals
1992	East Fremantle	South Fremantle	Robbie West (West Perth)	Kevin Caton (Swan Districts) Craig Edwards (South Fremantle) 48 goals
1993	Claremont	West Perth	Neil Mildenhall (West Perth)	Jason Heatley (Subiaco) 111 goals
1994	East Fremantle	Claremont	Ian Dargie (Subiaco)	Brenten Cooper (Perth) Andrew Lockyer (East Fremantle) 90 goals

*The early years are disputed.

Notes

Introduction: Divided by the Barassi Line

1 Throughout what follows, except where it is obvious, the term Rugby is used to include both Rugby (Union) and Rugby League. Usually football refers to Australian Rules football, as played or codified from time to time.

2 Ian Turner, 'The Ron Barassi Memorial Lecture 1978', in Garrie Hutchinson, *The Great Australian Book of Football Stories*, 1983, p. 290.

3 Jim Davidson, ed., *The Sydney-Melbourne Book* is the definitive summary of this complicated story. The chapter comparing sporting traditions is by Brian Stoddart. Refer also to the work of Lionel Frost in comparing the various Australian colonies, *Australian Cities in Comparative View*, McPhee Gribble, Ringwood, Vic., 1990.

4 Richard Cashman and Tom Hickie, 'The divergent sporting cultures of Sydney and Melbourne', *Sporting Traditions*, vol. 7, no. 1, November 1990, pp. 26–46; see also M. P. Sharp, 'Australian football in Sydney before 1914', *Sporting Traditions*, vol. 4, no. 1, November 1987, pp. 27–45.

5 Frank Hainsworth, Letter to the Editor, *The Age*, Melbourne, 3 June 1993, p. 14.

6 These five basic differences figure strongly in the April 1994 television campaign ('I'd like to see that!') to promote Rules in Sydney and Brisbane (*Herald-Sun*, Melbourne, 6 April 1994, p. 5).

7 Thomas V. Hickie, *They Ran with the Ball*.

1: The Laws of the Game

1 Susanne Gerraty, 'The Bloodbath Grand Final (and other stories)', p. 19.

2 Ian Turner, 'The Ron Barassi Memorial Lecture 1978', in Garrie Hutchinson, *The Great Australian Book of Football Stories*, 1983.

3 Garrie Hutchinson, *Great Australian Football Stories*, p. 96.

4 Chris McConville, 'Football, liquor and gambling in the 1920s', *Sporting Traditions*, vol. 1, no. 1, November 1984, pp. 38–54.

5 'Tape settles the lie of the land', *Sunday Age*, 16 October 1994, suppl. p. 24.

6 C. C. Mullen, *History of Australian Rules Football*, p. 144.

7 Associate Professor C. T. Stannage, interviewed by Robert Pascoe, Bassendean, W.A., 28 June 1993.

8 Leonie Sandercock and Ian Turner, *Up Where, Cazaly?*, p. 235.

9 *Sun-Herald*, 27 August 1994, suppl. pp. 10–11; *Weekend Australian*, 2–3 April 1994, p. 23.

10 Peter Burke and Leo Grogan, *This Game of Ours*, p. 34.

11 For the history of kicks, see Graeme Atkinson and Michael Hanlon, *3AW Book of Footy Facts*, pp. 195–196.

12 An excellent summary of the ambiguity in the rules is in Garrie Hutchinson, *Australian Rules Football: The Watcher's Guide*, pp. 8–19. The convention that players running into goal do not usually attract a call of 'travel' arose out of the Keith Forbes incident of Round 8 in 1940, when the Fitzroy forward was penalised for running too far into an open goal – the decision was judged by the League to be too technical a reading of the rules.

13 Johnny Quinn's story is told by Bernard Whimpress, *The South Australian Football Story*, pp. 121–122.

14 Richard Stremski, *Kill for Collingwood*, pp. 216–217.

15 Richard Stremski, *Kill for Collingwood*, pp. 233–235.

16 Paul O'Brien, 'The father/son rule', in Bob Stewart and Robert Pascoe, *Oval Logic*.

2: Teams, Positions and Players

1 Garrie Hutchinson, *Australian Rules Football: The Watcher's Guide*, pp. 20–57.

2 Brent Crosswell, 'Mongrel weapon victim of soft-shoe shuffle', *Weekend Australian*, 9–10 April 1994, p. 28.

3 The definition of a key player is one whose entry in Jim Main and Russell Holmesby, *The Encyclopedia of League Footballers*, is above-average in length. Naturally some subjectivity is involved in the selection, and it misses many talented interstate players.

3: Origins

1 The first is quoted in Geoffrey Blainey, *A Game of Our Own: The Origins of Australian Football*, p. 103, the second by A. Mancini and G. M. Hibbins, eds, *Running with the Ball: Football's Foster Father*. A photographic copy of the handwritten 1859 rules and those ratified in 1860 is displayed outside the MCC Archives at the MCG.

2 G. M. Hibbins, 'The Cambridge connection', *International Journal of the History of Sport*, vol. 6, no. 2, September 1989, pp. 172–192.

3 Joseph B. Oxendine, *American Indian Sports Heritage*, Human Kinetics Books, Champaign, Ill., 1988, pp. 60–65.

4 Jim Poulter, 'The Origins of Australian Rules Football', ms, February 1985, 5 pp. This manuscript was kindly provided by the author, Serpells Road, Templestowe. It is reprinted in Peter Burke and Leo Grogan, *This Game of Ours*, pp. 64–67.

5 M. F. Christie, *Aborigines in Colonial Victoria, 1835–86*, Sydney University Press, Sydney, 1979, pp. 16–17.

6 Beverley Blaskett, 'The level of violence: Europeans and Aborigines in Port Phillip, 1835–1850', in Susan Janson and Stuart Macintyre, eds, *Through White Eyes*, Allen & Unwin, Sydney, 1990, pp. 77–100.

7 Don Dennetts, comp., *Melbourne's Yesterdays: A Photographic Record, 1851–1901*, Souvenir Press, Medindie, S.A., 1976, p. 38.

8 Leonie Sandercock and Ian Turner, *Up Where, Cazaly?*, p. 24.

9 Martin Flanagan, *Southern Sky, Western Oval*, pp. 161–162.

10 Roslyn Brereton, 'Entertainment and recreation on the Victorian Goldfields in the 1850s', unpublished fourth year thesis, 1967, Department of History, University of Melbourne, p. 33. See also Blainey for details on Ballarat's football history.

11 Oswald Pryor, *Australia's Little Cornwall*, Rigby, Adelaide, 1962, p. 165.

4: Breaking from the Pack

1 Leonie Sandercock and Ian Turner, *Up Where, Cazaly?*, p. 184.

2 Richard Stremski, *Kill For Collingwood*, pp. 6–9.

3 John Lack, ed., *Charlie Lovett's Footscray*, pp. 69–70.

4 Leonie Sandercock and Ian Turner, p. 41.

5 W. F. Mandle, 'Games people played: Cricket and football in England and Victoria in the late nineteenth century', *Historical Studies*, vol. 15, no. 60, April 1973, pp. 511–535; see pp. 520–521.

6 C. C. Mullen, *History of Australian Rules Football*.

7 *Australasian Sketcher*, 3 October 1874, p. 147.

8 *Australasian*, 23 June 1888, quoted in Hutchinson, *Great Football Stories*, p. 44.

9 Geoffrey Blainey, *A History of Camberwell*, rev. ed., Lothian Publishing, Melbourne, 1980, pp. 58–59.

10 Ballarat *Courier*, November 1890, quoted by Weston Bate, *Lucky City: The First Generation at Ballarat, 1851–1901*, Melbourne University Press, Melbourne, 1978, p. 242.

11 Don Chambers, *Violet Town or Honeysuckle in Australia Felix, 1836–1908*, Melbourne University Press, Carlton, Vic., 1985, pp. 241–242.

12 Leonie Sandercock and Ian Turner, *Up Where, Cazaly?*, p. 258, note 1, ch. 3.

5: Victoria's Decade of Crisis

1 Mike Sutherland, Rod Nicholson and Stewart Murrihy, *The First One Hundred Seasons: Fitzroy Football Club, 1883–1983*, p. 1.

2 Richard Stremski, *Kill For Collingwood*, pp. 3–11.

3 Richard Stremski, pp. 12–16.

4 Richard Stremski, p. 16.

5 Richard Stremski, pp. 17–25.

6 Richard Stremski, pp. 26–27.

7 Stephen Rodgers, comp. *Every Game Ever Played: VFL Results 1897–1989*.

8 Ken Spillman, *Identity Prized; A History of Subiaco*, University of Western Australia Press, Nedlands, W.A., 1985, p. 103.

9 Chris McConville, seminar, Footscray, 12 May 1994, reprinted in Bob Stewart and Robert Pascoe, eds, *Oval Logic*.

6: Class Identity

1 C. C. Mullen, *History of Australian Rules Football*, pp. 112–113, 116.

2 Richard Stremski, *Kill for Collingwood*, pp. 28–31.

3 Richard Stremski, p. 32.

4 Richard Stremski, pp. 70–71.

5 Richard Stremski, pp. 33–45.

6 Richard Stremski, pp. 46–54.

7 Richard Stremski, pp. 140–141.

8 Leonie Sandercock and Ian Turner, *Up Where, Cazaly?*, p. 67. Chapters 6 and 7 deal with this period.

9 Leonie Sandercock and Ian Turner, *Up Where, Cazaly?*, p. 61.

10 Brian Hansen, *Tigerland: The History of the Richmond Football Club from 1885*, p. 27.

11 Gerard P. Dowling, *The North Story*, p. 47.

12 'Follower', writing in *The Age*, October 1908, reprinted in Garrie Hutchinson, *Great Australian Football Stories*, pp. 99–100.
13 *Sunday Age*, 13 February 1994, suppl. p. 28.
14 Edward Dyson, *Benno and Some of the Push*, Sydney, 1911. Quoted in Anthony Harvey, *The Melbourne Book*, Hutchinson, Richmond, 1982, p. 273; the short story is also cited in Hutchinson, op. cit. 'Cumby' refers to Cumberland, who played on to become the VFL's oldest player, but this is Dyson's artistic licence, as Cumberland in fact stood out of football for the 1905 season. Victor Barwick was a solidly built champion rover.
15 John Ritchie, 'John Worrall (1861–1937)', *ADB* (1891–1939) pp. 575–576.
16 *Argus*, 3 October 1936, quoted in Hutchinson, *Great Football Stories*, pp. 154–157.
17 *Football Final: South Melbourne vs Carlton, 1909*, National Film and Sound Archive, MOV 796.
18 Richard Stremski, pp. 66–68.
19 Detailed year-by-year accounts of VFL results are based mainly on Stephen Rodgers, comp., *Every Game Ever Played*.
20 Richard Stremski, p. 64.
21 The standard Western Australian reference is Geoff Christian et al., *The Footballers: From 1885 to the West Coast Eagles*, ch. 3. WAFL is used instead of the acronym WANFL throughout.
22 Robert Pascoe and Frances Thomson, *In Old Kalgoorlie*, W.A. Museum, Perth, 1989, p. 192.
23 Robert Pascoe and Frances Thomson, op. cit., p. 162.
24 Bernard Whimpress, *The South Australian Football Story*.

7: The Anzac Heritage

1 John Worrall, 'The opening day, 1920', *Australasian*, 1 May 1920, repr. in Garrie Hutchinson, *Great Australian Football Stories*, p. 135.
2 Leonie Sandercock and Ian Turner, *Up Where, Cazaly?*, p. 83.
3 Leonie Sandercock and Ian Turner, *Up Where, Cazaly?*, pp. 156–157.
4 C.A. Farmer, 'The character and social significance of the Richmond Football Club during the Depression', unpublished fourth year thesis, Department of History, University of Melbourne, 1978.
5 Jim Davidson, *Lyrebird Rising: Louise Hanson-Dyer of l'Oiseau-Lyre, 1884–1962*, Melbourne University Press, Carlton, 1994, p. 51.
6 Leonie Sandercock and Ian Turner, *Up Where, Cazaly?*, pp. 92–93.
7 Richard Stremski, *Kill for Collingwood*, pp. 68–70.
8 Tom Wanliss, interviewed by Robert Pascoe and Michael George at Collingwood, 23 December 1993.

9 Richard Stremski, pp. 59–61.

10 Richard Stremski, pp. 71–72.

11 Richard Stremski, pp. 77–86.

12 Richard Stremski, pp. 88–89.

13 Richard Stremski, pp. 91–92.

14 Richard Stremski, pp. 101–102.

15 Stephen Rodgers, *Every Game Ever Played*, pp. 128–210.

16 Marc Fiddian, *Devils at Play: A History of the Oakleigh Football Club*.

17 Leonie Sandercock and Ian Turner, *Up Where, Cazaly?*, p. 95.

18 *Australian Rules Football: Personalities of the 1920s and 1930s*, National Film and Sound Archive, MOV 883 (c) Doug McLaughlan.

8: Depression Football

1 The AFL lost sight of the date on which the Coulter Law finally disappeared, as no date for its demise is given in their publications, e.g., *Football Record*, Round 17, 1994.

2 Leonie Sandercock and Ian Turner, *Up Where, Cazaly?*, pp. 104–106.

3 Richard Stremski, pp. 114–117.

4 Richard Stremski, pp. 102–109.

5 Richard Stremski, pp. 110–111.

6 Richard Stremski, p. 37, p. 296 n. 21.

7 Richard Stremski, pp. 112–113.

8 Lynne Wrout, interviewed by Robert Pascoe, University of Melbourne, 7 June 1994.

9 Leonie Sandercock and Ian Turner, *Up Where, Cazaly?*, pp. 107–109.

10 Maya V. Tucker, *Kilmore on the Sydney Road*, Shire of Kilmore, 1988, p. 204.

11 John Murphy, *No Parallel: The Woorayl Shire, 1888–1988*, Hargreen, North Melbourne, 1988, p. 210.

12 Martin Flanagan, *Going Away*, McPhee Gribble, South Yarra, 1993, p. 70.

13 Leonie Sandercock and Ian Turner, *Up Where, Cazaly?*, pp. 161–162.

14 Rodgers, Stephen, *Every Game Ever Played*.

15 Richard Stremski, pp. 124–131.

16 Richard Stremski, pp. 132–138.

17 Lynne Wrout, interviewed by Robert Pascoe, University of Melbourne, 7 June 1994.

18 Jack Mueller, interviewed by Tom Wanliss, Camberwell, Vic., 11 November 1993.

19 Leonie Sandercock and Ian Turner, *Up Where, Cazaly?*, pp. 124–126.

9: Social Mobility

1 See detailed account in Richard Stremski, pp. 141–147.
2 Richard Stremski, p. 149.
3 Richard Stremski, pp. 150–155.
4 Alf Brown, 'Bill Hutchinson – a great rover', in Garrie Hutchinson, *Great Australian Football Stories*, p. 228.
5 Professor Eric Lund, interviewed with Harvey Reese by Robert Pascoe, Essendon, Vic., 12 November 1993.
6 'The peanut gallery loses an old friend', *The Age*, Melbourne, 16 December 1991.
7 Harvey Reese, interviewed with Eric Lund by Robert Pascoe, Essendon, Vic., 12 November 1993. The racist nickname was 'Blood-Stained Niggers'.
8 Based mostly on Michael Maplestone, *Flying High*.
9 Lynne Wrout, interviewed by Robert Pascoe, University of Melbourne, 7 June 1994.
10 Fred Morton, interviewed at East Melbourne by Robert Pascoe.
11 Richard Stremski, pp. 160–169.
12 Leonie Sandercock and Ian Turner, *Up Where, Cazaly?*, p. 122.
13 Victoria, Department of Community Welfare Services, *The Community Effects of VFL Sunday Football*, Office of Research and Social Policy, 1981, p. 44.

10: The Golden Rules

1 *Australian Football, 1951*, National Film and Sound Archive, MOV 45.
2 Martin Flanagan, 'Barassi: The man and the legend', *The Age*, 19 August 1994, suppl. p. 1.
3 Extract from the video history of Melbourne Football Club.
4 Richard Stremski, pp. 172–184.
5 Ajax history.
6 Tom Wanliss, interviewed by Robert Pascoe and Michael George at Collingwood, 23 December 1993.
7 Leonie Sandercock and Ian Turner, *Up Where, Cazaly?*, p. 148.
8 Leonie Sandercock and Ian Turner, *Up Where, Cazaly?*, pp. 136–138.
9 Leonie Sandercock and Ian Turner, *Up Where, Cazaly?*, pp. 226–227.
10 Leonie Sandercock and Ian Turner, *Up Where, Cazaly?*, p. 139.
11 Susanne Gerraty, 'The Bloodbath Grand Final *(and other stories)*', p. 15.
12 Brian Matthews, *Oval Dreams*, pp. 45–46.
13 Alf Brown, '6-goal burst puts Essendon in front', *Herald*, 25 May 1957, p. 33. Ironically, Hawthorn went on after three-quarter time to kick 7 straight goals and win the game, 11.8 (74) to 9.12 (66). The headline would have been changed accordingly! (Thanks to Sharon Welgus for this reference.)

14 Geoff Christian and others, *The Footballers*.

15 Leonie Sandercock and Ian Turner, *Up Where, Cazaly?*, pp. 180–181.

16 Leonie Sandercock and Ian Turner, *Up Where, Cazaly?*, pp. 132–134.

11: New Skills

1 Chris McConville, in Bob Stewart and Rob Pascoe, eds, *Oval Logic*.

2 Garrie Hutchinson, *Great Australian Football Stories*, p. 249.

3 Robert Walls, 'Sorry, they're all in a meeting', *The Age*, 1 April 1994, suppl. p. 4.

4 Alex Jesaulenko, quoted by Garrie Hutchinson, *Great Australian Football Stories*, p. 310.

5 Ron Barassi, interviewed by Robert Pascoe, by telephone, 1 September 1994. Barassi reveals the exact wording in his autobiography, written with Peter McFarline and due for publication in March 1995.

6 Jeff Wells, 'Barassi at the crossroads', *National Times*, 30 August 1985.

7 John Nicholls, with Ian McDonald, *Big Nick*, p. 44.

8 Lynne Wrout, interviewed by Robert Pascoe, University of Melbourne, 7 June 1994.

9 Heather Gridley, St Albans, Vic., MS.

10 Chris Beck, 'Ted Whitten: Footy legend', *The Age*, 21 August 1993, suppl. p. 2.

11 Martin Flanagan, *Southern Sky, Western Oval*, p. 107.

12 Richard Stremski, pp. 185–194.

13 Richard Stremski, pp. 204–211.

14 Graeme Atkinson and Michael Hanlon, *3AW Book of Footy Records*, p. 54.

15 Associate Professor C. T. Stannage, interviewed by Robert Pascoe, Bassendean, W.A., 28 June 1993.

12: 'Going the Long Bomb'

1 Leonie Sandercock and Ian Turner, *Up Where, Cazaly?*, pp. 180–182.

2 Richard Stremski, pp. 194–196.

3 Richard Stremski, pp. 218–220.

4 Neil Balme interviewed by Robert Pascoe and Michael George, East Melbourne, Vic., 2 December 1993.

5 Ian Turner, 'The Ron Barassi Memorial Lecture 1978', in Garrie Hutchinson, *Great Australian Football Stories*, p. 297.

6 Paul O'Brien interviewed by Robert Pascoe, East Melbourne, Vic., 9 December 1993.

7 Ray Carroll, *'Just Crackers': Keenan and Football*.

8 Richard Stremski, pp. 232–233.

9 John Powers, *The Coach*.

10 Ken Piesse, *The Complete Guide to Australian Football*, p. 15.

11 Richard Stremski, pp. 220–223.

12 Leonie Sandercock and Ian Turner, *Up Where, Cazaly?*, pp. 205–206.

13 Richard Stremski, pp. 237–249.

14 Richard Stremski, pp. 250–268.

15 Paul Ormonde, *A Foolish Passionate Man*, pp. 118–119.

16 Leonie Sandercock and Ian Turner, *Up Where, Cazaly?*, pp. 170–171.

17 Leonie Sandercock and Ian Turner, *Up Where, Cazaly?*, p. 173.

18 Leonie Sandercock and Ian Turner, *Up Where, Cazaly?*, pp. 160–161.

19 Marc Fiddian, *Devils at Play*, pp. 66–73.

20 Geoff Christian and others, *The Footballers*.

21 Stephen Rodgers, *Every Game Ever Played*.

13: Balanced Attack and Defence

1 Harvey Reese, interviewed with Eric Lund by Robert Pascoe, Essendon, Vic., 12 November 1993.

2 Jeff Wells, 'Working-class guru', *National Times*, 21–27 March 1986, p. 43.

3 Michael George, interviewed by Robert Pascoe, Armadale, Victoria, 14 June 1994.

4 Wells, 'Working-class guru', *National Times*, 21–27 March 1986, p. 43.

5 Richard Stremski, pp. 269–277.

6 Ross Topham, 'The Collingwood Football Club and Collingwood', in *Meanjin*, vol. 34, no. 2, pp. 157–163.

7 Victoria Department of Community Welfare Services. *The Community Effects of VFL Sunday Football*. Office of Research and Social Policy, Department of Community Welfare Services, Melbourne, 1981. [Copy at VFTS] The University of Melbourne academics commissioned to undertake this work were Ross King and Bruce Crawshaw.

8 Op. cit., pp. 44–45.

9 Some details are given by John Cain, 'Centrepiece for the people', *The Age*, 25 March 1992, suppl., p. 7. See also Lawrence Money, 'In the 'G we trust', *Sunday Age*, 22 January 1995, suppl. p. 6.

10 Joseph Johnson, *For the Love of the Game*.

11 Alan East, ed., *Eagles for the Flag*, Australian Sports Publications, North Perth, 1992, 1993, a glossy club magazine produced annually.

12 Stephen Rodgers, *Every Game Ever Played*.

13 Paul O'Brien, interviewed by Robert Pascoe, East Melbourne, Vic., 9 December 1993.

14 Martin Flanagan, interviewed by Robert Pascoe, Glenhuntly, Vic., 25 April 1994.

14: Possession at All Costs

1 Ironically, FIGHTBACK! for most middle-class Australians will be remembered as the hare-brained policy of the Liberals in the lead up to the 1993 Federal Election; only in Melbourne's west will the term be recalled as the dogged response to save Footscray Football Club.

2 Kerrie Gordon and Alan Dalton, *Too Tough to Die: Footscray's Fightback 1989*, p. 37.

3 Martin Flanagan, interviewed by Robert Pascoe, Glenhuntly, Victoria, 25 April 1994.

4 This elite also formed the local educational leadership; refer Chris McConville, *Rising in the West*, Western Institute, St Albans, Vic., 1991, pp. 5–8.

5 Gerard Wright, interviewed by Robert Pascoe, MCG, 28 September 1993.

6 Gerard Wright, interviewed by Robert Pascoe, MCG, 28 September 1993.

7 Gerard Wright, 'North Melbourne v Footscray: Bulldogs spoil North's party', *Sunday Age*, 29 August 1993, suppl. p. 15.

8 Neil Balme, interviewed by Robert Pascoe and Michael George, East Melbourne, Vic., 2 December 1993.

9 Gary Hughes, 'Barassi's Swan song', *Weekend Australian*, 1–2 May 1993, p. 17.

10 Mike Sheahan, 'Body of opinion behind Eagles', *Herald-Sun*, 6 June 1994, p. 92.

11 Ian Brayshaw, *Football's Magnificent Seven*; Ian Brayshaw and Ray Wilson, *Football's Magnificent Seven Ride Again*.

12 David Wheadon in Bob Stewart and Robert Pascoe, *Oval Logic*.

13 William H. Wilde, Joy Hooton and Barry Andrews, *The Oxford Companion to Australian Literature*, Oxford University Press, Melbourne, 1985, q.v. 'Australian Rules'.

14 A selection of Flanagan's journalism was published under the title *One of the Crowd: A Personal View of Newspapers*, Macmillan, South Melbourne, 1990; his first novel was *Going Away*, McPhee Gribble, South Yarra, 1993.

15 Martin Flanagan, *Southern Sky, Western Oval*.

16 Martin Flanagan, interviewed by Robert Pascoe, Glenhuntly, Victoria, 25 April 1994.

17 Chris McConville, seminar at Footscray, 12 May 1994, published in Bob Stewart and Robert Pascoe, *Oval Logic*.

18 An extract from the 'Coodabeen Champions' the week after Footscray, 11.23 (89), doubled the score of the much-fancied Essendon, 6.7 (43), at the Western Oval in Round 5 of 1991.

15: Zones and Set Plays

1 Scott Palmer, 'Barassi's brash predictions bear fruit', *Sunday Herald-Sun*, 25 April 1993, p. 78.
2 David Wheadon in Bob Stewart and Robert Pascoe, *Oval Logic*.
3 Martin Flanagan, interviewed by Robert Pascoe, Glenhuntly, Victoria, 25 April 1994.

Bibliography

Agars, Merv, *Bloods, Sweat & Tears. West Adelaide Football Club, 1887–1987*, Self-published, West Adelaide, 1987.

The Age, Melbourne, 1854–

Alford, Peter and Tony Allen, *Light Up and Burn: Aquinas Old Collegians Football Club, 1981–1990*, Aquinas Old Collegians FC, Ringwood, Vic., 1991.

Alomes, Stephen, 'Australian football as secular religion', in Ian Craven, Martin Gray and Geraldine Stoneham, eds, *Australian Popular Culture*, Cambridge University Press, Cambridge, 1994, pp. 46–65.

The Argus, Melbourne, 1846–1957.

Ashford, Michael, *Pride & Premiership: A History of De La Salle Old Collegians Amateur Football Club, 1955–1980*, Old Collegians, Melbourne, 1981.

Atkinson, Graeme, *Everything You've Ever Wanted to Know About Australian Rules Football*, The Five Mile Press, Canterbury, Vic., 1982; revised as Graeme Atkinson and Michael Hanlon, *3AW Book of Footy Records*, Matchbooks, South Melbourne, 1989.

Atkinson, Graeme, *The Book of VFL Finals*, The Five Mile Press, Canterbury, Vic., 1973 & 1981; revised as *The Book of Australian Rules Finals*, The Five Mile Press, Canterbury, Vic., 1983; and revised as *The Complete Book of VFL Finals*, The Five Mile Press, Canterbury, Vic., 1989.

The Australasian Sketcher, Melbourne, 1864–1957. [Also available in facsimile edition]

Australian Football Action, Melbourne, 1981–82.

Aylett, Allen, *My Game: A Life in Football As Told to Greg Hobbs*, Sun Books, South Melbourne, 1986.

Barnes, L., *A Fair and Honest Game: The History of the Brunswick Football Club*, Brunswick Community History Group, Brunswick, 1990.

Bartrop, Paul R., *Scores, Crowds and Records: Statistics on the Victorian Football League since 1945*, Historical Statistics Monograph No.4, History Project Incorporated, UNSW, Kensington, NSW, n.d., ca 1986.

Bartrop, Paul, 'The VFA and the search for an identity', *Sporting Traditions*, vol. 2, no. 2, May 1986, pp. 74–87.

Blainey, Geoffrey, *A Game of Our Own: The Origins of Australian Football*, National Australian Football Council, Information Australia, Melbourne, 1990.

Brayshaw, Ian, *Football's Magnificent Seven*, Cal Bruton, Subiaco, W.A., 1991.

Brayshaw, Ian and Ray Wilson, *Football's Magnificent Seven Ride Again*, Brayson Books, Attadale, WA, 1993.

Buggy, Hugh, *The Carlton Story: A History of the Carlton Football Club*, Earl White Associates, Melbourne, 1958.

Burke, Brian, 'The great Australian football dream fades' [The problems of building a Victorian Football League team in Queensland], *Australian*, 5 June 1987, p. 30.

Burke, Louise M. and Richard S. Read, 'A study of dietary patterns of elite Australian football players', *Canadian Journal of Sports Sciences*, vol. 13, no. 1, March 1988, pp. 15–19.

Burke, Peter and Leo Grogan, eds, *This Game of Ours: Supporters' Tales of the People's Game*, Eatwarlflemsd, St Andrews, 1993.

Cadigan, Neil, and others, *Blood Sweat & Tears: Australians and Sport*, Lothian, Port Melbourne, 1989.

Carroll, Ray, *'Just Crackers': Keenan and Football*, RayRon Books, Kilmore, 1982.

Carter, A., *The South Saga: The Official History of the South Bunbury Football Club, 1897–1976*, South Bunbury Football Club, Bunbury, W.A., 1977.

Cashman, Richard, and Tom Hickie, 'The divergent sporting cultures of Sydney and Melbourne', *Sporting Traditions*, vol. 7, no. 1, November 1990.

Christian, Geoff, Jack Lee and Bob Messenger, *The Footballers: A History of Football in Western Australia*, St George Books, Perth, 1985; revised as *The Footballers: From 1885 to the West Coast Eagles*, 1988.

Christison, Darren, ed., *Gaumont Football Yearbook 1991*, Gaumont Media Group, Melbourne, 1990. [See Main 1988, Main and Christison 1989.]

Christison, Darren, ed., *Gaumont Football Year Book 1992*, Gaumont Media Group, Melbourne, 1991.

Clare, John, 'Aussie Rules: A fad for fickle Sydney?', *National Times*, 25–31 July 1982, p. 46.

Conway, Sean, *Aussie Rules, OK: A Dictionary of Australian Rules Football*, Sky Publishing, Padbury, WA, 1989.

Cooney, Richard and Rob Pascoe, 'The steady invasion of the Irish Catholic Labor stamping ground' [Richmond], *The Living Daylights*, 19 February 1974, pp. 18–20.

The Coodabeen Champions Big Bumper Footy Book, Viking O'Neil, Melbourne, 1990.

The Cornwall Chronicle (Launceston) 1875–.

Corris, Peter, 'Demon in Swan's clothing: Ron Barassi, last hope for Australian Rules football in Sydney', *Time Australia*, 12 July 1993, pp. 46–8.

Costelloe, David, *Magpie Memories: A History of the New Town–Glenorchy Football Club, 1948–1990*, self-published, North Hobart, 1991.

Coward, Mike, *Men of Norwood: The Red and Blue Blooded*, Norwood FC, Adelaide, 1978, rev. ed. 1992.

Craven, John, ed., *Football the Australian Way*, Lansdowne Press, Melbourne, 1969.

Davison, Graeme, 'R.E.N. Twopeny and *Town Life in Australia*', *Historical Studies*, vol. 16, no. 63, October 1974, pp. 292–305.

Daws, A.G., 'The origins of Australian Rules football', unpublished fourth year thesis, Department of History, University of Melbourne, 1954.

Delbridge, Noel, ed., *The Bulldog Book: sons of 'Scray (1883–1983)*, Footscray Football Club, West Footscray, Vic.

Dowling, Gerard P., *The North Story*, The Hawthorn Press, Melbourne, 1973.

Duncan, Tim, 'A game of dynamic change: Australian Rules football', *Bulletin*, Sydney, 28 September 1982, pp. 34–40.

Dunn, Craig, 'The campaign for VFL membership: Hawthorn Football Club and the local community, 1919–1925', unpublished fourth year thesis, Department of History, University of Melbourne, 1987.

Dunn, John, ed., *How to Play Football Australian Style*, Rigby, Kent Town, SA, 1973.

Dunn, John, with Jim Main, *Australian Rules Football: An Illustrated History*, Lansdowne Press, Melbourne, 1974.

Dunstan, Keith, *The Paddock that Grew: The Story of the Melbourne Cricket Club*, Cassell, 1962, revised edn, Cassell, Melbourne, 1974.

Dyer, Jack, as told to Brian Hansen, *'Captain Blood'*, Stanley Paul, London, 1965.

Dyer, Jack, and Brian Hansen, *Captain Blood's Wild Men of Football*, Hansen, Cheltenham, 1993.

East, Alan, ed., *Eagles for the Flag*, Australian Sports Publications, North Perth, 1992, 1993.

Farmer, C. A., 'The character and social significance of the Richmond Football Club during the Depression', unpublished fourth year thesis, Department of History, University of Melbourne, 1978.

Farnham, John, intro., *Just for Kicks*, Swan Publishing, Nedlands, WA, 1992.

Feldmann, Jules and Russell Holmesby, *The Point of It All: The Story of the St Kilda Football Club*, Playwright Publishing, Melbourne, 1992.

Fiddian, Marc, *The Pioneers*, Victorian Football Association, Melbourne, 1977.

Fiddian, Marc, *Devils at Play: A History of the Oakleigh Football Club*, Pakenham Gazette, Pakenham, 1982.

Fiddian, Marc, *The Roar of the Crowd*, Victorian Football Association, Melbourne, 1987.

Fitzgerald, Ross and Ken Spillman, eds, *The Greatest Game*, William Heinemann Australia, Melbourne, 1988, repr. 1989, 1992.

Fitzpatrick, Peter and Barbara Wenzel, *Death in the Back Pocket*, Crossbow, Jolimont, 1993.

Flanagan, Martin, *Southern Sky, Western Oval*, McPhee Gribble, South Yarra, 1994.

Fogarty, J., *One Hundred Years of Football in Gladstone, 1882–1982*, Gladstone Football Club, Gladstone, Vic., 1982.

The Footballer: An Annual Record of Football in Victoria and the Australian Colonies, Henriques & Co, Melbourne, 1875–.

Football Life, Melbourne, 1968–1972.

Football Record, Victorian Football League, Melbourne, 1912–.

Gardner, G., *In Full Flight: The Magpies Story, Lake Boga F.C. 1892–1992*, Lake Boga Football Club, Lake Boga, Vic., 1992.

Garvey, Jim, 'Australian Rules football: Something of its history and character', *Recorder*, Melbourne, No. 163, July 1990, pp. 4–8.

Gerraty, Susanne, 'The Bloodbath Grand Final (and other stories)', unpublished fourth year thesis, Department of History, University of Melbourne, 1991.

Gillett, R., 'Where the big men fly: An early history of Australian football in the Riverina', *Sporting Traditions*, vol. 4, no. 2, May 1988.

Gordon, Harry, *The Hard Way: The Story of the Hawthorn Football Club*, Lester–Townsend Publishing, Sydney, 1990.

Gordon, Kerrie and Alan Dalton, *Too Tough to Die: Footscray's Fightback 1989*, Self-published, Melbourne, 1990.

Grow, Robin, 'Nineteenth Century Football and the Melbourne Press', *Sporting Traditions*, vol. 3, no. 1, November, 1988, pp. 23–36.

Handley, George, *The Great Grand Finals*, Walshe, Geelong, 1989.

Hankin, Wayne M., ed., *The History of Football in Ballarat*, 6 vols, mimeo, Melbourne Cricket Club Library, 1982.

Hansen, Brian, *Tigerland: The History of the Richmond Football Club from 1885*, Richmond Former Players and Officials Association, Melbourne, 1989.

Hansen, Brian, *The Magpies: The History of the Collingwood Football Club, from 1892 to 1992*, Semis Carla, Cheltenham, Vic., 1992.

Hansen, I.V., *Neither Free Nor Secular: Six Independent Schools in Victoria: A First Sample*, Oxford University Press, Melbourne, 1971, pp. 25–36, 119–125.

Harper, B., *Against the Wind: A History of Football, Hockey and Netball in Boort, 1888-1988*, B. Harper, Boort, Vic., 1989.

Harris, B., *The Proud Champions: Australia's Aboriginal Sporting Heroes*, Little Hills Press, Sydney, 1989.

Harrison, Frank and Jack Lee, *The South Fremantle Story, 1900–1975*, 2 vols, South Fremantle Football Club, Fremantle, c. 1975.

Hart, Royce, *The Royce Hart Story*, Thomas Nelson, Melbourne, 1970.

Hawke, Steve, *Polly Farmer: A Biography*, Fremantle Arts Centre Press, South Fremantle, 1994.

The Herald, Melbourne, 1839–

Hewart, T., *The Blues*, Carlton Football Club, Melbourne, 1982.

Hibbins, G. M., 'The Cambridge connection: The origin of Australian Rules football', *International Journal of the History of Sport*, vol.6, no.2, September 1989, pp. 172–192.

Hickie, Thomas V., *They Ran with the Ball: How Rugby Football Began in Australia*, Longman Cheshire, Melbourne, 1993.

Hobbs, Greg, *125 Years of the Melbourne Demons*, Melbourne Football Club, Melbourne, 1984.

Hogan, Bernie, *Follow the Game*, 1968, repr. Dene 1983.

Hopgood, Alan, *And the Big Men Fly*, Heinemann Educational, Melbourne, Vic., 1969.

Humphries, L. T., *History of a Great Football Club: Collegians Centenary 1892–1992*, Collegian, Albert Park, Vic., 1992.

Hunt, Rex, *The Football Bible '94*, Crossbow Publishing, Jolimont, 1993.

Hutchinson, Col, *Cat's Tales: Geelong Football Club, 1897–1983*, Geelong Advertiser, Geelong, 1984.

Hutchinson, Garrie, 'Football B.C. (before Collingwood)', *Age*, Melbourne, 27 March 1982, suppl. pp. 1–2.

Hutchinson, Garrie, *The Great Australian Book of Football Stories*, Currey O'Neil, Melbourne, 1983, repr. as *Great Australian Football Stories*, Viking O'Neil, Melbourne, 1989.

Hutchinson, Garrie, *From the Outer: Watching Football in the 80s*, McPhee Gribble, Fitzroy, Vic., 1984.

Hutchinson, Garrie, *Australian Rules Football: The Watcher's Guide*, William Heinemann Australia, Melbourne, 1988.

Johnson, Joseph, *For the Love of the Game: The Centenary History of the Victorian Amateur Football Association, 1892–1992*, Hyland House, Melbourne, 1992.

Jordan, David, 'Spin off from Swans may benefit the Sydney clubs', *Australian*, Sydney, 31 March 1982, p. 23.

Lack, John, ed., *Charlie Lovett's Footscray*, City of Footscray Historical Society, Footscray, 1993.

Laurence, L., *History of South Melbourne Football Club*, South Melbourne Football Club, Melbourne, 1963.

Laidlaw, Robert, *Central District Football Club: 30 Year Almanac*, Central District FC, Adelaide, 1994.

Lee, Jack, *Old Easts: 1948–1975*, East Fremantle Football Club, Fremantle, 1976.

McConnell, K. and D. Evison, *Korumburra Football Club, 1892–1992*, Korumburra Football Club, Korumburra, Vic., 1992.

McConville, Chris, 'Football, liquor and gambling in the 1920s', *Sporting Traditions*, vol.1, no.1, November 1984, pp. 38–54.

McDonald, John, *Football Year 94*, Pagemasters, Melbourne, 1994.

McGuire, Eddie and Jim Main, *Pants: The Darren Millane Story*, Celebrity Publishing, Melbourne, 1994.

McHale, J., A. E. Chadwick and E. C. H. Taylor, *The Australian Game of Football*, C. G. Hartley & Co., Melbourne, 1931.

Macintyre, Clement, 'The "Bouncing Game" in Fremantle: Australian football and community identity in Western Australia, 1885–1900', *International Journal of the History of Sport*, vol. 7, no. 1, May 1990, pp. 131–9.

McKenna, Peter, *My World of Football*, Jack Pollard, North Sydney, c. 1972.

McLean, A. R., *100 Years with the Magpies: The Story of the Port Adelaide Football Club*, Letterpress, Hindmarsh, S.A., 1971.

Main, Jim and Ken Piesse, *The A to Z of Football*, Wedneil Publications, Melbourne, 1982.

Main, Jim, ed., *1988 Football Year: The Year in Review*, Century Magazines, Melbourne, 1988.

Main, Jim and Darren Christison, eds, *1989 Football: The Year in Review*, Century Magazines, Melbourne, 1989.

Main, Jim and Russell Holmesby, *The Encyclopedia of League Footballers*, Wilkinson Books, Melbourne, 1992, rev. edn., 1994.

Mancini, A. and G. M. Hibbins, eds, *Running with the Ball: Football's Foster Father*, Lynedoch Publications, Melbourne, 1987.

Mandle, W. F., 'Games people played: Cricket and football in England and Victoria in the late nineteenth century', *Historical Studies*, vol. 15, no. 60, April 1973, pp. 511–35.

Mandle, W. F., 'The Gaelic Athletic Association and popular culture, 1884–1924', in Oliver MacDonagh, W. F. Mandle and Pauric Travers, eds., *Irish Culture and Nationalism, 1750–1950*, Macmillan, London, 1983, pp. 104–121.

Maplestone, Michael, *Flying High: The History of the Essendon Football Club*, Essendon Football Club, Melbourne, 1983.

Maplestone, Michael, *Those Magnificent Men, 1897–1987*, Essendon Football Club, Essendon, 1988.

Markoff, Barry, *The Road to 'A' Grade: A History of the Ajax Football Club*, Brownhall Prints, Clayton North, ca 1980.

Marshall, Barbara, comp. *The National Game in the National Capital*, ACT Australian Football League, Canberra, 1983.

Mason, Nicholas, *Football! The Story of All the World's Football Games*, Hicks Smith & Sons, Sydney, 1974, Chapter 5, 'Splendid isolation: Gaelic Football and Australian Football: 1858 to 1970', pp. 77–101.

Masters, R., 'The codes of football: You can tell a lot about a city by its football nuttiness: But Sydneysiders and Melburnites might not like what they hear', *Inside Sport*, Sydney, September 1992, pp. 62–71.

Matthews, Brian, *Oval Dreams: Larrikin Essays on Sport & Culture*, McPhee Gribble, Ringwood, Vic., 1991.

Mensforth, Shane, *Jarman Magic: The Andrew Jarman Story*, Jarforth Publications, North Haven, S.A., 1994.

The Mercury, Hobart, 1866–.

Morley, Clive, 'Going to the footy: VFL attendances 1950–1986', *Australian Marketing Researcher*, vol. 11, no. 2, February 1988, pp. 5–17.

Mullen, C. C., *History of Australian Rules Football, 1858 to 1958*, Horticultural Press, Melbourne, 1958.

Mulvaney, D.J., *Cricket Walkabout: The Australian Aboriginal Cricketers on Tour 1867–8*, Melbourne University Press, Melbourne, 1967.

Murray, Bill and Paul Bartrop, 'Victorian sports crowd attendances, 1925–1939', *Australian Historical Statistics*, no. 4, November 1981, pp. 46–54.

Murray, Bill, *Football: A History of the World Game*, Scolar Press, Hampshire, U.K., 1994.

Murray's Sports Series: Australian Football, Murray Books, Sydney, 1979.

Nadel, Dave, 'Aborigines and Australian Football: The rise and fall of the Purnim Bears', *Sporting Traditions*, vol. 9, no. 7, May 1993, pp. 47–63.

Nicholls, John, with Ian McDonald, *Big Nick*, Garry Sparke & Associates, Hawthorn, Vic., 1977.

Nowicki, Stan and Frank Filippone, *A Run Through the Runthroughs: VFL Cheersquads and their Banners*, Collins Dove, Blackburn, 1989.

Oakley, Barry, *A Salute to the Great McCarthy*, Penguin Books, Melbourne, 1970.

O'Dwyer, B. W., 'The shaping of Victorian rules football: From the 1850s to 1890s', *Victorian Historical Journal*, vol. 60, no. 1, March 1989, pp. 27–41.

O'Toole, Alan, *The Coach from the City*, Rigby, Adelaide, 1967.

Palmer, Scott and Greg Hobbs, *100 Great Marks*, Sun Books, Melbourne, 1974.

Parkin, David, Ross Smith and Peter Schokman, *Premiership Football: How to*

Train, Play and Coach Australian Football, Hargreen, North Melbourne, 1984.

Pavia, Grant, 'An investigation into the sociological background of successful South Australian footballers', *Australian Journal of Physical Education*, no. 63, March 1974, pp. 9–15.

Piesse, Ken, *The Complete Guide to Australian Football*, Pan Macmillan, Chippendale NSW, 1993.

Piesse, Ken, *Ablett: The Gary Ablett Story*, Wilkinson Books, Melbourne, 1994.

Pinchin, Ken, *A Century of Tasmanian Football*, Launceston, 1979.

Pinchin, Ken, *The Blues Story–100 Years of Competition Football, 1877–1977*, Ken Pinchin, Longford, Tas., 1977.

Pollard, Jack, ed., *High Mark*, K.G. Murray, Sydney, c. 1963.

Porter, Ashley, and the Adelaide Crows, *Crows' Tales*, HarperCollins, Pymble, NSW, 1993.

Porter, Dennis, comp., *A History of the Victorian Public Service Football Association, 1964–1983*, Self-published, Melbourne, 1983.

Powers, John, *The Coach: A Season with Ron Barassi*, Thomas Nelson, West Melbourne, 1978.

Pyke, Frank and Ross Smith, *Football: The Scientific Way*, University of Western Australia Press, Nedlands, WA, 1975.

Richards, Lou and Tom Prior, *The Footballer Who Laughed*, Hutchinson of Australia, Richmond, Vic., 1981.

Richards, Lou with Stephen Phillips, *The Kiss of Death*, Hutchinson Australia, Sydney, 1989.

Richards, Lou with Stephen Phillips, *Shooting from the Lip*, Magenta Press, Scoresby, Vic., 1990.

Roberts, Michael, *A Century of the Best: The Stories of Collingwood's Favourite Sons*, Collingwood Football Club, Melbourne, 1991.

Rodgers, Stephen, *The Complete Book of VFL Records*, Self-published, Melbourne, 1987.

Rodgers, Stephen, *Every Game Ever Played: VFL Results 1897–1989*, Viking O'Neil, Melbourne, 1983, rev. edn, 1990, 1992.

Rowell, Ted, 'Series of talks by Ted Rowell about Sport on the Eastern Goldfields in the Early Days', broadcast on ABC Radio, 1954. Typescript at Battye Q796.

Sandercock, Leonie and Ian Turner, *Up Where, Cazaly? The Great Australian Game*, Granada, London, 1981.

Scott, Alan, *Football for Boys*, Golden Press, Potts Point, NSW, 1971.

Sharp, M. P., 'Australian football in Sydney before 1914', *Sporting Traditions*, vol. 4, no. 1, November 1987, pp. 27–45.

Sheedy, Jack with Darcy Farrell, *My Football Life*, Self-published, Perth, 1969.

Slattery, Geoff, and others, *At Last! Collingwood, Premiers 1990*, Text Publishing Company, East Melbourne, 1990.

Stewart, Bob, *The Australian Football Business: A Spectator's Guide to the VFL*, Kangaroo Press, Melbourne, 1984.

Stewart, Bob, 'Sport as big business', in Geoffrey Lawrence and David Rowe, eds, *Power Play: Essays in the Sociology of Australian Sport*, Hale & Iremonger, Sydney, 1986, pp. 64–84.

Stewart, Bob and Robert Pascoe, eds, *Oval Logic*, Victoria University of Technology, Footscray, 1994.

Stoddart, Brian, 'Sport and Society 1890–1940', in C. T. Stannage, ed., *A New History of Western Australia*, University of Western Australia Press, Nedlands, W.A., 1981, pp. 652–780.

Stoddart, Brian, 'Sport: The horses started in different directions', in Jim Davidson, ed., *The Sydney–Melbourne Book*, Allen & Unwin, Sydney, 1986, pp. 247–58.

Stoddart, Brian, *Saturday Afternoon Fever: Sport in the Australian Culture*, Angus & Robertson, North Ryde, NSW, 1986.

Street Ryan and Associates, *Socio-Economic Impact of Australian Football*, National Australian Football Council, Melbourne, 1993.

Stremski, Richard, *Kill for Collingwood*, Allen & Unwin, Sydney, 1986.

Sutherland, Mike, Rod Nicholson and Stewart Murrihy, *The First One Hundred Seasons: Fitzroy Football Club, 1893–1983*, Fitzroy Football Club, Melbourne, 1983.

Taylor, E. C. H., *100 Years of Football: The Story of the Melbourne Football Club*, Melbourne Football Club, Melbourne, 1958.

Taylor, K., *Footystats 1993: Australian Football League Statistics, 1897–1992*, Fast Books, Sydney, 1992 [and 1993, 1994 updates].

The Times, London, 1857–.

Topham, Ross, 'The Collingwood Football Club and Collingwood', fourth year thesis, Department of History, University of Melbourne, 1974, published in *Meanjin*, vol. 34, no. 2, June 1975, pp. 157–163.

Victoria. Department of Community Welfare Services, *The Community Effects of VFL Sunday Football*, Office of Research and Social Policy, Melbourne, 1981.

Victorian Football League, *League Football in Victoria*, VFL, Melbourne, 1972.

Warren, John, *Australian Football Fundamentals*, Reed, Frenchs Forest, NSW, 1982, rev. ed., 1983.

Warren, John, *Australian Rules Football*, Cambridge University Press, Cambridge, 1988.

Weightman, Dale with Bruce Eva, *Saving Our Skins, And Other Tiger Tales*, Floradale Productions, Kilmore, 1991.

Wheadon, David, *Drills and Skills in Australian Rules Football*, Longman Cheshire, Melbourne, 1988.

Wheadon, David, *Tactics in Modern Football*, Longman Cheshire, Melbourne, 1990.

Whimpress, Bernard, *The South Australian Football Story*, South Australian National Football League Inc., Adelaide, 1983.

Williams, L. and C. Greenwood, *From the Ashes: A History of the Mid-Gippsland Football League*, Morwell, Vic., 1985.

Williams, Lynette, *Birth of the Blues: A History of the Beulah Football Club, 1891–1991*, Beulah Football Club, Red Cliffs, Vic., 1991.

Williams, Ron, comp., *North Launceston Football Club, 1899–1990: The Robins*, North Launceston Football Club, Launceston, Tas., 1991.

Wood, John, *Bound for Glory: The Story of the Port Adelaide Football Club, 1939–1990*, John and Wendy Wood, Glenelg, S.A. 1991.

Wood, John, *S.A. Greats: The History of the Magarey Medal*, John and Wendy Wood, Plympton, S.A., 1988.

Wood, John, *Gentleman Jack: The Johnny Cahill Story, 1958–82*, John and Wendy Wood, Plympton, S.A., 1982.

Young, Ray and Dave Pincombe, *Footy Facts: All-Australia Guide to Aussie Rules, 1986–87*, Information Australia, Melbourne, 1987.

Index

Abikhair, Dick 60
Ablett, Gary 37, 202, 204, 217, 247
Abley, John 158
Aboriginal football 12, 47, 48–9, 52, 247
  players 60, 125, 203, 205, 218
Adams, Frank 'Bluey' 25
Adamson, L. A. 'Dicky' 86, 208–9
Adelaide Crows Football Club 9, 23, 217
'Aintree' (C. L. Stopford) 104
Ajax Football Club 144
Albert Park Football Club 56
Albiston, Alec 40, 129
Albress, William 60
Alexander, Ron 213
Alves, Stan 31
amateur football 126, 127, 208–9
Anderson, Frank 29
Andrew, Bruce 31
Anti Football League 232
Anzac legend 91–3
Armstrong, Ken 191, 194, 210
Arnold, Paul 194
Arthur, Graham 33
Atkins, Simon 230
attendances 72, 99, 236
Atwell, Mal 174–6, 190–1
Austen, Colin 29
Austin, Rod 'Curly' 30
Australian Capital Territory football 234

Australian Cricketer's Guide 47
Australian Football League (AFL) 218–19,
243–4
  statistics 260–1
  see also Victorian Football League
Australian Rules football
  codification of 47–8, 51, 59
  cultural determinants 47–52
  initial development xv
  official origin 47
  spread of 55–60
Aylett, Dr Allen 183, 201
Ayres, Gary 30, 202

Baggott, Ron 118
Bagley, Ken 171
Bairstow, Mark 204, 212, 216
Baker, Leon 202, 211
Baldock, Daryl 34, 161
ball characteristics 8
ball-up (bounce-down) 11, 16, 66
Ballarat football 50, 58
Ballarat Football Club 58
Ballarat South Football Club 58
Balme, Neil 38, 184–6, 224–5
Banbury, Vernon 94
Banks, Norm 92
Barassi Line xiii
Barassi, Cliff 117

Barassi, Elza 141
Barassi, Mario 117
Barassi, Ron jnr 19, 41, 96, 140–2, 144, 149, 161–3, 165–8, 187, 196, 205, 225, 230, 239
Barassi, Ron snr 19, 117
Barker, Syd 41, 123
Barker, Tim 170
Barnes, John 204
barrackers *see* supporters
Barrot, Bill 32, 165
Bartlett, Kevin 'Hungry' 24, 40, 184–5
Barwick, Victor 285
baseball curtain-raisers 110
Beames, Percy 40, 118
Beard, Colin 191
Beasley, Simon 210, 215
Beazley, W. D. 65
Beckton, Norman 105, 123
Beckwith, John 4, 26
Bedford, Peter 167
Belcher, Vic 37
Bennett, Darren 12
Bentley, Perc 38
Bentley, Perc 118
best and fairest medals 18
    see also Brownlow Medal; Magarey Medal; Sandover Medal
Beveridge family 19
Billings, Ken 188
Birt, John 152
Bisset, George 187
Blackwell, Wayne 211
Blight, Malcolm 11, 33, 187, 199, 205, 209, 214, 216
boot inspection 42
bounce-down *see* ball-up
Bourke, David 19
Bourke, Francis 19, 30
Bourke, Frank 19
Box, Peter 32
Boyd, Dave E. 157–8
Boyd, Johnnie 123
Bradley, Craig 42, 216
Breen, Barry 34, 163
Brehaut, Greg 210
Breman, Todd 212
Bremner, Ian 28
Brennan 226

Brereton, Dermott 15, 23, 34, 202, 217
Brereton, Harry 11
Brewer, Ian 148, 174
bribery allegations 94
    see also gambling
Brisbane Bears Football Club 23, 212
Britannia Football Club 56, 64–5
Brittingham, Bill 27, 129–30
Broadstock, Jack 136
Brosnan, Gerald 34
Brown, Alf 122–3, 150–2
Brown, Mal 174, 176–7, 190–3, 209, 211
Brownless, Billy 204
Brownlow Medal 99
    medallists 255–61
Brownlow, Charles 57, 99
Bruns, Neville 215
Brunswick Football Club 65
Buckenara, Gary 17, 194, 210, 216
Buhagiar, Anthony 203
Bunton, Haydn jnr 157, 170, 171, 172, 174–5, 178, 191, 211
Bunton, Haydn snr 40, 113, 119–20, 140
Burgess, Reg 123
Burley (football) 8
Burnie Football Club 233–4
Burns, Peter 37
Burton, Peter 195
Burwell, F. W. 87
Busustow, Peter 211
Buttsworth, Fred 135, 153

Cable, Barry 40, 172, 175–7, 190–1, 193–5, 209
Cahill, Bill 112
Cahill, John 206, 234
Cahill, Laurie 157
Cain, John 308
Cairns, Dr Jim 189
Camberwell Football Club 58, 103
Cameron, Ern 39
Campbell, Blair 11
Campbell, 'Garney' 123
Campbell, Graham 193
Cananore Football Club 110
Canterbury Football Club 58
Capper, Warwick 24
Cardwell, Jim 187, 239

Carey, Wayne 34, 247
Carlton Football Club 8–9, 55, 56, 57, 58, 73, 123–6
  administration 189–90
  formation 49–50
  origins 21
  premierships 82, 84–6, 116, 128, 129, 165–6, 196, 199, 214, 216
  supporters 110–11, 144, 167–8
  see also Victorian football
Carman, Phil 188–9
carnivals see interstate competition
Carr, Barney 105
Carroll, Dennis 31
Carroll, Tom 160
Caspar, Harry 131
Castledine, Fred 171, 174
Catholic school football 144
Cazaly, Roy 39, 41, 98–9, 112, 128
Central District 235
  see also South Australian football
Chadwick, Albert 28, 105
Chadwick, Derek 175
Champion of the Colony 28, 35, 39, 63
  see also Brownlow Medal
Chandler, Newton 30
Chapman, Charles 105
cheer squads 206–7
Chipp, Don 241
Chitty, Bob 28
Churchett, C. J. 137
City Football Club (Launceston) 112
City South Football Club (Launceston) 112
Claremont Football Club 119, 132, 134, 135, 226–7
  see also Western Australian football
Clarence Football Club 233, 234
Clark, Manning 229
Clark, Norm 'Hackenschmidt' 29
Clark, Sammy 119
Clarke, Ern 188
Clarke, Jack 32, 155, 173
Clarkson, Jack 123
class identity 46, 51, 60, 71–7
Clay, Richard 'Dick' 31
Clayden, George 28
Cleary, 'Gentleman' Jim 27
Cleary, Phil 241

Clegg, Ron 29
Cloke, David 34
Clover, Horrie 11, 34, 98–9, 103
club nicknames
  Blood and Tars 136
  Blood-stained niggers 124n9
  Bombers 116
  Bulldogs 116
  Dons 123
  Fuchsias 96
  Gorillas 246
  Hawks 128
  Maroons 75
  Mayblooms 95
  Old Easts 210
  Pivotonians 84
  Purloiners 65
  Redlegs 102
  Same Olds 72
  Sharks 210
  Shinboners 78
  Students 72
  Tricolours 56
  Young Easts 86
coaches 4, 26, 43–4, 82, 94–5
  captain-coaches 43
coaching styles 224–5, 228
Coburg Football Club 103
Cockatoo-Collins, Che 203
Coleman, Bob 173
Coleman, John 27, 36, 130–1, 137, 145, 200
Coles, Sir Edgar 188
Collard, Herb 111
Collard, Tony 111
Collegians 209
Collier, Albert 'Leeter' 29, 95, 103, 110, 115
Collier, Harry 40, 95, 115, 140
Collingwood Football Club 8, 9, 11, 56, 91, 94–7, 126, 188–9
  administration 115, 143, 188–9, 206
  club loyalty 74–5, 96–7, 143
  club song 77
  colours 65
  formation of 64
  nicknames 65
  origins 22–3
  premierships 66, 75, 80, 86, 97, 102–3, 114, 115, 153, 146, 148, 217

supporters 76, 110, 169, 206
tactics 46, 74, 78, 80
see also Victorian football
Collins, Andrew 25
Collins, Jack 36, 146, 148
Collis, Gordon 29, 162
Colreavy, John 192
Combden, Bruce 'Bugsy' 26
Cometti, Denis 210
Compton, J. 'Froggy' 119, 162
Condon, Richard 39, 74
Connolly, Rohan 222
Considine, Ed 202
Coodabeen Champions 231
Cook, Fred 36
Cookson, Bill 122
Cooper, Ian 35
Copeland, Ern 65, 66
Corbett, Bob 101, 105
Cordner, David 19
Cordner, Denis 29, 142
Cordner, Don 41
Cordner, Harry 84
Cordner, Ted 19, 84
Cornes, Graham 196
Couch, Paul 19, 32, 216–7
Coulter Law *see* player payments
Counihan, Noel 69
country football 50, 51, 111–12, 125, 150
Couper, Murray 194
Coventry, Gordon 'Nuts' 27, 36, 95, 98, 101–3, 114, 116, 129
Coventry, Syd 38, 95, 102, 116, 140
Cover, Ian 232–3
Cransberg, Alan 211
Crawford, Hector 188
Crawley, W. S. 65
Crimmins, Peter 24, 40
Crisp, Micky 124
Crosswell, Brent 19, 23, 34, 115, 188, 205
Cubbins, William 27, 105
Culpitt 128
Cumberland, Harry 'Vic' 41, 285
Cummeragunja Football Club 125
Curtin, John 239
Curtis, Harry 95, 115
Cuzens, Dave 172

Daicos, Peter 35, 217
Dalwood, P. A. 136
Dandenong Football Club 190
Daniel, Peter 210
Daniher family 202
Davie, Harry 99
Davis, Allan 35
Davis, Barry 28, 187
Davis, Bob 13, 159
Davis, Robert 'Woofa' 33
Day, Barry 192
De La Salle 209
Deacon, Bert 29, 124, 129
Dean, Ken 161
Dean, Roger 26, 162
Dear, Greg 38
Dempsey, Gary 38, 163, 197
Dench, David 27
Devine, John 205
Devonport Football Club 234
Dick, William 41
Dimattina, Frank 19
Dimattina, Paul 19
DiPierdomenico, Robert 'Dipper' 31
District Football League 95
Ditterich, Carl 38
Dixon, Brian 31, 241
Dobrigh, Len 'Gus' 96
Doig, Charles 87, 120
Doig, George 133
Dolan, Jerry 135
Domnus, Brother 187
Don, Donald 40
Donald, Wally 26
Donohue, Larry 198
Dornau, Irwin 158
Dorrington, Grant 209
Doull, Bruce 28
Dowdell, Harry 66
Drohan, Edward 30
Drummond, Tom 'Chick' 96
Duckworth, Bill 202
Duncan, Alec 96
Dunne, Ross 'Twiggy' 34
Dunstall, Jason 37, 202, 216–17
Dunstan, Don 241
Dunstan, Keith 232
Duperouzel, Bruce 191

Dwyer, J. J. 87–8
Dwyer, Laurie 31
Dyer, Jack 'Captain Blood' 11, 29, 38, 42, 104, 109, 111, 118, 128, 130, 137, 140, 145, 158, 221, 223
Dyson, Edward 81
Dyson, Kevin 225

Eakins, Lee 188
Eakins-Stannage, Rev. James 170
Eason, Alex 105
East Fremantle Football Club 8, 67, 73, 86, 87, 119, 120, 121, 132, 133, 134, 135, 226–7
    see also Western Australian football
East Perth Football Club 86, 91, 94, 132, 134
    see also Western Australian football
Easton 199
Ebbs, Alan 132
Edelsten, Dr Geoffrey 206
Edmonds, 'Tubby' 95
Edwards, Brendan 32
Eicke, Wellesley 29
Elliott, Fred 'Pompey' 41, 83
Emselle, Ray 117
Epis, Alex 28
equalising competition 18, 240, 244, 246
Essendon Football Club 8, 9, 10, 47, 56, 122–3
    Mosquito Fleet 46, 122
    nicknames 72, 123
    origins 21
    premierships 647, 99, 127, 130, 161, 163, 203, 215
    recruiting 202–3
    tactics 45, 46, 98, 228
    see also Victorian football
Eustice, Ken 179
Evans, Neil 177
Evans, Ron 123, 149–50, 173
Evans, Vic 176
Excell, Gavin 204
exhibition games 8, 9, 75, 77, 80, 114, 145, 158, 199
Ezard, Alan 202

fairest and best medals see best and fairest medals

Fanning, Fred 35, 92, 118, 128, 142
Farmer, Graham 'Polly' 13, 25, 38, 40, 153–4, 156–7, 160–1, 164, 172, 176–8, 192, 205
Farmer, Ken 104, 120, 136,
father/son rule 19–20, 245
Featherby, Peter, 177, 191
Fenner, Gary 178
field dimensions xvii-xviii, 5–6
field markings
    boundary line 3–4
    centre square 7, 191
    50-m arc 14
    goal square 7
Figgins, Murray 111
finals systems 67, 77, 80, 99–100, 112–13, 196
    Argus system 80
    McIntyre final four 112–13
Fisher, Charlie 35
Fitzgerald, Len 35
Fitzmaurice, Tom 37
Fitzpatrick, Mike 39, 125, 177, 191–2
Fitzroy Football Club 6, 9, 12, 47, 56
    amalgamation with Footscray 219–20
    nicknames 75, 246
    origins 22
    premierships 67, 81, 85, 86, 98, 128
    tactics 78
    see also Victorian football
Flanagan, Fred 34
Flanagan, Martin 112, 218, 220, 229, 230, 247
Flanagan, Tom 112
Fleiter, Fred 41
Fleming, Eric 104
Fletcher, Dustin 19, 27
Fletcher, Ken 19
flick-pass 12
Flood, David 202
Flower, Robbie 24, 31, 205–6
Flynn, Jim 37
Foley, Brian 156
folk football 47
Fontaine, Fred 35
Football Park (SA) 235
Football Record 79
football cards 69, 178
Foote, Les 32

Footscray Football Club 6, 8, 12, 46, 56, 73, 91, 94, 230–1, 244
  amalgamation with Fitzroy 219–20
  colours 56
  joins VFL 100
  nicknames 56, 116
  origins 22
  premiership 142, 220–1
  see also Victorian football
Forbes, Charles 'Tracker' 37
Forbes, Keith 105
Fordham, Tom 163
Foschini, Silvio 19
Fothergill, Des 35, 118, 121, 129, 136
Foulds, Gary 202
Fowler, Laurie 30
Franks, Albert 37
Fraser, 'Mopsy' 29
Fraser, Ken 34, 123
Fraser, Malcolm 167
Freake, James 36
Fred, Mulga 77
free kicks *see* rules, infringements
Fremantle Dockers Football Club 23, 226
Fremantle Football Club 73, 86
  see also Western Australian football

Gabelich, Ray 13, 38, 172
Galbally, David 188
Galbally, Frank 188
Galbally, Jack 110, 169
Gale, Alan 'Butch' 41, 141
Gallagher 152
gambling 65–6, 73, 77–8
Gardiner, Vin 35
gate-takings 20
Gavin, Hugh 28
Geddes, Alan 30
Geelong Football Club 6, 8, 9, 55, 56, 57
  longest winning sequence 145
  nicknames 84
  origins 21
  premierships 101, 113, 116, 145, 161
  recruiting 204–5
  tactics 145, 204–5
  see also Victorian football
George, Max 192
Gerovich, John 154, 157

Gill, Frank 27
Glass, Don 155
Gleeson, Brian 148
Glendinning, Gus 19
Glendinning, Ross 19, 29, 191, 199
Glenelg Football Club 104, 120
  see also South Australian football
Glenorchy Football Club 234
goal kicking tallies 18
  see also relevant Leagues' statistics
goal posts 6–7, 14
Goggin, Bill 40, 161, 205
Golden Rules 46, 139–40, 224
Goldsmith, Fred 11, 27, 147
Goninon, George 36, 131, 145–6
Goodwin, Andy 234
Goold, John 'Ragsy' 30, 185
Gordon, Peter 219
Gormans, Eric 173
Gotz, Martin 29
Grace, James 36
Grace, Michael 35, 82
Grace, Sid 68
Greene, Russell 31
Greening, John 17, 33
Greenwood 168
Greeves, Edward 'Carji' 32, 99
Greig, Keith 31, 197
Grgic, Ilija 221, 244
Grieve 119
Griffiths, A. 88
Grinter, Rod 225
Grljusich, Tom 175
Groom, Ray 241
ground conditions 150

Hafey, Tom 26, 184–6, 189, 198, 203, 205, 214, 228
Hagger, Lloyd 101
Hale, Jack 40
half-time entertainment 76–7
Hall 168
Hall, Alec 'Joker' 39
Hamilton, Jack 27
Hamilton, Paul 202
Hammersley, W. J. 47–9
Hammond, Charlie, 37

handball 11, 12–13, 56–7, 67, 83, 96, 105, 140
Hands, Ken 'Solvol' 34, 124
Hanks, Ray W. 136, 157
Hardie, Brad 26, 215
Hardy, Charles 105
Harmes, Wayne 40
Harrington, Tom 111
Harris, George 163, 189
Harris, R. 128
Harrison, Barry 'Hooker' 142–3
Harrison, H. C. A. 47, 49
Hart, Royce 34, 164, 184–5, 226
Harvey, Mark 202
Hawke, Neil 156
Hawker, Glenn 202
Hawkins, Doug 168
Hawthorn Football Club
    colours 144
    joins VFL 100
    nicknames 95, 128
    origins 22
    premierships 160, 167, 198, 199, 214, 215, 216, 217
    tactics 45, 202, 214
    see also Victorian football
Hay, Phil 27, 202
Hay, Sted 27, 202
Hayes, Neville 158
Hayes, Robert 220
Head, Lindsay 179–80
Heal, 'Popsy' 133–4
Healey, Des 31
Healy, Gerald 35
Heard, Shane 202
Hector, Norm 10
Henderson, Herb 27
Henfry, Ern 32, 130, 154
Hepburn, Stan 105
Herald 151, 221
Herald Sun 223
Herbert, Barney 93
Heywood, Doug 224
Hickey, Harry 128
Hickey, John 189
Hickey, Pat 75
Hickey, Reg 29
Hinkley, Ken 28

Hird, Alan jnr 19, 188
Hird, Alan snr 19
Hird, James 19
Hocking, Gary 'Buddha' 42, 204
Hocking, Steven 204
Hogg, Bruce 142
Holten, 'Mac' 126
Hopkins, Alan 32, 105
Hosking, 'Shine' 104
Hotham Football Club 56
Howard, Ray 155
Howell, 'Chooka' 38, 130
Howell, Verdun 27, 190
Hudson, Paul 19
Hudson, Peter 19, 30, 36, 164–5, 167, 198
Hughes, Danny 216
Hughes, Frank 'Checker' 39, 93–4, 118, 163, 203
humour 68–9, 231–3
Hunt, Rex 221
Hunter, Ken 30
Hutchinson, Bill 38, 40, 122–3, 145, 147, 152
Hutchinson, Ross 133–4
Hyde, Albert 105, 145

Imperials Football Club 58
Industrial Football League 111
Ingersoll 152
injuries 24
interchange players 104
    see also Nineteenth Man; Twentieth Man
intercolonial competition 57
international ambitions 55, 158, 246
interstate competition 88, 158, 171, 180, 213, 218
Ironmonger, John 211
Irving, Dean 226

Jack Oatey Medal 180
Jackson, Eddie 125
Jackson, Mark 37
Jackson, Syd 33, 175, 190, 203
Jakovich, Allen 4, 36, 226, 227
Jakovich, Glen 29
James, Benjamin 49
James, Hugh 97
James, John 29, 125, 160

Jenkins, Frank 'Scranno' 132, 133–4
Jesaulenko, Alex 30, 199–200
Jess, Jim 29
Jewell, Tony 26
Johns, R. F. 178
Johnson, Alan 25, 210, 216
Johnson, Bob jnr 172–3, 175, 190
Johnson, David 202
Johnson, Edward 101, 105
Johnson, 'Mocha' 124
Johnson, Robert 38, 105
Johnston, Gregory 105
Johnston, Wayne 42
Jones, Chris 224
Jones, Dennis 191
Jones, Peter 'Percy' 38, 145, 166
Jordon, Ray 'Slug' 184, 187
journalism 68–9, 78–9, 92, 150–2, 159–60, 221–3
Joyce, Alan 177, 191, 194, 231
Judkins, Stan 30
junior football 110, 126, 127, 243

Kalgoorlie football 87–8
Kavanagh, Tom 19
Keane, Gavin 202
Keenan, Peter 'Crackers' 19, 38, 186, 188
Kelly, Des 153
Kelly, Phil 194–5
Kemp, Dean 42
Kennedy, John jnr 19
Kennedy, John snr 19, 38, 144, 240
Kennedy, Rick 27
Kenny, Peter 211
Kerley, Neil 'Iron' 178–9, 196
Kernahan, Stephen 34, 216
Kerr, Cecil 105
Kettlewell, Laurie 152
kick-outs 15, 66
Kickett, Dale 203
Kickett, Derek 33, 212
kicking styles 11–12, 46, 80, 96, 140
Killigrew, Alan 158, 161, 175
Kilmurray, Ted 154
Knights, Peter 29
Krakouer, Jim 40, 210, 218, 247
Krakouer, Phil 40, 210, 218, 247
Kyne, Phonse 38, 126, 130, 143

La Fontaine, Allan 32
Lahiff, Tommy 230
Lambert, Harold 123
Lane, Gordon 'Whoppa' 123
Lane, Tim 221
Langdon, Don 173
Langford, Chris 27, 202
Langford, Dick 66
language of football 61
Larcombe, Jack 135
Larkin, Phillip 229
Latrobe Football Club 233
Launceston Football Club 112, 234
Lawrence, Ray 173
Lawrence, Ron 155
Lawson, Joe 171
Le Brun, Norm 121
Leach, Frederick 31
'League Teams' 159
league ladder 17–18
Lee, Dick 85, 98
Lee, Mark 233
Lee, Walter 'Dick' 36, 66, 97
Leonard, Tony 232–3
Lewington, Clive 153
Lewington, Neil 132, 134–5
Lewis, Chris 33, 226, 247
Lewis, Percy 104
Libbis, William 40
Liberatore, Tony 40
Lindner, Bruce 204
Lindner, Don 179–80
Little League 177
little mark 67
Lockett, Tony 37, 216
Lockwood, Ted 76
Loewe, Stewart 34
Lofts, Wes 27
Long, Michael 13, 33, 203, 247
Longerigan, Mike 'Mad Mick' 30
Lord, Alistair 32, 160–1
Lord, Stewart 160
Loveridge, Richard 214
Lovett, Glenn 225
Lovett, Wally 125
Luke, Kenneth 158, 183
Lund, Eric 122
Lyon, Garry 'Dollars' 6, 35

Macdonald, Ranald 206
Madden, Justin 39
Madden, Michael 81
Madden, Simon 39, 202
Madden, Sir John 95
Maffina, 'Sonny' 153
Magarey Medal 104, 136, 137, 263–70
Magee, Stewart 192
Magro, Stan 26
Maher, Frank 40, 104
Mainwaring, Chris 31
Makeham, Robert 35
Malarkey, Gary 27, 191
Malone, Mick 177
Malthouse, Michael 26, 186, 215, 225
Manassa, Phil 13
Mann, 'Hassa' 41, 162, 176–7
Manning, Peter 171
Mantello, Albert 30
Marchbank, Jim 37
Margitich, George 103
Marinko, Don 156
marking the ball 12
Marmalade, Trevor 232
marn-grook 12, 48–9, 50, 247
   see also Aboriginal football
Marriott, J. E. 137
Marsh, Steve 132, 153–4, 156
Marshall, Denis 32, 161, 176, 190
Marshall, T. S. 49, 66
Martin, Harold,4
Martini, Percy 35
Martini, Raymond 123
Martyn, Mick 27
Mason, Angus 105
Matera, Peter 13, 31
Matthews, Brian 151
Matthews, Harold 29
Matthews, Herb 31, 116, 118–9
Matthews, 'Lethal' Leigh 40, 189, 197, 202, 215
May, Charles 'Chooka' 32, 157
Mayman, Bill 88
Maynard, Colin 171
McAlister, Alan 206
McAlpine, Ivan 31
McAullay, Ken 191
McCallum, Firth 33

McCarthy, Con 37, 94, 96
McClelland, Dr William 92, 158
McClure, 'Bluey' 146
McClure, Bob 38
McConnell, Roy 29
McCormack, Peter 27
McCracken, Alex 63
McCrae, Hugh 'Splash' 69
McDermott, Chris 42, 217
McDonald, Norm 28, 203
McDonald, 'Runty' 133
McDonnell, Marty 156
McGrath, J.P. 'Shane' 27
McGregor, Bruce 104
McGregor, Rod 32
McGuane, Michael 13, 42
McHale, Jock jnr 188
McHale, Jock snr 31, 43, 94–5, 110, 115, 116, 117, 126, 130, 143, 144, 203
McInerney, Jack 66
McIntosh, Ashley 30, 226
McIntosh, John 172
McIntosh, Merv 134, 153–4
McIntyre, Kenneth 112–13, 196
McKay, Joe 195
McKenna, Guy 28, 226
McKenna, Peter 36, 196
McKenzie, Jack 37
McLean, Bob 158
McMahen, Noel 28
McNamara, Dave 12, 19, 34, 81, 99, 187
McSperrin, Billy 13
Melbourne Cricket Club (MCC) 56, 208
Melbourne Cricket Ground (MCG) 5, 6, 9, 57, 208, 240, 243
Melbourne Football Club 9, 56
   amateur status 64, 72, 73, 109
   nicknames 96
   origins 21
   premierships 73, 80, 96, 102, 112, 117, 118, 129, 147, 148, 149, 150, 162
   role in rules formulation 47, 48
   tactics 46, 78, 203–4, 205, 224–5, 228
   see also Victorian football
Melrose, Graham 210–11
Menzies, Sir Robert 167, 206
Merifield, Kevin 152
Merrett, Roger 34, 202

Merrett, Thorold 31
Merrick, Robert 98
Metropolitan Amateurs 111
Metropolitan Junior Football Association 208
Mew, Chris 30
Michael, Stephen 171, 195, 210–11
Michalcyzk, Richard 191
Middlemiss 145
Midlands Junction Football Club 86, 87
Miller, Ian 193
Minogue, Dan 37, 40, 94, 96
Mitchell, Bill 69
Mithen, Laurie 32
Modra, Tony 37
Moffat, David 41, 93
Mohr, Wilbur 'Bill' 36
Moloney, George 36, 119
Monkhorst, Damian 39
Monohan, Jack 28, 74, 81
Monteath, Bruce 209
Moore, Don 111
Moore, Kenny 111
Moore, Peter 39, 189, 199, 215
Moriarty, Don 104
Moriarty, Jack 36, 113
Morris, William 38, 130, 145
Morrisey, James 35
Morrison, Albert 35
Morrow, Allan 38
Morton, Fred 123–5
Moss, Graham 39, 43, 193, 198, 211
Motley, Geoff 158
Mueller, Jack 36, 116–18
Mullen, Cec 92
Murdoch, Joe 29
Murphy, Eddie 66
Murray, Dan 172
Murray, Kevin 30, 172, 174–5
Murray, Robert 27

Nankervis, Bruce 41
Nankervis, Ian 26
Narkle, Phil 210–11
Nash, Laurie 34, 111–12
Nathan, Sir Maurice 183
National Australian Football Council 77, 140
national draft 18–19, 20
Nauru government 22, 246

Naylor, Bernie 132, 134, 153, 155
Neagle, Merv 202
Neale, Kevin 'Cowboy' 34–5
Neesham, Gerard 227–8
Neesham, Harry 177
Nettlefold, William 41
New Norfolk Football Club 233, 234
New South Wales football 57, 80, 88, 158
New Zealand football 88
Newman, John 'Sam' 38
Nicholls, Doug 60
Nicholls, John 38, 167–8
Nineteenth Man 24, 42
Niven, Col 105
Norm Smith Medal 30
Normanby Football Club 63
North Adelaide Football Club 88, 120, 136
  see also South Australian football
North Fremantle Football Club 86
North Hobart Football Club 234
North Launceston Football Club 233
North Melbourne Football Club 9, 10, 56, 73,
186–8
  nicknames 78
  origins 22
  premierships 78, 197, 198
  tactics 228
  VFA record 78
  violent reputation 78, 100
  see also Victorian football
North Tasmanian Football Association 112
Northcote Football Club 112
Northern Tasmanian Football League 233
Northern Territory football 120, 234
Northey, John 33, 186, 205–6, 216, 224–5
Norwood Football Club 55, 88, 104, 136
  see also South Australian football
Nowotny, Stan 211

O'Brien, Paddy 28
O'Brien, Paul 186, 217
O'Dea, Jim 17
O'Donnell, Gary 202
O'Neil 119
O'Neill, Kevin 26
Oakleigh Football Club 103–4, 190
Oakley, Ross 201
Oates, Max 19

Oates, Michael 19
Oatey, Jack 43, 136, 157, 178–80, 186
Officer, Edward 27
Ogden, Percy 39
Old Melburnians 209
Old Paradians 208
Old Scotch Football Club 208
Oliver, Harold 104
Oliver, Norm 121
Olliver, Arthur 41, 156
Olsen, Mark 194
Ongarello, Tony 11
Oppy, Max 26
Orbost Football Club 125
Ormond Football Club 209
Outen, Albert 105
Ovenden, Dick 69, 123

Pagan, Denis 26, 223, 228
Page, Percy 118
Pannam, Albert 40
Pannam, Charles 30, 74, 101
Park, Roy 35, 85
Parkin, David 26, 192, 228
Parkinson, John 175
Parratt, Percy 33
Patterson, Mike 179
Peake, Brian 193, 204–5
Pearson, Charles 'Commotion' 12, 49
Peck, John 'Elvis' 36, 161–3
Pelly, Jim 111
Peos, Paul 226
Perkin, Graham 222
Pert, Brian 19
Pert, Gary 19
Perth Football Club 8, 86, 132, 133, 134, 135
  see also Western Australian football
Petchell, J. H. 105
Peters, Vic 104
Phillips, H. R. 136
Pianto, Peter 172
Picken, Bill 29
Platten, John 40, 216
player identification numbers 24
player payments 18–19, 66, 71–2, 73–6, 109–10
  Coulter Law 18, 109
  Western Australian 134

player transfers 19, 46, 187, 209, 245
playing gear 23–4
playing positions 25–42
  back pocket 25–6
  centre 31–3
  centre half-forward 33–4
  centre half-back 28–9
  defenders 29–30
  follower 41
  forward pocket 26
  forward 35
  full-back 7, 15, 26–7, 36
  full-forward 7, 26, 35–7
  half-back flank 28
  half-forward flank 33
  interchange 42
  rover 26, 39–40
  ruck 26, 37–9
  ruck-rover 41–2
  utilities 29
  wing 30–1
Pola, J. 120
police involvement 3, 17, 114, 161, 215
Pool, Ted 105
Port Adelaide
Port Adelaide Football Club 46, 73–4, 88, 104, 120, 136, 140
  colours 65
  joins AFL 22, 235
  see also South Australian football
Port Melbourne Football Club 46, 56, 78, 94, 140, 187
Porter, Don 135
Potter, Edward 30
Power, Tom 49
Prahran Football Club 100
Pratt, Bob 36, 103, 114, 167
pre-season matches 14, 17
Preston Football Club 103
Price, Barry 32
Prince Imperial Football Club 56
professionalism 18, 47, 63, 65–6, 69, 71–6, 77
Protestant Churches Association League 111
Proudfoot, Bill 25, 29, 66, 74
Pryor, Geoff 188
punching the ball 11, 12
Pye, Brother 120

Quinlan, Bernie 'Superboot' 36, 189, 215
Quinn, Johnny 16

radio 92, 159, 221, 231, 232–3
Raines, Geoff 32
Ralph, Warren 210–11
Ranson, Trevor 112
Rantall, John 28, 187
Rattray, Gordon 33
Ray, Allan 141
Rayson, Noel 147
Reese, Harvey 123
Regan, Jack 27, 95, 125
Reilly, Stephen 222
religious influences 21, 22, 93, 94, 144
Reserves football 97, 112
Reynolds, Colin 171
Reynolds, Dick 40, 116, 118, 122–3, 127
Rhys-Jones, David 233
Richards, Lou 30, 40, 137, 159, 230
Richardson, Barry 27
Richardson, Viv 88
Richmond Football Club 56, 93–3, 184–6
   joins VFL 72, 78, 82
   origins 22
   premierships 94, 96, 98, 113, 114, 128,
   164, 165, 185, 197, 200
   supporters 206
   tactics 45, 186
   see also Victorian football
Richmond, Graeme 68, 184–5, 206
Riley, 'Mick' 68
Rioli, Maurice 195, 210, 247
Roach, Michael 36, 200
Roberts, Michael 19
Roberts, Neil 19, 148
Roberts, William 105
Robertson, Austin 172, 175, 176–7, 192
Robran, Barrie 179–80
Rohde, Peter 225
Roos, Paul 29
Rose, Bob 19, 40, 143
Rose, Robert 19
Round, Barry 38
Rowe, Percy 38
Rowell, Ted 27, 74
Royal, Brian 220
royal families of football 19

Rudolph, George 104
Rugby 24, 48, 51, 57, 89, 240–1
rules
   changes 56, 66, 239–40
   duration of game 9–10
      final siren (bell) 10
      time on 9, 10
   15-m penalty 16, 154
   50-m penalty 16–17
   formulation xvi-xvii, xix, 3–20
   free kicks xvii, xviii, xix, 4, 12, 15–16, 66
      from kick-out 15
   infringements 15–17
      holding the ball 16
      holding the man 16
      relayed free kick 132
      reports 17
      running with the ball 13, 16
      secondary infringements 17
      throwing the ball 11, 13, 16
      time-wasting 154
   out of bounds 4, 13, 14, 15, 16, 33, 66, 96,
   101, 104, 165
      out of bounds on full 177
   principles of interpretation 16
   send-off power 17, 78
   shepherding 16
   standing the mark 12
   tackles 15, 16
runners 43
Rush, Bob 26, 115, 143
Ruthven, Alan 'Baron' 40

salary cap 18–19, 245
Salmon, Paul 202
Sampson, Brian 177
Samson, V. 105
Sandland, John 196
Sandover Medal 119, 134–5, 273–9
Sandringham Football Club 103
Sandy Bay Football Club 234
Sarich, Eric 177
Saunders, Hary 96
Saxon, Lee 187, 189
Scaddan, John 87, 241
Scanlan, Paddy 101
Schimmelbusch, Wayne 33
Schmidt, Bill 13, 32

Schofield, Ray 155
Schultz, Graham 202
Schultz, John 150
Schwab, Alan 184
Schwarz, David 19
scoring
    behinds 6, 7, 11, 14, 15, 66
    goals 14
Scott, Don 38, 40, 185
Scott, Ray 135, 153
Screaigh, Merv 152
Seal, Paul 173
Sekem 8
Sellers, Bob 105
Sergeant, Cec 220
Serong, Bill 32, 144
Sharland, Wally 'Jumbo' 92
Sharp, James 29
Sharrock, John 33
Shaw, Derek 195
Shaw, Tony 32
Sheedy, Jack 132, 137, 154–5, 172, 174,
176–7
Sheedy, Kevin 26, 186, 203, 223, 227–8
Sheehy, Maurice 96
Shelton, Ian 'Bluey' 29
Sherrin (football) 8
Sherrin, Tom 169
Silvagni, Sergio 19, 41, 60, 168
Silvagni, Stephen 19, 27
Sime, Charlie 'Buffer' 66
Simmonds, Roy 29
Simpson Medal 132
    see also Western Australian football
Simunson, Bob 179
Skilton, Bob 40, 149, 161, 165
Slater, Joe 29
Slater, Keith 171–3
Smallhorn, Wilfred 'Chicken' 31, 113
Smith, Arch 'Snapper' 66
Smith, B. 194
Smith, Bernie 26, 131
Smith, Dave 34
Smith, Ken 209
Smith, Len 46, 139–41
Smith, Mike 211
Smith, Norm 19, 30, 36, 118–19, 140–3,
146–7, 162–3, 166, 187, 225

Smith, Peter 19, 142
Smith, Ross 40, 164, 191
Smith, T. H. 47, 48
Somerville, John 17
Somerville, Peter 202
Sorrell, Ray 173, 174
South Adelaide Football Club 88
    see also South Australian football
South Australian football 71–2, 73, 234–5
    colours and nicknames 235
    1900s 88–9
    1920s 104
    1930s 120
    1940s 135–7
    1950s 157–8
    1960s 178–9
    1970s 179, 195–6
    statistics 262–71
    wartime amalgamations 135–6
South Fremantle Football Club 46, 86, 87,
119, 121, 132, 133, 134, 135, 226–7
    see also Western Australian football
South Launceston Football Club 112, 233
South Melbourne Football Club 56
    'Foreign Legion' 109, 114
    origins 22
    premierships 83, 86, 109, 114
    Sydney relocation 201, 225, 244
    see also Victorian football
Southby, Geoff 27, 185
Southern Sky, Western Oval 230
Spalding 8
Spargo, Bob 174
Sparrow, Frank 155
Spencer, Baldwin 92
Spencer, Jock 36
Spencer, Stuart 40
Sporting Globe 151
Sproule, Paul 32
St Kilda Football Club 56, 97
    colours 93, 114
    origins 21
    player revolt 84
    premiership 163
    see also Victorian football
Stannage, Tom 169, 170–1
Stephen, Bill 26
Stevens, Arthur 105

Steward, Peter 177, 190–1
Stewart, Bob 239
Stewart, Ian 32, 163, 167, 190
Stewart, James Finley 33
Stockdale, Greg 99
Stoneham, Barry 34
Stopford, C. L. 104
Stretton, Alan 92
Strickland, Bill 65
Sturt Football Club 88, 120
    see also South Australian football
Stynes, Jim 17, 39, 216
Subiaco Football Club 65, 86, 87, 133, 134
    see also Western Australian football
Sumich, Peter 227
Sunday Age 223
supporters 4, 60–1, 68, 111, 230, 232, 244
    see also cheer squads
Sutton, Charlie 142, 147
Swan Districts Football Club 6, 67, 119, 131, 132, 134
    see also Western Australian football
Swift, Fred 27
Sydney SwansFootball Club 22, 212, 225, 244
    see also Victorian football

tactics 45–6, 78, 139–40, 160, 166, 178, 186, 202, 214, 224
Taggart, Andrew 187
Tandy, Mark 39
Tannock, Peter 172
Tasmanian football 110, 112, 233–4
Tasmanian Football League 110, 233–4
Taylor, Brian 215
Taylor, Dick 105
Taylor, Jim 38
Taylor, Kevin 195
Teasdale, Graham 39, 198
Teasdale, Noel 38
television 159, 160, 190, 223–4, 231–2, 233
Templeton, Kelvin 199–200
The Club 189
The Coach 230
The Footballer 56
'The Footy Show' 232
The Greatest Game 229
Thomas, Bill 94
Thomas, Hugh 95, 121

Thomas, Len 32
Thomas, Ted 104
Thomas, William 'Sonna' 28
Thompson, J. B. 47, 48
Thompson, Len 18, 38, 188–9, 196
Thompson, Mark 'Bomber' 30, 202
Thomson, Michael 202
Thorp, Vic 27, 93
Thurgood, Albert 12, 35, 78, 80
Tilbrook, John 'Diamond Jim' 18
timekeepers 9–10
Titus, Jack 34, 94, 118
Todd, George 'Jocka' 27
Todd, John 154, 156, 171, 174–5, 190–1, 193, 210, 213
Todd, Ron 36, 116, 118, 121, 136
Toms family 64
Toms, Edward Vincent 64
Toms, George 63–4
Topping, George 33
Torney, Hugh 38, 123
trades clubs 73
traineeships 227–8, 245
trainers 4
Tresize, Neil 40, 241
Trotter, Percy 39
Truscott, Bluey 124
Truth 223
Tuck, Michael 41
Tuddenham, Des 18, 19, 33, 166, 188
Tuddenham, Paul 19
Turnbridge, Geoff 33
Turner, Ian xiii, 117, 185, 221, 229, 244–5
Turner, Kenneth 33
Turner, Michael 31
Twentieth Man 42
Twomey, Bill snr 96
Tymms, William 105
Tyson, Charlie 96, 152
Tyson, E. 119

Ulverstone Football Club 233
umpires xviii, xix, 15, 42–3, 105, 236
    boundary 4, 13, 66–7, 80
    goal 14
    reports 17
    signals 10, 14, 16, 77
Under Nineteens competition 126, 129

University Blacks 208
University Football Club 72–3, 82, 84, 85, 91

'Vagabond' 68
Valentine, Viv 39
Vallence, Harry 'Soapy' 11, 36, 103, 116, 124
Valli, Bill 177
Van Der Haar, Paul 34, 217
Victorian Amateur Football Asocciation 208–9, 233
Victorian football
  1890s 67
  1900s 79–83
  1910s 83–6, 97
  1920s 97–103
  1930s 112–18
  1940s 118–19, 127–30
  1950s 130–1, 144–9
  1960s 149–50, 160–5
  1970s 165–7, 196–9
  1980s 200
  1980s 213–17
  1990s 217
Victorian Football Association (VFA) 1, 63, 64–6, 77
  club performances 73
  expansion in 1920s 103–4
  formation 56
  innovation 104
  reductions in team size 30, 78
  rivalry with VFL 72, 78, 126–7, 208
  statistics 251–3
  television 190
  violence in 78, 104
Victorian Football League (VFL) 4, 7
  1st season 67
  1908 admissions 72
  1925 admissions 100
  1987 expansion 215
  administration 158, 183–4, 201
  established for professional competition 18, 47
  fixtures 17–18, 116, 207
  formation 63, 64, 66
  fundraising 184
  night competition 8, 9, 190
  statistics 253–60, 261
  Sunday matches 190, 207–8

team colours 21–3
  Waverley Park 183–4, 235, 243
  see also Australian Football League
Victorian Rules 47
Victorian Women's League 246
Vinar, Paul 'the Swede' 12
violence 3, 17, 19, 96, 118, 185
  1910 Grand Final 75, 84
  1945 Grand Final 121–2, 128
  in VFA 78, 104
Violet Town Football Club 59
Vosti, Jack 27, 105, 123

Waddell, Rod 205
Wade, Doug 36, 160, 162, 164, 187, 197
Walker, Bill 171, 174–5
Wallace, Terry 32
Wallis, Dean 202
Wallis, Stephen 28
Walls, Robert 34, 197, 199, 224, 228
Walsh, Brian 26
Wanganeen, Gavin 26, 202
Wanliss, Tom 95
Ware, Norman 38
Warne-Smith, Ivor 36, 102, 105
Waterman, Chris 226
Watson, Colin 32
Watson, Mark 212
Watson, Tim 41, 202
Watters, Scott 226
Watts, John 173
weather influences 5–6, 8–9
Wednesday Football League 111
'WEG' 69
Weidemann, Murray 34, 188
Weightman, Dale 40, 233
West Adelaide Football Club 88, 104, 136
  see also South Australian football
West Coast Eagles Football Club
  formation 212–13
  origins 23
  tactics 45, 186, 213, 225–6
  see also Victorian football
West Perth Football Club 86, 87, 119–20, 132, 133, 134, 135
  see also Western Australian football
West Torrens Football Club 23, 88, 120, 136
  see also South Australian football

Western Australian football 59, 67–8, 71, 73, 233
    1900s 86–8
    1930s 119
    1940s 119–20, 131–4
    1950s 134–5, 152–7
    1960s 156–7, 170–1, 172–6
    1970s 177–8, 190–5
    1980s 195, 209–13
    statistics 271–9
Weston, Paul 203
Wheadon, David 227
Wheeler, Terry 26, 219, 228, 231
Whelan, Marcus 32
White, H. J. 105
White, Lindsay 36
Whitten, Ted jnr 19
Whitten, Ted snr 12, 19, 34, 142–3, 147, 168–9
Wight, Sean 216
Wiley, Robert 211
Wilkins, Bill 103
Wilkins, Harry 104
Williams, Don 29
Williams, Fos 136–7, 145, 157, 158, 196, 234, 247
Williams, Geoff 28
Williams, Greg 'Diesel' 32, 205
Williams, John 187
Williamson, David 189
Williamstown Football Club 8, 56, 65, 94, 118, 140
Wills, T. W. 47, 49
Wilson, Bill *see* Proudfoot, Bill
Wilson, Brian 32, 214
Wilson, Charles 65
Wilson, E. L. 65
Wilson, Garry 40

Wilson, Percy 39
Wilson, Peter 226
Winmar, Nicky 31
Wittman, Stan 'Bunny' 35
women's football 246
Wood, Bryan 31
Woods, Bervyn 126, 130, 143
Woodville Football Club *see* South Australian football
Woodville-West Torrens Football Club 235
    see also South Australian football
Woolfe 152
Wooller, Fred 34
'World of Sport' 159
Worrall, Jack 63, 82–5, 91
Worsfold, John 'Whoosher' 30, 226
Wraith, Frank 115, 126, 143
Wren, John 73, 78, 95, 143
Wrensted, Murray 212
Wright, Duncan 17
Wright, Gerard 221–2
Wright, Roy 38, 145, 146
Wright, Steve 234
Wrout family 115
Wrout, Jack 115, 124, 167, 189–90
Wynd, Scott 39
Wynne, John 177

Yarraville Football Club 94
Yeates, Mark 217
Young, George 33
Young, Henry 'Tracker' 37
Young, Morrie 152, 172
Young, William 147

Zeldin, Theodore 68
zoning 19, 72, 76, 77, 150, 184, 245
Zucker, Lloyd 158